THE COMEDY OF ENTROPY

Patrick O'Neill

THE COMEDY OF ENTROPY: Humour, Narrative, Reading

UNIVERSITY OF TORONTO PRESS

Toronto Buffalo London

© University of Toronto Press 1990
Toronto Buffalo London
Printed in Canada

ISBN 0-8020-2737-7

Printed on acid-free paper

Canadian Cataloguing in Publication Data

O'Neill, Patrick, 1945–
The comedy of entropy

Includes bibliographical references.
ISBN 0-8020-2737-7

1. Comic, The, in literature.   2. Narration
(Rhetoric).   3. Fiction – 20th century – History
and criticism.   I. Title.

PN3352.C6054 1990   809'.917   C90-093234-1

This book has been published with the help of a grant from the
Canadian Federation for the Humanities, using funds provided by
the Social Sciences and Humanities Research Council of Canada.

For Trudi,
who has been humouring me for years;

Conor, Owen, Brian, and Siobhán,
who carried on regardless;

and Maxwell's Demon,
patron saint of taxonomists.

Contents

Figures

Acknowledgments

This project developed out of a seminar on black-humour fiction that I conducted in 1980 under the auspices of the Program in Comparative Literature at the University of British Columbia. I am grateful to the participants in that seminar for their criticism of the initial stages of the project.

My thanks are due to the University of British Columbia for research assistance during the early stages of this undertaking and to the Social Sciences and Humanities Research Council of Canada for generous research assistance on several occasions. My special thanks are also due to both for making possible a year of sabbatical leave during 1985–6, when much of the manuscript took shape.

An initial outline of this project appeared in 1983 in the *Canadian Review of Comparative Literature;* some of the material in part 2 has previously appeared in *Acta Litteraria* (Budapest 1987); and the analysis of *Der Prozess* first appeared in a longer version in *Franz Kafka (1883–1983): His Craft and Thought* (1986), ed. Roman Struc and J.C. Yardley.

Introduction

Large areas of twentieth-century writing, both literary and non-literary, are pervasively informed by one variety or another of what this book calls the *comedy of entropy*. Entropic comedy may be defined as the expression – literary or otherwise – of a form of humour whose primary characteristic is its own awareness of its status as essentially *decentred* discourse. The emergence of this form of humour is a relatively recent phenomenon in intellectual history, becoming noticeable only about the beginning of the eighteenth century, burgeoning rapidly during the early nineteenth century, and increasing exponentially in importance in the thinking of twentieth-century modernism and postmodernism. A very salient factor in this process, moreover, has been the degree to which humour, traditionally relegated to the margins of serious discourse, has increasingly impinged on areas where its presence would once have been unthinkable – to the point, indeed, where there are now few areas of thought in the human sciences that have not been touched by it to a greater or lesser degree. This continuing development in our understanding of humour and its role in our thinking represents a paradigm change of major significance in the way we see the world around us, and this book sets out to explore in turn (a) the broader implications of this phenomenon in the context of our general cultural practice, (b) its specific implications for twentieth-century literary theory, especially narrative theory, and (c) its practical implications for the reading of one particular mode of twentieth-century literary narrative.

The book is consequently divided into three separate parts, each of which explores in its own quite different way various ramifications of the comedy of entropy. Part 1, 'Contexts: Entropy and Humour,' focuses on an analysis of the systemic affects of entropic thinking on our modern and postmodern perception of what constitutes humour and what its role may be. Part 2, 'Pretexts: Humour and Narrative,' analyses the systemic effects of that conceptual reorganization of humour on our modern and postmodern perception of what constitutes the literary text, focusing specifically on the production and reception of narrative. Part 3, 'Texts: Narrative and Reading,' turns from theory to a fairly extensive critical analysis of a set of narrative texts illustrating, in terms of narrative structure, a taxonomy of the comedy of entropy.

The book is fairly evenly divided between theory and practice, part 3 being roughly as long as the first two parts together. I should perhaps emphasize, however, that each of the three parts, though intimately connected with each of the others, also has its separate identity and separate concerns, so that each to a degree can be read as one of three parallel discourses in different though closely related domains. Any attempt to read the two theoretical parts merely as an introduction to the final extended exercise in practical criticism is consequently very likely to be entirely unsatisfactory. Part 2, moreover, which attempts to situate modern and postmodern textual theory in the context of a general theory of humour and the ludic, is of necessity the least accessible of the three discussions. Readers who have had their fill of theory by the end of part 1, however, should feel free to proceed with an easy conscience directly to part 3 if they so desire, leaving part 2 for another day. Taken in a very narrow sense, the three parts of the book could be read as addressed to three quite separate audiences, namely humour theorists, narrative theorists, and literary critics respectively – each of them potentially impatient with the excessive interest of the author in the other two. The ideal reader, not surprisingly, would turn out to be someone with a very strong family resemblance to the author and would be equally fascinated by all three aspects – humour, narrative, and reading alike – all three of which are treated here as essentially tributary to the consideration of the central concern, the comedy of entropy.

A Note on References

I have dispensed with footnotes and endnotes throughout. All necessary references are instead included parenthetically in the text and are cued to the full concluding bibliography. In parts 1 and 2 texts are cited (and where necessary quoted) either in the original language (Kafka's *Prozess*) or in English translation (Kafka's *Trial*), as seems most appropriate and useful under the particular set of circumstances involved. In part 3, however, where the emphasis is on the critical analysis and interpretation of the individual texts involved, all quotations from the texts under discussion are given first in the original language of composition (followed by a parenthetical reference to the original version as listed in the bibliography), and if the original language is not English, then in a translation (followed by a parenthetical reference to the published English translation of the work as also listed in the bibliography). Translations not followed by a parenthetical reference are my own work: I have also silently amended published translations where this was considered necessary.

In parenthetical references divided by a slash, page numbers before the slash refer to the text in the original language, and page numbers following the slash refer to the published English translation.

Part One

CONTEXTS:
Entropy and Humour

1 Entropy: The Loss of Certainty

The syndrome known as life is too diffuse to admit of palliation. For every symptom that is eased, another is made worse. The horse leech's daughter is a closed system. Her quantum of wantum cannot vary.

Samuel Beckett

Goethe's Faust, with the unshakeable confidence of a Renaissance man in his own ability to succeed, sets out to discover no less than 'was die Welt im Innersten zusammenhält' (20) / 'what holds the world together at its core,' the innermost, central, cohesive principle of the universe. If Faust had set out on his heroic quest for certainty in more modern times rather than in Goethe's version of the dawn of modern thinking, he might well have chosen to do so only after a thorough academic training as a physicist, for up until the middle years of the nineteenth century, at least, physics seemed increasingly capable of producing final, authoritative answers about the basic building blocks out of which the physical universe and everything in it was constructed. In our own rather more disillusioned days the dream of reaching the rock-bottom of reality is generally agreed to have been just that, a dream, an illusion. Rather than reaching the solid rock-bottom of reality, physics could only watch, as Arthur Koestler's novel *The Call-Girls* (1972) puts it, as 'the rock turned into a bottomless mud-bank.' For Koestler's physicist, Nikolai Solovief, himself a disillusioned would-be Faust, the 'beguiling vision' of classical physics 'had disintegrated into a mad Wonderland ... All traditional, human notions of space, time, and matter had gone overboard, followed by the sacred principles of logic which linked cause and effect; all certainties had vanished from the universe, to be replaced by statistical probabilities; ... the harmony of the spheres had turned into a cacophony' (44).

Apocalyptic thinking, in its various shadings, is nothing new: as Nikolai Solovief himself wryly comments, Ecclesiastes 'dates from the Bronze Age and God was still supposed to be alive then' (67). Closer to our own time we find outbursts of apocalyptically tinged uncertainty in various periods of cultural history. The late Middle Ages, the Baroque, the *Sturm und Drang* of the 1770s in Germany, some of the more extreme strands of European Romanticism all suffer from (and revel in) what Emile Durkheim called *anomie* in varying tinctures – the disorientation, that is, resulting from the disintegration of normative codes of thinking. But throughout the history of human endeavour the Preacher's realization that 'all is emptiness and chasing the wind' has been balanced and, at least in the West, outweighed by the Greek optimism of an Archimedes, whose boast 'Give me a place to stand and I will move the earth' has been the rallying cry of Fausts since time immemorial. That Archimedean point of purchase has been looked for and discovered successively in nature worship, tribal gods, an omniscient personal God, the power of human reason and common sense, the power of human and natural creativity, the power of scientific, educational, and industrial progress. The certainty of the one firm spot in a turbulent world has unfailingly enabled us to survive with ever-renewed optimism the ravages of plague, famine, and war throughout the ages, even down to the refinements of our own day, in the name of God or king or country.

It is a commonplace that the twentieth century, to the extent that its intellectual climate can be gauged from the discourse of its philosophers, artists, and intellectuals, has pervasively lost its ability to trust in that saving certainty. Few poetic utterances, it seems, could be considered more emblematic of the age, or have found a more general resonance, than Yeats's lines from 'The Second Coming':

> Turning and turning in the widening gyre
> The falcon cannot hear the falconer;
> Things fall apart; the centre cannot hold;
> Mere anarchy is loosed upon the world.

> (*Collected Poems* 210–11)

When, and where, it might seem reasonable to ask, did things begin to fall apart, as seen from the vantage point of our own time? A common-sense question, certainly – and that fact alone should be enough to make us wary, for common sense too has become suspect in the general falling apart. Perhaps the major point of convergence, indeed, among researchers in both the human and the physical sciences over the past century or so has been precisely the untrustworthiness of that traditional bulwark of civilized society, common sense. But let us for the moment, provisionally, set that consideration aside and attempt none the less to locate that Archimedean point where the undermining precisely of the validity of Archimedean points began. In one sense, it is apparent, we can go as far back in human history as we choose, for it is possible, after all, to locate the catalytic point in the first coherent thought formulated by a human brain, since the very notion of coherence – the germ of the Faustean quest for 'what holds the world together at its core' – enables also the counternotion of incoherence. We can abbreviate the narrative of our own quest for coherence, however, and find a dramatic emblem of the modern consequences of the eating of the fruit of the tree of knowledge, by beginning our story no further back than that other Faustean figure in the history of human endeavour, Copernicus. For 'Copernicus and his cronies started taking the cosmic jig-saw to pieces,' as Koestler's failed Faust puts it, 'and all the king's horses and all the king's men could not put it together again' (88).

In the halcyon pre-lapsarian days before Copernicus, our story would then begin, man (for woman did not count for much in this untroubled scheme of things), the crowning glory of God's creation, sat securely in the centre of a cosmos whose singing spheres eternally circled to the greater praise of God and the greater confirmation of the centrality of man and his concerns. For if God existed, in theory at least, as the primary object of man's attention, man very definitely existed also as the primary, if not indeed the only, object of God's attention – as witnessed by the frequency with which the Creator intervened miraculously in human affairs to right some transient wrong or verify some lasting truth. Copernicus's suggestion of a heliocentric rather than a geocentric world-picture was not only earth-shattering, it was heaven-shattering as well, for the decentring of man in astronomical terms could be read as a decentring of man also in the mind of God, as if man, in other words, were only one of numerous concerns of this suddenly very much more distant though still almighty and omniscient father. Perhaps, even, the thought grew over the next few centuries, though valiantly contested by the Church, perhaps the primary focus of man's attention should be man himself rather than a god who no longer took any meaningful part in human affairs. Perhaps this god was less a benevolent father than an ingenious watchmaker, who, having put together the world for his own amusement, now watched with idle interest as it ran out its clockwork course. And in that case, was man not freer than he had ever been before? And what if the reason for God's loss of interest was quite simply that God was dead? Our drastically foreshortened fable has taken us in a few lines from the high Middle Ages to 1883, when the death of God was formally announced (though it had been the subject of numerous rumours previously) in Friedrich Nietzsche's *Thus Spoke Zarathustra*. But the fable is of course only half over: the second part concerns man's newly won freedom and what he did with it, now that he had re-established his centrality in the scheme of things.

Thomas Pynchon's short story 'Entropy' (1960) operates on two levels in an apartment building in Washington, DC. Downstairs one Meatball Mulligan's 'lease-breaking party' (277) threatens to slide from 'a sustained, ungodly crescendo' (291) into total chaos. Upstairs an ageing intellectual named Callisto and his girl-friend Aubade inhabit a 'hothouse jungle it had taken him seven years to weave together. Hermetically sealed, it was a tiny enclave of regularity in the city's chaos, alien to the vagaries of the weather, of national politics, of any civil disorder ... What they needed from outside was delivered. They did not go out' (279). Callisto is obsessed by the laws of thermodynamics:

> As a young man at Princeton ... Callisto had learned a mnemonic device for remembering the Laws of Thermodynamics: you can't win, things are going to get worse before they get better, who says they're going to get better. At the age of 54, confronted with Gibbs' notion of the universe, he suddenly realized that undergraduate cant had been oracle after all. That spindly maze of equations became, for him, a vision of ultimate, cosmic heat-death. He had known all along, of course, that nothing but a theoretical engine or system ever runs at 100% efficiency; and about the theorem of Clausius, which states that the entropy of an isolated system always continually increases. It was not, however, until Gibbs and Boltzmann brought to this principle the methods of statistical mechanics that the horrible significance of it all dawned on him: only then did he realize that the isolated system – galaxy, engine, human being, culture, whatever – must evolve spontaneously toward the Condition of the More Probable ... He was aware of the dangers of the reductive fallacy and, he hoped, strong enough not to drift into the graceful decadence of an enervated fatalism ... Nevertheless, ... he found in entropy or the measure of disorganization for a closed system an adequate metaphor to apply to certain phenomena in his own world.
> (282–3)

The story ends with a narrative chiasmus. Downstairs the wild party, contrary to expectations, gradually sobers down. Upstairs Callisto is increasingly demoralized, first of all by his failure to revive a sick bird by warming it against his body – by putting heat transfer to constructive use, that is to say – and then by the fact that the temperature outside has now been at a steady thirty-seven degrees for the last several days, suggesting to Callisto the final heat-death of all life and all matter. In the end it is Aubade who puts an end to 'this Rousseau-like fantasy' (279) by smashing out the glass of the window 'with two exquisite hands which came away bleeding and glistening with splinters; and turned to face the man on the bed and wait with him until the moment of equilibrium was reached, when 37 degrees Fahrenheit should prevail both outside and inside, and forever, and the hovering, curious dominant of their separate lives should resolve into a tonic of darkness and the final absence of all motion' (292).

Callisto was not the first to be disturbed by the concept of entropy. In the late 1800s when the consequences of the second law of thermodynamics were being considered in a number of fields (cf. Brush), considerable pessimism was engendered among philosophers and, more especially, theologians, as religious feelings attempted to come to grips with the antiteleological thrust of a concept based on the necessary dissipation of energy and the necessary randomization of all matter, as opposed to an ultimate harmonizing of a disorderly world. Christianity, after all, depended on the concept of ultimate order, a stage of development when all accounts would be harmoniously balanced. The notion of entropy suggested chaos as the ultimate destiny of all things. The roots of such apparently millennial pessimism, perhaps surprisingly, go back to so overtly innocuous a source as early nineteenth-century attempts to understand the nature and functioning of heat, which was a problem of more than merely theoretical interest in the early days of the Industrial Revolution (Jammer; Whitrow). Out of these attempts came the formulation of the three laws of thermodynamics, the first and second of which have had the most interesting repercussions outside the field of thermodynamics.

The first law states that in any closed system – any system, that it to say, theoretically isolated from the rest of the universe – the total quantity of energy remains constant. This is generally known as the principle of the conservation of energy, and implies that energy can be neither created nor destroyed, but only transformed. Heat can be converted into work (and work can be converted into heat), but the total amount of heat (or work, or energy) in a closed system remains constant. The third law states that every substance has a definite quantity of available energy to do work and that that quantity approaches zero as the temperature approaches absolute zero. The second law, the most interesting one for our purposes, focuses on the quality rather than the quantity of such energy available for doing useful work. In the classic formulation of Rudolf Clausius in 1854, 'entropy' – Clausius coined the expression from the Greek *tropē* 'transformation' – is a measure of the mechanical unavailability of energy (Prigogine, 117; Whitrow, 526). In a closed system (such as nature, for example), that is to say, though the quantity of energy remains constant, *available* energy tends to become unavailable energy, a process that is unidirectional, irreversible, and leads inevitably to a 'heat death' or total unavailability of energy, complete inert uniformity and equilibrium. A red-hot poker, for example, cools gradually while heating up the air or water around it until their temperature is the same. A scotch on the rocks, left to sit, will degenerate from its original dual form of whisky on the one hand and ice-cubes on the other as the ice melts and the molecules of water mix randomly with the molecules of whisky. Moreover, if it is left to its own devices (that is, without the application of outside energy), the watery scotch will never revert spontaneously to scotch on the rocks. More formally stated, all matter moves towards molecular chaos in the absence of external energy sources. As Ludwig Boltzmann later formulated it, ordered arrangements (of molecules) tend to degenerate into disordered ones (quoted in Whitrow, 527; Wiener, 12). Entropy, moreover, as we have seen, cannot diminish, it can only continually increase towards an equilibrium state, which is therefore the state of maximum probability, the object of Callisto's paranoia.

In this book, like Callisto, I am going to use the notion of entropy as a metaphor for the crumbling of ordered systems, the breakdown of traditional perceptions of reality, the erosion of certainty. As well as its purely metaphorical connotations, though, the notion of entropy has a more precise and more interesting application for literary studies – and particularly for the study of humour in literature. The connection comes from the second major area where the concept of entropy plays a considerable role, namely the field of information theory. The migration of the concept of entropy from thermodynamics to information theory is generally dated to the attempt of James Clerk Maxwell in 1871 to contradict the universality of the second law of thermodynamics (Jammer, 116; Wiener, 28–30). Maxwell hypothesized a vessel filled with gas in an equilibrium state. The vessel is divided into two parts by a central partition which contains a very small hole. By the hole sits a very small but intelligent being (who has since come to be labelled 'Maxwell's Demon'). The demon is small enough to be able to see individual molecules and, being of a methodical turn of mind, sets out to sort them into two classes. He opens and closes the central hole so as to allow only the faster moving, 'hotter' molecules to pass in one direction and only the slower moving, 'colder' molecules to pass in the other. Eventually, Maxwell argued, the temperature of the two halves of the vessel would differ sufficiently that the difference would generate energy available for useful work. The entropic process would therefore, and contrary to the second law of thermodynamics, be reversed, since no external application of energy would have taken place. More than half a century was to pass before theorists were able to demonstrate that no contradiction of the second law is involved if the demon is construed as acting on *information* received and thus, in effect, transforming information (namely his classification of molecules) into negative entropy (Campbell, 48–9).

In other words, if entropy is a measure of disorder, information is a measure of order. Entropy, as a measure of disorganization, of randomness, becomes also a measure of *lack* of information – information theorists consequently use the somewhat unfortunate coinage 'negentropy' (that is, negative entropy) to denote a measure of information. Entropy, by the same logic, becomes a measure of the *disruption* of information, a measure, that is to say, of what the information theorists call 'noise' (Campbell, 43–52). Noise is the distortion factor in any communication system – the electrical interference, for example, that causes static on the radio or snow on the television screen, eroding the information content of the signal. All communication is a function of what Aubade, to return to Pynchon's 'Entropy' again, thinks of us as 'that precious signal-to-noise ratio' (287). Callisto, we remember, is obsessed by the implications of the concept of entropy in the thermodynamic sense; another character in the same story, one Saul, is more disturbed by its implications for communication theory, for his wife has left him after a marital quarrel about this very topic. For Saul, noise is the villain.

> 'Tell a girl: "I love you." No trouble with two-thirds of that, it's a closed circuit. Just you and she. But that nasty four-letter word in the middle, *that's* the one you have to look out for. Ambiguity. Redundance. Irrelevance, even. Leakage. All this is noise. Noise screws up your signal, makes for disorganization in the circuit.'
>   Meatball shuffled around. 'Well, now, Saul,' he muttered, 'you're

sort of, I don't know, expecting a lot from people. I mean, you know.
What it is is, most of the things we say, I guess, are mostly noise.'

(285–6)

Meatball, in his noisy way, puts his finger on what most of us, unless
we are as heroically paranoid as Callisto, instinctively realize, namely
that all communication, whether linguistic or otherwise, is essentially
a question of compromise, Aubade's 'precious signal-to-noise ratio'
(287). Total order is just as sterile and deadly as total chaos. Life,
language, literature are all possible only because of the *exploitation* of
noise. Jeremy Campbell puts it well in his discussion of information
and entropy in language and life: 'Biologists as well as philosophers
have suggested that the universe, and the living forms it contains, are
based on chance, but not on accident. To put it another way, forces of
chance and of antichance coexist in a complementary relationship. The
random element is called entropy, the agent of chaos, which tends to
mix up the unmixed, to destroy meaning. The nonrandom element is
information, which exploits the uncertainty inherent in the entropy
principle to generate new structures, to inform the world in novel ways'
(11). The most appropriate metaphor for the life process, Campbell
further suggests, may thus not be the traditional pair of rolling dice or
a spinning roulette wheel, but rather the sentences of a language,
conveying information that is always partly predictable and partly
unpredictable (12).

If this is true of the everyday language we use in everyday situations,
it is true a fortiori of narrative language, which will be one of our
concerns in what follows, and humour, which will be the other.
Humour, in very overt fashion, and literature, especially narrative, in
rather less overt fashion, are very centrally a function of the exploitation of uncertainty, the incorporation of noise as an essential component, even *the* essential component, of the signal. In the narrative texts
examined later in this book we shall be looking for the dual exploitation
of the notion of entropy, as used in both thermodynamic and information theory. In the former sense the term metaphorically suggests that
erosion of certainty which is the thematic thread linking all our texts;
in the latter sense the term points to that exploitation of uncertainty
which is the key technique of humour and narrative alike.

What we are calling the erosion of certainty, that is to say the erosion
of traditional notions of order and truth, might well seem to belong
primarily or wholly in the context of the tragic rather than the comic.

Morris Kline, for example, begins his history of mathematics, which carries the title *Mathematics: The Loss of Certainty* (1980), with the following statement: 'There are tragedies caused by war, famine and pestilence. But there are also intellectual tragedies caused by limitations of the human mind. This book relates the calamities that have befallen man's most effective and unparalleled accomplishment, his most persistent and profound effort to utilize human reason – mathematics' (3). Traditionally mathematics had 'provided a firm grip on the workings of nature, an understanding which dissolved mystery and replaced it by law and order' (4), for truth was in essence a series of mathematical laws. From Copernicus through Kepler, Galileo, Descartes, Pascal, Newton, and Leibniz to Euler, the great mathematicians and philosophers of the fifteenth to eighteenth centuries affirmed what Leibniz called pre-established harmony. The universe was the most perfect conceivable, the best of possible worlds, and logical thought would unfailingly reveal its immutable beauty, clarity, and symmetry. The key to this sovereign reality, however, was lost, after more than two thousand years, about the beginning of the nineteenth century, when strange new geometries and algebras forced mathematicians to realize that spatial and temporal reality, reality as experienced by us all every day, could find a satisfactory fit in several *different* geometries or algebras that were mutually completely contradictory. These strange new discoveries included Karl Friedrich Gauss's work in non-Euclidean geometry, William Rowan Hamilton's algebraic theory of quaternions, Hermann von Helmholtz's conclusion that only experience, *not* the workings of some supernal principle, can tell us where and when the laws of arithmetic do and do not apply (92). 'All could not be truths ... This realization was the first of the calamities to befall mathematics' (4), and 'disaster struck again in 1931 in the form of a famous paper by Kurt Gödel,' the foremost logician of the twentieth century, 'in which he proved, among other significant and disturbing results, that the logical principles accepted by the various schools could not prove the consistency of mathematics' (5–6). Mathematical statements, in other words, might well be unassailably 'true' within the bounds of the particular logical framework adopted by a particular school or approach, but opposing statements might be equally 'true' within the terms of reference of a different school or approach – and there was no way to decide finally which of the opposing truths constituted the 'real' truth, even assuming there might be such a thing any longer.

Gödel's deconstructive achievement, which succeeds in turning against themselves the most basic assumptions of classical mathematics as a science (Hofstadter, 17–19), is the most dramatic result of a renewed awareness in the early twentieth century of a very old thorn in the side of mathematicians, namely *paradox*. From earliest times, mathematicians and philosophers have both amused and mystified themselves and others by demonstrating the limits of reason when it comes to certain mathematical and logical problems. The pre-Socratic philosopher Zeno of Elea assembled a celebrated collection of paradoxes in the fifth century BC that are as effective today, in their own terms, as they were 2500 years ago. His best known paradox, the Achilles paradox, to take only one example, demonstrates that even the swiftest moving object can never overtake an object in front of it, however slowly the latter moves. Achilles, relates Zeno, can run ten times as fast as the tortoise, whom he therefore generously gives a head start of one hundred paces in a somewhat unlikely sporting event. Achilles sprints the hundred paces while the tortoise laboriously moves ten; he sprints those ten paces while the tortoise is able to cover only one; he leaps the single pace while the tortoise can only struggle one-tenth of a pace further on – but by now Achilles should be realizing that the joke is really on him, for by the time he covers the remaining tenth of a pace the exasperating tortoise is still one-hundredth of a pace ahead, and so on in infinite regress. However fast he runs, Achilles can never catch the elusive tortoise.

Such age-old conundrums came back to haunt mathematics (and philosophy) in the early years of the twentieth century. Even before Gödel's bombshell, the work of Georg Cantor in set theory, specifically on infinite sets, had unleashed an awareness of the pervasiveness of paradox hitherto unparalleled, not just in the fairly rarefied field of set theory, but throughout classical mathematics and throughout ordinary language (Hofstadter, 20). Following the rules of logic, it now suddenly appeared, would not necessarily lead to some Platonic ideal truth but perhaps just as easily to total self-contradiction. Suddenly philosophers were once again busying themselves with questions uneasily reminiscent of medieval scholastic deliberations as to the exact number of angels that could be accommodated on the point of a pin. Can an omnipotent being create an indestructible object? Of course, if he is omnipotent; of course not, since if he is omnipotent he can destroy anything he wants to. What about the old Epimenides or liar paradox: 'This sentence is false'? If it is true, then what it says is true, so it must be false; if it is false, then this is what it says, and so it is true. Or what about 'All rules have exceptions'? Since the statement itself is a rule it must accordingly also have exceptions – therefore there must be at least one rule that does not admit of exceptions. These innocent-looking puzzles, reminiscent of children's teasers, would have far-reaching effects for mathematics, once the unchallenged and untroubled Queen of Sciences. Gödel, as Douglas Hofstadter observes, in one sense simply applied the Epimenides paradox – 'This statement is false' – to mathematics. Gödel's theorem, as rephrased by Hofstadter, amounts to saying that 'all consistent axiomatic formulations of number theory include undecidable propositions' (17). Mathematical logic, in other words, can never lead to complete certainty; the attempt to eliminate paradox from mathematical thinking had, with Gödel, definitively failed. For Kline, these results are nothing short of tragic, 'amazing' (261), 'shattering' (263).

Kline's account of the erosion of certainty in mathematics is of compelling interest, not least because of the author's perhaps unconscious narrative strategy and his undiscussed presuppositions: the story is a linear progression from a pre-lapsarian, originary state of untroubled order and authority, a mathematical Eden, to a fallen state of rampant disorder rapidly approaching maximum entropy. But there are clearly other stories that could be written which would show the whole history of mathematics and scientific knowledge in general to be entirely the result of the exploitation of this tragically perceived loss of certainty, the rewriting of maps once regarded as corresponding to an undisputable reality. What is more interesting for our immediate purpose here is rather the at least potentially *comic* aspect of this erosion, which has taken place gradually over the centuries and then with precipitous rapidity in our own time. The history of science is a history of the abandonment of positions once judged impregnable for new positions previously held to be ludicrously mistaken. In the last half-century the adoption of ludicrous positions and their abandonment for even more ludicrous ones has become so rapid and so commonplace that rather than feeling the awe that primitive peoples must once have felt for the power of their shamans, or even the astonishment that people could still experience in the fifties when the first earth-satellite was successfully launched, our reaction nowadays to the latest miracle of space exploration or medicine or computer technology tends increasingly to be a mixture of *déjà vu* and something like incredulous *laughter*. Science, in fact, has long since passed beyond the bounds of the reasonable into domains that can no longer be taken *seriously*, any more than we take seriously jokes such as Epimenides' 'This sentence is false' or Alice's adventures in Wonderland. As any introductory book on particle physics will demonstrate, to take another obvious example, the micro-world upon which our comfortably solid everyday world is constructed is one saturated through and through with dazzling paradoxes, one where the only constant seems to be the often quoted comment of the Nobel Prize–winning physicist Niels Bohr, which might just as well have come from one of Alice's playmates: 'The madder the better.'

Quantum physics is not just a layman's conundrum either, it seems; even for the quantum physicist it is ungraspable in any sort of real terms. More than one writer has observed that while the subject is solidly buttressed by both experimental evidence and a coherent body of theory, it still rests upon a foundation that defies human understanding and is consequently related to certain kinds of religious faith (Zukav, 23). That it shares a dimension with the worlds of fiction and humour, pretend worlds of the imagination, could equally well be observed. That it shares a dimension with our own, real, solid world of everyday experience is far harder to believe. That world, the world of experience, is built up on hard facts and clear distinctions – here and there, then and now, yes and no, true and false. This division has been one of the sturdiest planks in the conceptual platform of classical philosophy since Aristotle; the so-called law of the excluded middle, which states that propositions must state their colours clearly, must be *either* true or false, *either* one or the other, not both at once. The realm of humour, of course, has always been at least tacitly felt to be beyond the reach of this reasonable dictum – in recent years, however, it has become necessary to exclude more and more areas of the serious business of the real world as well. But, in that case, how real *is* the real world?

The real world and its chief bulwark, common sense, have in fact been taking a very considerable battering since Nietzsche, a century ago, declared that not only was God dead but that truth was a fraud. Truth, said Nietzsche, was nothing more than a marching army of metaphors whose metaphoricity had been forgotten ('On Truth' 174). Truth, in other words, is not an absolute value, an ontological given, but a set of conventions, a negotiated agreement. Over the intervening years we have had the chance to become more and more aware of Nietzsche's contention, as the discourse of common sense becomes increasingly relativized and provisionalized by the conflicting discourses of theoretical investigation in both the physical and the social and human sciences. Linguists, anthropologists, psychoanalysts, and philosophers join theoretical physicists and mathematicians in suggesting that there *is* in fact no longer any such thing as an objective, unchanging real world 'out there.' Rather what we experience as the real world is our own attempts to organize a meaning in what is essentially, in itself, as meaningless as a Rorschach blot. Oscar Wilde notoriously accused Wordsworth of being able to discover sermons in stones and tongues in the running brooks only because he had previously hidden them there. If we are able to discover structures of meaning in the randomness of existence, it is likewise because we have previously taken the trouble to plant them there. Not only is the world, in Rilke's phrase, always a 'gedeutete Welt' (20), a 'world interpreted'; in a very real sense we in fact *invent* the world we inhabit. The concerted thrust of the main movements in continental European philosophy over the past century or so has been to explode the comfortable notion of some original point of meaning, truth, fixity, plenitude – the originary Logos, 'In the beginning was the Word,' of St John's gospel – that would give shape and form and coherence to the world and to existence, that would, in a word, establish and fix ultimate reality, the ultimate molybdenum bar resisting all temptation to be anything other than exactly itself, and against which all else might once and for all be measured. As opposed to fixity, we are now offered only fictions: our ultimate realities are our own invention. We ourselves, at the same time, are as little independent of the world we inhabit as it is of us: the classical picture of the self-sufficient Archimedean in-dividual has been just as effectively exploded in half a dozen different discourses, Marx, Nietzsche, Freud, and their continuators having demonstrated in their different contexts that far from being sublimely untouched by our social and cultural surroundings we are deeply and centrally a product of them. Our certainties are houses built on sand, our truths are myths and illusions, our individuality is woven of forces utterly beyond our personal control: thus the concerted philosophical thrust of our times.

First, as it might seem, came the demise of God, then comes the demise of man – for if in one sense the decentring and peripheralizing of the individual dates back to Copernicus at least, in a much more compelling sense Nietzsche's laughing onslaughts with the philosophical hammer mark the crucial and emblematic turning point in the history of the modern psyche. After Nietzsche, the individual mind, for the leading thinkers of the time if not for the man in the street, definitively ceases to be the organizing centre – the Cartesian 'Cogito, ergo sum' – around which reality predictably circles, and becomes instead a mere buffeted scrap of flotsam carried along willy-nilly on a current it can do little or nothing to control. The reversal labelled here for convenience' sake with Nietzsche's name, however, has in fact been signalled from many different though complementary discourses over more than a century now. Marx, for example, was able to write as early as 1859 that the individual is completely submerged in the determinism of the economic basis: 'It is not the consciousness of men that determines their being, but on the contrary their social being that determines their consciousness' (1: 74). For the American philosopher Charles Sanders Peirce, it was not economics but semiotics that provided the context of dissolution, but the result was the same: the individual, 'man,' was just one more sign among the myriads of signs that constitute the semiotic web of existence, just as for Heidegger, in yet another context and another philosophical tradition, man is flotsam in the stream of language and cultural tradition. More and more the goal of the human sciences came to be seen as being 'not to constitute man but to dissolve him,' in the words of the anthropologist Claude Lévi-Strauss (quoted in Culler, *Pursuit* 33). The psychoanalyst Jacques Lacan, developing Freud's position, goes so far as to see the thinking individual as a mere empty space, an 'empty subject'; a subject defined, that is to say, only as a locus of interrelationships, a sort of crossroads or intersection of multiple and conflicting functions. For Lacan, Freud's work decentred the human being just as effectively as Copernicus decentred the cosmos; as a result of Freud's work, he writes, 'the very centre of the human being was no longer to be found at the place assigned to it by a whole humanist tradition' (114), for in challenging the Cartesian basis of liberal humanism, Freud 'challenged the concept of personality determined by conscious subjectivity, the transcendent mind of the unique individual' (Belsey, 130). For the philosopher and cultural historian Michel Foucault man is an afterthought, 'a recent invention ... like a face drawn in sand at the edge of the sea' (386, 387). For the philosopher Jacques Derrida it is our stubborn insistence on the centrality of the human mind and its ability to experience and understand what it perceives as reality that is the major factor limiting our apprehension of the world around us – a disturbing 'humanist' insistence that, in spite of our always fragmentary and discontinuous experience, somewhere 'there must exist a redeeming and justifying *wholeness*, which we can objectify in ourselves as the notion of Man, and beyond ourselves as the notion of Reality' (Hawkes, 146). All of these currents of thought, and others besides, combine to form the central axiom of current theoretical research in the human sciences, which is, in summary, 'that the individuality of the individual cannot function as a principle of explanation, for it is itself a complex cultural construct, a heterogeneous product rather than a unified cause' (Culler, *Pursuit* 53).

In this general disappearance of man from the scene, language, paradoxically, comes to occupy a role of more pervasive importance than had ever been the case before. Philosophical thinking, indeed, has very largely become primarily a thinking about language. Traditionally, language had been seen as transparent and unproblematic, a neutrally objective tool for the description of an equally unproblematic reality. As that reality grew less certain and more troubled, so did language. On the one hand, its unproblematic fit with the real world came gradually to be seen as illusory, while on the other language itself was to *become* the only reality for various schools of thought. Nietzsche, again, had suggested that all being is linguistically posited; for poststructuralist thinking this suggestion becomes the central article of faith. Linguistic being is the only being we are permitted to know, and by its very nature it is pervasively and irreversibly characterized by the condition of undecidability. For if Freud decentred the psyche, as Marx had the individual in history and Nietzsche the individual as locus of philosophical authority, the Swiss linguist Ferdinand de Saussure decentred language in demonstrating it to be essentially a web of differences without positive terms: language's tie to the real world is essentially an arbitrary one, and words mean what they do not because of some ontologically certified and unalterable relationship of the linguistic sign and its non-linguistic signified, but rather because we recognize the word in question as being different from other words. 'Their most precise characteristic is in being what the others are not' (117). For poststructuralist thinkers like Derrida, meaning, being linguistic, is thus always a shifting, moving system of differences, is always 'deferred,' as Derrida puts it, always absent, never present and graspable. The human subject – no longer enjoying the dignity of being a 'self' – is 'itself' merely one strand in this linguistic text, and all non-linguistic notions such as value, meaning, order, consciousness are merely comfortable illusions. All our knowledge is linguistic knowledge, and as such is utterly devoid of all claim to truth or finality. The only certainty we can possess is the *aporia*, the knowledge of the complete uncertainty, relativity, and provisionality of all knowledge, the awareness of the infinite play of linguistic difference. René Wellek no doubt expresses the alarm of many in observing with some asperity that for these new philosophers of language, with Derrida at their head, 'knowledge is only a freeplay with words and their etymologies,' while 'motifs from Nietzsche, Freud, and

Heidegger, together with a strain from Dadaism combine to result in a complete skepticism and even self-proclaimed nihilism' (317).

The other most striking feature of this brave new world is that it is a participatory world; that is to say, the role played in it by the individual as *observer* is far more nuanced, more productive, than in the traditional nineteenth-century realist and positivist scheme of things. However, that said, it must be observed that the realist scheme of a neutrally objective observer operating on a docilely passive reality, while typical of nineteenth-century realism, had already been unsettled as early as the eighteenth century. Kant's shifting of emphasis from the fixity of 'objective' reality to the subjectivity of perception can be seen as the Copernican revolution ushering in the Age of Indeterminacy in which we currently find ourselves. Even before Kant, indeed, Berkeley had argued that nothing can exist unless it is perceived by a mind – in the well-known formula: 'esse est percipi' / 'to be is to be seen to be.' Berkeley's formula, of course, had little in common with the deconstructive ambitions of twentieth-century thinking: it was intended as a proof of the existence of God, with matter redefined as an extension, or rather a projection, of the divine mind, which therefore served as the point of final anchorage and ultimate meaning. For the positivist thinking of the nineteenth century, the 'real world' itself formed the objective reality, solid and unchanging, while the scientific observer of this reality was held to be capable of registering it with complete detachment, in the same totally objective way that a camera (as long as we disregard the cameraman) registers what it finds before its lens. Twentieth-century thought draws the conclusion from Kant that 'reality' is in fact very largely determined by the perceiving subject. This is the position most notably expressed in Werner Heisenberg's principle of indeterminacy in physics: here the observer/observed relationship ceases to be a common-sense matter of a clearly defined observing subject operating on a clearly defined and clearly separate observed object. Rather, as the experimental physicists tell us, 'reality' is actually shaped by the very act of observing it: the observing scientist can *choose*, for example, depending upon his immediate purposes, whether a ray of light is observed as an energy wave or a stream of individual particles. However, if 'life is what you make of it' in a very real sense here, as the old saw has it, you are also what life makes of you. The subject/object relationship, in other words, is not unidirectional, but rather, as the philosopher Edmund Husserl, for example, argued, a two-way exchange, a sort of negotiated settlement, to use that phrase again, where both subject and object are redefined and altered by virtue of their relationship to each other. This paradoxical relationship, which again reflects the disappearance of any once-and-for-all fixed point of purchase or authority – be it God, reality, or the autonomous self – around which to organize meaning, has very deeply affected twentieth-century hermeneutic theory. The hard facts so beloved of positivist and common-sense thought now tend to be regarded rather as provisional contentions, as positionally coloured phenomena, whose factual existence, as well as their interpretation as 'tragic' or 'comic' or merely 'neutrally' evaluated bits of information, is seen as depending very largely if not entirely on how they are seen, by whom, under what circumstances, for what conscious or unconscious purpose. The evaluating subject, by contrast, is wholly a product of that reality it presumes to evaluate. This paradox – life is what you make of it, as long as it allows you to do so – seen as inherent in modern hermeneutic theory, is a very large part of the reason why so much of modern theoretical discourse seems constantly poised on the edge of comedy, and why so much of that comedy seems to lead us back inevitably to the notion of entropy.

Which brings us back as well to what might be seen as the crucial question for our present concern, namely how one should *evaluate* this entropic erosion of certainty – the death of God, the disappearance of man and reality, the insurrection of language, the disaffection of philosophy, the incomprehensibility of the sciences and their attempts to explain 'what holds the world together at its core.' The answer to this question is, of course, part of the problem rather than a solution, for entropy, like humour, is always, to some extent, in the eye of the beholder. Disorder, no less than the comic or the tragic, is not a wholly objective property, so the observer who measures the entropy of a given system – or evaluates that measurement as tragic or comic – cannot be excluded from the observation (Campbell, 32). If we have 'decided' to see disorder or comedy or tragedy, in short, then that is what we will find – and it can certainly be argued that as long as we can mount a convincing argument for our findings we have every right to find whatever we want. Modern philosophical thought, and with it literary criticism, has increasingly moved in influential ways towards the view that there are no standpoints that a priori can be considered privileged: to put it the other way around, as Paul de Man does, 'all structures are, in a sense, equally fallacious' (10).

Whether we regard such developments as tragic or not clearly depends on our attitude to the necessary centrality of the sovereign individual and the concomitant humanist values implied by this centrality. If that centrality is held to be an undebatable necessity, then there are many reasons for concluding that our age of entropy is also a tragic age – not an age that produces tragedies, but an age in which we are characters in a tragedy. Wimsatt and Brooks quote Joseph Wood Krutch in *The Modern Temper* (1929) on what is the necessary condition for tragedy, and for Krutch as for many it is faith in the greatness of man: 'A tragic writer, he says, does not have to believe in God, but "he must believe in man." Thus, our modern failure to write tragedies springs, not from our loss of faith in the supernatural, but from our loss of faith in the worth of human nature' (561). But if we no longer write tragedies in the traditional sense, comedies in the traditional sense are hardly written any longer either. For both tragedy and comedy in the traditional sense are firmly anchored in a solid system of commonly accepted values: the tragic hero and his mirror image, the comic butt, both transgress against a received code of values, both are wrenched willy-nilly back into line, and in both cases, via the agency of tragic or comic catharsis respectively, the validity of the prevailing norms (or at least of the norms that are desired to prevail) is therapeutically and trenchantly reconfirmed. In our own time tragedy as a genre has indeed beaten a retreat, and where we might expect to find it we tend to find instead not comedy in the traditional sense, to be sure, but varieties of comic writing whose affinity to tragic writing is so marked as to disorient completely our stock responses to traditional tragedy and comedy and disrupt totally the traditional cathartic reaffirmation of the norms of an ordered societal system.

These norms seem well and truly shaken in our time. There is a marked entropic – not to say apocalyptic – quality in the work of many contemporary thinkers, the suggestion of the end of an era, where the philosophical, metaphysical, and even physical fictions that have been in operation since Plato seem to have reached a point of exhaustion, while the future remains veiled in undecidability. Traditional norms, constructed in traditional ideology, no longer hold, but, to quote Catherine Belsey, 'it is not immediately clear how to contemplate the alarming prospect of a world in which there are no final and uncontested divisions because there are no ultimate determinable meanings, no transcendental signified' (145). Michel Serres has drawn our attention to the importance of considering the role of thermodynamic thinking as opposed to classical Newtonian mechanical thinking in evaluating the shift in our perception of history that has been taking place since the middle of the nineteenth century. The Newtonian model of history, based on the physics of mechanical devices, saw time as moving from point to point on the face of the cosmic clock, each point a new point of presence, complete in itself and identical in this respect to all the others. This archeological or geological conception of history, as it might be called, visualizing history as a layering of successive presences, was radically shaken by the middle of the nineteenth century by the new notions of thermodynamics, based on a physics of heat and fire rather than a physics of mechanical devices, which substituted, in Eugenio Donato's words, 'a notion of history based upon the metaphors of decay, decadence, corruption; in a word, a notion of history based upon any metaphor that can be read as abolishing differences' (236). Thermodynamics ushered in 'an episte-mological nihilism that denounces the possibility of ever attaining an essential knowledge of the world' (237), as demonstrated in the new concept of history: 'Origins are forever erased, differences disappear, and the end foreseen is an indifferent universe governed by the laws of chance and statistics' (238). While the Newtonian universe was theo-retically knowable in its totality, the new entropic universe is end-lessly indeterminate, undefinable, unknowable – except as to what its final end will be. Points of origin disappear in favour of chance; notions of presence give way to infinite mutability; anthropocentrism gives way to indifference and statistical probability; epistemological opti-mism gives way to implicit nihilism. The end, however, is unequivo-cal: universal equilibrium, eternal stasis, maximum entropy.

Serres writes in the French poststructuralist frame of reference; and poststructuralist thinking is entropic through and through, leading inevitably – as its detractors claim and its practitioners triumphantly proclaim – to nihilism. For the triumphant proclaimers, nihilism is no longer a negative value, associated with futility and despair, but a positive value associated with liberation from the authoritarian shib-boleths of the 'logocentric' past ('logocentric' being Jacques Derrida's coinage for a fixation on stable points of reference). Nihilism, after centuries underground, so to speak, takes up its rightful place in the sun again, for nihilism, in the words of one of its proclaimers, Hillis Miller, 'is an inalienable alien presence within Occidental metaphysics' (447). For this entropic world-picture the emblematic figure would no longer be a Faust who believed in his own ability to seize and comprehend the universe at its very core; rather it would be Flaubert's stumbling pair of amanuenses, Bouvard and Pécuchet – to whose memory, not inciden-tally, Koestler's *The Call-Girls* is dedicated. Two office clerks who earn their living by copying documents, Bouvard and Pécuchet, through an

unexpected legacy, suddenly find themselves in possession of a respect-
able-sized fortune and set out à la Faust – 'Je voudrais bien savoir
comment l'univers s'est fait!' (139) / 'I should like to know how the
universe is constructed' – to achieve an encyclopaedic understanding
of the totality of human knowledge by systematically exploring its
various domains, from agriculture through medicine, literature, and
politics to philosophy. Their inevitable – and comic – failure forces
them to realize that *any* such act of totalization must by definition be
not only impossible but of necessity marked at every stage by accident,
chance, and randomness. Having finally recognized and admitted their
failure, they return to their old occupation of copying documents. But
this time, rather than copying systematically and purposefully, they
randomly copy everything and anything that comes to hand: cigarette
papers, stray notices, old letters, random newspaper items – a grotesque
parody, in fact, of their earlier attempt at totalization, and one even
more obviously doomed to failure, since the impossible final copy of
the universe would have to include an infinitely regressing copy of
itself to complete the task. As Flaubert wrote in his plan for the end of
the novel (for, ironically, he died before completing it): 'Pas de réflexion! copions! Il faut que la page s'emplisse ... – égalité de tout, du bien
et du mal, du beau et du laid ... Il n'y a de vrai que les phénomènes' (443)
/ 'No more reflection! Keep on copying! The page must be filled ...
Everything is equal, the good and the evil, the beautiful and the ugly ...
There is no truth but facts, phenomena.'

Bouvard et Pécuchet (1881) would have good claim to stand emble-
matically at the head of any attempt at a historical account of what we
may call entropic comedy in modern narrative, for in it we find just that
blend of nihilism and humour which, as we shall see, is the characteristic of the genre. The nihilism of the entropic tradition in modern
thought, from Nietzsche and Flaubert to the poststructuralists, is
characterized precisely by this association with comedy: rather than
being offered the stoic's dagger, we find ourselves invited to join in the
game, to play, to laugh. The idea of non-significance has become a
commonplace of entropic thinking: the world is neither meaningful
nor meaningless, neither tragic nor, in the grimmer sense of the exis-
tentialists, absurd – it simply *is*. Alain Robbe-Grillet points this out in
his *Pour un nouveau roman* of 1962, for example, just as Ludwig
Wittgenstein did half a century before in beginning the *Tractatus
Logico-Philosophicus* of 1921 with the lapidary opening sentence 'Die
Welt ist alles, was der Fall ist' (30) / 'The world is everything that is the
case' (31). Simply being, however, without meaning (as I shall argue in

more detail at a later stage), tends inevitably in the direction of comedy. Life is what you make of it, indeed, but since of itself it means nothing, anything we can 'make' of it will overtly be a form of fiction, and its production a form of play, however earnest and non-comic our intentions may be. These substitute worlds that we conjure up will be seen by those of an idealist turn of mind as demonstrating the triumphant victory of form over the void; for those of a more existential turn of mind the inevitable final triumph of the void over all form will still remain the primary consideration. What has become increasingly evident in both literary and critical texts alike over the last few decades, however, is precisely the increasingly pervasive awareness of the element of play itself, and with it of entropic comedy, of the fictionality of all discourse, of the status of all discourse as a version of the Epimenides paradox, 'This discourse is false.'

2 Humour: Reconstructing a Spectrum

Mieulx est de ris que de larmes escripre,
Pour ce que rire est le propre de l'homme.

Rabelais

It is better to write of laughter than tears,
For laughter is what is special about mankind.

Having looked at the growing importance of entropic modes of thought over the last century or so, we will investigate in this chapter the development and the conceptual reach of a form of humour that I will call *entropic humour* because its most salient characteristic is the degree to which it is influenced precisely by entropic modes of thought. Over the last few decades, notoriously, there has been a spate of this kind of humour in all sorts of areas, from TV and newspaper cartoons to modern art and, most interestingly for our present concerns, literature too. Over the last twenty-five years or so this kind of humour has generally come to be identified under the somewhat rough-and-ready label of 'black humour' and has given critics considerable difficulty in situating it with regard to more 'normal' forms of humour, whether literary or otherwise. Things in general have a marked tendency to become particularly interesting around the edges, and humour is no exception. An initial investigation of what exactly the rather vague term *black humour* may be (and has been) said to *mean*, consequently, will provide us at this point with a useful point of entry into the investigation of the larger question as to the reach of humour as a whole and the place in that conceptual spectrum occupied by the various branches of what we will be calling entropic humour, a term that is at once wider and more specific than notions of the largely indeterminate 'blackness' of particular forms of humour.

The phrase *black humour*, we can fairly say, is one that crops up reasonably frequently in everyday conversation as well as in literary criticism, but there is little or no general agreement as to what exactly this so-called black humour may be. In one sense, of course, this is hardly surprising, for the same can be said of the application of humour terminology in general. Words like 'humorous,' 'ironic,' and 'satiric' are commonly bandied about with very little regard for the nature and the nuances of their interrelationship. Indeed, as almost all investigators of humour phenomena have at some time or other had occasion to remark, the lack of an agreed upon taxonomy or terminology of humour is one of the most irritating stumbling blocks in humour research. None the less, most people are reasonably sure – though they might well contest the equal sureness of their friends and neighbours – that they know what humour is when they come across it, and the researchers, from Plato's day to our own, have continued undaunted their efforts to explain and if possible systematize the field.

The notion of 'black' humour enjoyed an upsurge of interest in North America especially during the 1960s, and an excellent brief treatment of its impact on the literature of the time can be found in an extended article – summarizing the findings of an earlier book – by Max F. Schulz in the *Encyclopedia of World Literature in the 20th Century* (1975). To summarize Schulz's position, 'black humor describes a state of mind as much as a body of literature; both are an expression predominantly of the 1960s' (45), more precisely of the American sixties. The decline of belief in socially accepted norms of behaviour and thinking that had been under way since at least the mid-nineteenth century found its culmination, writes Schulz, in the disillusionment of the sixties, and exercised in those years a 'widespread cumulative impact on the form and theme chiefly of American, and peripherally of European, fiction' (46). The disillusionment is comprehensive, involving a loss of faith in psychological, sociological, and metaphysical systems alike, as well as in our own ability to replace the ailing systems by satisfactory surrogates. The resulting thematic characteristics, as far as fiction is concerned, include the following: most important, the 'refusal to treat tragic materials tragically' (48) but rather to subject them to comic, even grotesque distortion; this accompanied by a detached, uninvolved observation of the despairing, the fantastic, the outrageous, a mocking apocalyptic tone of cosmic irony in which no attempt at the correction of vices or the praise of virtues can be discerned, and an ironic undercutting of the fictional undertaking itself, which is thus implied to be no more trustworthy than any other intellectual system. Characters are one-dimensional, settings minimal, plots disjunctive, fact and fiction irretrievably blurred. There is a self-conscious delight in artistry and artifice, frequently resulting in a penchant for omnibus, encyclopaedic pluralism of both form and content.

Schulz, we notice, consciously sidesteps any real attempt to define the humour content of black humour; rather he finds the expression primarily useful as a convenient, if not very precise, label for the work of certain American writers of the sixties whose work conforms to the general outline just given. 'Black Humor has never been a programmatic movement,' however, for 'authors tagged as Black Humorists range from surrealistic symbolists like John Hawkes to comic realists like Friedman, from metaphysical speculators like Borges to whimsical moralists like Vonnegut' (46). The label, indeed, since it is also used in connection with 'existentialist literature, absurd theater, happenings, gallows humor, sick humor' (46), and so on, seems finally to have a lot in common with the disembodied grin of the Cheshire Cat: 'it hardly needs emphasizing that Black Humor as a critical term and as an historical appellation alludes to so heterogeneous a range of material that it is almost useless taxonomically' (46).

The notion of black humour as a home-grown American intellectual current had been popularized by Bruce Jay Friedman, in a mass-market paperback anthology tersely called *Black Humor* (1965). Friedman avoids defining his specific conception of black humour, but suggests that what holds his collection together is a shared feeling of insecurity, of a 'fading line between fantasy and reality,' a sense of 'isolation and loneliness of a strange, frenzied new kind,' and above all the element of virulent satire in a world gone mad. A new 'chord of absurdity has been struck' in the sixties, according to Friedman, who finds a 'new style of mutative behavior afoot, one that can only be dealt with by a new, one-foot-in-the-asylum style of fiction' (ix), since the normal role of the satirist has of necessity been pre-empted by the daily newspapers. The writers of the new sensibility, says Friedman, move in 'darker waters somewhere out beyond satire' (x).

Friedman, though he obviously sees black humour as a predominantly contemporary and American phenomenon, suggests that in a wider perspective black humour 'has probably always been around, always will be around, under some name or other, as long as there are disguises to be peeled back, as long as there are thoughts no one else cares to think' (xi). Douglas M. Davis, in a rather more systematic anthology published in 1967, *The World of Black Humor*, broadly agrees with Friedman's position but situates recent examples of the genre much more firmly in a historical tradition. Aristophanes, Erasmus, Shakespeare, Jonson, Pope, Voltaire, Swift, Céline, Kafka, Musil, Beckett, Ionesco – all of these find their place in Davis's wider conception of a typological tradition of black humour in Western literature. 'The least we can conclude, in fact, is that Western Literature regularly offers us a view of man, his affairs, and his cosmos as nightmarish and unreasonable' (15). Black humour 'in its specifically satirical moments was and is savage, brooking no compromise with its subject' (14); however, 'it is not ultimately the perfectibility of man that goads these writers on, but the hostility of the universe' (65); black humour, in short, 'laughs at the absurd tragedy which has trapped us all, man, woman, child, self' (14). For Robert Scholes, likewise, in his *Fabulation and Metafiction* (1979), black humour should be viewed as both a modern movement (in life as in literature) and a development in a continuing tradition: the intellectual comedy of Aristophanes, the flourishing satire of imperial Rome, the humanistic allegories and anatomies of the later Middle Ages, the picaresque narratives of the Renaissance, the metaphysical poems and satires of the seventeenth century, and the great satiric fictions of the Age of Reason – all of these are ancestors of modern black humour, and since understanding and evaluating depend so completely on our sense of genre, this pedigree is not something we can afford to ignore (143). Black humorists, as Scholes observes, are often misjudged as failed satirists, or as deliberately choosing to be flippant rather than to attempt 'seriously' to alter the world for the better (156), but, as he acutely phrases it, the black humorist is concerned not with what to do about life but with how to take it. In this respect black humour has certain affinities with some existentialist attitudes, roughly distinguishable in terms of the difference between seeing the universe as absurd, a fate best countered by what Camus, in *The Myth of Sisyphus*, called 'scorn,' and seeing it as ridiculous, a joke, with the point being one's ability to enter into the joke, 'get' it, and laugh (Scholes, 147).

Though pointing to varying degrees to a wider cultural context, however, these American critics all stress a particular decade in a particular country. It is instructive to compare the understanding of the notion of black humour in Europe. 'Humour noir' as a term in

French literary criticism traces its origins to André Breton's *Anthologie de l'humour noir* (1939). Breton prides himself in the foreword to the 1966 edition on having been father to the phrase: 'Qu'il suffise de rappeler qu'à son apparition les mots "humour noir" ne faisaient pas *sens* ... C'est seulement depuis lors que la locution a pris place dans le dictionnaire' (7–8) / 'Suffice it to remember that when it appeared the words "black humour" did not make *sense* ... It is only since then that the expression has taken its place in the dictionary.' He is unwilling to attempt to provide a definition, but, whatever definition we may choose to give it, it has become an inalienable part of the modern sensibility:

> Il est de moins en moins certain, vu les exigences spécifiques de la sensibilité moderne, que les oeuvres poétiques, artistiques, scientifiques, les systèmes philosophiques et sociaux dépourvus de *cette sorte* d'humour ne laissent pas gravement à désirer, ne soient pas condamnés plus ou moins rapidement à périr.   (12)

> It is less and less certain, in view of the specific demands of the modern sensibility, that poetic, artistic, or scientific works, philosophical or social systems devoid of *this sort* of humour are not seriously deficient, are not condemned, more or less rapidly, to oblivion.

Though only recently named, moreover, black humour, according to Breton, has been an identifiable factor in literature throughout the ages, and in painting as well – he mentions Hogarth, Goya, Seurat – though it is only in our own day that it has managed to break free of the didactic, moralizing bent of satire and begin to exist in a 'pure state.' For Breton, black humour is above all subversive, a 'révolte supérieur de l'esprit' (16), a 'higher spiritual revolt,' disruptive of accepted values and systems, an aggressive weapon against a world gone mad. The satirical element is almost always very strong in the selections Breton chooses as exemplary of black humour, and in most cases the subject-matter is one that in polite society would be considered definitely taboo. Breton casts a wide net over the field of European literature since 1700, and his list includes forty-five authors in all, three eighteenth-century (Swift, Sade, Lichtenberg), and the remainder fairly evenly divided between the nineteenth and twentieth centuries. There are selections from, among others, to give a sense of the flavour of the collection, Thomas de Quincey, Grabbe, Poe, Baudelaire, Lewis Carroll, Villiers de l'Isle-Adam, Nietzsche, Lautréamont, Huysmans, Rimbaud, O. Henry, Gide, Synge, Jarry, Roussel, Apollinaire, Picasso, Kafka, Jakob von Hoddis, Marcel Duchamp, Hans Arp, Jacques Prévert, and Salvador Dali.

Faced with this large selection of extracts all allegedly illustating various facets of black humour, the reader may well pause at certain points for purposes of comparison and to reflect especially on the comparative 'blackness' of the humour. If we attempt to use Max F. Schulz's definition that black humour essentially refuses 'to treat tragic materials tragically' ('Black Humor' 48), for example, then one or two of Breton's selections seem hardly 'black' enough to have qualified for inclusion at all – Lichtenberg's deconstructive squib on the possibility of a bladeless knife without a handle, for example, or Alice's adventures down the rabbit hole, seem relatively unthreatening, relatively unlikely to inculcate guilt feelings in the mildly amused reader. At the other end of the spectrum, however, and far more representative of Breton's collection, there are the excerpts from Swift's *Modest Proposal*, Sade's *Juliette*, or Lautréamont's *Chants de Maldoror*, where the 'blackness,' so to speak, is overwhelmingly in evidence, the 'humour,' by contrast, next to impossible to discern for most readers, one might imagine, certainly if by 'humorous' we mean something like 'funny.' But here we must pause, for to make a claim like this is to broach whole endless areas of humour research: Does 'humorous' necessarily mean laughable? Do any two readers laugh at the same time and for the same reason? Is there a 'national' sense of humour just as there is an individual one? And so on. We shall return to such questions at a later stage; for the moment, however, let us look at two of the less obviously 'funny' excerpts, from Swift and Sade respectively.

'Tout le désigne, en matière d'humour noir, comme le véritable initiateur' (25), Breton writes of Swift. 'Everything points to him, as far as black humour is concerned, as being the true initiator.' Breton sets the *Modest Proposal* (1729) at the very beginning of his collection, thus, to some extent, setting also the tone for what follows. The *Proposal* begins, in the tone of many an early-eighteenth-century tract, as an urbane and enlightened essay on the alleviation of the distress of the Catholic Irish poor, only to metamorphose suddenly and without overt change of tone into the appallingly rational argument that serving the better nourished of the infants, properly cooked and seasoned, on the tables of the better classes would at once provide a piquant change of fare for the latter and a source of honest income for the over-productive and destitute peasantry – many of whom, the narrator adds as if in passing, would no doubt consider themselves better off if they too had been cannibalized quickly as children rather than slowly and excruciatingly throughout their wretched lives. These few pages have an enormous, almost a frightening impact. Partly the impact is due, no doubt, to the suggested revelation of the self-centred barbarity and inhumanity of the *soi-disant* cultivated classes; no doubt too though, the impact is also partly the result of the shock value involved in the incongruous fusing of the overt rationality of urbane satire and the apparent understatement of irony on the one hand with the flaunted irrationality and exaggeration of the alleged solution on the other, the reformer's apparent care for the improvement of the lot of suffering humanity on the one hand with the hint of a perverse glee in the fictive debasing of that same humanity on the other. To what extent, however, the reader of Breton's collection might well ask, is it justified to speak of 'humour' here? Is it not rather simply a horrifying example of extreme bad taste, even if undertaken for no doubt worthy ends?

The extract from Sade's *Juliette* (1796) faces the reader with similar problems. Sade, 'cet esprit le plus libre qui ait encore existé' (51) / 'the freest spirit who ever existed,' as Breton calls him, quoting Apollinaire with approval, has his Russian giant Minski take Swift at his word. Minski, otherwise known as the Ogre of the Appenines, satisfies his depraved tastes by having appropriately cooked and dressed human babies served up to him at his table; even the table contributes to the debasement of human dignity, however, for the table is human too, made up of the naked buttocks of a number of young women who are forbidden on pain of immediate and excruciating death to make even the slightest movement as the searingly hot chafing dishes burn into their flesh. While most readers will no doubt react primarily with disgusted rejection of Minski's tastes, many will no doubt also be distressed by the *potentially* comic reading of the situation; for there is certainly the same element of the comic – the potentially comic, of course – present here as is present in most 'dirty' jokes, that is to say, the sudden and grotesque juxtaposition of the human person endowed with all the rights and privileges we would like to think appropriate and the human body as a mere worthless object among objects to be used with total lack of compunction for our momentary pleasure, even if that pleasure is entirely fictional. It is possible, if the reader chooses to do so, to read the Minski episode, as it is to read Swift's horrifyingly 'modest' suggestion, as enlightened satire aimed at the dehumanizing practices of an emerging high capitalism. 'Ce que vous avez la folie de nommer dépravation,' shrugs Minski philosophically, 'n'est jamais que l'état naturel de l'homme' (60) / 'What you have the folly to call depraved is never anything other than man's natural state.' What militates against a reading as well-intentioned satire is the narrator's obvious pleasure, in this as in other texts of the Marquis de Sade, in compiling his endless and exhausting lists of sexual perversions, making the comfortable solution of classifying the text as satire an uneasy one and continually compelling the 'normal' reader to balance an incipient comic reaction (such as that evoked by the punchline of a scatological joke) and, in many cases at least, an immediate repression of what is felt to be a forbidden pleasure.

Our 'normal' reader – assuming merely for the sake of the argument that such may somewhere exist – may well experience a similar reaction to, say, many of the savage vignettes of Lautréamont's *Chants de Maldoror* and at least some of Kafka's texts – 'In der Strafkolonie' ('In the Penal Colony'), for example, where the condemned man's punishment is to have his sentence inscribed on his own flesh by the machine that kills him in the name of justice. What makes all of these texts interesting at this point in our discussion is that none of them is in any way immediately and overtly humorous in the conventional meaning of the term – and this is what makes them a more useful place to begin an analysis of the nature of entropic comedy than most of the texts of the black humorists of the American sixties in at least one sense, for most of the latter texts, while frequently horrifying, are also usually overtly humorous. This is not at all to claim that all entropic comedy is necessarily horrifying. The overtly horrifying, however, marks one useful boundary from which to begin a consideration of the character of black humour – which is exactly what another European anthologist, Gerd Henniger, attempts, in his *Brevier des schwarzen Humors* (1966).

Misanthropy, contempt, and loathing, perversely yoked with the comic, are the very yardstick of black humour in its purest manifestation for Henniger, whose book attempts to develop and systematize Breton's conception. For Henniger, black humour at its highest pitch of intensity eliminates laughter altogether, or rather translates what might have been laughter into inarticulate despair: 'schwarzer Humor ist, wenn man trotzdem nicht lacht' ('Zur Genealogie' 20) /

'black humour is when in spite of everything you do *not* laugh.' His archetypal black humorists in this vein are Swift and Sade, Büchner and Poe, the visions of Lautréamont's Maldoror,and the anonymous early-nineteenth-century German narrative, the *Nachtwachen des Bonaventura*. The characteristics of black humour for Henniger are essentially threefold: the situation subjected to comic treatment is tragically unchangeable; this subject-matter is very frequently taboo, sacrosanct, unspeakable; and our incipient laughter is immediately strangled, 'ein Lachen, das keines ist – oder Lachen in des Menschen höchster Potenz' (*Brevier* 7) / 'laughter that is no laughter – or laughter at the highest pitch of human intensity.'

Finally, to complete our survey of anthologies of black humour in literature we may note briefly Cristóbal Serra's *Antología del humor negro español* (1976). Serra is not at all interested in definitions of black humour. Rather he operates on the simple premise that if what Breton's anthology contained can be described as black humour, then so can the work of many, if not most, of the major writers in Spanish. Spanish black humour, however, does not result in the vague, intellectualized, neurasthenic products that, by implication, are to be found north of the Pyrenees; rather it is a spontaneous and healthy product of a salty native sense of humour. This rich vein, for Serra, runs uninterruptedly from the anonymous picaresque narrative *Lazarillo de Tormes* of 1554 through Cervantes, Quevedo, and Gracián, down to Espronceda and Larra among the Romantics, and Unamuno, Valle-Inclán, Machado, Juan Ramón Jiménez, and José Bergamín among twentieth-century authors.

It is clear, then, that as a label 'black humour' designates a disturbingly elastic range of heterogeneous connotations. For some of our anthologists and critics it suggests primarily a virulent mode of satire (Davis), possibly with a somewhat hysterical tinge (Friedman); for others it represents primarily an attitude of sarcastic pessimism (Serra), a response to the horror of existence (Henniger), a generalized revolt against an oppressive world (Breton), a response to an intellectual and philosophical pluralism (Schulz), or even evidence of the irrepressible and indomitable joy of fabulation (Scholes). For some the humour is primary (Scholes), for others it can be simply ignored as peripheral (Schulz), unproblematically assumed as self-evident (Serra), or held to be paradoxically self-deconstructive (Henniger). Emulating Maxwell's Demon, let us see if we can establish some degree of order by attempting at this point to situate the regional phenomenon of 'black' humour within the global phenomenon of humour as a whole.

Let us attempt then to assign this so-called 'black' humour a place in the realm of humour in general, both diachronically (by sketching the historical development of humour as a cultural phenomenon) and synchronically (by suggesting a spectrum of the communicative reach of humour in our own time). The question 'What is black humour?' in other words, is seen as logically dependent upon the answer to the question 'What is humour?' and it is possible to give a perfectly satisfactory dictionary definition as an answer to this latter question. My *Webster's New Collegiate Dictionary* (1977), for example, defines *humour*, in the sense we are interested in here, as 'a) that quality which appeals to a sense of the ludicrous or absurdly incongruous; b) the mental faculty of discovering, expressing, or appreciating the ludicrous or absurdly incongruous; c) something that is or is designed to be comical or amusing.' This is a perfectly adequate description of what humour means for most of us in everyday parlance. As soon as we attempt to explore the notion in more detail, however, grappling – if only at second or third hand – with the hundreds of books that exist in English alone on the subject of humour and wit, the comic, the ludicrous, and the laughable, not to mention such intersecting sub-realms as irony, satire, parody, or sarcasm, we are perhaps more likely to be reminded of another famous definition. In 'The Analytical Language of John Wilkins' – Wilkins being a seventeenth-century English philosopher who attempted to devise an analytical language of ciphers that would accurately account for and catalogue all of creation – Jorge Luis Borges refers to 'a certain Chinese encyclopedia entitled *Celestial Emporium of Benevolent Knowledge.* On those remote pages it is written that animals are divided into (a) those that belong to the emperor, (b) embalmed ones, (c) those that are trained, (d) suckling pigs, (e) mermaids, (f) fabulous ones, (g) stray dogs, (h) those that are included in this classification, (i) those that tremble as if they were mad, (j) innumerable ones, (k) those drawn with a very fine camel's-hair brush, (l) others, (m) those that have just broken a flower vase, (n) those that resemble flies from a distance' (142). Attempts to categorize the innumerable categorizations of humour types and situations that have been penned since the days of Plato tend to have a strong family resemblance to this benevolent (if dubiously authentic) taxonomy, and are certainly enough to cause humour researchers to tremble as if they were mad, if not even to smash flower vases. One can at any rate very readily see the appropriateness of Michel Serres's nomination of Hermes as the deity of comedy, paralleling Nietzsche's nomination of Dionysos as the father of tragedy: Hermes the swift and elusive messenger, the intermediary, shifter, trickster, impossible to pin down on the one hand, but on the other a perennial communicator in border territories where landmarks cease to be obvious and clear outlines blur.

In the English-speaking world, at least, there is a well-established tendency to associate humour as a concept with notions of Dickensian good cheer and *bonhomie*, the expansiveness and good-natured tolerance of postprandial laughter over the old port and good cigars. There are those theorists too who also regard humour and laughter as being primarily a benign instinct of the human animal, an instinct primarily amiable and genial in nature. This is a minority position, however: most humour theorists see humour as originating in a distinctly less humanitarian zone of the human mind and as being connected with a variety of the less pleasant and less comfortable sides of human nature. When we look for laughter – and the attitudes towards it – in the Bible or in the classics or in the oldest vernacular literatures such as Old Irish, for example, we find little to remind us of Pickwickian good cheer or Sternean whimsy. Biblical laughter certainly seems to be born predominantly of scorn and mockery, and is assigned no very honourable place in the gamut of human expressive capacities: laughter, as Ecclesiastes has it, is as the crackling of thorns under a pot, an activity for fools and children, and unworthy of the serious-minded (7.6). The earliest recorded reference to laughter in the classics appears to be to the unfeeling and uncontrollable hilarity of Homer's Olympians as they heartlessly mock the hobbling gait of the lame Hephaestus limping up and down the hall (*Iliad* 1.599). In our own enlightened times, where it is no longer considered acceptable to laugh at the physically, mentally, or financially handicapped, it is easy to forget that this Olympian laughter has echoed through history at the stocks and pillories of the Middle Ages, at the fools, dwarfs, and hunchbacks of Renaissance courts, in the pleasure trips of eighteenth-century nobility to taunt the inmates of the local lunatic asylum. In early medieval Ireland this essentially malicious and overtly derisive humour clearly showed its closeness to the malevolent charms of black magic: a bard who was skilled in his craft was expected to be able to compose on demand an *áer*, or satire, sufficiently venomous to raise blisters of shame on the face of its victim and force him into ignominious exile or even suicide (Mercier, *Irish Comic Tradition* 106).

Classical writers on humour and laughter considered them both to be base and ignoble. Aristotle wrote in the *Poetics* that comedy was essentially a representation of inferior people, as opposed to tragedy, which showed man at his noblest. Laughter, he continued, was a species of the base or ugly, provoked by some ugliness of body or baseness of character in its victim (19–21). Plato, in *Philebus*, held humour to arise from delight in the sufferings of others (338–9), and three hundred years later Cicero, in *De oratore*, similarly adopted the position that the province of the ridiculous lay in a certain baseness, ugliness, or deformity. Most people nowadays would probably be deeply offended if they were accused of having no sense of humour; in Aristotle's day they would no doubt have considered it a compliment. Laughter might well be the distinguishing mark of the human animal, as Aristotle himself observed, but it was scarcely something to be proud of and needed to be handled with caution if at all. Both Plato and Aristotle regard laughter as a politically dangerous activity, apt to disrupt the careful web of social order – comedy, as a result, like strong liquor, was something that responsible adults might be trusted to indulge in, in carefully regulated doses, but should be kept away from the impressionable and all too easily corruptible young.

The classical view of laughter as essentially the product of malicious joy, gloating, derision, ridicule, and self-satisfied mockery is the oldest and most tenacious general theory of humour and laughter we have, and it was stated most forcefully in modern times – no less than two thousand years later – by the English philosopher Thomas Hobbes in his *Leviathan* (1651). 'Sudden glory is the passion which maketh those grimaces called laughter; and is caused either by some sudden act of their own that pleaseth them; or by apprehension of some deformed thing in another, by comparison whereof they suddenly applaud themselves' (27). Laughter, in other words, is essentially a function of (perceived) superiority: we laugh when we see somebody else falling down a flight of stairs and suddenly, gloriously, realize that it could just as easily have been ourselves. This is the laughter of power, the jungle roar of triumph and the stripping of the teeth in the snarl of defiance, as later ethologists, following Hobbes, have pointed out. For Hobbes, no sentimentalist, war was the natural state of humanity, yielding only gradually and grudgingly to an always threatened process of uneasy civilization. Life was a *bellum omnium contra omnes*, a war of everybody against everybody, the individual was perforce *homo homini lupus*, a wolf to his fellow man, and laughter – the mark of those who possess power – simply a socially acceptable device for showing one's teeth.

The superiority theory, as it is generally called, no doubt owes its longevity to its powerful simplicity – it still survives in our own time in more sophisticated versions such as that propounded in Henri Bergson's essay on laughter, where, even though incongruity is advanced as the primary key to humour phenomena, humour and laughter are still essentially seen as a punishment inflicted on the unsocial or at least as a castigation of stupidity. While the superiority theory may possibly have furnished an adequate explanation of humour and laughter in ancient Athens, however, it seems clear enough to us today that it can account adequately only for a particular *kind* of humour and laughter, namely precisely that kind traditionally associated in literature with the derision of satire. It can certainly be argued that even by the time Hobbes was formulating the theory it was already, as we can see by virtue of hindsight, drastically inadequate as an account of much of the humour, for example, of Chaucer and Rabelais, Shakespeare and Cervantes.

Louis Cazamian has argued convincingly that modern humour 'hardly came into its own till the Renaissance; prior to that time the mental complexity which it requires was not very widely diffused' (4). The mental complexity in question concerns the ability to see laughter – or, more generally, comic response – as deriving from something more complex than the simple and linear laugher/victim, subject/object, one-way relationship of purely derisive humour. The Renaissance, in fact, sees the beginnings of the emergence of that more differentiated, more complex *sympathetic* laughter which by the eighteenth century would come to be seen as the only true form of 'humour,' even to the extent of displacing its derisive ancestor and relegating it largely to the contrasted realm of 'wit.' Though the eighteenth century glorification of sympathetic humour was eventually to be as one-sided in its turn as the earlier inability to conceive of any form of humour other than the derisive had been, its first stirrings during the Renaissance mark a highly significant stage in the historical development of humour. For the earlier forms of derisive humour the laugher and the victim were clearly distinct, the laugher rooted in a sense of his own unimpeachable worth and his belonging to an orderly value system, regulated by generally accepted norms of behaviour and belief, from which the victim was by definition excluded. For the sympathetic humorist the relationship was, incipiently at least, a much more complex one, for sympathetic humour rests finally on the hypothesized identity of laugher and victim, just as derisive humour rests on the distinction between them. The derisive humorist finds his victim's weakness laughable because of his own strength; the sympathetic humorist sees himself as the potential victim. The variety of positions available between the two extremes is endless and makes for the much more differentiated forms of humour that begin to appear in the works of such writers as Chaucer and Rabelais as early as the fourteenth and fifteenth centuries, not to mention the subtleties of humorous shading that we find in Cervantes's portrayal of Don Quijote and Sancho Panza or Shakespeare's treatment of such characters as Falstaff. Cazamian makes the very useful point, however, that even though the Renaissance period marks a decisive stage in the development of humour the phenomenon of humour itself still lacked any major 'degree of self-realization,' still lacked 'an individual name for itself' (103). The finding of an individual name for the new phenomenon of a laughable experience that was not purely derisive in character did not in fact take place until about 1700, when there was, as Cazamian puts it, a sudden flowering of consciousness of humour as a distinct instrument (103), a product in part of the increasing awareness of the newly perceived virtues of enlightened tolerance and understanding as a way of life.

So far we have not been making any distinction between laughter and humour, as if one always involved the other, but at this point we need to start using a more carefully differentiated vocabulary. In modern usage the word *humour* covers all shades of what we have been calling both derisive and sympathetic humour – but this certainly was not always so. The eighteenth century, for example, as we have just noted, made a clear distinction between 'humour' and 'wit.' Moreover, the word *humour* certainly does not cover all of the range of experiences that make us laugh, as even a very brief moment's reflection shows. We laugh (sometimes) when we are tickled, when we are embarrassed, when we are terrified, when we inhale laughing gas, and in all sorts of other situations that cannot be comprehensively accounted for by theories of humour alone. Nor, of course, does humour always make us laugh: one person may become helpless with laughter at something that another person – or even the same person under slightly different circumstances – may only smile at, or register unsmilingly as vaguely amusing, or simply just not find funny at all. The overt linguistic association of humour and laughter dates back in fact no further than the Renaissance. For the Greeks laughter was laughter – and for the philosophers at least a distinctly disreputable affair – and there was apparently no such concept as 'humour.' What made you laugh was what Aristotle in the *Poetics* called *to geloion* 'the laughable' (19), and that was the end of it – the verb *gelan* 'to laugh' is related to the English *yell*, and one could read this association as reflecting the uncomplicated straight-forwardness of ancient laughter, no more problematic than the yell of pain when you hit your thumb with a clumsily wielded hammer. As for *humour*, it started its conceptual career far from the laughable at its Latin face value as meaning a moisture or liquid – a meaning it still retains in modern medical usage, where a humour is a normal functioning bodily fluid or semifluid such as blood or lymph. In medieval physiology it came to be specifically applied to the four cardinal fluids seen as entering into the constitution of the body and determining by their relative proportions a person's health and temperament. The four humours were blood, phlegm, choler ('yellow bile'), and melancholy ('black bile,' the 'black humour' in a very different sense), and a preponderance of one or the other of these led to individuals *being* of a sanguine or phlegmatic or choleric or melancholy humour. Here we see at work the extension of meaning from the fluid that allegedly determined a person's temperament to the temperament itself – and of course this meaning still lives on too, independently of any risible connotations, when we describe someone as being in a good or a bad or a filthy humour. The further extension, linking humour and the laughable, is an easy one, occurring when an individual's temperament is seen as sufficiently eccentric and exaggerated that it becomes an object of ridicule and satiric laughter. The key figure at this stage in the development of the English concept of humour, as Cazamian argues, is Ben Jonson, whose 'comedy of humours' castigates the ridiculous eccentricities and affectations of upper-class fools, and also prepares yet another extension of the notion of humour. For Jonson a 'humorist' was an individual *affected* by a particular ridiculous humour; the next step in the continuing semantic shift was for the humorist to become the individual who *detects* this exaggerated humour and makes it into an object of laughter. It is this particular shift from the observed to the observer, we may note, that accounts for the modern lexicographer's problematic need to define *humour*, in paradoxical terms, both as something that has an apparently objective existence in itself and as something that is created only by the subjective act of observing it. Cazamian sees the course of this change of semantic focus as 'roughly speaking spread over the seventeenth century and the first half of the eighteenth, though its earliest symptoms can be detected before the end of the sixteenth' (319), and as reflecting the dawning awareness of a mental attitude hitherto unknown, 'the realization of the humorous attitude as an aspect of thought' (319), an awareness most obvious, says Cazamian, in the work of Shakespeare. Among Shakespeare's many comic characters perhaps the most interesting and complexly humorous is Falstaff, who is a humorist in both the Jonsonian and the modern senses, and in both roles the humour involved is a complex blend of the derisive and the sympathetic: as a Jonsonian butt Sir John is cruelly exposed to ridicule, but the complexity of his character constantly reminds the laugher of the similarities between observer and observed, just as Falstaff's own brand of humour blends the punitive and the amiably genial.

It is in one sense ironic that the most forceful statement of the superiority theory of laughter should have been the work of an Englishman, for the crucial transformation making possible our modern notion of humour was very much an English affair. Cazamian associates the development with the reflective mood of seventeenth-century England after the excitement of the Elizabethan age, an introspective and analytical mood that involved – and was involved with – the increased intellectual complexity and greater skill in the distinction of shades of meaning that made the new mode of thought possible. He points out that similar developments were very close to taking place in both Italy and France – Cervantes was the grand exception in Spain – but were eventually pre-empted in England (325–30). The English pedigree of European humour is attested to by the fact that almost all of the major Western languages turned to English for their word to describe this new phenomenon: Italian *umore*, Spanish *humor*, German *Humor*, Russian *jumor*, even French *humour* – which was borrowed in the early eighteenth century from English, while the native *humeur*, itself actually the etymological ancestor of the Middle English *humour*, was felt to be inadequate as a vehicle for the new intellectual development. As early as 1690 Sir William Temple's essay *Of Poetry* refers in self-congratulatory vein to 'Humour, a Word peculiar to our Language ... and hard to be expressed in any other' (quoted in Wimsatt/Brooks, 210).

It might strike one as odd that Hobbes so obviously disapproved of laughter at a time when these far-reaching new developments were in progress in the realm of humour and the laughable. But in fact Hobbes was by no means alone among his contemporaries in his disapproval of laughter – a position, moreover, wholly sanctioned by the ancients. Over the hundred years between 1650 and 1750 numerous voices were raised in England against laughter. Swift is said to have been able to recall having laughed only twice in his entire life. Jonson declared that 'the moving of laughter is a fault in Comedie' (quoted in Wimsatt/Brooks, 209). Pepys and Pope and Dryden and Addison all seem to have been similarly agelastic (to employ the splendid seventeenth-century locution for those not given to laughter; those who were prone to overindulgence in the vice of laughter were described as 'hypergelasts'). The polite smile was commended; laughter, by contrast, was condemned. Lord Chesterfield warned his son against the vice of laughter in the most stringent terms in 1748: 'In my mind there is nothing so illiberal, and so ill-bred, as audible laughter' (quoted in Boston, 172). Hobbes's attitude seems in fact to have been quite typical of the low esteem in which the more overt forms of humour had come to be held by the middle of the seventeenth century. One can suggest two interconnected reasons why this disapproval should have come about. First, as Richard Boston points out, there was undoubtedly a reaction to the hypergelastic excesses of the sort of humour loosely thought of as 'Rabelaisian.' Boston notes that Sir Thomas Urquhart, the translator of Rabelais, is popularly supposed to have died in 1660 as the result of an uncontrollable fit of laughter on hearing of the restoration of Charles II (24). The later Middle Ages had seen the burgeoning of various genres of extremely robust humour, demanding an equally robust, belly-shaking response – the digestive and excremental humour of many of the chapbooks of the period, for example, very aptly described in German as *grobianisch*, 'vulgarian,' and very often linked with a strong vein of overt cruelty. The second reason, undoubtedly, grows precisely from a reaction against such cruelty, just as the first was connected with a reaction against vulgarian excess. With the stirrings of the new concept of humour and its concomitant liberalism and tolerance, in short, the unvarnished and unabashed aggression of purely derisive laughter could only fall increasingly into disrepute.

The association of humour and sympathy, pathos, and sentiment during the eighteenth century has been explored by Stuart Tave in his study *The Amiable Humorist* (1960). Tave chronicles the displacement of the ridicule, raillery, and punitive satirical wit of the Restoration period in England by the good-natured, good-humoured, portrayal of good-natured, good-humoured, amiable 'originals' (one of the key terms of the new concept of humour), 'whose peculiarities are not satirically instructive,' as they had been in the case of Jonson's eccentric humorists, 'but objects of delight and love' (viii).

Fielding's Parson Adams and Sterne's Uncle Toby appear on the scene in the 1740s and 1750s and are followed by ever-increasing numbers of similar gentle eccentrics whose whimsical oddities of character are chronicled not with scorn and derision but with an affectionate chuckle, for their oddities are seen in the new scheme of things not as antisocial vices demanding the lash of satire, but as human failings that as fallible humans ourselves we have the obligation to understand and treat with benevolent sympathy. A philanthropic combination of laughter and tears now became a desirable norm as the new awareness of the range of humour grew. Nor was it just a question of new literary eccentrics being produced to fit the new conception of laughter, from Parson Adams, Uncle Toby, and the Vicar of Wakefield down to Mr Pickwick, Aunt Betsey Trotwood, and Mr Micawber; older characters now began to appear in a new light as well, as Tave shows. Falstaff and Don Quijote especially became standard-bearers of the new awareness, appearing now as lovably human and complex eccentrics rather than as the ridiculous buffoons they had represented for audiences a century earlier. The duty of the laugher was now, in a word, no longer to laugh *at*, but to laugh *with*; no longer to excoriate folly but to marvel smilingly at the reach and diversity of human nature. By the end of the eighteenth century laughter and humour were completely rehabilitated. Once regarded as unworthy of a gentleman, laughter, in its new and humanitarian guise, would be seen by the Romantics as an essential buffer against the slings and arrows of existence.

None of this is to suggest that the new conception of laughter and humour quickly routed the traditional view of laughter. Far from it, indeed: the debate between the rival adherents of 'wit' and 'humour' grew to be one of the most protracted and vigorous *causes célèbres* of the eighteenth century. For every champion of the new live-and-let-live democratic virtues of humour there was another who extolled the more disdainfully aristocratic pleasures of fine satire, likened by Dryden to 'the fineness of a stroke that separates the head from the body, and leaves it standing in its place' (quoted in Wimsatt/Brooks, 207). It is also worth noting that even though the word *humour* is borrowed by the French (according to Larousse) as early as 1725, the *Encyclopaedia Britannica* carries no definition of *humour* in either of its first two editions (1771 and 1783), only cross-references to *fluid* and *wit* respectively. The third edition, in 1797, defines humour as bearing a 'considerable resemblance to wit,' but as being 'more wild, loose, extravagant and fantastical,' and doubts whether humour can be considered 'perfectly consistent with true politeness' (quoted in Cazamian, 409). In spite of this conservative judgment on the part of the learned encyclopaedist, however, the new humour was certainly here to stay and had in fact already found a theoretical explanation several decades before. Shaftesbury's 'Sensus Communis: An Essay on the Freedom of Wit and Humour' (1709) seems to mark the beginning of the theoretical re-evaluation of humour, but the honour of suggesting a general theory of humour and laughter that would be capable of replacing the Hobbesean superiority theory – insofar, at least, as the latter could not adequately account for the newer forms of humour – seems to belong to the Scottish poet and philosopher James Beattie, in his 'Essay on Laughter' of 1776. Beattie's contribution, later elaborated by Kant and Schopenhauer among others, is generally known as the incongruity theory, according to which laughter arises not so much from considerations of superiority and inferiority as from the perception of two or more objects or events or concepts whose relationship, if they are regarded as constituting a single complex entity rather than as being separate and unrelated items, is markedly incongruous, inconsistent, or unsuitable (603). Kant, in the *Critique of Judgment* (1790), emphasized that the element of surprise and unexpectedness is vital: 'Laughter is an affectation arising from the sudden transformation of a strained expectation into nothing' (225). Schopenhauer, in *The World as Will and Idea* (1818), wrote in similar vein that humour occurs when 'two or more real objects are thought through *one* concept; ... it then becomes strikingly apparent from the entire difference of the objects in other respects, that the concept was only applicable to them from a one-sided point of view' (76–7) – in other words, when there is a mismatch between conceptual understanding and perceptual experience. For Hazlitt, too, in his *Lectures on the English Comic Writers* (1819), 'the essence of the laughable is the incongruous, the disconnecting of one idea from another, or the jostling of one feeling against another' (7).

The incongruity theory, in other words, shifts the emphasis from the emotional reaction of the superiority theory to the cognitive reaction. Where Hobbes had stressed the duality or contrast between the superiority of the laugher and the inferiority of the victim, the more modern view stressed the fact of duality, contrast, incongruity itself. The Hobbesean laugher laughs because he is superior to the contrasted object of his laughter; for the newer theorists the illogicality, unexpectedness, inappropriateness of the contrast itself is central. There had been elements of the incongruity theory present in the superiority theory from Aristotle on, of course, in the sense that contrast is necessarily central to the superiority theory as well. Only in the eighteenth century, however, with the new emphasis on liberalism, tolerance, reason, and humanitarianism, was the ground ready for such a conceptual shift, and a less punitive and more playful view of laughter called for. The incongruity theory, in a word, pulled the teeth of the Hobbesean *homo homini lupus* and turned him into *homo ludens*.

The new emphasis on the ludic possibilities of contrast per se found a particularly sympathetic response among the Romantics, with their concern for the contrast between the real and the ideal, the temporal and the eternal, the finite and the infinite. And among the Romantics it was the Germans above all who seized upon the new conception of humour and elevated it into a metaphysical system. Jean Paul Richter was Sterne's most enthusiastic German champion and set out, in his *Vorschule der Ästhetik* (1804), to develop a theory of the new humour – which he called 'das Romantische Komische' / 'the Romantic form of the comic' as opposed to the cold derision of classical satire – based on incongruity, which would also serve as a Romantic metaphysical system. In humour situations the intellect, like an artist, toys deliciously with alternative possibilities, dancing back and forth in delightful freedom. On the higher levels of freedom attained through humour the laughable becomes a link with the transcendental, measuring the finite no longer against the equally finite but against the infinite and finding the contrast infinitely ludicrous. Finiteness itself is annihilated in the contrast with the idea of infinite reason, by virtue of the mere fact of the contrast: 'Der Humor... vernichtet nicht das Einzelne, sondern das Endliche durch den Kontrast mit der Idee' (125) / 'Humour annihilates not the individual, but the finite, through the contrast with the ideal.' In the presence of infinity all are alike and all equally nothing, and the laughter that arises consequently contains both 'sorrow and greatness.' Friedrich Schlegel makes a similar use of the laughable, although he calls it not humour but rather irony – we will return at a later point to the relationship between these two terms. Wimsatt and Brooks summarize Schlegel's arguments succinctly: 'Irony was a succession of contrasts between the ideal and the real, a technique by which the "transcendental ego" was capable of mocking its own convictions and its own productions. It was ultimate self-parody. It remained aloof from fixation or satisfaction at any level of insight. It was an avenue to the infinite, the expression of man's appetite for the boundless; it was expansiveness, it was megalomania. Life at its most incandescent phase destroyed itself as it created' (379–80). For Heine and the aesthetician K.W.F. Solger, irony, as Wimsatt and Brooks observe, becomes so further subtilized that it becomes coextensive with all art, an almost mystical energy of creation, a translation of the insufficient world of experience into the artist's dream world (380). For Baudelaire laughter is likewise a token of the essentially contradictory nature of the human condition, torn between 'an infinite grandeur and an infinite misery' (249–51).

Humour, in other words, became for the Romantic sensibility a very serious business indeed, having very little to do with the cosiness and whimsy of an Uncle Toby or a Mr Pickwick. Indeed as the nineteenth century progresses two quite distinct traditions of humour pursue separate and parallel existences. On the one hand there is the sunny, whimsical, comfortable tradition of English humour that we associate with the tea-and-crumpets world of a Mr Pickwick. There is the hearty humour of a Carlyle, who declared that 'no man who has once heartily and wholly laughed can be altogether irreclaimably bad' (quoted in Boston, 224); there is the sunny humour of Lamb, the early Dickens, the early Mark Twain, George Eliot at least sometimes, and G.K. Chesterton; there is the cosiness and whimsy of such later benevolent humorists as Beatrix Potter, A.A. Milne, and P.G. Wodehouse (cf. Carlson). By contrast, we have the hollow, gloomy laughter of a Baudelaire, for whom 'the wise man laughs only with fear and trembling,' for his laughter, provoked by existential contradiction, is essentially aimed at the discordances of the human condition itself; or there is Nietzsche, for whom 'man alone suffers so excruciatingly in the world that he was compelled to invent laughter' (Goldstein/McGhee, 20); there is Byron, for whom 'if I laugh at any mortal thing, 'tis that I may not weep' (Goldstein/ McGhee, 58); there is the later Mark Twain, for whom 'the secret source of humor itself is not joy but sorrow' (ibid); there is the whole series of black humorists collected in André Breton's anthology. The darkening of humour in the later nineteenth century – and increasingly so in the twentieth, where laughter is only relatively rarely without its blacker side – has suggested to some historians of humour that the comfortable eighteenth- and early-nineteenth-century humour we may usually think of as peculiarly English should be seen as merely a passing episode in the history of laughter. Stuart Tave, for example, sees sympathetic humour in this sense as 'a historical event with a beginning and an end' (ix), the beginning situated in the early eighteenth century, the end in 1914. Ronald Knox similarly concludes that derisive laughter, being both international and of all ages, is a normal function of human genius, while sympathetic humour may be seen as something of a perversion or at least a highly specialized offshoot of the satirical impetus. 'The humorist,' says Knox apophthegmatically, 'is a satirist out of a job' (62).

There are almost as many theories of humour and laughter as there are writers on the subject, but the superiority and incongruity theories may be called general theories, in that many individual explanations are variants of one or the other. One can speak of three of these general theories, the third in chronological order being the so-called relief theory that came into its own during the second half of the nineteenth century, partly at least as a response to what one might call the re-emergence of the darker, more aggressive, unsympathetic, Hobbesean side of laughter. The relief theory sees laughter primarily as a sort of safety valve, a venting of excess energy. Herbert Spencer, the English philosopher, suggested in 1860 that laughter was primarily a physiological affair, due to an overflow of surplus energy through the facial muscles and the respiratory system. Serious expectations are not met, and the laugher's attention is diverted to something that by comparison is frivolous – in Spencer's own formulation, laughter occurs 'when consciousness is unawares transferred from great things to small' (310). Once again, as we can see, the heart of the theory is the fact of contrast, but the emphasis is now shifted a second time, this time both from the laugher's perceived superiority to the contrasted object of ridicule and from the cognitive perception of the contrast itself to the psycho-physiological results of a sudden release from tension as the contrast is perceived. The beginnings of this third general conception of laughter, we may note, can be found already hinted at at least as early as Shaftesbury's essay of 1709, where laughter is associated with the bursting free of the *constrained* human spirit. Kant too, as we may remember, derived laughter from 'the sudden transformation of a *strained* expectation into nothing' (225; my emphasis). Charles Darwin was another who accounted for laughter in primarily physiological terms, and George Meredith introduced the notion of humour as a regulatory *social* safety valve, deflating the pompous, exposing the hypocrite, making the frightening more tolerable. But the most influential version of the relief theory has certainly been that of Freud. In his celebrated treatise of 1905, *Jokes and Their Relation to the Unconscious*, laughter is presented as the physiological result of a psychological triumph over prohibition, over the thou-shalt-not of the censorious superego. Humour phenomena, in other words, constitute the venting of aggressive and/or sexual feelings and anxieties in a disguised, subdued, sublimated, playful, socially accepted way, thus circumventing the heavy-footed superego and disarming the guilty conscience. There is a strong Hobbesean element in Freud, who consistently stresses the nastier origins of laughter: we laugh only because it is no longer acceptable to bite. In spite of its brutish origins, however, humour is still essentially a safety valve, an agent of civilization, of psychic and social good health, a redirection of potentially dangerous energies into useful and therapeutic work. Freud's explanation of humour phenomena, as one might say, is couched in thermodynamic terms, a thermodynamics of the psyche, conserving and transforming psychic energy. Psychic energy, stockpiled to deal with an imminently threatening situation as the ego seems about to be swamped by the atavistic urgings of the id, is not merely dissipated uselessly, but is transformed into a substitute, simulated gratification. Humour, in short, fully partakes of the overall program of psychoanalytic practice: 'Wo es war, wird ich sein' / 'Where id was, will ego be.' The good-housekeeping metaphor is an appropriately negentropic one: the overriding task of humour in Freud's system is the preservation of order.

The preservation and the possible disruption of order, indeed, play an important, even a vital role in all three of the general theories of humour that have emerged since classical times. None of the three seems to be able to account comprehensively for humour; each of them explains a particular type of humour most adequately; and each of them to some extent overlaps with each of the others. All three, however, as we have seen, place a central emphasis on the existence of contrast – and contrast is always associated with an implicit or explicit notion of order. 'To detect eccentricity you must have a centre,' as L.J. Potts admirably puts it (quoted in Wimsatt/Brooks, 55). The Hobbesean satirist laughs scornfully because his position is so obviously *right*, so obviously superior to the clearly *wrong* position of the victim of his gleeful ridicule. The laugher knows what is right and proper (such as *not* falling into a swimming-pool with your clothes on), and his laughter, which can easily slide over into overt contempt, proves it. The laugher of the incongruity theory similarly knows what relationships between objects and events and happenings are the normal, right, and proper ones, and his laughter signifies his sudden perception of the abnormal apparently masquerading as the norm. Unlike the superior laugher, who is locked into derision, the laugher at incongruity has the option of laughing derisively or sympathetically as he chooses, but each of them is equally certain as to what constitutes the norm of psychological and social order and what does not – and this certitude is not altered by the fact that another individual, or even society at large, may radically disagree. The laughter of relief, finally, is very much the consequence of a successfully averted disruption of the rules of order, as we have just seen. Indeed, all three of our traditional macrotheories deal with the *prevented* disruption of order. Etymologically a norm (from the Latin *norma*) is a carpenter's square – in humour situations the rectitude of the right angle is challenged. In what we may call the humour of order, however, the challenge to the orthogonal, to rectitude and right thinking, is received as only a temporary, inessential, easily reversible deviation, 'comic relief,' as the traditional phrase has it, from the four-square, logical, rational, controllable, common-sense world of law and order. The humour of order, that is to say, is *normative* humour. What if the threat to the regulated system could not be averted, though? What if the ninety degrees of the right angle came to be relativized as merely a conventional arrangement rather than an axiomatic, ontologically assured given? To what extent, in other words, can we speak of a comedy of entropy as well as a comedy of order?

We have reached the point where we can suggest an answer to the first part of the project stated in the opening sentence of this chapter, namely the situation of black humour in the diachronic development of humour. The darkening of humour during and after the Romantic movement is, as we have seen, well attested. Both Breton and Henniger, however, the only critics so far to have looked in any detail at the historical development of black humour as a literary form, see the early eighteenth rather than the nineteenth century as marking its emergence as a coherent force in literary history. Various critics, as we have also seen, have pointed to yet earlier occurrences of very dark strains of humour ranging back as far as Ecclesiastes, but the very fact that Swift and Sade could write with such an extreme of black humour as they did in the age of enlightenment, tolerance, rationality, and confidence is particularly startling – all the more so since this was precisely the point at which the general conception of humour was beginning to shift towards the other, more benign, end of the spectrum. If writers like, say, Sterne and Goldsmith employ a form of humour inextricably linked with sympathy and goodwill, Swift's and Sade's humour seems equally inextricably linked with contempt and loathing. It is *possible*, as already discussed, to read Swift's and Sade's humour as an extreme of Hobbesean corrective satire, as an extreme form of satire designed to jolt a jaded readership into a new and shocked realization of man's inhumanity to man, as a fevered defence, in other words, of the same sense of order, wholeness, and cosmos that Sterne and Goldsmith whimsically celebrate. Such a reading lacks persuasiveness, however, as already suggested, precisely because of the *pleasure* that both Swift's and Sade's narrators so clearly derive from their accounts, the scrupulous attention to detail of the one, for example, or the fanatically encyclopaedic accumulation of enormities of the other. If these are satires, the object of the satire is the very notion of order itself.

During the Christian Middle Ages, as Gerd Henniger observes, when belief had hardened into a hidebound system untroubled by doubts or rational qualms, humour may frequently have been drastic, but it was never black in the Swiftean or Sadean sense (*Brevier* 9). Modern humour, with its sudden awareness of the fact of incongruity itself as a laughable phenomenon, is ultimately derivable from the breakdown of the medieval world-picture and the consequent intensification of the sense of discrepancy between the real and the ideal. The sense of disorientation thus engendered, combined with the contrary thrust of Renaissance optimism, leads ultimately to the new psychological phenomenon of a sense of humour that is conceptual rather than merely physical, as found in varying tinctures in the works of Rabelais, Cervantes, and Shakespeare. Only when the gap between the real and the ideal begins to be perceived as extreme, when humour begins to be self-consciously aware of the futility of its own gestures towards reconciliation of the opposites, does black humour fully emerge, as Henniger argues, not any longer as a force for reconciliation but as an exacerbated reflection of the separation. This 'crisis of humour,' Henniger further argues, though prefigured throughout the history of literature in the case of individual isolated outsiders, and in full swing since the breakdown of a firmly institutionalized morality during the late Middle Ages, reached its fullest development only during the eighteenth century, and black humour was born, as a fundamental criticism of human affairs, sprung from the new, exhilarating, and terrifying freedom of rational thought ('Zur Genealogie' 27), the result of the confrontation with the idea of absolute freedom and with the consequent problem of the ultimate meaning of life itself, a question now fully answerable neither by the new reason nor, any longer, by the old faith.

The 'crisis of humour' can be seen as one expression of the larger crisis of the European consciousness in the early years of the eighteenth century as documented by Paul Hazard. Humour, which for thousands of years had been, by and large, a brutally simple affair of your falling down and my laughing uproariously, suddenly became a much more intriguing affair, as reflected in the emergence of new forms predicated on sympathy and a sharpened awareness of the function of contrast. But if Shaftesbury has some claim to be the father of sympathetic humour, Swift has certainly a strong claim, as Breton observed, to be considered the father of black humour – Shaftesbury, incidentally, knew and detested Swift, whom he considered obscene, profane, and a 'false wit' (Tave, 37). Humour, in other words, was in the final stages of a polarization with regard to the concept of an ordered universe by the beginning of the eighteenth century, the literary emergence of the joyous affirmation of the sympathetic humorists counterbalanced by the rejection of psychological and social norms on the part of the new black humorists, comedians of entropy. The benign and the black alike were thus latent in that humour whose dominant expression was derisive until at least the end of the seventeenth century, infrared and ultraviolet regions just beyond the edges of the narrow visible spectrum. It would take another two centuries or so before the 'new' entropic humour would be seen in perspective: Cazamian, we remember, argued that the self-awareness of the benign humour of the eighteenth century, and the subsequent flowering of consciousness of humour as a distinct instrument, came only with the finding of an individual name for the 'new' psychological phenomenon (103). Black humour would have to wait until the 1940s before Breton, by giving it a name, made possible its incorporation in the known spectrum.

The relationship in synchronic terms of black humour to humour in general emerges from a consideration – along lines suggested by Northrop Frye's procedure in the *Anatomy of Criticism* – of the structure of that spectrum. We may see the range as beginning – typologically, not historically – with the most benign forms of sympathetic humour, for which God is indeed in his heaven and all right with the world. This is humour in its celebratory aspect. The norms of psychological and social order are unshakeably established, and the laugher's reaction to any deviation from the norm is one merely of sympathetic amusement and benevolent understanding. The next band in our spectrum is occupied by the various shadings of increasingly aggressive, derisive humour, where the laughter is increasingly cold, intolerant, unsympathetic, where deviation from the norm is regarded as a dangerous and incipient threat to order and the response is one of increasingly sharp rejection and punitive correction. This is humour in its apotropaic aspect. In spite of their essential difference, the benign and the derisive forms of humour share one important characteristic, however: they are both essentially self-congratulatory, self-reassuring, springing from an ordered world of unshaken norms; the humour of those inside and safe rather than outside and lost, the humour of those who can still put their trust in compasses. Both the benign and the derisive aspects of humour see the self optimistically as a controlling agent in an orderly world. They may differ in their mode of expression, the warmth of the one reflecting its unthreatened norms and the coldness of the other reflecting a militant defence of the same norms; they are alike, however, in that they are both expressions of the humour of certainty, the humour of cosmos. Black humour contrasts with both of these in that it is the humour of uncertainty, lost norms, lost confidence, the humour of disorientation, the comedy of entropy.

The band of values associated with sympathetic or celebratory humour in our spectrum would range from the beatific smile of the Buddha to the mildly ironic, wordly-wise shrug of amused acquiescence; derisive or apotropaic humour would range from the gentle smile of avuncular reproach to lacerating ridicule. Entropic humour similarly has its range, and it is a range that *can* accommodate the untrammelled ferocity of a Swift or a Sade at one extreme, and at the other the apparently so completely different work of a Nabokov or a Borges. As the humour of order is divided into the proclamation and celebration of order in the sympathetic mode and the militant rejection of disorder in the derisive mode, so the humour of entropy may be seen as divided into two correlative modes or phases (to employ Frygian vocabulary again), moving between the apocalyptic and anomic rejection of all order at the 'blackest' extreme (thus Swift or Sade) and the parodic celebration of disorder – or rather the active *replacement* of a vanished order with a new and overtly humorous *fictional* order – at the other (thus Nabokov and Borges). It is towards *metahumour*, in other words, self-reflective humour about humour itself, that our spectrum of entropic humour moves, from the rejection of all norms to the celebration of parodied norms. We may observe moreover that the relationship between anomic humour (based on the rejection of order) and parodic (meta)humour (growing out of the celebration of disorder) exactly parallels the relationship between the thermodynamic and the information-theory concepts of entropy, the former predicated on the erosion of certainty, the latter on the exploitation of uncertainty.

To the extent that *all* humour, however self-confident, in a sense exploits uncertainty, all humour can be said to tend towards the reflexivity of metahumour, of course, suggesting a more complex interrelationship between the humour of order and the humour of entropy than can be accommodated in the tidy scheme just advanced (and diagrammed in figure 1). This fact alone should be enough to make us properly suspicious of the beguiling symmetry of the theory (or explanatory fiction) proffered over the last few paragraphs. All explanation, after all, is indeed a fiction in the sense that it constitutes a *narrative* – and narrative, like humour, is predicated also on the exploitation of uncertainty. The analogue of the spectrum is, of course, only a suggestive one, a metaphoric one, useful mainly for pointing to primary emphases, and in so doing it finds it more convenient to ignore the fact that even the most self-confident forms of the humour of order can, given appropriate conditions, be read as containing more than a hint of what we are calling entropic humour here, and vice versa, especially in the case of what we are calling metahumour. One could perhaps better illustrate (narrate) this particular insight by abandoning the story of the spectrum and visualizing the comedy of order and the comedy of entropy as intersecting cones instead, along the lines of Yeats's gyres in *A Vision*. The gyres – intersecting cones, with the apex of each touching the centre of the base of the other – represent for Yeats the antithetical elements in all of human nature, insofar as the intersecting cones are at any point inversely proportional to each other and never mutually exclusive. A cross-section of either, at any point, always contains something of the other, though no two cross-sections will have identical proportions. Neither the humour of order nor the humour of disorder necessarily excludes the other, it must be remembered, in one very important way: namely, as soon as we choose to see humour from the perspective of the receiver rather than the sender in a situation where both are present. Sufficiently determined readers, as we have already observed, *can* read Sade's texts as brilliant satires on man's inhumanity to man, or on Enlightenment optimism, or on the marginalization of women in a male society, and the thrust of contempo-

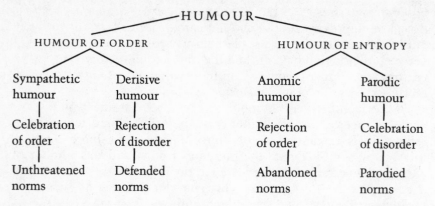

Figure 1. The spectrum of humour

rary interpretive theory is that they will be as right or as wrong as the combination of their critical skills and their chosen context of operation allows them to be. The tale – as we saw with Zeno's (mis)treatment of Achilles and the tortoise – is in the telling, and the telling is *shared* by its author and its reader: the author *tells* the expectant reader which narrative facts are relevant, and from these facts the reader can *tell* how and why the narrative develops as it does. Another alternative telling of our tale of humour can be advanced to incorporate the insights of both the spectrum metaphor and the cone metaphor if we choose to regard our spectrum as inscribed on a Möbius strip. A Möbius strip is constructed by taking a piece of paper, twisting it once, and taping the ends together. The result is a topological paradox, a surface with only one side. If we allow one side of the strip (before taping, that is) to represent the normative, orderly face of humour and the other the entropic face, we can traverse the strip in either direction, starting on either the side originally that of order or disorder, and the result is the same. 'Each' side paradoxically becomes the 'other,' at least as long as we choose to continue playing the game. The two original sides, however, verifiably still exist in the sense that at any point on the strip (that is, if we refuse to play the game of traversing it) the paper still obviously has two sides – you cannot cut one side without cutting the other as well, for example. This two-faced telling of the tale not only associates normative and entropic humour at all points, as does the gyre story, it also suggests – to follow Frye one more time (239) – that when you move far enough in the direction of the reflexive end of entropic humour you do not necessarily fall off the edge of the spectrum, but end up, after passing through what one can only call a humour warp, in the realm of celebratory humour all over again.

How can we resolve the duplicity of the dual narrative presented by the model of the Möbius strip? It is evident that the particular interpretive game we choose to play determines which result we obtain – a cautionary parable for all critics, no doubt, but especially for those dealing with humour. It is evident too that the 'spectrum' of humour that we have constructed in this chapter has no claim at all to any sort of ontological (as opposed to metaphorical, that is to say, narrative) truth. It exists only as the net result of a particular way of reading the history (which is to say, the historiography) of humour phenomena of various kinds, especially literary, over the last few centuries. By employing this particular way of thinking about humour as an enabling fiction in our further reading of certain literary texts we shall also obtain certain more or less persuasive results, and these results too will be provisional and positional, the results of interpretive choices taken and not taken. No apology is called for that this should be so, for, after all, this situation is wholly appropriate to the nature of humour, which is never primarily concerned with how things 'really are,' but rather always with how they can be *told* as being and *read* as being. Even the simplest form of humour situation, in other words, constitutes an elementary narrative situation as well, and we shall return to this point and its implications for both humour and narrative at some length in another chapter. Before exploring the more narrowly technical aspects of the relationship from a narratological point of view, however, let us first return to the question already raised in our opening chapter and examine some more general implications of the role of humour as a pervasive force in modern thinking.

3 Boundaries Blurred: The Importance of Being Earnest

Since the Romantics, and increasingly in the twentieth century, it has become a commonplace that we *need* laughter, that humour is a necessary component of our lives rather than a peripheral activity of a merely frivolous and essentially wasteful character. Byron's contention that 'if I laugh at any mortal thing, 'tis that I may not weep,' or Nietzsche's that man 'suffers so excruciatingly in the world that he was compelled to invent laughter,' or Oscar Wilde's that 'life is much too important to talk about seriously,' or even Freud's that humour is an essential safety-valve – all of these subscribe generally to the Romantic dictum, as systematized by Richter and Hegel, that all humour, black or white, is primarily affirmative. In Hegel's terms: 'Inseparable from the comic is an infinite geniality and confidence, capable of rising superior to its own contradiction' (quoted in Shipley, 214). Or as Richard Boston puts it: 'We need laughter, just as we need love. Were we entirely rational, and without any hang-ups, neuroses or tensions, then we would need neither. Laughter is like the pearl which the oyster forms around the speck of irritation. The entirely healthy oyster produces no pearls, and the inhabitants of Utopia ... do not laugh. Laughter exists in an imperfect world, and it makes us rejoice that it *is* imperfect' (239).

In the Western tradition, however, as we have seen, humour and laughter, as represented by the theorists at least, were regarded in a much less favourable light from the earliest times down to the beginning of the eighteenth century and even longer. Laughter and the comic were traditionally distrusted, stigmatized as buffoonery ill suited to any but the low-bred, and generally perceived as a threat to the serious business of living. The importance of being earnest, to borrow Wilde's phrase, is self-evident for Aristotle and Plato (in *Philebus*, at any rate), as we have seen, and this is reflected in their ostentatious privileging of tragedy over comedy. Tragedy is high, comedy low; tragedy is serious, comedy flippant; tragedy is *important*, in a word, involving us in cathartic consideration of eternal verities, while comedy is merely a passing amusement, allowing us at best to let off steam. In Plato's *Symposium*, to be sure, Socrates argues that the genius of comedy is the same as that of tragedy, action demanding tragic seriousness, while contemplation demands comic wisdom, but most literary theorists over the next two millennia or so tended to agree rather with Horace, who seemed to have real doubts in his mind as to whether comedy (and its near neighbour, satire) should even be admitted as qualifying for the status of 'real literature' (Wimsatt/ Brooks, 86).

Even in our own day one still sometimes encounters this traditional view that tragedy, because of its inherent seriousness, is somehow *superior* to comedy in that the latter, by choosing to employ humour as a vehicle, wantonly cuts itself off from the mainstream of both literary and social endeavour. This view was in fact, however, effectively exploded more than a century ago by Friedrich Nietzsche, who, in his ground-breaking essay on *The Birth of Tragedy* (1872), took up Plato's suggestion in the *Symposium* in postulating a common root for tragedy and comedy. Repudiating the then received wisdom that Greek tragedy was essentially 'Apollonian' in character, marked by detachment, serenity, and contemplation, Nietzsche maintained that it was in fact rooted rather in 'Dionysian' impulses traditionally associated with the comic, in instinctive and irrepressible impulses, that is, towards wild abandon, revelry, licentiousness, and intoxication. In addition, however, by conceiving of tragedy as essentially a pattern of *tensions* Nietzsche also provided for the possibility of formal arguments as well for the drawing together of tragedy and comedy. Wimsatt and Brooks, in their brilliant chapter on 'Tragedy and Comedy,' see Nietzsche's work as the beginnings of a complete re-evaluation of comedy, which continues with the work of Bergson and Koestler. First, they rightly point out the parallelism between Nietzsche's conception of tragedy and Bergson's conception of comedy in his essay 'Laughter' (1900). Like Nietzsche before him and Freud after him, Bergson traced art ultimately to the dark, instinctive side of the mind. And as Nietzsche saw tragedy as functioning in terms of a pattern of tensions, so Bergson saw comedy (that is to say, the comic) as the result of a similar conflict between the Apollonian (that is, the level of intelligence) and the Dionysian (or level of instinct). For Bergson, developing Baudelaire's concept of humour as based on the discrepancy between the physical and spiritual aspects of the human condition, the comic resulted from the encrustation of the mechanical upon the organic: a man falling down a flight of stairs is behaving not as a human being should but as an automaton might be expected to function. The comic response involves superiority as well as incongruity, however, demands distance, perspective, suspension of sympathy for the victim – what Bergson calls a temporary 'anaesthesia of the heart' (64). The Apollonian stratum of intelligence and social cohesion, that is to say, recognizing and deriding the personal and social inappropriateness of falling down flights of stairs, subdues the instinctive (Dionysian) identification with the sufferer (Wimsatt/Brooks, 567–9). Arthur Koestler's *Insight and Outlook* (1949) undertakes to push even further the similarity between tragedy and comedy, to establish 'the direct connection between the comic and the tragic, between laughter and crying, between humour and art' (430). The key to these connections is what Koestler terms the 'Eureka effect,' which consists in the 'bisociative' treatment of a phenomenon: a phenomenon, that is to say, regarded as a habitual member of one field of ideas is suddenly *seen* to be also a member of a contrasting field of ideas, as when Archimedes reportedly discovered that the volume of displaced bathwater had a hitherto quite unsuspected connection to the apparently unrelated problem of measuring the volume of solid bodies. For Wimsatt and Brooks Koestler's work marks the culmination of the development initiated by Nietzsche: the subsumption of tragedy and comedy 'under one pattern, a pattern of bifurcation, of resistances acknowledged and transcended' (579).

The effects of the re-evaluation of comedy in the Nietzschean tradition have been far-reaching, as Martin Esslin's work on the theatre of the absurd, for example, clearly shows. A companion re-evaluation of the relationship between the tragic and the comic has also been taking place more recently, however, from a quite different perspective, one of considerable interest to our present concern, associated with the name of the Russian literary theorist and historian Mikhail Bakhtin. During the Middle Ages the classically separate decora of tragedy and comedy, as is well attested, were largely abandoned: Dante's *Divina commedia*, innumerable miracle and mystery plays, even cathedral architecture, as Bakhtin observes, all frequently demonstrate a distinct vein of grotesquerie, a mingling of the sacred and the sublime with the profane and the all-too-human, low, funny, and by modern standards even disgusting. In terms of the historical development of humour this incongruity should no doubt be read as still an expression of a sense of cosmos, of wholeness, rather than of entropy, a feeling for the cosmic interrelatedness of all created things, an attitude similar, in fact, to the traditional fourfold method of scriptural exegesis, where a single original text – the text of scripture, the text of creation – admitted of multiple readings that in a superficial sense might appear unrelated and even mutually contradictory, but seen in the relevant interpretive context were wholly complementary facets of a unitary meaning, for the world, in all its aspects, was merely an expression of the radiant order, beauty, harmony, and hierarchy of divine creation (Wimsatt/Brooks, 151). Laughter, in short, becomes what Bakhtin calls 'one of the essential forms of the truth concerning the world as a whole, concerning history and man; it is a peculiar point of view relative to the world; the world is seen anew, no less (and perhaps more) profoundly than when seen from the serious standpoint.' Indeed, for Bakhtin, 'certain essential aspects of the world are accessible only to laughter' (*Rabelais* 66).

Bakhtin develops this notion in his *Problems of Dostoevsky's Poetics* (to which all subsequent page references in this paragraph refer), tracing this new attitude to life to the close of classical antiquity, when there arose, as opposed to the more 'serious' genres of tragedy, epic, and history, a new realm called by the ancients themselves the *spoudogeloion* 'serio-comic' (106). The new realm included certain forms of mime, the Socratic dialogue, and the so-called mennipea or Menippean satire that would eventually spawn the European picaresque novel as well as the satires of Rabelais, Swift, and Voltaire (116). These new genres, according to Bakhtin, are all characterized by what he calls a 'carnival sense of the world' and an atmosphere of 'joyful relativity' (107). The serious genres are *monologic*, or *homophonic*, as Bakhtin phrases it: they presuppose an integrated and stable universe of discourse. The *spoudogeloia*, by contrast, are *dialogic*, or *polyphonic*: they deny the possibility, or at any rate the experience, of such integration. The serious forms attempt to comprehend human endeavour; the serio-comic forms are based on human inability to know and contain our fate. Socrates is Bakhtin's main exemplar of the dialogic or polyphonic nature of truth and human thinking about truth (110, 132). There is no ready-made monologic truth: truth is 'born *between people* collectively searching for truth, in the process of their dialogic interaction' (110). Socratic irony, a 'reduced carnival laughter' (132), is thus a model of the dialogic search for truth, by negotiated settlement, as it were. Bakhtin's notion of 'carnivalization' has attracted considerable attention in recent years with its emphasis on the

provisional inversion of traditional structures of hierarchy and authority, its *'joyful relativity* of all structure and order' (124; emphasis
Bakhtin's), its focus on parodic doubling and the implications of this
for the development of literature. Carnival, where fool's licence is
general, is a turning upside down of normal everyday reality, where all
authority and fixity are relativized and the norms of accepted order are
temporarily and parodically reversed. The first generic impact of
carnival on literature, says Bakhtin, was in the *parodia sacra*, blasphe-
mous (but tolerated) inversions and perversions of sacred liturgy, and
this iconoclastic parodic strand, together with related strands deriving
from the traditions of Socratic irony and Menippean satire, constitutes
the root specifically of that form of modern narrative that Bakhtin calls
dialogic or polyphonic fiction. More generally, however, the 'great
function of carnivalization in the history of literature' was that it
'constantly assisted in the destruction of all barriers between genres,
between self-enclosed systems of thought' (134–5). Generic development, in other words, is not the result of some abstract logic or
taxonomy; generic development is itself dialogic, the seriousness of
tragedy *provokes* the comic rejoinder.

The distinction between tragedy and comedy, in other words, once
so obvious, has, it is quite clear, become increasingly blurred during
the twentieth century. Earlier ages certainly saw blendings and
minglings of the two – one has only to think of Shakespeare or, even
more so, some of the Jacobean dramatists like Webster, Middleton, or
Tourneur. In most of these cases at least, though, what is happening is
a provocative *juxtaposition* of the tragic and the comic; in our own
time it is less a question of juxtaposition than *identity*. It has become
a critical commonplace that what J.L. Styan calls 'the ethical conven-
tionality of tragedy' (33) seems today impossible to adopt without very
considerable reservations, and material that in earlier, more stable
times and societies would automatically have been given tragic form
seems almost equally automatically to be treated as comic. Arthur
Koestler argues for the interchangeability of tragedy and comedy: since
the similarity in 'intellectual geometry,' as he calls it, is so marked, a
great weight comes to be placed on the 'emotional charge' of the work,
which now becomes the major yardstick by which we differentiate
between tragedy and comedy – just as it determines whether we decide
to treat the account of an acquaintance falling into the river as
warranting solicitude or hilarity.

The importance of being earnest is comparable to the importance of
an unwavering belief in Euclidean geometry. Within their self-im-

posed limits the systems work very well indeed; but they fail to suggest adequate answers to problems couched in terms of norms and perspectives other than their own. The outsider, notoriously, has become a stock figure in modern writing, and his (or her) emergence is certainly related to the emergence of a new conception of humour. We can see Archimedes as the patron saint of a long line of these humorist-geometers looking for places to stand from which to move the earth. Humour provides that vantage point in our times in a way that religion or magic once did, demonstrating the 'joyful relativity' of everyday norms, charting the everyday from new and unsuspected points of perspective. The re-evaluation of the relationship of tragedy and comedy is certainly related to the historical emergence of what we have been calling entropic humour, and both are related in turn to the re-evaluation of humour itself, increasingly since Nietzsche, as constituting a major rather than a peripheral strand in modern social discourse. One can go further, indeed, and say that the realignment of tragedy and comedy is only one aspect of a more general modern realignment, namely that of the relationship of humour and literary discourse in general, the re-evaluation of both writing and reading, in other words, that the re-evaluation of humour involves.

The course of literary history over the last century or so, reflecting a general shift from late-bourgeois confidence to post-bourgeois scepticism, provides ample evidence of the growing role of the non-serious, marked as that history is by the succession of realism by modernism in the early years of the twentieth century and the passage of modernism since the 1950s into what it has now been generally agreed to call postmodernism. For my present purposes, in fact, and even at the high cost of drastic oversimplification, I will use the terms *realism, modernism, postmodernism,* and their respective derivatives in a consciously schematic sense – cutting across the normal use of these terms as labels for periods of literary history – as usefully illustrating *positions* on an ideational scale of literary production and reception ranging from the most 'serious' to the most 'non-serious.' I will also assume (a) that both authors and readers can be classified as realists, modernists, or postmodernists according to their respective practice as producers or receivers of literary texts; (b) that a reader of any individual text can – subject to various restraints – theoretically adopt any one of these positions whether or not that position is the same as that adopted by the author of the text in question; and (c) that the practice of real authors and readers has always been very much more complex than allowed for in this deliberately attenuated scheme, which is concerned only with the relationship of the 'serious' and the 'non-serious.' I am therefore, for example, emphatically *not* making the simplistic claim that the great realist writers were grimly and totally devoid of all humour; far from it. However, realist writing was *in principle* very consciously a bourgeois art-form, and its program in consequence was a resolutely anti-romantic decision to emphasize the stability of things as they were. The realist writer's task was perceived, in principle, as the faithful representation of a common-sense reality where the ground was solid under foot and romantic doubts and questionings as to 'ultimate' stability or the lack of it were by and large firmly quashed – whether naïvely or with due reservation – as irrelevant to the serious business of getting on with it. Nor is this statement any less true in principle because of the large number of exceptions we could easily think of, for example, in the practice of writers classified by literary history as realists. Emma Bovary or Anna Karenina might experience life as tragic, Mr Pickwick or Tom Sawyer might live it as a comedy, but the distinction and its consequences were *primarily* the result of individual temperament or social realities rather than a reaction – whether on the part of the characters or on that of the narrative instance animating them – to an existence experienced as unstable in itself. For the archetypal realist *reader*, moreover, these were less characters in texts than people in 'real-life' situations, and he or she was well advised to learn from their mistakes and profit from their experience. The fictional world was no less real than the tangible reality of the everyday world, each validated by the other, and each unshakeably guaranteed by a central authoritative instance, whether called God, King, or Country in the one world or authorial intention in the other. The fit – whether consciously or unconsciously, ironically or naïvely constructed – was unproblematic *in its own terms*, and this was hardly surprising, since it was underwritten by the most obvious common sense.

The central thrust of modernism was precisely the criticism of the nineteenth-century bourgeois social order and the comfortable assumptions of its self-confident world-view. In this endeavour the modernists could draw not only on the darker and more disturbing insights of certain of their romantic ancestors but also on the newer currents that had given rise to the thought of Nietzsche and Marx, Freud and Durkheim, Husserl and Saussure, Einstein and Heisenberg. The artistic strategy of modernism, as handily summarized by John Barth, after Gerald Graff, was 'the self-conscious overturning of bourgeois realism by such tactics and devices as the substitution of a "mythical" for a "realistic" method,' as when Joyce and Thomas Mann, for example, parodically set off their modern-day Ulysses and Faust against their Homeric and Goethean forbears; the 'radical disruption of the linear flow of narrative' and the 'frustration of conventional expectations concerning unity and coherence of plot and character and the cause-and-effect "development" thereof,' foregrounding the fictivity and irreality of the textual world; the 'deployment of ironic and ambiguous juxtapositions to call into question the moral and philosophical "meaning" of literary action; the adoption of a tone of epistemological self-mockery aimed at the naive pretensions of bourgeois rationality; the opposition of inward consciousness to rational, public, objective discourse; and an inclination to subjective distortion to point up the evanescence of the objective social world of the nineteenth-century bourgeoisie' ('The Literature of Replenishment' 68). Like the romantics too, the modernists insisted on the notion of the artist as 'outsider,' as observer of rather than participant in the affairs of the workaday world. Coupled with their foregrounding of language, technique, and fictivity for their own sake, this pose put the modernist writer in a relationship to society markedly different from that of the realist. If the realist writer's task was to bolster the status quo by its faithful reproduction, the modernist relativized the everyday world by projecting alternative, fictional worlds where different norms obtained – where a man might wake up one morning, for example, and find himself, like Kafka's Gregor Samsa, metamorphosed into a monstrous insect. If the realists' characters were real people leading lives one could identify with and learn from, the modernists' characters, however psychologically accurate their portrayals might be – and could one ever know another person in as intimate detail as Joyce provides us with for Bloom? – were essentially fictional constructs, the sum of narrative choices taken and rejected. If the realist reader's reaction – and, once again, *real* readers' reactions might be far less predictable than those of our prototypical construct – was the passive reception of an authoritative message buttressing his confidence in himself and his society, the modernist reader, faced with the radical discrediting and parody of authoritative norms for determining meanings and messages, is forced willy-nilly into the active construction of his or her own meaning from the multiple, overlapping, and contradictory meanings proffered by the text. (A realist reader, at the same time, is likely to read such modernist texts as realist works gone wrong – hence the repeated proclamation of the widely lamented 'death of the novel.') If the realists' fictional worlds and their real world reciprocally validated each other as real and fixed and certain, the modernists' texts demonstrated themselves to *be* precisely texts and nothing else and by implication pointed to the erstwhile real world as merely an interpretive convention as well. The fit between the fictional world and the everyday world as suggested by the modernists is to this degree a parallel (with the sign reversed) to the realist fit, but it is, unlike the latter, far from unproblematic and not at all calculated to buttress confidence in the traditional norms of the realist world-view – which, of course, lived on and lives on regardless in large areas of the Western world as the obvious and common-sense approach to reading literary texts, undisturbed by the growing rumours of its own demise.

If seriousness was a distinguishing mark of realism, then a shift in the direction of humour is certainly a distinguishing characteristic of modernism. By this distinction I do not just mean that most modernist writers were more prone to the comic than most realist writers, though this is very likely true as well. Rather I mean that realism was 'serious,' devoid of any suspicion of flippancy, in that it theoretically provided an exact replica of what it saw to be reality, provided a mirror image, free of distortion. The modernist, by contrast, worked not with a mirror but with a set of prisms, bending and refracting the light emitted by an all-too-solid reality stoutly refusing to acknowledge its own lack of objectivity. The realist writer was the mouthpiece of his society, and consequently he wrote always essentially as a participant in, rather than as an external observer of, his society and its concept of reality. The archetypal realist text, in other words, admits of no distance and no difference between itself and the reality it reproduces; the modernist text is a product precisely of this distance and difference. (We may note in passing that distance and difference are the two essential conditions constituting a situation likely to be actualized as humour. We shall return to this point in the next chapter.)

The modernist position consciously distanced itself from the common-sense referentiality of realism. Postmodernism – which we can see as coming to the fore in fiction with the emergence of the *nouveau roman* in France in the 1950s, continuing largely in the United States in the sixties in the form of an intensified fascination with fictionality, and spreading to Germany (Grass, Handke, Bernhard), Italy (Calvino), and Latin America (Cortázar, García Márquez) – sees itself in reaction both to realism's emphasis on referentiality *and* modernism's emphasis on formalist, mythical, and symbolist alternatives. However, in one sense at least postmodernism is a direct continuation and intensification of the program of modernism, namely in its consequent insistence on the essential fictivity of writing. Where the modernist writer tended to see himself or herself as writing in conscious opposition to the realist stance, however, as providing an alternative to a rejected position, postmodernist writing is characterized by a flaunted disengagement, by the production of texts that lay claim neither to realist referentiality nor to modernism's symbological alternatives but simply to existing as 'non-significant surfaces,' ostentatiously unteleological, innocent of 'deeper meanings' or authorial messages. Where the modernist reader's task was to recuperate epiphanic or mythical or symbolic alternatives to realist referentiality, the postmodernist reader's task is to *react* to the text, to play with it, to construct a plurality of meanings rather than a single authorized meaning, to use the text as a springboard for further creation, to continue rather than conclude its gamelike workings. The importance of parody grew with modernism's ironic distancing of writing from the more or less naïve referentiality of (much) realism; for postmodernism parody is paramount, omnipresent, and inescapable. Fictivity for modernism was an engaged, polemical alternative; for postmodernism fictivity is all there is. If modernism moved away from the 'seriousness' of realism in the direction of an incipiently 'humorous' view of reality, postmodernism completes the process: the postmodernist view of reality is essentially a comic one, and 'the joy of the observer is allowed to prevail as the primary quality of the experience' (Stevick, 210).

The movement towards comedy over the last century or so as demonstrated in this foreshortened and drastically simplified survey of literary history is paralleled, not surprisingly, by a similar movement in literary critical methodology. The realist reader's predilections were canonized in traditional and largely positivist approaches to the literary text: the diligent and objective accumulation and analysis of factual information would unfailingly reveal, with a greater or lesser degree of sophistication, the author's intentions and consequently the nature of the particular message he had to convey about life in the world. The modernist reader's more sophisticated approach was enshrined in, above all, Anglo-American New Criticism, where the seat of authority was shifted from the godlike author to a gemlike text characterized by complexity, ambivalence, autonomy, and, above all, irony, which for the New Critics became the very touchstone of literary discourse. Russian Formalism and later Czech and Parisian Structuralism, by focusing attention on the *systemic* nature of the literary transaction, helped to transfer further the locus of authority from the text to the reader. Although psychoanalytic criticism and other non-formalist approaches such as Marxist and feminist criticism make full use of this further displacement in their critical practice, it is in the various forms of poststructuralism, and especially in that strand of it known as deconstruction, that the full consequences of the displacement are felt. Roland Barthes's *S/Z* (1970), the first classic of poststructuralist criticism, draws a seminal and much quoted distinction between texts that are *lisible* 'readable' or 'readerly' and texts that are *scriptible* 'writable' or 'writerly,' between traditional realist texts (*lisible*), that is to say, where the reader's task is the preplanned conclusion of the work of the text, and modernist and, even more so, postmodernist texts (*scriptible*), where the reader becomes an active co-producer of the unfinished, open text. The text, for Barthes, is 'a galaxy of signifiers, not a structure of signifieds' (5), and the reader's task is 'to multiply the signifiers, not to reach some ultimate signified' (165). The reader's work, in other words, is *play*, and it is only through this play that the text can approach its potential. Rather than the traditionalists' authorially determined message (both fixed *and* closed) or the New Critics' multivalent but still unitary meaning, the Barthesean text is comparable to a musical score, where only the barest, formalized notation of the text's potential can be set down on paper, awaiting its liberating (and endlessly variable) performance by a suitably skilled reader. Jacques Derrida vastly complicates this position by in effect asking to what extent either the musical score or the player of it can be regarded as fixed, since both score and player, text and reader alike are themselves simply 'characters' in an all-embracing macro-text, namely language itself, beyond which there is nothing. The deconstructive approach espoused by Derrida and his many followers not only assumes that all texts *are* infinitely extensible, but that it is impossible that it should be otherwise: no text, however brief, simple, direct, or 'realist' it may appear to be, *can* be literal or closed or final, for all texts are products (or rather, processes) of language. Language, however, is not, as traditionally supposed, an orderly, determinable structure, a transparent sheet laid over and merely *naming* an ontologically stable reality, but a limitless web of endlessly shifting and slipping relationships, where meaning can never be pinned down finally to a determinable signified but is always only a temporary spin-off of a potentially endless play of signifiers, words defining not essences, but only other words. There can be no transcendent meaning, no ultimate origin against which all else can be measured, no centre of gravity towards which all else irresistibly rushes. What there is, and all there is, is language in endless 'freeplay,' as Derrida calls it, eternally resisting gravity and the 'serious,' eternally deconstructing.

Poststructuralist hedonism, as Frank Lentricchia observes (145), may be the most extreme expression of the Kantian theory of art as purposiveness without purpose, and the traditionalist approach to it has been to accuse it of self-satisfied solipsism, unbridled subjectivism, unrestrained relativism, wilful irrationalism, and even out-and-out nihilism. Much the same reproaches have been levelled against postmodernist writing, as when Gerald Graff charges that 'postmodernism may be defined as that movement within contemporary literature and criticism which calls into question the claims of literature and art to truth and human value' (219). The postmodernist answer to such charges is undoubtedly simply to carry on writing. The poststructuralist answer is undoubtedly to echo the Nietzsche of *Thus Spoke Zarathustra*: 'He who climbs upon the highest mountains laughs at all tragedies, real or imaginary' (68), as Zarathustra proclaims; 'I have canonized laughter; you Higher Men, *learn* – to laugh!' (306). In our post-Nietzschean, post-Einsteinean, postmodernist, poststructuralist day comedy has come in from the cold, has moved from the periphery of cultural discourse towards where the centre may once, in less self-reflective times, have been. But it can hardly be said to have displaced or replaced tragedy; rather it has swallowed it whole. The systematic re-evaluation of humour that has been taking place over the last three centuries or so has seen a massive realignment of areas once considered unproblematically 'serious' or 'non-serious.' Ionesco speaks for many when he declares that 'the comical is tragic, and the tragedy of man derisory. For the modern critical spirit nothing can be taken entirely seriously, nor entirely lightly' (quoted in Merchant, 64). The result, as we have already seen, is a comedy of entropy and a laughter that lacks the untroubled simplicity and unshaken self-confidence of both the traditional derisive and the traditional sympathetic expressions of humour. We are as apt to laugh at our tragedies as we are to weep at our comedies. Humour has never been so consistently disturbing, perhaps, but it has perhaps also never been so central and so vital a part of our cultural discourse. Not so overtly, at any rate; there is, after all, little new under the sun, and in the end, perhaps, after an arduous (though fascinating) journey, we have merely regained the position espoused some twenty-three centuries ago by the Hindu sage Valmiki, to whom the Sanskrit epic of the *Ramayana* is traditionally ascribed. 'There are three things,' wrote Valmiki, 'which are real: God, human folly, and laughter. Since the first two pass our comprehension, we must do what we can with the third' (*Ramayana* 276).

Part Two

PRETEXTS:
Humour and Narrative

4 Theoretical Worlds: Humour, Play, and Narrative

So far we have examined both the systemic effects of entropic think-ing on our modern perception of what constitutes humour and the extent to which this new entropic humour has not only gradually become the dominant mode of humour in our time but has also come to inform whole areas of discourse that were previously regarded as entirely foreign to the realm of humour in every way. It is now time to turn, in part 2, to the second of the three major objectives of our overall project, namely the analysis of the systemic effects of that newly developed humour on our perception of what constitutes the literary text, focusing our attention specifically on narrative. If our primary concern in part 1 was with the theory of humour, in part 2 it will be with the theory of narrative and its reading. (In part 3, finally, we will focus our attention not as theorists but as literary critics on a selected set of texts chosen to illustrate the positions developed in the theoretical discussion.) Before looking at the relationship of hu-mour and narrative, however, it will first be necessary at this point to examine in some detail the relationship of humour, play, and games.

Poststructuralist ludism, where the text is viewed as 'a game affording both author and reader the possibility of producing endless meanings and relationships' (Mistacco 375), is the most ostentatious example in recent years of the literary transaction considered in terms of play. It is by no means the only example, however. The applicability of theories of play and games in literary criticism has in fact been the subject of considerable discussion in several different critical contexts over the last few years, and gamelike qualities have been noted in literary texts on a spectrum ranging from the thematic (many texts *contain* games as elements of the plot) to the structural (many texts, perhaps *all* texts, are structured *as* games) and beyond, as in the poststructuralist concept of the game of language itself, in which author, text, and reader alike are mere pawns. Somewhat surprisingly, the usefulness to these discussions of the related field of humour theory has been, to my knowledge, left completely unexploited. Yet arguably it is precisely the re-evaluation of humour and the associated realignment of the 'serious' and the 'non-serious' over the last century or so that has made this widespread interest in the relationship between literature and play a defensible strategy of critical discourse.

It is evident that in a very traditional sense art and literature are indeed forms of play. They are clearly forms of play rather than work in the sense that art is a cultural luxury rather than a necessity: faced with the choice of decorating the walls of his cave or going hunting for meat, it was obvious to the cave-dweller which was the primary and which the secondary occupation, even allowing for the magical potential of his drawings to alter the course of events in the real world and draw the bison towards the hunter. It is evident too, though hardly of any great interest, that all literature is indeed a form of game, in that the events and feelings depicted are 'only pretend': Don Quijote, Hamlet, Anna Karenina are no more 'real people' than are Mickey Mouse and Donald Duck. It is obvious that poetry is a playing with words, just as it is clear that in some forms of narrative (if not all) the author is playing an overt game of hide-and-seek with the reader: the point of most detective novels, for example, is clearly that the reader should be prevented from discovering the clues carefully hidden by the author until the latter is willing to allow it. The current interest in, one could even say fascination with, the theory of play and games as part of the discussion of literature is funded not only by such fairly obvious traditional insights, however – which assume, incidentally, that we know exactly what we mean when we talk about 'play' and 'games.' Robert Rawdon Wilson has attempted to unravel the various strands, to some degree quite incompatible with each other, that contribute to current discussion of play and game concepts, and I will follow his distinctions here in general terms for purposes of orientation.

First and foremost, serving as backdrop, as it were, there is a philosophical tradition, dating back to classical times, that treats play as *paideia*, a mode of education: through playing games children 'nonseriously' rehearse roles they might be called upon to play 'seriously' in adult life, learn the arts of social interaction, and learn to gauge their own abilities. The most important development in this tradition for our purposes dates back at least to Schiller's essay *On the*

Aesthetic Education of Man (1793), where play (Schiller's *Spieltrieb*) is held to be both central and fundamental to human experience, for it is only in play that human beings can both fully realize themselves and make real their highest ideals. Johan Huizinga's *Homo Ludens* (1938) considerably develops this line of thinking in arguing that *all* human culture rises upon a basis of play.

A number of twentieth-century developments have served to expand and differentiate the notion of play propagated in this general tradition. First, psychoanalysis since Freud has made us aware of the obscurity and the unreliability of overt motivation: the unconscious is seen as manipulating, playing with, or playing through the conscious surface of things. The conscious surface is read as a visible game constituted by invisible rules. If this is true of language in general, it is a fortiori true of the literary text. Second, since Wittgenstein's *Philosophical Investigations* (1953) there has been a widespread tendency to subject all human activity to an atomistic analysis in which discrete behavioural segments may be described as isolatable games, each operating according to its particular set of specialized constitutive rules – as Wilson observes, the various recent applications of speech-act theory (that is, the detailed analysis of linguistic exchanges between characters) to literary criticism may be regarded as an example of this particular type of game theory. Third, the invention in the 1940s of mathematical game theory (that is, the logical and mathematical analysis of strategies of decision-making) has prompted a diverse application of its specialized terminology (if perhaps not much else) to a variety of situations involving the game-like adversarial relationship of author and reader. Fourth, the fairly recent development of research into fantasy literature, romance, science fiction, and the like, where the laws of physics governing the real world can be rewritten at will, suggests that by analogy all evocation of fictional worlds in literary texts is a form of game: this development is supported by the formalist, including the New Critical, position that all literary texts are autonomous, auto-teleological, self-contained, and self-referential. Fifth, finally, and perhaps most significantly, there has been the development within poststructuralist thought in general and in deconstructive theory in particular of the notion of textual freeplay, as already discussed.

The implications of these positions differ quite radically from one to the other, as becomes clear, for example, if we look at the extent to which the element of literary play is considered to be voluntary or involuntary and the degree to which this distinction affects the identity of the players involved in the literary transaction. Derridean freeplay sees language itself as the dominant but involuntary player playing *through* author, text, and reader alike, a play of uncontrollable energy, as when one speaks of the play of waves or the play of light (Wilson, 'Palamedes' 192). The psychoanalytic tradition would see the unconscious, be it that of author, narrator, character, or reader, as the dominant player, a puppet-master strategically manipulating their respective conscious, but only partly voluntary response. The Wittgensteinean tradition would see all aspects of the literary encounter as marked by an attempted reconciliation of free and determined strategies – even the most brilliant chess master cannot legally decide to move his bishop other than diagonally, for example, though within that constraint he can exercise a great deal of individual freedom. The position of mathematical game theory would be similar to that of the Schillerean tradition in allowing for a free, voluntary, intentional, rationally controlled contest between author and reader or between character and character. The formalist tradition of textual autonomy would cast the reader in the role of voluntary player, but his relationship to the text would be largely limited to pushing the button that made the machine run: some minor fine-tuning would be permitted, but essentially the reader's role would be a passive one, that of an admiring onlooker.

Quite apart from these specifically focused theories of play and games, moreover, the various branches of the vigorous field of reader theory over the last few years have made us aware of at least one comprehensive way in which the reading of a literary text is always a game, a strictly regulated form of play, for the properly trained and equipped reader. Games have a way of substituting their play-reality for everyday reality, a way of becoming more real than the reality they temporarily displace. Our no doubt largely instinctive adoption of a particular critical methodology as readers, however, should not blind us to the fact that any critical approach to literature is itself a fiction, a particular game played in a particular context for particular stakes as a result of particular constraints and choices. Even those readers who completely 'reject theory' are playing a particular interpretive game, admitting certain rules as valid while refusing to acknowledge others, and as a result obtaining specific – but always provisional – results. As long as we are prepared to admit that our favourite approach is no more than a particular way of looking at texts, which will respond differently according to the particular strategies we employ, we can, as reader theory (itself a fiction, of course) shows us, change baseball for tennis, structuralism for feminism, game for game.

Twentieth-century theories of humour have brought a new awareness of the relationship between humour and play. In a sense this relationship is of course already quite obvious, and is attested to quite clearly (as Richard Boston has observed) in the semantic linkage between humour, play, and games in our everyday language. Humour is 'funny,' games are 'fun,' play is 'in fun.' *Fun* itself seems originally to have been a verb meaning 'to hoax' or 'to trick.' Something 'amusing' makes us laugh, but an 'amusement' will not necessarily do so. Games provide 'ludic' pleasure without necessarily being 'ludicrous.' An Italian *gioco* and a Spanish *juego* are not jokes but games; an Italian *commedia* or a Spanish *comedia* is not necessarily a comedy, but is necessarily a play. A German *Scherz* can be a play as well as a joke; a French *jeu* is either play or sport. To *juggle*, a form of play, derives from the Middle French *jogler* and Latin *joculari*, meaning to joke. Boston observes that in Chinese the ideogram *wán* is common to the words for amusement, play, fun, game, and laughter (38), and so on. Relatively few theorists of humour, however – perhaps Max Eastman's *Enjoyment of Laughter* (1937) is the best-known exception – have stressed the simple joy, pleasure, high spirits, and delight that link humour and play. Eastman sees humour as being funny precisely because it 'derails' the everyday and puts it in an amusingly and obviously false perspective. D.H. Monro's *Argument of Laughter* (1951) similarly stresses the delight in novelty, new perspectives, relief from the boredom of the unchanging everyday with its monotony and sameness, as a primary stimulant of laughter. Students of children's behaviour point not only to the presence of elements of superiority, incongruity, and relief but also to the element of sheer high spirits and what may seem to be spontaneous joy in otherwise apparently unmotivated shrieks of laughter.

Theories of humour that link humour and play clearly subscribe to the general incongruity theory developed during the eighteenth century, and clearly also this notion traces its more immediate ancestry to the Kantian tradition of 'purposiveness without purpose.' Kant's 'Copernican revolution' as a philosopher was to displace the accent in the relationship between the perceiving subject and the experienced world from the latter to the former, from the unchanging objectivity of the external object to the shaping subjectivity and creativity of the knowing mind, and in so doing effectively to usher in the age of relativity and reflexivity where both play and humour would move from the periphery into a position of new and previously untenable prominence. Aesthetics played a central role in Kant's view of the world, as demonstrated in his *Critique of Judgment* (1790). On the one hand, there was the external world of physical objects and events, brought under control by imagination, scientific understanding, and, above all, reason. On the other hand, there was the internal world of moral choice, brought under control by the categorical imperative. Serving as an area of mediation between these two worlds was the realm of aesthetic values, the realm of the beautiful and the sublime, the realm, that is to say, of subjective values with objective expression in the external world. The sublime, *das Erhabene*, blended a natural awe in the face of the uncontrollable energy of the natural universe and an exultation at being none the less safe and unthreatened. The beautiful, by contrast, *das Schöne*, was characterized by a 'purposiveness without purpose,' a 'Zweckmässigkeit ohne Zweck,' a feeling of utterly harmonious oneness of sense and spirit, external and internal, matter and form. The beautiful was a form of secularized *unio mystica*, in fact, and was accordingly also the external symbol of the morally good and of ultimate truth, as celebrated in the triune ideal of German classicism, *das Wahre, Schöne, Gute*, the true, the beautiful, the good. Contemplation of the beautiful is a disinterested act, undertaken for its own sake, just as the beautiful, though purposive, is without purpose. The experience of art is, in fact, a form of play: our mental powers engage each other in a 'lively' and 'indeterminate' activity of 'play,' to no end except an 'internal feeling' of 'harmony' (51–4). Like play, the beautiful is both in the world and yet removed from it; it is both a 'non-serious' activity without practical purpose and simultaneously an activity whose regenerative powers enable one to undertake with renewed vigour the serious business of the everyday world.

With Kant the non-serious, as we have been calling it, play, became a completely respectable area of intellectual endeavour, and one whose possibilities both Goethe and Schiller were quick to realize. 'True art,' according to Goethe, 'can only spring from the intricate linking of the serious and the playful,' while for Schiller, 'man only plays when he is in the full sense of the word a Human Being, and he is only human when he is at play.' Schiller's essay *On the Aesthetic Education of Man* follows Kant closely in seeing all art as arising out of two separate impulses that are balanced in infinitely various ways by a third: the finite material impulse, or *Stofftrieb*, and the infinite impulse of the formative idea, the *Formtrieb*, are harmoniously reconciled in the free 'play' of the creative human mind, in what Schiller calls the *Spieltrieb*, the play impulse. In his essay on *Naive and Sentimental Poetry* (1795) he develops this idea in a consideration of what he sees as the growing role of reflexivity, self-consciousness, and subjectivity in modern literature. *Naive* writing, classical writing, was primarily characterized by its direct, uncomplicated relationship to nature; *sentimental* writing, that is to say romantic, post-Kantian writing, was complicated by its own awareness of itself as writing and of the problematic relationship between the writer and reality. (The last word was far from having been said, though, for a century later the next round would be fought out between the realists and the modernists.) While Schiller developed his concept of play in the Kantian tradition of 'purposiveness without purpose,' a new concept of humour was simultaneously being developed, along similar lines, by such contemporaries as Jean Paul Richter and the Schlegels, as we have seen above, similarly emphasizing the role of the comic as an area of mediation between the world of the everyday and the realm of the ideal.

The implications of the relationship between play and humour were not really explored by the Romantics, nor were they indeed by Schiller's most thoroughgoing modern continuator, Johan Huizinga, in his classic study of the play impulse, *Homo Ludens* (1938). Though Huizinga's broad-ranging thesis is that all human culture bears the character of play, he is not at all interested, surprisingly enough, in humour phenomena. Indeed, he sees little useful or interesting relationship between play and humour, to which he devotes only two or three paragraphs on the grounds that play is 'by no means necessarily comic' (6). Without examining the extent to which humour, conversely, might necessarily always be a form of play, he none the less notes that the 'rationale and mutual relationships' of humour and play phenomena 'must lie in a very deep layer of our mental being' (6). Let us examine his thesis in a little more detail.

Play, says Huizinga, is characterized by *freedom*, that is to say it is voluntary, unnecessary, superfluous. It is a *stepping aside* out of the normal or 'real' life, that is to say it is a pretence. It is played out within certain *limits of space and time*, 'temporary worlds' (10) within the ordinary world. It is a *creator of order*, of an area of limited perfection in an imperfect world. Finally, it is *governed by rules* and accompanied by feelings of tension, joy, and the awareness of its unreality (10–28). Play is older than culture, since animals play too, and human civilization has added no essential feature to the general idea of play: conflicting definitions notwithstanding, as Huizinga puts it, the essential element of play is *fun* (3). The great archetypal activities of human society are all permeated with play from the start, and 'it is through this playing that society expresses its interpretation of life and the world' (46). Language itself is a continuous 'sparking' between matter and mind: 'Behind every abstract expression there lie the boldest of metaphors, and every metaphor is a play upon words. Thus in giving expression to life man creates a second, poetic world alongside the world of nature' (4). Myth is play, for in myth too the outer world is transformed, 'imagined,' grounded in the divine. 'In all the wild imaginings of mythology a fanciful spirit is playing on the borderline between jest and earnest' (5). Ritual too is play, and from myth and ritual spring 'law and order, commerce and profit, craft and art, poetry, wisdom and science. All are rooted in the primaeval soil of play' (5). 'Genuine, pure play is one of the main bases of civilisation,' lying 'outside the antithesis of wisdom and folly, and equally outside those of truth and falsehood, good and evil' (6).

As for the specific relationship of play and literature, Huizinga is suggestive rather than systematic. Poetry always falls within the play sphere, though its ludic character may not always be outwardly preserved (143). The lyric mode is most closely allied to the original play sphere in that it is the language of mystic contemplation, oracles, and magic – the poet is inspired, closest to supreme wisdom – 'but also to inanity' (142), as the surrender of reason and logic tends towards non-sense and the exorbitantly exaggerated. 'That comedy and tragedy both derive from play is obvious enough' (144). As for philosophy, that it was a game was already clear to both the ancient Sophists and to Plato, who followed their lead, as well as later to Nietzsche: the antilogic or double reasoning of the Sophists, and other forms of reasoning closely related to riddles, hinted at the perpetual ambiguity of every judgment made by the human mind (152). The Sophists, in other words, institutionalized the notion that Bakhtin calls carnival: the 'official' world of everyday convention, reason, and logic is relativized by the juxtaposition of an oppositional, unofficial world where these norms are no longer valid.

Huizinga's conception of play though sweeping in scope in one sense is interestingly limited in another, which perhaps goes some way towards explaining why he was so little interested in the intersection of play and humour. The play-element in culture, Huizinga laments at the end of his book, though almost solely responsible for that culture, has been on the wane ever since the eighteenth century, when it was in full flower. The nineteenth century smothered the play-element in utilitarianism, efficiency, and the bourgeois ideal of social welfare. 'Never had an age taken itself with more portentous seriousness' (192). The nearer we come to our own times, however, the 'more doubts arise as to whether our occupations are pursued in play or in earnest, and with the doubts comes the uneasy feeling of hypocrisy, as though the only thing we can be certain of is make-believe' (191). Rather than seeing this blurring as a verification of his thesis, however, Huizinga curiously denies the existence of any marked play-element in twentieth-century art precisely because of its overt reflexivity. 'When art becomes self-conscious, that is, conscious of its own grace, it is apt to lose something of its eternal childlike innocence,' writes Huizinga, echoing Schiller's dichotomy of the naïve and the sentimental and Kleist's essay on the puppet theatre, *Über das Marionettentheater* (1805), and this is exactly what Huizinga sees happening in the Europe of his time, where 'the constant striving after new and unheard-of forms impels art down the steep slope of Impressionism into the turgidities and excrescences of the twentieth century' (202).

Huizinga's play is primarily 'childlike,' unreflected, that is to say naïve rather than sentimental in Schiller's terms, and one of the weaknesses of this pioneering study is therefore its inability to distinguish adequately between relatively unstructured forms of play and highly structured games, which also fall under the general rubric of 'play.' Roger Caillois attempted to rectify this failure twenty years later in another classic study, *Man, Play, and Games* (1958). Caillois broadly accepts Huizinga's markers of play situations, but clearly tailors them to game situations rather than to the more unstructured forms of play: play is *free*, in that it is not undertaken under duress; it is *separate*, in that it has fixed limits in space and time; it is *uncertain*, in that its course and result cannot be determined beforehand; it is *unproductive*, in that it generates neither new wealth nor goods in the everyday world; it is *governed by rules*, under conventions that suspend ordinary laws and temporarily establish new and binding legislation in their place; it is *make-believe*, in that it is accompanied by a special awareness of a second reality separate from ordinary reality (9–10). Caillois's major new contribution to the discussion was to suggest a comprehensive classification adequate for all games, which he did by arranging games under four rubrics: *agôn*, or games involving competition; *alea*, or games involving chance; *mimicry*, or games involving simulation, impersonation, role-playing, and the like; and *ilinx*, or games involving vertigo or a sense of giddiness, such as those involving swings, slides, roller-coasters, and the like. Individual games may belong to more than one classification, and within each classification there is a range from *paidia*, that is to say unstructured, spontaneous play, to *ludus*, or regulated games involving structure, rules, and discipline.

Caillois's classification of games is exemplary, but his distinction between play and games is still not quite adequate. When, in other words, does *paidia* become *ludus*? Bernard Suits's *The Grasshopper* (1978) provides the most satisfying answer so far to this question. Quite simply, as soon as at least one constitutive rule is added, says Suits, play becomes game: thus hanging from a branch by one hand for simple amusement's sake is play; doing it to see how long you can last is a game. Games, for Suits, who coins the term *lusory* to mean 'proper to games,' are further defined by four necessary conditions, namely a *pre-lusory goal*, *lusory means*, *constitutive rules*, and a *lusory attitude*: 'To play a game is to attempt to achieve a specific state of affairs [pre-lusory goal], using only means permitted by rules [lusory means], where the rules prohibit use of more efficient in favour of less efficient means [constitutive rules], and where the rules are accepted just because they make possible such activity [lusory attitude]. I also offer the following simpler and so to speak, more portable version of the above: playing a game is the voluntary attempt to overcome unnecessary obstacles' (41). Suits makes one further and very useful distinction between *closed games*, where the achievement of the goal (such as crossing a finishing line or mating a king) ends the game, and *open games*, whose goal is precisely not the ending but the prolongation of the game (such as games of make-believe, for example) (133). An open game, in other words, is 'a system of reciprocally enabling moves whose purpose is the continued operation of the game' (135). The conflict of an open game (heroes 'against' villains) is purely dramatic; the conflict of a closed game (one opponent against another) is genuinely competitive (137).

Suits makes no attempt to explore the implications of any of this for literary criticism, but we may note that in these terms the traditional, 'realist' approach to reading – in the schematic sense in which I am using the term *realist* – is always a closed game, a contest for the stakes of meaning between the reader and the authorial artefact. What Barthes calls the 'writerly' rather than the 'readerly' reading experience, by contrast, is always an open game, even though it may (as in the case of detective fiction and the like) *contain* one or more closed games. Indeed the search for a work's 'true meaning' in traditional realist terms must be seen as a form of work rather than play, for, as Suits puts it, work is instrumentally valuable, while play is intrinsically valuable: work is 'doing things we value for the sake of something else' (such as reading novels for the sake of moral self-improvement or the acquisition of factual historical information), while play is 'doing things we value for their own sake' (15). Postmodernist reading, in this perspective, is utopian: in a utopian world, where only activities intrinsically valued would be engaged in, Aesop's grasshopper, once the model of improvidence, would be metamorphosed into the exemplification of the life most worth living, and playing games would be the essence of that life.

It seems evident that the reason why humour theory has played little or no part in these already well-developed theories of play and games is that humour and the comic tend to be run together, and play, as Huizinga says, is certainly not necessarily comic. It is easy enough, however, to define a working distinction between humour and the comic: humour *is* not necessarily comic, but it *evokes* the comic under the right circumstances. To put it more formally: a potentially actualizable *humour situation* may or may not, subject to contextual restraints, evoke a *comic experience* which, in its turn, and again subject to contextual restraints, may or may not provoke *comic pleasure*. The relationship might be diagrammed as a triangle: the relationship between the humour situation and a possible comic experience is direct, as is the relationship between the comic experience and a possible comic pleasure; the relationship between the humour situation and comic pleasure, however, is always indirect (figure 2). The humour situation, in other words, makes comic response (experience and possibly pleasure) possible, but does not guarantee it. A humour situation, however, may alternatively provide what we may call a *pre-comic* humorous experience and pleasure: irony, for example, is a form of humour situation that is not necessarily or even usually actualized as comic experience. The kind of 'black' humour that we associate with Swift or Sade, however, achieves its effect precisely by evoking comic experience while inhibiting comic pleasure. The distinction between comic and pre-comic humour is of course lost if we simply conflate humour and the comic (as more than one book on literary comedy has done). The distinction, however, is a crucial one in terms of the relationship of humour situations and the

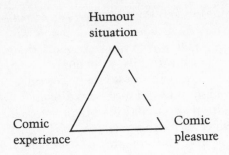

Figure 2. Humour and the comic

literary text, as we shall see. As to what constitutes a 'humour situation' in the first place, meanwhile, and as to what its relationship to play and game situations and to the literary text may be, we can profitably turn to the notion of *possible worlds*, as first suggested by Leibniz and developed in modern semantic theory.

The theory of possible worlds rests on the elegantly simple notion that when describing the hypothetical developments of a given situation, where any one of an indefinite number of possible states of affairs might at some point obtain, it is sometimes useful to think of individual states of affairs as constituting a 'possible world,' which may or may not coincide with the description of the actual world at some point (Lyons, 163). 'Let's hope it won't rain,' for example, evokes one possible world at a future point in time in which it is not raining and a second possible world at the same point in time in which it *is* raining, and expresses the hope that a third possible world, coinciding with a future state of the real world of the speaker, will also coincide with the first (dry) world rather than the second (wet) world. Possible worlds, in other words, and for all the ponderousness of the explanation just given, are habitually and obviously evoked (and invoked) in wishes ('Get well soon!'), curses ('The hell with it!'), threats ('Just you wait!'), and fears ('I'm going to be sick!'). Less obviously, perhaps, but no less habitually, as the semanticists tell us, we invoke possible worlds in all matters involving verbal tenses, moods, and modalities (Lyons, 787ff.). Similarly, an ambiguous sentence, for example, is one 'that might be true under one interpretation and false under another interpretation in some possible state of the universe, i.e. in some possible world' (Lyons, 169), while a homonym like *seal* denotes an aquatic mammal in one possible world, an imprint on wax in a second, a device for closure in a third, and so on.

Leibniz, we remember, convinced Pangloss at least that the Creator, out of the infinity of possible worlds available to an omnipotent
divine being, had chosen to activate (actualize, create) the single one
that is the 'best of possible worlds' (Voltaire, 138). 'God,' wrote
Leibniz in the *Theodicy* (1710), 'would not have created the world, if
it were not the best of all possible worlds' (128). The Creator, we note,
is by definition external to his creation. As observers, we too remain
by definition external to the possible worlds we project and contemplate (including, theoretically, the 'real' world we inhabit at any given
point in time), just as a fictional narrator remains external to the
narrated state of affairs (or possible world) that he presents. It is clear
that the notion of possible worlds can provide us, in fact, with a
comparative perspective in its own terms on the relationship between play, games, humour, and literary discourse – not to mention
myth, magic, religion, ritual, and, of course, lies. It is also clear that
this notion draws our attention with exemplary force to the importance of the observing subject. Every one of these discourses depends
on the hypothesized existence of worlds alternative to the everyday
world for its very existence. They are *ludic* worlds, play worlds, in the
sense that they are *hypothetical projections*. We shall find it useful to
use the term *ludic* to refer to play in this generalized sense (that is,
play as *langue*), and Bernard Suits's term *lusory* to refer to individual
examples of play and games in the recreational sense (play as *parole*).
In this extended sense 'ludic' worlds include a broad range from the
most 'serious' (for instance, religion) to the most 'non-serious' forms
(such as puns and jokes). It is of course clear that some of these ludic
worlds are received as being more lusory in character than others: a
game of cops and robbers, or soccer, or chess is usually (though
certainly not always) felt to be more 'playful' in character than are
religious ceremonies or the swearing in of a president, for example.
There is a range of response, that is, from 'non-serious' lusory pleasure for its own sake to 'serious,' or what we may call *pre-lusory*,
satisfaction for the sake of some contextually determined psychological or social end. Serious pleasure (satisfaction) shades gradually into
what we are calling pre-comic pleasure, and pre-comic into comic
pleasure – but though we need the distinction in theoretical terms
here, in practical terms it is clear enough that there will be many
cases where it will no longer be possible to distinguish between
serious satisfaction or pleasure and non-serious or humorous pleasure. A philosophical investigation of paradox or a scholarly treatise
on humour, for example, may well provide comic pleasure by way of

the various examples of jokes and paradoxes it may provide, but our comic pleasure is likely to be subsumed in the dominant feeling of intellectual satisfaction evoked by the text's handling of its subject-matter. There is undoubtedly a 'sense of play' just as there is a 'sense of humour,' and between them they determine whether situations are experienced as more or less lusory, more or less comic.

What constitutes the essence of the ludic situation as defined here is the *relationship* of the postulated alternative world to (or in other words, its difference from) the standard of the everyday world. The observer in all cases is free to decide how to classify the relationship – but only to the extent that the conventional code of his or her community allows that freedom. The observer may 'decide' to enter without reservation into the ludic or fictive world, becoming a participant rather than an observer, as if it were the 'real' world. Myth, magic, religion will persuade the believer of their entire ontological reality; a bitterly contested game of football may obliterate everything outside it for a dedicated player; a well-told lie will fool us completely as long as we are unaware of its falsehood; a skilfully told narrative of star-crossed lovers will have readers sharing every nuance of their suffering as long as the reader forgets that it is all 'only a story.' In all of these instances the constitutive difference of the ludic world is ignored, the observer becomes a participant, a character in the story, and in consequence it ceases, for him, to *be* a ludic world and becomes a real world. The greater the degree of self-awareness on the observer's part, the less chance there is of this happening. We may rather self-consciously dress up for a social ritual such as a wedding, for example, or an academic graduation, fully sympathize with its symbolic power and social necessity, and yet simultaneously feel silly: we are operating, half-observer, half-participant, in both worlds simultaneously, and we may or may not reflect that the activity is a 'playful' one. We may note that highly structured *games* (Caillois's *ludus*) tend to encourage the absorption of the observer while more overtly *play* activities *(paidia)* do not. For the most part, however, our attention is not at all focused primarily on the *relationship* between the ludic world and the real world, even though we may be aware of the simultaneous existence of both worlds. In the case of humour, however, it is precisely this relationship, this difference, that is stressed.

All the major traditional theories of humour are, with various weighting, posited on the existence of an initial formal incongruity.

The psychological explanations as to why we do or do not derive pleasure from this constitutive incongruity have differed through history, as we have seen, invoking perceived superiority or surprised recognition or sudden relief or whatever, but the initial spark is always an incongruity – or, more accurately, a *perceived* incongruity under appropriate contextual restraints. In terms of the possible-worlds model a *potential* humour situation *always* exists as soon as a possible alternative world is projected. 'Let's hope it won't rain!' could be devastatingly funny in the middle of the Sahara or in the middle of a downpour or in the middle of an air-raid or in dozens of other contexts we could imagine. In fact *anything* at any time can be *made* funny given the right context, a fact by means of which professional comedians routinely make their living. The reason why *everything* is not *always* hilarious is quite simply that we already know beforehand that certain things, events, and relationships are everyday and ordinary, part of the serious world of working and eating and sleeping. There's nothing funny about them. We know this because we have already agreed on these things as a community — though different communities will agree on different things. The British sense of humour is notoriously different from the American, the German from the French, the Oriental from the Occidental, the modern from the medieval. What has been presented in an earlier chapter as a historical or diachronic sequence of derisive, sympathetic, and entropic modes of humour taking over from each other in turn can equally well be seen as the emergence over time of synchronically different (and overlapping) interpretive communities, to use Stanley Fish's phrase (14), who favour different conventions as to what may be considered comic. Derisive humour is by no means dead in our time; neither is sympathetic humour; but by and large the influential interpretive community determining what is the mainstream of humour in recent decades has been the one subscribing to the enabling conventions of entropic humour.

In terms of the possible-worlds model, then, a potential humour situation is always generated by every projection of an alternative possible world, and at this point appropriate contextual restraints come into play, dominating all that follows: if the relationship of the possible worlds is perceived as incongruous it becomes an actual (as opposed to a potential) humour situation, which may, as we have seen already, either evoke a pre-comic form of humorous experience such as irony, or evoke a comic experience, which in its turn may provoke comic pleasure, which, finally, may result in laughter, a smile, or just vague amusement. The sequence of reactions might be diagrammed as in figure 3.

The possible-worlds model also allows us to relate humour to play and games, and all three of these to the literary text, in a potentially fruitful way. The primary concept of ludic play is seen as encompassing both 'serious' play phenomena (such as, magic, religion) and 'nonserious' and as including at one end of its less serious range the more engaged forms of games, whose participants are 'trapped' in the world of the game in the same way that characters in a realistic narrative have no escape from their narrated reality. In the centre of the range we may see the less engaged, more playful forms of what Caillois called *paidia* rather than *ludus*. Here the participant's involvement is less intense, less real, more provisional, with only one foot in the world of play and the other anchored in the world of normality. (A narrative analogue here would be the use of *mise en abyme* to allow a character the possibility of the sort of insight into his own situation usually only possible on the level of the narrator rather than that of the character: an example would be Josef K.'s opening the lumber-room door in Kafka's *Trial* to find a 'miniaturized' version of his own narrative situation in progress.) At the least 'serious' end of the spectrum of play, finally, we have humour, which is wholly a matter of observation rather than participation – or, in narrative terms, it is a function of the act of narration rather than the content of the narration, the level of discourse rather than that of story, the telling rather than what is told.

The relationship of humour, games, and play (as *parole*) within the discursive system of ludic play (as *langue*) is dynamic rather than static, and any one of the terms of the relationship can quickly metamorphose into either of the other two. Play and games owe their difference to the presence or absence of a single game-constituting rule; humour and the lusory to a single constitutive factor, the factor of observation. Games and play, like anything else, can easily become forms of humour, while humour always has an element of the lusory in it, whether as a form of play with the logic of the everyday or, like all jokes, as a form of game. All forms of play, finally, we may note, including humour, make possible ludic pleasure; games make possible specifically lusory pleasure as well, while humour similarly can provide both ludic and specifically humorous pleasure of either a pre-comic or comic character. The aesthetic text, and most especially the

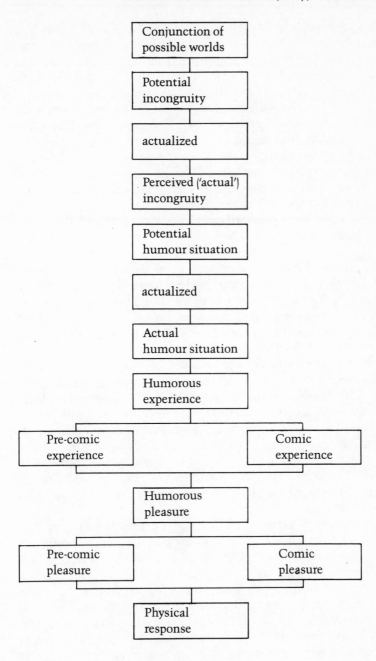

Figure 3. The generation of humorous response

literary text, depends for its existence on this interplay of lusory and humorous experience. This is indeed hypothetically true in an attenuated sense of *any* fictive world-projection in that the hypothesis of conflated or conjunctive worlds always has potential lusory content and humour content, depending on the circumstances of reception. It is true, however, in the strongest sense of the literary text, which most overtly draws attention to its own fictivity. The more reflexive the literary text becomes, and the more it points metalinguistically to its own fictivity, the more it realizes its own humour potential as well as lusory potential. The literary text is capable of providing ludic, both pre-lusory and lusory, *and* both comic and pre-comic pleasure, and the extent to which this capability obtains even in the case of texts not necessarily designed or designated as overtly comic will form the subject-matter of our next section

We can examine the comedy of entropy in modern narrative on two levels of inhibition. The more overt level presents themes, situations, stories that tend in varying degrees to evoke comic experience but inhibit, or at least qualify, comic pleasure; on a less overt level there is an exploitation of what we have been calling the pre-comic factor in literary discourse. The former level has to do primarily with the content plane of the narrative expression, the *story*; the latter level has to do primarily with the formal plane of narrative expression, the *discourse*. Both levels provide ludic experience that would be fully comic given an appropriate context, but convention inhibits the reader a posteriori from accepting the invitation to comic pleasure of the story plane and suppresses a priori the comic potential of the discourse plane. The comedy of entropy in modern narrative is a function of the intersection of two different readings of Barthes's reference to the narrative text as 'the comical that does not make us laugh' (*Pleasure* 30).

Entropic comedy is not at all limited in its expression to narrative, as can be seen from a number of well-known studies on the grotesque in art and literature (Kayser), on the theatre of the absurd (Esslin), on nonsense in verse (Sewell), and so on. Narrative fiction, however, has been a particularly fertile breeding ground for various forms of entropic humour over the last half-century or so, and this fact in itself would constitute a sufficient pragmatic reason for using it as a focus for a study of entropic comedy. A more attractive reason, however, is that the form of narrative itself, or more precisely, the structural relationship of narrative levels, allows us to explore in an exemplary way a typically pre-comic moment in *all* literary texts, namely the relationship between *what* the text 'is all about' and *how* this material is presented to the reader. There is a sense, admittedly, in which even non-narrative literary forms such as drama or the lyric must be seen as the utterance of a narrative instance or narrating agent, but only in specifically narrative fiction do we find the potential of this narrative instance fully exploited. One of the consequences of this exploitation is the generation in all narrative of an intriguing variety of possible narrative worlds.

The study of narrative has burgeoned to an unprecedented extent over the last twenty years or so, and one of the key distinctions upon which all recent narrative theory rests, as already mentioned, is that between narrative content (the tale as told, *l'énoncé, das Erzählte*) and narrative form (the telling of the tale, *l'énonciation, das Erzählen*). The Russian formalists called these narrative levels *fabula* and *sjužet*, or *fable* and *sujet*, and the most useful terms in English are those suggested by Seymour Chatman, *story* and *discourse*: 'The story is the *what* in a narrative that is depicted, discourse the *how*' (19). Story answers the question 'What happens next?'; discourse answers the question 'How will what happens next be told?' Story is the narrative signified, in other words; discourse the narrative signifier (Genette, 27). A number of theorists go a step further and follow Gérard Genette in further subdividing discourse into two levels, *récit* and *narration*, the former referring to the text as we actually read it, the words upon the page, and the latter referring to the act or process of producing the text. The most acceptable terms in English for these two levels are those suggested by Shlomith Rimmon-Kenan (1983), *text* and *narration*. In these terms, text refers to the discursive handling of time, characterization, and the angle of vision through which the story is filtered, while narration refers to the narrative levels and voices involved in the communication situation. *Text*, in other words, answers the question 'How will what happens next be told?' in terms of the 'downward' arrangement of the discourse, that is to say insofar as it refers to the story of the characters, while *narration* answers the same question in terms of the 'upward' arrangement of the discourse, that is to say insofar as it refers to the role of the narrating agent. We could rephrase our questions, in fact: story answers the question 'What happens next?'; text answers the question 'How will the account of what happens next be arranged?'; and narration answers the question 'Who is speaking?' Story is to text is to narration as what is to how is to who.

The question of narration leads us, of course, to another question as well: 'Who is being addressed?' A narrative is a *communication*, and as such it presupposes two basic parties, a *sender* and an *addressee* or *receiver*. Common sense identifies the sender with the author of the text we are reading and the receiver with ourselves, namely the reader; theory improves on common sense by dividing each of these parties into a variable number of symmetrically corresponding personages. By the application of Ockham's razor we can limit the dissection of each party to three personages. On the sending end of the communication we then have the *real author*, the *implied author*, and the *narrator*; on the receiving end, in inverse order, we have the *narratee*, the *implied reader*, and the *real reader* (Chatman, 28, 151; Rimmon-Kenan, 86). (We shall return to these distinctions in due course.) The abstraction of the semiotic model, however, omits precisely the one personage in the whole transaction with whom the naïve reader will instinctively identify, namely the 'hero' or 'heroine,' and all those other fictional denizens of the story world whom, for short, we can call characters. Our complete list of *dramatis* (or *narrationis*) *personae* can thus be arranged as in figure 4.

The personality of these *personae* makes it unlikely, of course, that they could ever all take a bow together on the same stage. Though there are certainly readers (and even more certainly television viewers and film audiences) for whom such figures as Don Quijote or Anna Karenina or Hercule Poirot are more real than their shadowy creators, it is still clear enough that Cervantes enjoyed at least one major advantage that the Knight of the Dolorous Countenance did not: Cervantes was free to choose whether he would attempt to create Don Quijote or not. Cervantes could reach into Don Quijote's world and change it, godlike. Generations of readers could similarly reach into the errant knight's world and readjust it according to their own desires and designs. To be a character is to be caged in the world of story, to have the freedom to do only what has been irrevocably prescribed (or, in the reader's rearrangement of things, *post*scribed), to have inscribed the sentence Kafka's condemned man in *The Penal Colony* is to learn to read with his body: 'Honour thy superiors!' (197).

Now, admittedly, on the one hand it could be objected that this is mere playing with words; on the other, so is all literature and literary criticism. We know very well that Emma Bovary never existed and yet we tend intuitively, naïvely to think of her *story* as being in some sense more real, more primary, than the particular discursive strate-

Real author	Implied author	Narrator	Character	Narratee	Implied reader	Real reader

Figure 4. Narrative personalia

gies used to present it. And yet the text, the textual presentation, is all we have, in a very real sense: 'there is not, *first of all*, a given reality, *and afterward*, its representation by the text. The given is the literary text; starting from it, by a labor of *construction* ... we reach that universe where certain characters live, comparable to the persons we know "in life"' (Todorov, 27). Likewise, it is also through the text, and only through the text, that we can acquire knowledge of the narration, namely knowledge of the process of its production. The relationship between both text and story, on the one hand, and text and narration, on the other, is a paradoxical (or pre-comic) one, however, for 'the narrative text is itself defined by these other two aspects: unless it told a story it would not be a narrative, and without being narrated or written it would not be a text' (Rimmon-Kenan, 4).

This ludic, metonymic, and paradoxical relationship of the levels of narration of the narrative text is reflected in the complex interrelationship of the narrative personalia already mentioned and enables equally complex utilization of the pre-comic potential of narrative as a discursive system. To speak of narrative personalia is, of course, merely a metaphor. Neither characters, narrators, narratees, nor implied authors or readers are real persons in any but a metaphorical sense: they are *narrative agents*, narrative instances, and the most appropriate pronoun for each of them is *it* rather than *he* or *she*. (This awareness, however, need not necessarily prevent us from occasionally having our narratological cake and eating it as well. Where it seems appropriate to our purposes they will consequently be referred to in anthropomorphic terms; however, this usage should be read as meaning that they are conceived of not *as* persons but *as if* they were persons.)

Working outwards in concentric circles from the centre of our diagram of *dramatis personae* we move from the level of characters to that of narrator and narratee. It is true, of course, that characters can themselves be narrators *within* the story and address their narratives to other characters who then serve as narratees, and we shall return to this aspect. For the moment, however, let us concentrate on the basic hierarchy of narrative structure, situating characters in stories, which are narrated by and for entities on a higher level of the structure. It is perhaps unnecessary to point out that the narrator is not the real author: only the most hard-line traditionalists, to repeat a point made earlier, would still insist on confusing Marcel with Proust, for example. Nor is the narratee the real reader: rather he (it) is the semiotically necessary receiver of the narrator's discourse. Every word in the text is 'spoken,' or, as in the case of directly reported speech, at least presented by the narrator, who, after all, might have chosen to omit such information. Similarly, however inconspicuous his presence, the narratee is never absent, every word of the narrator's being intended for him (it) alone. Between them these two agents construct the text that discourses the story of the characters, the narrator's discourse evoked by the presence of the narratee as receiver. Their relationship to the world of the characters is godlike, for, in view of the hierarchical relation between the two levels, one negative word of the narrator would in principle be sufficient to alter radically the entire meaning of the world of the story (Bal, 149). Like any projector of a possible world the narrator remains external to the world he creates and can change it with a word.

If the characters' relationship to the narrator of their story is indeed that of 'flies to wanton boys,' the narrator's freedom is by no means unlimited either: common sense reminds us that the narrator is himself a fictional creation of an author. Indeed he is a fiction of a fiction, for between narrator and author there is one more narrative level, that of the implied author and his counterpart the implied reader. Theorists disagree as to how the existence of the implied author should be viewed, whether as an anthropomorphic entity, 'the author's second self' (Booth, 71), or as a semiotically necessary but abstract construct inferred and put together by the reader on the basis of all the components of text, narration, and story (Chatman, 148). For our present purposes the dispute is not a crucial one: it is clear that an author 'may embody in a work ideas, beliefs, emotions other than or even quite opposed to those he has in real life; he may also embody different ideas, beliefs and emotions in different works' (Rimmon-Kenan, 87). Indeed it is clear that in one sense at least the real author's ideas, beliefs, and emotions *must* to some degree differ in each of his or her texts, since authors too are situated in a web of time and space. Corresponding to the implied author is the implied reader, the hypothetical reader perfectly attuned to every textual nuance woven into the narrative by the implied author. We never *see* or *hear* the implied author; we can only infer his presence informing the narrator's narration. The only *voice* we ever hear is the narrator's

– but sometimes, for example, we may feel that the narrator is not completely trustworthy, that in some way he is diverging from what we accept as the values and norms of the narrative as a whole. In such a case, as Chatman puts it 'the unreliable narrator is at virtual odds with the implied author; otherwise his unreliability could not emerge' (149). The implied author, in other words, situates the narrator with regard to the discourse delivered by the narrator.

On the hierarchical level immediately superior to that of the implied author and his counterpart the implied reader we finally encounter the real author and the real reader, and we might be tempted to heave a sigh of relief at reaching solid ground again after the narrative parade of ghostly presences. The relief would be premature, however, as we have seen in other chapters: the traditionalist notion of the objectively receptive reader unproblematically quaffing of the vessel of meaning previously and unproblematically poured full by a sovereign author has turned out to be as riddled with paradox as any other level of the narrative transaction. None of these levels is independent; each is metonymically constituted by its difference from its neighbours, just as its neighbours are in turn constituted by their difference from it. Even on the individual narrative levels the relationship between agent and message is determined by paradox: the narrator constitutes the text and is simultaneously constituted by it; the implied author determines the process of narration and is in turn determined by the narration; the author in turn operates through the exercise of control over language – language whose wall-to-wall uncontrollability has become an axiomatic given for increasingly larger areas of literary theory.

In the light of this view of the narrative process, our curtain-call of narrative personages must be recast as a series of nested frames, as in figure 5. Each of the narrative frames constitutes a narrative world, a possible world that could have been projected quite differently had the narrative agency of any one of the higher-ranked worlds so 'chosen' – but this 'choice' would also have involved a chain reaction of differences in the superior levels of the hierarchy as well. The controllers in the narrative god-game are controlled by what they control. The four levels of our diagram represent only the tip of the iceberg, however, as far as narrative complexity is concerned. The narrator may well 'focalize' his narrative through the eyes of one (or several) of the characters rather than his own, for example (Genette, 186–94), thus relativizing both his own voice and their vision in a polyvocal act of narration. Characters in a story regularly narrate stories them-

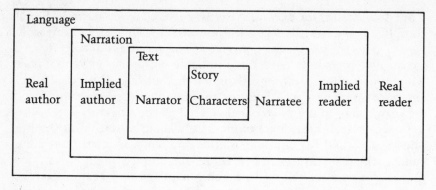

Figure 5. Narrative worlds

selves about other characters: 'diegetic' characters, that is to say, conjure up 'hypodiegetic' stories one level lower in the narrative hierarchy (Genette, 228; Rimmon-Kenan, 91–2), narratives within narratives. It is an over-simplification to think in terms of merely two levels here, however, for in constructing and recounting his own narrative a fictional character does not just become a diegetic narrator; he becomes a diegetic real author. The mind reels at the complexity of possible worlds involved in these terms in, say, John Barth's bravura passage – one of many – from *Lost in the Funhouse* (150), as discussed by Chatman (255–6):

> '''''''Speak!' Menelaus cried to Helen on the bridal bed," I re-
> minded Helen in her Trojan bedroom,' I confessed to Eidothea on
> the beach," I declared to Proteus in the cavemouth,' I vouchsafed to
> Helen on the ship," I told Peisistratus at least in my Spartan hall,' I
> say to whoever and where- I am. And Helen answered:
> '''''''Love!'''''''

Here we have a potential infinite regress in a straight line, as it were. Circular paradoxes are also often found in such writers as Sterne, Flann O'Brien, Cortázar, or Borges in the form of what Genette calls 'metalepsis' (234), where characters 'escape' from their rightful narrative level to a higher one, as in Flann O'Brien's *At Swim-Two-Birds*, where the 'author' character Dermot Trellis is tried while asleep by his own characters for alleged injustices perpetrated upon them. 'All these games,' writes Genette, 'by the intensity of their effects, demonstrate the importance of the boundary they tax their ingenuity to overstep, in defiance of verisimilitude – a boundary *that is precisely the narrating (or the performance) itself*: a shifting but sacred frontier between two worlds, the world in which one tells, the world of which one tells' (236; Genette's emphasis). Such games flaunt for comic purposes the pre-comic structure of narrative itself, and the comedy is entropic, for 'the most troubling thing about metalepsis indeed lies in this unacceptable and insistent hypothesis,' as Genette puts it, 'that the extradiegetic is perhaps always diegetic, and that the narrator and his narratees – you and I – perhaps belong to some narrative' (236).

And of course we *do* belong to 'some narrative,' several of them, in fact: the narratives of language, of history, of culture, of society, and, for millions of orthodox believers, any of the various narratives of salvation that have been and are being written. In Umberto Eco's novel *The Name of the Rose* (1980) a medieval monk becomes a ruthless murderer in order to prevent the discovery of a manuscript hidden in a secret room at the centre of a labyrinthine library. The manuscript turns out to be the lost second book of Aristotle's *Poetics*, which undertakes to discuss comedy as extensively as tragedy was in the first book. The monk turns murderer to prevent its discovery, for such a book, he believes, lending classical authority to so volatile and dangerous a thing as comedy and laughter, would eventually destabilize and undermine all authority, human and divine alike. Many a beleaguered humanist facing the relentlessly advancing postmodernist, poststructuralist hordes might experience a sneaking feeling of sympathy for the resolutely agelastic cleric. With due respect for theological sensibilities, however, it is clear that – from a narratological point of view at least – God, as the ultimate self-reflective narrator and creator of possible worlds, is by that definition also the ultimate humorist. Barthes quotes Flaubert as asking 'When will someone write from the point of view of a *superior joke,* that is as God sees things from above?' (*Image* 111). Much modern narrative exploits precisely the fact that in one sense *all* narrative responds to Flaubert's demand.

To the degree that narrative is always a multiple play of levels and metalevels it is also always a form both of play and of (pre-comic) humour. Narrative is lusory in that the narrative discourse always plays with the story, always adopts a particular mode of presentation and arrangement where many other arrangements would have been equally possible. Recent metafictional narrative merely makes playfully overt what has always, of necessity, been narrative practice, as when John Fowles offers the reader three alternative endings to *The French Lieutenant's Woman* (1969) or Julio Cortázar provides a table of instructions for alternative readings of *Hopscotch* (1963). The comic potential of such play becomes more apparent as the play becomes more ostentatious: take Raymond Queneau's *Exercises in Style* (1947), for example, where a minimal and totally banal story is given no less than ninety-nine separate narrative treatments. The character in any story is an actor; the narrator is an observer. The character's milieu is sequentiality, uncertainty, unpredictability; the narrator's is arrangement, certainty, predictability. The character operates on what Jakobson ('Two Aspects') called the syntagmatic or metonymic axis, the axis of syntax and 'just one damn thing after another'; the narrator operates at right angles to this time-bound world and privileges instead the paradigmatic or metaphoric axis, the axis of semantics and interpretation. Even if narrative is conceived of simply as a two-level structure involving level and metalevel, history and its telling, it is still always potentially comic because of the element of discursive *choice* involved. Seen as a multilevelled structure involving not only a narrator but an implied author and a real author as well, together with their three receptive counterparts, the comic potential increases proportionately, each of the narrative levels serving as metalevel to the one immediately below it: the narrator's discourse is itself 'story' to the implied author's discourse, which is in turn 'story' to the authorial discourse. The complexity as well as the amount of the information transmitted and received increases at each higher level, the whole constituting not just a structure, but a structure of structures (cf. Barthes, *Elements* 89–94). In diagrammatic terms it would thus look something like figure 6.

In this system of nested narrative worlds there are no absolutes. The agents on every level exist only to the extent that they are *discoursed* on a higher level as existing. If we adopt a simple system of notation to convey the suggestion of nested worlds, it is clear that a character (C) is never simply

$$C = (C),$$

that is, a character existing in an absolute and unmediated world, but is always both

$$C = (N(C)),$$

that is, the character as discoursed by the narrator (N), and

$$C = ((C)N'),$$

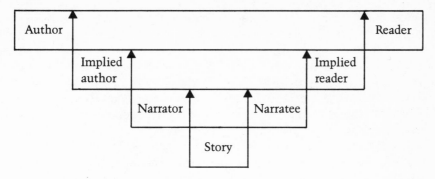

Figure 6. Nested worlds

that is, the character as received by the narratee (N'). Indeed to be more accurate, the character is

$$C = (N((C))N'),$$

that is, constituted by the discourse of one narrative agent and the reception by another. Once we introduce the implied author (A') and the implied reader (R'), our character metamorphoses into

$$C = (A'((N((C))N'))R').$$

The introduction of the real author (A) and the real reader (R) involves seeing the character as

$$C = (A((A'((N((C))N'))R'))R);$$

and if we choose to regard both author and reader as irremediably embedded in language (L) we finally obtain the monstrous but suggestive formula

$$C = (L((A((A'((N((C))N'))R'))R))L).$$

Splendid as it may be, though, our final formula could be argued as being in a sense perfectly irrelevant, for if authors and readers alike are inescapably embedded in language then so are we all, and since this is true we might just as well ignore the fact. This is exactly the sort of argument against which contemporary critical theory most eagerly takes up arms, however, explaining with many accents – Marxist, feminist, psychoanalytical, sociological, deconstructive – that 'reality' is 'written,' that consciously or unconsciously we are all inscribed in discourses that may or may not be largely or even totally beyond our capacity to alter, but whose existence at least it is possible and necessary to be aware of. Awareness, 'distance,' suspicion – Shklovsky's *ostranenie*, Brecht's *Verfremdung* – have become the critical order of the day in a concerted attempt at least to analyse the frames that define our world(s) and determine what is 'real' and what is 'fiction.' The American sociologist Erving Goffman has suggested in his *Frame Analysis* (1974) that ultimately the distinction may not be possible and that in the end 'that which is sovereign is relationship – not substance' (561).

We have looked at how a possible-worlds model might cast some light on the extent to which play and humour situations operate in narrative. At this point we can also attempt the reverse procedure and look more closely at the extent to which play and humour situations can be read as constituting 'narrative' situations. First of all we need to recall the relationship between play situations and humour situations – or play and humour *texts*, for, as we have seen, the distinction is very largely one of 'reading' the given situation. Together they constitute ludic or non-serious texts read as offset against the serious world, the 'real' world of work as opposed to the 'unreal' escape worlds of ludic play. Figure 7 will help to clarify their overall relationship.

We may begin by looking at lusory texts, since their relationship to narrative is probably the most intuitively obvious. A game (Caillois's *ludus*), we will assume, has a diegetic story (the encounter between opponents, or between a single player and the rules) and an extradiegetic discourse (the game is interpreted, or analysed, or framed, as *being* a game rather than, say, a form of judicial combat or tribal warfare or religious drama of some sort). The player who becomes completely caught up in the game – as a good player should – is unaware that the game *is* a game. The rules of the game take over from the norms of everyday behaviour, and the game, for the totally absorbed *player*, is no longer a game but a real world, alternative to the reality felt to exist by non-players. This latter category includes the player himself, of course, once the game is over or the spell is broken by some unforeseen interruption from the outside world – if somebody spills his beer all over the chess-board, for example. Once the spell is broken, the player crosses the threshold between the 'real' world of the game in which he performed the role of diegetic character and enters the world of the extradiegetic observer in which the game is interpreted as just that, just a non-serious, 'unreal' pastime. If we provisionally reserve, for convenience' sake, the interpretation 'real/unreal' for the diegetic world and the interpretation 'serious/

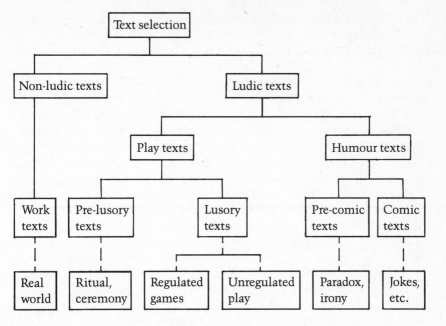

Figure 7. Work, play, and humour texts

non-serious' for the extradiegetic world, we arrive (employing the same system of notation as before) at the formula

(1)   Game text = (This is non-serious (This is real)).

Perhaps our player is not really as committed to his game-world as he might be, though – perhaps he is just *playing at* the game rather than playing the game, perhaps, say, to amuse a small child. Here not only does the extradiegetic observer regard the diegetic world-text as non-serious; even the intradiegetic participant regards it as unreal. We may, in fact, differentiate game and play situations, *ludus* versus *paidia*, on precisely this difference, for

(2)   Play text = (This is non-serious (This is unreal)).

But on another occasion perhaps our player friend isn't just amusing his three-year-old on a Sunday afternoon. Perhaps he is in fact a professional football player whose commitment to the game ensures that as player he sees the diegetic world text as very real, while his stockbroker ensures that as extradiegetic observer he also interprets the game as a very serious form of work. This solidly non-ludic variation provides us with

(3)   Work text = (This is serious (This is real)).

Purely lusory play is not the only domain where the intradiegetic actor perceives the diegetic world to be unreal, however. There are many conventions whose nature is recognized as essentially arbitrary – eating one's peas with a fork rather than a soup-spoon, for example – but whose existence is accepted as a useful contribution to everyday, real-world living. These would include not only table manners but also all systems of politeness and good manners, all moral codes, all philosophical, political, and critical systems, all religious creeds – unless, of course, they are regarded by a particular individual as being absolute rather than relative, in which case they are, for him, undifferentiated real-world texts like any other, such as brushing your teeth or boiling an egg. For those who regard them as arbitrary though necessary conventions whose value is relative rather than substantial they are a form of inverted game text, which, as already suggested, we may call *pre-lusory* texts: the intradiegetic actor recognizes the world-text as unreal, and the extradiegetic observer none the less accepts it as part of serious real-world living. In other words,

(4)   Pre-lusory text = (This is serious (This is unreal)).

To the extent that almost all social discourse has over the last century or so come to be seen as conventional, and all attempts at theoretical explanation to be merely provisional, the pre-lusory can be said to have invaded ever larger areas of social discourse. The prelusory, that is to say, has a similar relationship to the purely lusory as the pre-comic has to the purely comic. (I owe the term *pre-lusory* to Bernard Suits, but while Suits uses it in a contrastive sense as meaning 'non-lusory' or 'extralusory,' I employ it in a relative sense to designate a text potentially but not actually lusory.)

These four categories, seen in terms of the relationship of participation and evaluation, story and discourse, level and metalevel, are not absolute or substantive; rather they are categorized relatively – that is to say by their difference from each other. Non-ludic and prelusory texts, or, as we might say, real-world and conventional or ritual situations, differ from the two kinds of lusory texts (game and play situations) only in degree, not in kind, and any one of the four can easily metamorphose into any one of the other three. On both textual levels there is an evaluative decision hinging on a simple binary opposition, real/unreal or serious/non-serious. However, we have been using these separate terms only for terminological convenience in distinguishing between the two textual levels of our model. They are in fact interchangeable: what is *real* relates to 'things as they really are' (Latin *res* 'thing,' 'fact'), to what is fixed, permanent, immovable, essential, fundamental, important, or, in other words, serious; what is *unreal* relates to what is lacking in solidity, substance, genuineness, gravity, to what is artificial and illusory, or, in other words, non-serious. It thus becomes clear that the relationship between our two textual levels hinges on whether the *same* decision is made on the diegetic and extradiegetic levels. If we allow 'S' to represent what is evaluated as serious and '–S' ('not S') to represent what is evaluated as non-serious, we can rewrite our four formulas, starting at the 'serious' extreme of the diagram in figure 7:

(5)   Work text = $(S(S))$

(6)   Pre-lusory text = $(S(-S))$

(7)   Game text = $(-S(S))$

(8)   Play text = $(-S(-S))$

Both comic and pre-comic texts, as we have seen already (cf. figure 3), derive from a humorously experienced incongruity. An incongruity, it has also been suggested, is the result of a particular *perception* of a conjunction of possible worlds. The perceiver's world, that is to say, determines the congruity or incongruity of the perceived world. Once again there is an extradiegetic and a diegetic world, the latter functioning as level to the metalevel of the former. A perceived incongruity, that is, has the formula

(9)   Perceived incongruity = $(W_1$:This is not so $(W_2$:This is so$))$.

The diegetic world (W_2), that is, presents as a proposition ('This is so') a situation that the extradiegetic world (W_1) refuses to accept ('This is not so'). A perceived incongruity, however, as we know, is as yet only a *potential* humour situation. In order to be experienced as an actual humour situation (text) there must be a further process of perception that extradiegetically treats the perceived incongruity of formula 9 as a diegetic text:

(10)   Humour text = $(W_0$:$(W_1$:This is not so $(W_2$:This is so$)))$

The evaluation of the new extradiegetic world (W_0) determines whether the humour text is experienced in pre-comic or comic terms. If the evaluation is 'This is serious,' then we have the formula for pre-comic humour:

(11)   Pre-comic text = (This is serious (This is not so (This is so))).

As we have seen, this is the world of paradox, irony, metaphor, all tropological use of language, indeed language itself as seen by poststructuralist writers. It can include other discourses such as satire and parody as well, though either of these can also easily mutate into comic texts. Comic texts differ from pre-comic texts only in that the evaluation in the extradiegetic world W_0 is 'This is not serious' rather than 'This is serious.'

(12)   Comic text = (This is non-serious (This is not so (This is so))).

Comic experience, as we have seen, requires favourable 'appropriateness conditions,' as the speech-act theorists say (we shall return to this point in more detail in the next chapter), but is no different in this respect from other forms of textualizing experience. Both the decision between 'This is serious' and 'This is not serious' and the psychological consequences deriving from this decision are always matters involved with appropriateness conditions, and our conception of what constitutes good manners or play (as opposed to, say, brawling) is no less conditioned by our notions (in W_0) of what constitutes appropriate norms of behaviour than are our notions of what is funny. The more obvious types of black humour achieve their effect by inducing us to ignore appropriateness conditions, thus balancing, as we have seen already, the evocation of comic experience and the inhibition of comic pleasure.

One of the advantages of the possible-worlds model is its ability to illustrate the very close family relationship between play texts and humour texts as twin branches of the ludic impulse. The relationship becomes even clearer if we choose to interpret the statement '(W_1:This is not so (W_2:This is so))' as meaning simply '(W_1:This is unreal),' for in that case the formulas for *paidia* (unregulated play) and the comic are exactly the same, just as the formulas for the pre-lusory and the pre-comic are exactly the same. In that case

(13)   Pre-lusory *or* Pre-comic text = (S(−S))

and

(14)   Play *or* comic text = (−S(−S))

while both work texts and game texts refer to diegetic real worlds, giving us, as before,

(15)   Work text = $(S(S))$

and

(16)   Game text = $(-S(S))$.

Though this conflation is useful for analysing the closeness of the formal relationship between play and humour, however, it is preferable if we wish to distinguish humour from all other types of possible-world conjunctions to retain the three-level definition of humour, $(W_0(W_1(W_2)))$. For, as we have seen before, while all possible-world conjunctions are based on the simultaneous *existence* of two or more possible worlds, only humour emphasizes precisely the *relationship* between them.

In this sense one could argue that humour is structurally more similar to the narrative text than are games or play, even though the argument might seem counter-intuitive. Humour, like narrative, requires a greater nesting of textual levels than do games or the various forms of lusory play. Like narrative, humour maximizes the information content of any message and *contains* various forms of play and games existing and interacting simultaneously. On this basis humour and narrative are also comparable to the extent that they both tend towards informational entropy, towards the retardation of story and the proliferation of discourse, towards the slowing down of time and the privileging of observation, towards a comedy of stasis.

Narrative is essentially an ironic, that is to say a pre-comic genre, an affair of message and metalinguistic commentary, with each message and commentary being relativized by the next higher levels in the narrative hierarchy. At the level of story all is serious, all is real: 'This is so.' At the level of text the narrator essentially says 'This is *not* so,' for by his (its) employment of all the tricks of the narrative trade, flashbacks and flashforwards, manipulation of duration and order, repetitions and omissions, focalization on this character instead of that one, and so on, the narrator shows that in his world there is no one real or substantial story holding the entire narrative structure together but only a series of events whose relevance is their arrangeability. The narrator's discourse is in its turn relativized by the implied author, whose world is relativized by the author, whose world is relativized by language itself.

Roman Jakobson famously observed that poetic language involved the projection of the vertical or paradigmatic axis of language onto the horizontal or syntagmatic axis ('Closing Statement' 358). Narrative, like humour, involves the projection of the horizontal axis onto the vertical. *Tristram Shandy* (1760–7) is the archetypal example of narrative's tendency *not* to tell the story – which a naïve reader might well think of as the entire *raison d'être* of the narrative in the first place – but rather to reflect on its own process of production. Tristram's narrative pace is so discursive and his shaping of his own story so complicated that its completion becomes an impossibility, for 'the more I write the more I shall have to write' (230). Zeno would have approved.

5   Homologous Worlds: The Literary and the Ludic

So far the global relationship of literary discourse and humour as crea-tive acts has been argued on the basis of their being similar but separate products of the same ludic impulse to project fictive possible worlds. It can be argued that the relationship is a more intimate one, however, and that literary discourse is in fact a *form* of humour – a form whose major difference from jokes consists in the type of hu-morous pleasure (pre-comic as opposed to comic) typically made available. The argument of this chapter is that there is a continuum of potential humour experience from the simplest non-verbal comic situation (the proverbial man slipping on the banana skin) to the most Byzantine ramifications of the most sophisticated aesthetic text. This continuum is underwritten on the one hand, as we shall see, by the *textualizing* nature of all ludic experience, whether humorous or aesthetic or both, as constituted by the receiver from the raw material of situational observation or linguistic signalling, and on the other hand, though interdependently, by the ludic element in all linguistic, and especially all literary, signalling.

Literature, to be sure, abounds in various forms of the comic both in generic and thematic terms, and there is of course an enormous body of critical literature available discussing literary comedy in terms of both its history and its techniques. 'Literature' and 'hu-mour,' that is, are traditionally regarded unproblematically as sepa-rate but intersecting systems, the area of intersection including the multiple forms of specifically literary comic devices, themes, and genres. There has been considerably less discussion of the problem that will concern us in this chapter, however, namely the degree to which 'humour' and 'literature' as a system of discourse can be seen as semiotically homologous discourses or communicational systems, functioning within like textual and contextual restraints, or, to go further, the degree to which literary discourse can be seen as itself a *form* of humour. Freud's work on their common psychological origin and Arthur Koestler's on the connection between the logical processes involved in creative thinking whether in the context of science, art, or humour are among the few works that have so far associated humour and the more 'serious' forms of creative endeavour.

Giambattista Vico, in his treatise of 1725 on *The New Science*, anticipated modern literary and philosophical theory in regarding what he called *sapienza poetica* or 'poetic wisdom' as the one genuinely distinctive and permanent human characteristic: 'the capacity and the necessity,' as Terence Hawkes puts it, 'to generate myths, to use language metaphorically: to deal with the world, that is, not directly but at one remove' (15). Not surprisingly for his time, Vico makes no reference to humour in this context, but clearly there is a sense in which humour can be argued as belonging to *sapienza poetica*, the power of constructive, creative thought. Social anthropologists and literary historians, as Wylie Sypher points out, agree in tracing literature and art to a common origin in magic, myth, and ritual (*Comedy* 215). Vivian Mercier, for example, following Huizinga's lead, has examined the interrelations of humour, literature, magic, and myth in the early Irish comic tradition and concluded that humour, in the Irish tradition at least, can be seen as originating in non-verbal magic and in myth, giving early Irish literature its characteristic colouring of the fantastic, the macabre, and the grotesque. He sees word-play as originating later, in verbal magic, and becoming wit as the magical elements disappear. Satire similarly develops out of injurious spells as the druidic wizard becomes bard or poet, and parody appears in Mercier's scheme as the poet becomes more self-awarely conscious of the possibilities of formal technique (1–5).

Humour shares with magic and myth as governing psychological function the impulse and the ability to restore order and balance. Lévi-Strauss has discussed in his *Structural Anthropology* (1958) the power of shamans to cure physical pain by reintegrating what seems incoherent and arbitrary into an orderly world where everything is meaningful. 'That the mythology of the shaman does not correspond to an objective reality does not matter' (197). Humour, like mythology, provides an explanation, what Lévi-Strauss calls a *language* 'making it possible to undergo in an ordered and intelligible form a real experience that would otherwise be chaotic and inexpressible' (198). Mythical thought, as argued by Lévi-Strauss, always progresses from the awareness of oppositions towards their resolution. This is also the most characteristic feature, as we have seen, of humour as well, whether it be derisive, sympathetic, or entropic in expression. Humour indeed, like mythical thought, to borrow another of Lévi-Strauss's concepts, is a kind of *bricolage*. In *The Savage Mind* Lévi-Strauss distinguishes between the 'engineer,' who uses rational, scientific thinking to find the most professionally acceptable and appropriate solution to a problem, and the 'bricoleur' or do-it-yourself man, who employs unprofessional but none the less effective means towards a solution whose appropriateness will be of quite a different nature. Humour is a kind of intellectual *bricolage*, a papering over the cracks by ludic methods where more 'serious' intellectual engineering work might involve a total restructuring of the entire edifice. Humour, in other words, like magic and myth and religion, like philosophy and art and literature, is a way of coping with an uncertain reality, a way of bringing the essentially intractable under at least the fictive control of the imagination, that *sapienza poetica* that Vico talks about and whose essential task is the integration of difference, the interpretation of uncertainty. Humour is a protective mode, a control device allowing us to accept what we would otherwise reject. Humour, like tragedy, reveals life as paradox in that it always points implicitly to the simultaneous existence of mutually contradictory yet apparently fundamental truths, but where tragic catharsis reconciles us to the pain of existential paradox, humour can take us straight to the heart of paradox itself (Collins, 6).

Freud's theory of humour in *Jokes and Their Relation to the Unconcious* (1905) is central to any consideration of the relationship of humour and art. Freud preceded Huizinga in the implications of his research on jokes for the relationship between literature and the ludic. Modern psychologists are divided on the merits of Freud's theory of psychic economy as the central motive factor of comic response – humour, that is to say, as essentially fuelled by excess psychic energy stored in readiness for a threatening eventuality that fails to materialize. His scheme is highly suggestive, however, in its implication that humour phenomena, dreams, and artwork alike are derived from this unnecessarily stockpiled inhibition-energy towards the end of producing pleasure, dreams operating via the unconscious, humour via both the unconscious and the preconscious, and aesthetic production via the conscious mind. Even more interestingly for our present purposes, Freud also points to the element of parodistic metacommentary in jokes: like dreams, he notes, jokes operate through two major mechanisms of juxtaposition, condensation and displacement, but unlike dreams jokes foreground these mechanisms and reflect their own paradoxical structure.

Condensation, for Freud, means that the material to be processed as dreamwork, jokework, or artwork experiences a startling compression: in terms of Jakobson's seminal distinction in his essay 'Two Aspects of Language' (1956) we could call this a juxtaposition of worlds on the paradigmatic (or metaphoric) axis, the axis of similarity. Displacement, by contrast, means that events that may have played a major role in a dream, for example, may be consciously perceived as something entirely peripheral in the waking state: this lack of proportion would constitute a juxtaposition of worlds on Jakobson's syntagmatic (or metonymic) axis, the axis of contiguity. Both axes are characterized, in other words, by incongruous juxtaposition. Why are all dreams not perceived as comic, in that case? Well, many of them are, but in most cases what is missing is the receptivity factor, the appropriateness conditions. The dreamer as character in his own dream-world is unaware of the incongruity of his world, while the dreamer who recollects is more concerned to sort out rather than re-experience the remembered incongruities. For much the same reason, jokes that have to be retold to listeners who failed to understand the punch line, or cartoons that have to be explained to an unresponsive reader, immediately lose most or all of their comic potential – unless, of course, they regain it by becoming metajokes, as it were; witness the unintended hilarity of many of Freud's earnest explanations of his own sample jokes.

In *Beyond the Pleasure Principle* (1920) Freud discusses the *fort/ da*, now-you-see-it-now-you-don't game played by his little grandson, who would spend hours throwing a toy away only to haul it back again triumphantly by the string to which it had been attached all the time. Freud does not discuss this concept in connection with humour; rather he sees it as the infant's symbolic mastery of its mother's absence. The situation is one very cognate to the humour situation, however, in that a pretended loss, a pretended irruption of disorder, is played with, flirted with hypothetically, ludically, before the possible threat is defused and the uncertainty triumphantly reintegrated in the realm of order and security. Terry Eagleton has observed that the *fort/da* game can also be read as the first glimmerings of narrative – an object is lost, and then recovered (a theme to which Milton, for example, did very ample justice): 'Something must be lost or absent in any narrative for it to unfold: if everything stayed in place there would be no story to tell' (185). Narrative is thus a source of consolation (for the lost mother's body, origin of all desire; for paradises lost; for the irreversible tendency of closed systems towards randomness) and pleasurable, if surrogate, recovery. As Eagleton observes, the classical realist narrative operates precisely on this comforting triadic principle of loss or absence leading to desire leading to recovery and presence, while many modernist and postmodernist texts undercut the resolution, accepting, as it were, 'the reality of castration, the ineluctibility of loss, absence and difference in human life' (186). Precisely the same relationship obtains between what we have been calling the humour of order and the humour of entropy: the former operates on the comforting triadic principle of perceived disruption leading to humorous response leading to at least fictive reintegration; the comedy of entropy not only accepts but celebrates the ineluctability of loss.

In *Jokes and Their Relation to the Unconcious* Freud had attempted a distinction between jokes (providing relief from inhibition), the comic (providing relief from what Kant had called 'strained expectation'), and humour (providing relief from the need to feel sympathy). Jokes, he observes, are made for an audience, but do not necessarily need a victim; the comic is discovered, is limited to human beings and their environment, and needs a victim though not an audience; humour, which is the most skimpily treated of the three, is also discovered, specifically in situations where sympathy was felt to be called for but proves not to be necessary, and needs only one person, namely the humorist, the observer. The terminological distinction here need not detain us, since we are concerned with humour as a global phenomenon rather than with its sub-genres – Freud was of course using the word *humour* in its regional sense rather than as a global concept. In a later paper on 'Humour' (1927), by which time he had replaced his dichotomy of conscious versus unconscious with the threefold scheme of id, ego, and superego, Freud adapted his earlier model. Now jokes are seen as allowing the id some harmless penetration of the ego's's/defences; the comic becomes the ego's own comparison between two different ego processes; while humour arises in the elevated relationship of the superego vis-à-vis the struggling ego. The global humour situation, that is to say, is visualized in terms of a 'narrative' situation, with the ego, as Norman Holland says, acting like an *eiron* (52). The superego operates as controller, tester, observer on the level of discourse, the ego fights out the continuing battle with the marauding id on the level of story, and in the distance between the two worlds lies the difference essential for humour. Freud's account of the comic as the ego's *own* comparison between two different ego processes is a *mise en abyme* of the super-ego/ego relationship: the ego (like Josef K. opening the lumber-room door) escapes momentarily, provisionally, fictively, from the level of struggle, the level of story, to the level of observation, the level of discourse. Freud's later model of humour, in other words, describes the humour situation simultaneously in terms of a game, as the superego impassively plays cat-and-mouse with the struggling ego, and in terms of an elementary narrative structure, where the 'narrator' figure of the superego is safely insulated against the trials undergone by the ego as 'character.'

To say it once again, our interest here is essentially in the *structural* functioning of humour rather than in the psychological responses (superiority, surprise, relief, and so on) that provoke or inhibit particular comic response in individual cases. We are not so interested, in other words, in *why* people laugh as in the structural features of the humour situation that make it conventionally acceptable for them to do so in the first place. And here the multitude of available humour theories, however widely their explanatory positions may vary in psychological orientation, seem to agree at least on the basic structural constellation, which in its most general and least useful form could be expressed as: '*Sombody* finds *something* to be *funny.*' There is a particular cognitive stimulus, in other words ('something'), provoking a particular range of subjective response ('funny,' which can include pre-comic as well as comic response) in a particular perceiving subject ('somebody'). The cognitive stimulus is always a perceived difference, a perceived incongruity, a formal discrepancy, whether verbal or non-verbal; it is always perceived as such by an observer; the observer's reaction is always enabled by contextual restraints, by what the speech-act theorists call appropriateness conditions, that is (Pratt, 81), and which will include the cumulative impact of all forms of social and psychological pressures obtaining in the observer's community in his or her given place and time as well as the state of his or her own individual temperament and intellect both in general and at that particular place and time.

The notion of a formal discrepancy, an incongruous juxtaposition, is therefore central to all our notions of humour. But what is incongruity? In a universe without perceiving subjects there could be no incongruity, for incongruity is a function of perceived deviation from an accepted norm. Hence our difficulty, for example, in understanding humour deriving from cultures other than our own. It has been suggested that many of the parables in the New Testament 'are' jokes, but that we cannot see them in this light because we do not know the social structure that would define them as joking, as non-serious rather than serious – for example, the vineyard owner who pays his workers the same wage whether they work one hour or twelve (Holland, 94). Objects and events in themselves, in short, *are* never incongruous; they have incongruity thrust upon them. Nor *are* objects and events in themselves ever comic; they have humour thrust upon them. D.H. Monro has succinctly ordered the various types of situation that normally evoke comic response in our own culture, whichever psychological model we may adopt to explain why: any breach of the usual order of events, and especially if this involves breaking a rule of morality, etiquette, or decent behaviour; the introduction into any situation of what belongs in another; anything masquerading as something it is not; word-plays and nonsense; small misfortunes without serious consequences; want of skill; and, finally, skilfully veiled insults ('Humour' 90–1). Each of these situations is commonly deemed to be funny because of a departure from a norm, a difference from a prescribed course of behaviour, a relationship, in other words, where the expectation that things will continue to function exactly as they are supposed to function is abruptly threatened. To this extent a humour situation always represents a form of disruption, breakdown, uncertainty, threatened entropy; and entropic humour is in one sense distinguishable from the more self-confident forms of humour largely by the extent to which it is prepared to *play* with the threatened danger, to inflate it to overwhelming dimensions before plugging the gap in the dike. Entropic comedy is in this sense an example of the type of game Caillois called *ilinx*, a flirting with vertigo, with uncertainty, with the abyss. Uncertainty, of course, plays a dominant role in all games (including the game of narrative), a fact that is hardly surprising, perhaps, since life itself, tied to the arrow of time, is a function of uncertainty. All forms of humour are forms of ludic play as well, but entropic comedy, as we shall see, has a greater tendency to be specifically lusory as well, since its focus on uncertainty is more self-reflexive than that of its more self-confident (because more engaged) neighbours.

The textualizing function of the reader has been a matter of major concern for a number of years now for several different varieties of literary critic (cf. Suleiman; Tompkins). Approaches based on the premises of linguistic speech-act theory have been particularly enlightening in drawing attention to the constitutive role of the reader –

the 'textualizing' role, as I am calling it here – in determining the 'literariness' of given texts and thus effectively becoming their active co-producer rather than remaining simply the passive recipient of a finished product. Speech-act theorists of literature specifically argue against the formalist position – in a tradition ultimately deriving from the Kantian idea of the autonomous nature of aesthetic artefacts – that literature is formally and functionally distinct in its usage of language as opposed to the 'ordinary language' of everyday dealings. In so doing the speech-act theorists point the way towards the possibility of a unified theory of discourse, for once we take into account the institutionalized aspect of literature, that is to say the fact that a particular community of readers has *selected* particular texts as constituting a literary canon, 'the "special-ness" of literature, which poeticians have long been at pains to demonstrate empirically, does not have to be proved at all' (Pratt, 123). In other words, 'it is people, not properties, that "make a verbal message a verbal work of art" – people writing, editing, revising, reading, and judging. The specialness is in the context' (124), and the context is their central characteristic of being known literary 'display texts' (143). Once we *know* a text is a literary text, in other words, we *treat* it as a literary text – if only for fear of social loss of face if we do otherwise. Many jokes similarly establish their position *as* jokes by standard opening formulas – 'Did you hear the one about ...' – designed to elicit an appropriate response, just as fairy tales advertise their status by beginning with 'Once upon a time ...' and television newscasters signal that their narrative should *not* be treated as fictional by advising us that 'Here is the six o'clock news.' As the last example suggests, display texts exist as commonly outside as inside the realm of aesthetic discourse. Nor need they be verbal, it should be added: we constitute a mountain as a display text, for example, as soon as we admire its wild grandeur or line it up for a photograph.

Intentional deviation from 'ordinary language' on the part of authors of literary texts for purposes of heightened effect, often argued by formalist critics as the very essence of poetic language, in fact occurs routinely outside of literature, as Pratt argues, in everyday conversational narratives, and therefore cannot be held to be constitutive of literature. The same argument holds for fictivity, which, far from being a form of exclusively poetic deviance, is also 'readily found in almost any realm of discourse' (200). Taking narrative fiction as her literary norm, Pratt advances the claim that 'the unmarked case for the novel is the one in which the fictional speech situation reproduces the speech situation obtaining in real world narrative display texts: a Speaker addresses to an Audience a narrative utterance whose point is display and whose relevance is tellability' (205). While such narrative situations are regulated by a system of conventional rules, moreover (the so-called Cooperative Principle), both in non-literary and in literary narrative the point of the utterance can be precisely the deliberate breaking of these rules. In everyday conversation among intimates, for example, 'it is common for terms of abuse to serve as terms of endearment or as compliments precisely because among intimates it would be almost impossible for the genuinely abusive use of the word to occur' (216). A literary analogue would be the numerous *nouveaux romans,* anti-novels, metafictional narratives, and the like, where the stable relationship between author and reader, speaker and hearer, is deliberately flouted or put in jeopardy. For Pratt this constitutes a secondary game ('verbal jeopardy') superimposed on the primary game ('the tellability game of natural narrative'), and over the last half-century or so this double game has become the most favoured technique in modern and postmodern writing. 'The drastic deviance which we encounter in the new novel amounts to a declaration of war on the unmarked narrative and literary norms the novel presupposes and on the interpretation of experience which those norms have been used to affirm in our culture' (222).

These unmarked norms of traditional literary discourse invite further scrutiny, however. The deliberate flouting of rules once held to be inviolate and self-evidently true is central to the emergence of the new modes of literary humour in our time, but this is not to say that it is a new phenomenon. One of the chief rules constituting the Cooperative Principle enabling social interaction to take place at all, according to the speech-act theorists, is that the speaker's utterances are held (theoretically at least) to be true. And yet, though it would no doubt be overly cynical to claim that experience shows lying to be at least as common as truth in social discourse, it is certainly true to say that every utterance is at least in principle *potentially* false. While the practicalities of everyday living make the distinction between truth and falsehood a vital one, however, literature has traditionally been held by critics of a formalist persuasion, at least, to be unaffected by the practical rule that discourse should be truthful: literature is neither true nor false in the real-world sense of the distinction, and thus, as Sir Philip Sidney famously put it, the poet 'nothing affirmeth, and therefore never lieth' (quoted in Wimsatt/Brooks, 171), a formalist retort to Plato's charge that all literary endeavour, being literally a figment of the imagination, is ultimately founded on lies. Realist writing (and reading) largely ignored this constitutive polyphonality of the literary text as merely a matter of common sense; modernism and postmodernism, increasingly privileging discourse over story, narration over the narrated, increasingly focused also on the text's dialogic potential as simultaneously true *and* false, thus privileging those aspects of literary discourse most overtly funded by prevarication, namely irony and parody.

Irony is a humour phenomenon, as both Bergson and Freud recognized: in Freud's terms it is a subspecies of the comic, using joke techniques to convey the opposite of the utterance apparently intended (*Jokes* 73, 174). It is a subspecies in the sense that it is not usually fully actualized as comic experience; it is experienced instead as a pre-comic form of humour, as we have already seen. As Louis Cazamian put it, commenting on the inextricability of humour and irony, they 'answer to one and the same broad mental attitude' (52). 'To all practical purposes,' he continues, 'irony is a parallel method to humor, with a somewhat different atmosphere. It takes its rise in the same inner duality of perception and meaning; and the two psychological and aesthetic attitudes shade off into each other' (199). For the New Critics of the thirties and forties irony became not just a way of saying one thing and meaning another but an overall tactic that allowed the poet to live out Sidney's dictum, escaping all assertion, avoiding all stance-taking, engaging in a sovereign play with verbal textures founded on an aloof awareness of the incorrigible multiplicity of experience. Irony becomes the very 'synonym for complex awareness' (Lentricchia, 234), aesthetic autotelism, Kantian purposiveness without purpose. Cleanth Brooks, in *The Well-Wrought Urn* (1949), one of the classical New Critical statements, observed the similarity between irony in this expanded sense and paradox: the superfluity of equally privileged attitudes, impulses, and concepts, that the poet attempts to juggle tends towards a limit state of informational entropy, total equiprobability of all messages, stasis and ultimate silence. For Northrop Frye, in the *Anatomy of Criticism* (1957), this modernist concept of wall-to-wall irony becomes the dominant mode of Western literature in the twentieth century.

Thirty years later it is likely that most critics would name parody rather than irony as the dominant mode of our time, but arguably the distinction is essentially one of degree rather than of kind. Irony has its origins in a rhetorical trope; parody's pedigree is generic; both, however, functionally involve a doubled communication in which the semantic information is ostentatiously relativized by the signal-information. Parody is a development of the ironic attitude in that it effectively sharpens the reader's awareness of the literary medium itself, employing the devices of its target text while simultaneously, in Shklovsky's phrase, 'laying them bare' (30). 'In general the parodic method is the extension, in various directions and to various degrees, of the device of laying bare the device. In its attempt to expose that illusion which it originally tries to conceal, parody has a close affinity with irony' (Rose, 45). Parody is also a development of the ironic attitude in that it too is characterized by an oppositional or disjunctive structure, by a play on difference. Both, irony and parody, are structured as the simultaneous assertion and relativization of the identity of the terms of a binary opposition: the semantic information of the utterance states an identity, 'This is what I mean,' while the signal-information metalinguistically undermines and ostentatiously relativizes the statement – a formula that, as far as it goes, is also that of humour. Both irony and parody, indeed, to this extent share a strong family resemblance not only with joke structures but with paradox as well.

Parody, most overtly in its metafictional mode, is, by virtue of its overt commentary on its own form, an intensification, a heightening of literary discourse, and to this extent, 'in so far as literature turns back on itself and examines, parodies, or treats ironically its own signifying procedures, it becomes the most complex account of signification we possess' (Culler, *Pursuit* 36). By the same token, *all* literary discourse can be seen as tending towards parody, for 'major literary works are all comments on their own form, on the generic tradition or traditions from which they take their being' (Scholes, *Semiotics* 33). If language, as post-Saussurean linguistics tells us, is a structure of differences circumscribing an absent centre, then the literary text, essentially ironic, is a structure of differences to a higher degree, while parody is a third-order differential structure.

From its historical beginnings parody has been closely associated with the comic. The scholiasts spoke of it as a 'device for comic quotation' (Rose, 20) and described its main functions as being the juxtaposition of the tragic and the comic, the substitution of words, and paraphrase. One form of parody given early recognition was the pun. From its beginnings too parody was felt to belong to the genus of satire and thus to perform the double task of correction and ridicule – in the Horatian view of literature as being ideally both pleasurable and profitable, *dulce* and *utile*, parody thus (theoretically at least) constituted an exemplary literary form. The comic effect of parody is a function of the perception of an incongruity, a discrepancy, between the parodied text and its new context (Rose, 23). Two texts rather than a single text are offered within one work, in other words, balancing identity and difference, sympathy and criticism, playing off the evocation of audience expectations against the destruction of these expectations, as in the Kantian definition of humour. Notoriously, parody has contributed enormously to the postmodernist conception of writing and reading, in the same sense that modernist texts are pervasively informed by the global concept of irony – see, for example, Linda Hutcheon's *A Theory of Parody* (1985). With the help of Shklovsky's work on *Tristram Shandy* as the exemplary form of the novel and Foucault's *The Order of Things* parody has come to control norms of literary production and criticism and to canonize concepts such as intertextuality, metafictionality, and narrative discontinuity and obstruction as characteristic of modern (and especially postmodern) fiction. The notion of intertextuality, indeed, the concept that all texts can refer only to other texts and are woven only of other texts, turns the notion of parody as depending parasitically on a primary target text on its head and transforms parody instead into the fundamental principle of all literature. All literature, all writing, all language, writes Roland Barthes, becomes in this context parody, imitation, mimicry, not of 'reality' but of itself, 'quotation without quotation marks' (*Pleasure* 31). Writing, *all* writing, has become comedy, lacking only an overt comic response on the part of an audience shaped by traditional norms and conventions. Writing, as Barthes says, to repeat, is 'the comical that does not make us laugh' (*Pleasure* 30).

Parody is the most overtly ludic (and lusory) form of literature, and because of its dominant position in current critical discourse our attention is continually drawn to the ludic (and potentially comic) aspects of texts, aspects that in an age less conscious of parody would no doubt have escaped critical attention. One major new tenet of criticism, as Jonathan Culler notes, is thus 'the convention that we should regard most or all interesting works of fiction as self-reflective, self-critical, and try to read them in this way' (*Pursuit* 128). Our attention, that is to say, is continually focused on what one might call textual hypocrisy: the expression owes its origin to the Greek *hypokrisis*, meaning both 'dissembling' and literally 'playing a part on stage.' As in any joke or humour situation there are always at least two lines of communication going on simultaneously in this sort of reading: the naïve or untrained reader may well be aware of only the overt line of communication, the semantic information, while the reader attuned to the ludic possibilities of the text is simultaneously aware of the more covert signal-information continually relativizing the overt communication. Roman Jakobson's well-known formalist definition of literariness ('Closing Statement') essentially sees the literary text in these 'hypocritical' terms: isolating the six constitutive features of any communicative act as being sender and receiver, contact and message, code and context, Jakobson suggested that literariness consists essentially in a transformation of the message itself, namely by the message's dominant emphasis on its own formal structure rather than on its communicative or cognitive content. The communicative process is thus deliberately subverted, deformed by the aesthetic message, literary language becoming a sort of duplicitous game where the message simultaneously means and does not mean 'what it says.' Jakobson's view of literariness corresponds very closely to the New Critics' emphasis on the poem as essentially an ironic structure. Robert Scholes has proposed an extension of this strictly formalist definition: we sense literariness in an utterance, he suggests, when any *one* of the six features of communication loses its simplicity and becomes multiple or duplicitous (*Semiotics* 21).

One area where the duplicity of literary texts (and the potential for associated humour) has been traditionally felt, long before the current pre-eminence of parody in critical discourse, has been the question of tropes or 'figures of speech.' Strictly speaking, of course, tropes are by no means a purely literary affair, but from the days of Homer's 'wine-dark sea' and 'rosy-fingered dawn' the literary text has offered them a congenial home. Now clearly, thinking of dawn as having fingers at all, rosy or not, has an element of the comic about it, even though, recognizing it as a literary trope, we do not usually react to it as if it were 'actually' comic. Aristotle observed that metaphor is like a riddle and went on to associate it with various forms of other verbal 'jokes' like paronomasia. A.W. Schlegel, much later, and fired by Romantic enthusiasm for the transcendental virtues of humour, defended the pun – the 'lowest form of wit,' as tight-laced Victorians would later call it – as a small-scale model of all poetic endeavour. Fired by no such transcendental ambitions, Jakobson ('Two Aspects') characterized all 'poetic language' as drawing pre-eminently and typically on two basic rhetorical modes, metaphor and metonymy – both of which, we may note, are structured on an 'ironic,' pre-comic opposition of the type 'A is (not) B,' a play once again on the relativization of a stated identity.

Clearly many classical rhetorical devices are constructed on potentially comic incongruities. Catachresis, for example, involves the ostentatious usage of what is the 'wrong' word for the given context, as when Milton talks in *Lycidas* of 'blind mouths' or Hamlet takes up arms against a sea of troubles. Synaesthesia plays on the perception of one sense modality in terms of another, as when Lorca talks of the 'viente verde,' 'green wind.' Oxymoron makes 'pointedly foolish' use of incongruity, as when Baroque poets speak of 'icy flames' and 'cruel kindness.' Even though such figures are by no means limited to literary discourse – no one thinks it odd to talk of tables as having 'legs' or houses and football teams as having 'wings' – they are in practice the most obvious instances of literary discourse's concern with its own form, and they also contribute most obviously to the openness and ambiguity of literary texts as a result of what Jonathan Culler calls 'the potential reversibility of every figure' (*Pursuit* 78) since any such figure can (theoretically at least) be read referentially *or* rhetorically. Culler uses the example of a phrase like Burns's 'Her brow is like the snowdrop' to illustrate the point. Referentially this can be read as approval of the physical qualities of the beloved's forehead, as well as, by an automatic interpretive convention, her modesty, innocence, purity, and so on; rhetorically, in its figurality, 'it indicates a desire to see her as she is not' (78), namely as a flower. Naturalistically this is a preposterous suggestion: if she really did have a head like a snowdrop she would be a monster. Artists such as Hieronymus Bosch, indeed, who employ a grotesque mode of expression, are quick to seize upon the unactualized humour content and the potential comic effect in such a comparison – the particular effect centrally capitalized upon by the grotesque mode is precisely the reader's or viewer's unwillingness either to accept wholly or wholly to reject the combination of the monstrous and the comic. Surrealist writers and artists actualized the humour content by parodically poking fun at the convention – an effect easily gained here by substituting for Burns's 'snowdrop' any overtly incongruous expression also connoting whiteness, such as 'teacup' or 'toothpaste.' The incongruity in such a case would be patent precisely because of its breaking of conventional 'poetic' rules, as when Eliot writes that 'the evening is spread out against the sky / Like a patient etherized upon a table' (3). Even here though, so strong is the convention that poetic texts should be poetically received, we are far more likely to attempt to incorporate the incongruous image into some appropriately 'poetic' reading of the text than we are to actualize the incongruity as comic – as we very likely *would* do if it were related to us as a typical remark of an eccentric acquaintance, for example. The literary reading of such ruptures of empirical reality as Burns's snowdrop necessitates a willing 'suspension of disbelief' that is part of the literary game, ironizes the figurality of the trope, goes along with the joke, and implicitly points to the artificiality of all literary discourse.

More radically, recent critics have been pointing the finger at the artificiality of all linguistic discourse. There is an intuitive tendency to think of figurative language as being an artificial, secondary idiom of connotation arbitrarily imposed on a literal, primary language of denotation that straightforwardly 'means what it says.' Recent critics, however, following a line of thought already adumbrated by Rousseau in his *Essay on the Origin of Languages* as well as by Vico in the *New Science*, argue paradoxically that the contrary is true, that language originates in metaphor and that figurative language precedes literal language just as pictographic writing precedes phonographic alphabets. Literal language is thus, like 'literal meaning,' nothing but an erosion of figurative language, a forgetting of an initial figurality (Culler, *Pursuit* 203). Nietzsche's definition of truth as a 'moving army of metaphors, metonymies, and anthropomorphisms' is the most pointed statement of the consequences of this view: 'Truths are illusions whose illusionary nature has been forgotten, metaphors that have been used up and have lost their imprint and that now operate as mere metal, no longer as coins' ('On Truth' 174).

Umberto Eco, in a discussion of rhetoric from a semiotic viewpoint, observes that since classical rhetoricians viewed their discipline as the art of persuasion the various rhetorical figures therefore have as their primary function the focusing of attention by way of creating sudden and unpredictable connections, peacock displays acting as 'embellishments by means of which the discourse acquires an unusual and novel appearance, thus offering an unexpectedly high rate of information' (*Theory of Semiotics* 278). Rhetorical devices may also be seen, however, rather than as externally assumed embellishments, as being a liberation of the inherent ambiguity and consequently the latent potential for incongruity inherent in language itself, as being, in other words, ostentatious displays of language's inherent tendency to actualize its humour content, to move towards comedy.

Language as a semiotic system, as the semioticians and semanticists tell us, is permeated throughout by what might be called a capacity for prevarication. All of semiotics, as Eco himself puts it, is 'in principle the discipline studying everything which can be used to lie' (*Theory* 7), to the extent that 'the possibility of lying is the *proprium* of semiosis just as (for the Schoolmen) the possibility of laughing was the proprium of Man as *animal rationale*' (59). Linguistic signals, according to the linguists, typically convey at least three different kinds of semantic information, descriptive, social, and expressive, and the triple interpenetration of these is crossed by another set of distinctions between verbal and non-verbal signalling (Lyons, 50–63). Utterances may thus be modulated by superimposing upon them a particular attitudinal colouring, indicative of the speaker's involvement in what is being said, and this modulation may on occasion completely reverse the apparent information content of the verbal utterance (Lyons, 65): literary discourse institutionalizes this feature as irony, and many joke types depend on it entirely. Utterances may also of course be deliberately designed to deceive or misinform, and many semioticians consider that prevarication must be ranked as one of the most important properties distinguishing language from all other signalling systems (Lyons, 83).

Even where there is no intentional prevarication it is clear that the particular context of utterance can radically influence the sense of an utterance. The set of implications accepted by one speaker as following from a given utterance may differ radically from the set of implications accepted by another speaker as resulting from the same utterance. Many perfectly acceptable utterances are inherently ambiguous, to the point where, for example, the sentence 'They passed the port at midnight' is subject to totally different interpretations according to whether *port* is taken to refer to a harbour or to a fortified wine (Lyons, 397). Two utterly different possible worlds are generated, that is to say, incongruously held together by the 'same' utterance. Further ambiguities may be introduced by what the semioticians would call channel noise, or by deficiencies in the language-users' competence or performance, or by the particular contexts in which the utterances occur – consider a party of maritime revellers enjoying their dessert wine as they slip past the nocturnal harbour, for example.

Eco argues that 'usually a single sign-vehicle conveys many intertwined contents and therefore what is commonly called a "message" is in fact a *text* whose content is a multilevelled *discourse*' (*Theory* 57) – poststructuralist criticism, as we have noticed, sees literary texts as being most centrally an institutionalization of this inherent instability of language. Eco sees the 'sememe' (that is, the minimal unit of semantic content) as functioning less like a dictionary, with relatively rigid definitions of exact and unchanging meanings, than as an encyclopaedia, its meaning constituted by a network or 'compositional tree' of relationships of mutually opposed denotative and connotative features (84, 113). Like Barthes, Eco sees a central characteristic of aesthetic achievement in the 'programmed intertwining' (114) of the overlapping possible readings or paths constituting the spectrum of meaning of the individual linguistic sign-vehicles: the artistic achievement, however, is centrally an intensification of forces already at work in all linguistic utterance, namely the complexity and unpredictability of sign production springing from the format of the semantic universe (*Theory* 142). 'One might well ask,' writes Eco, 'whether the communicative process is capable of subduing the circumstances in which it takes place' (*Theory* 150). Poststructuralist critics, especially deconstructive critics, would answer the question with a resounding No.

Language, that is, far from being a limpid medium for the undistorted transmission of information, is grounded in paradox, in logical contradiction. Logical contradictions are counter-informative, uninformative, in the paradoxical sense not that they have too little, but that they have too much content (Lyon, 48). If we are told that an acquaintance is an unmarried man who is happily married, for example, or that a particular circle is a square, we experience a form of informational short circuit, baffled by being presented with more than we can accommodate in our everyday conceptual scheme of things. We are in fact presented with a latent humour situation, typical of many jokes and riddles of the 'When is an egg not an egg?' type, which we may or may not choose to (or be able to) convert into a comic response. The thesis of the unpredictability of language implies that, far from being something rare, quirky, and peripheral to the serious business of daily endeavour, paradox informs every word we speak or write and every thought we are capable of thinking. What should amaze us is not that paradoxes are every now and then discovered like rogue elephants by intrepid hunters stalking the far reaches of post-Einsteinean physics or deconstructive theory, but rather that common sense and rational thought ever succeeded in the first place in staking out clearings, where language behaved as if it were actually tamed, in the surrounding jungle of informational superabundance, overplenitude, and entropic proliferation. Language, it seems, is never more true to its own nature than when it says, with Epimenides, 'This sentence is false.'

Language in this perspective is seen as always about to precipitate the paradox of informational overkill, always about to generate an incongruous conflation of possible worlds, always potentially comic if the receiver, within his or her contextual restraints, is led (or is *allowed*) to regard it as such. If this is arguable of language, of course, then it is arguable a fortiori of the literary text, which flaunts its status as a linguistic artefact, and even more so of those texts that ostentatiously privilege irony and parody, as do an ever-increasing number of texts as realist conventions of reading and writing give way to modernist and postmodernist conventions.

Whatever humour potential the literary text may have as a result of its linguistic being, however, this potential will remain unrealized without the reader who, as it were, switches it on. In fact, semiotic accounts of the process of reception of an aesthetic text on the part of its reader are highly suggestive of the similarity of humour and literature as communicative systems and support the argument for their similarity advanced earlier on the basis of parallel reception of display texts. That semiotic accounts of the literary transaction (for example, Eco) may seem to attach greater weight to formalist arguments as to the primacy of the text itself as poetic language than do accounts based on speech-act theory (for instance, Pratt) does not detract from the validity of the comparison – indeed, if anything the comparison becomes more suggestive, for Eco's conception of textual authority, as we shall see, is a far cry from that of the formalists of an earlier persuasion. The aesthetic text, as Eco puts it, 'represents a sort of summary and laboratory model' (*Theory* 261) of all the aspects of sign-production. To summarize, the aesthetic text involves a particular self-focusing manipulation of the linguistic expression; this manipulation releases (and is released by) a reassessment of the content; this double operation releases what Eco calls a process of code changing; the entire operation frequently produces a new type of awareness about the world; and the whole, finally and most important, represents a complex and dynamic network of communicational acts between sender and addressee, author and reader (*Theory* 261). The multiple ambiguities of the text may or may not be noticed by the reader, and if noticed may simply produce confusion, but, writes Eco, when an ambiguity 'focuses my attention and urges me to an interpretive effort (while at the same time suggesting how to set about decoding) it incites me toward the discovery of an unexpected flexibility in the language with which I am dealing,' and it produces an aesthetic experience when 'the shock received by the breaking of certain rules forces the hearer to reconsider the entire organization of the content' (*Theory* 263). Eco is here drawing explicitly on the formalist contention as formulated by Shklovsky ('Art as Technique') that *ostranenie*, 'defamiliarization,' the 'device of making it strange,' is a central characteristic of aesthetic texts: 'in order to describe something which the addressee may have seen and recognized many times, the author unexpectedly uses words ... in a different way. One's first reaction is a sense of bewilderment, of being unable to recognize the object. Somehow the change in expressive device also changes the content' (Eco, *Theory* 264). Thus art, as Shklovsky says, 'increases the difficulty and the duration of perception' ('Art' 12) and describes the object 'as if one were seeing it for the first time' (13), so that 'the aim of the image is not to bring closer to our understanding the meaning it conveys but to create a particular perception of the object' (Eco, *Theory* 264). (In Brecht's exploitation of Shklovsky's notion for political ends, incidentally, it is interesting to note that the defamiliarizing effect achieved by the *Verfremdungseffekt* is very frequently obtained through the use of humour.)

The aesthetic effect is therefore seen as generated primarily, in semiotic as in formalist terms, by a self-conscious textual violation of norms; but the element of reflexivity is also crucial – and here the similarity to the speech-act theorists' position becomes apparent again – for it is in calling the reader's attention to its own shape that the message creates the context in which it may be received as 'aesthetic.' The parallel here with the comic experience is clear: Shklovsky's suggestion that the object of aesthetic pleasure is seen as if one were seeing it for the first time is equally applicable to comic pleasure. 'Finding connections between things we usually keep in separate compartments of our minds' may well be regarded as 'the ultimate source of all humor' (Monro, 'Humor' 91). The perceived violation of empirical or conventional norms or expectations, glimpsed via the experience of ludic defamiliarization, constitutes the potential humour content of a given situation just as it constitutes the potential aesthetic content of a given text, and their actualization as comic or aesthetic experience (or, of course, both) will be determined by context, convention, and the competence of the receiver – for just as an incompetent reader may receive little or no aesthetic pleasure from a text regarded by other readers as being of high aesthetic value, so there are notoriously people with 'no sense of humour.'

It might of course be objected that there is no element of self-focusing or reflexivity involved in a non-verbal situation such as that of the proverbial man who hits his thumb with the hammer, and that this marks a major distinction between the comic experience and the aesthetic experience. However, one could retort that in fact humour is always self-reflective, for as object language it trades in incongruity, while metalinguistically it comments on its *own* incongruity in that all humour is reducible to a single unitary function, the preservation of order (congruity) by means of the flaunted defusing of a hypothesized attack on social, linguistic, and/or logical convention. Moreover, *ex negativo*, there are many cases where aesthetic texts incorporate objects or events from 'real life,' such as the use of unaltered clippings from newspapers in a novel such as Döblin's *Berlin Alexanderplatz* (1929): how do these *disjecta membra* acquire their 'literariness'? Here the notion of the display text, once again, provides the most satisfactory answer – and helps to make clear the homologous reception of comic and aesthetic situations.

For speech-act theorists, we remember, texts *are* aesthetic primarily because a particular community has *selected* them as such: 'it is people, not properties, that "make a verbal message a verbal work of art" ... The specialness is in the context' (Pratt, 124), and the context is precisely that they have been selected, as 'display texts,' for the full readerly 'treatment.' Display texts, that is to say, are put in a 'frame,' set aside for intensified contemplation, just as a Duchamp snow-shovel by being *declared* an objet d'art *becomes* one. The reception of a given situation as comic is in these terms clearly analogous, though this may not be immediately obvious: we tend to think of the comic reaction as spontaneous, immediate, generated by the ludicrousness of the incongruity serving as stimulus. Yet *all* incongruities are not received as comic, as we well know: a well-dressed man slipping on a banana peel may be hilarious, but an elderly man, for example, or a pregnant woman slipping on the same banana peel is quite unlikely to be regarded as comic at all. We *select*, in other words, what we are *prepared* to consider comic, even though the process of selection may only take a fraction of a second. Our selection is not, however, free, for it is prompted both by the initial stimulus and by contextual considerations; similarly the selection of a text as warranting reading as an aesthetic artefact is prompted by features, textual and extratextual, bearing both on the text's own individual form and its relationship to the previously selected canon of aesthetic texts.

The humour situation, in other words, is a display text, whether verbal or otherwise, and like all texts its 'reading' is a function neither solely of its formal characteristics nor solely of the interpreter's performance; it is rather a function of the interactive *relationship* between its formal characteristics and the reader's performance. (Here again it might be objected that Duchamp's snowshovel, for example, is totally lacking in formal aesthetic characteristics and is thus completely 'reader produced'; but it is precisely its flaunted total refusal of aesthetic form, its parodic difference from the traditional canon, that paradoxically constitutes *ex negativo* its dominant formal characteristic.) The display text, whether received as aesthetic or comic or both, in other words, *becomes* such only as the result of a complex interaction or process of negotiation: partly as a result of its own conventionally suggestive formal characteristics, and partly as a result of the receiver's state of receptivity, which itself is largely determined by his or her contextual knowledge both of general convention (as established by other readers and other texts) and of the immediate situational context, for example the known comic or aesthetic intention of the sender. The receiver relies, within these constraints, as he or she does at every moment as a speaker of the language, on his or her knowledge of appropriateness conditions (Pratt, 83) as a guide to the interpretation of a given utterance or situation. The individual receiver may of course choose (or be led) to regard a given situation or text as comic or aesthetic or both in cases where such a response would not be shared by others, but until his response loses its idiosyncratic nature by being adopted by a larger interpretive community it will be regarded as being to a greater or lesser degree aberrant, and the offender will be regarded as lacking in good taste or good sense or both.

The humour text – a phrase already anticipated in the previous chapter as synonymous with the 'humour situation' – and the aesthetic text are both forms of ludic play, and the similarity of their ludic character emerges clearly from the treatment of them both as display texts. In each case the receiver *constitutes* the field of play by *regarding* the text as a message whose formal properties demand that they be regarded as a major (or *the* major) factor in the semantic information transmitted (Pratt, 136–48; Eco, *Theory* 271). Once this is recognized as the constitutive framework within which formal features operate, it is not surprising that Shklovsky's defamiliarization process or Mukařovský's notion that the poetic utilization of language depends on the systematic violation of the norm of 'ordinary' language (quoted in Pratt, 200) is as applicable to humour texts as to aesthetic texts. The argument as advanced by Pratt that no hard and fast dividing line can be drawn between literature and non-literature can similarly be paralleled by the contention that no hard and fast division can be established between humour and non-humour – or the serious and the non-serious, as has been argued on other grounds in an earlier chapter. Finally, the receptive processes producing humour texts and aesthetic texts, given the climate of our times and the realignment of areas formerly held to be serious on the one hand and non-serious on the other, can be seen as very naturally entering into an alliance favouring humorous forms of literary discourse – witness once again the dominant position of parody in the postmodern aesthetic. The dominance of parody is paralleled by what might be seen as the transfer of literary authority from the realist author to the post-modernist liberated reader, and in the process writing has become predominantly a *form* of humour. Writing does not have to be overtly comic to be a form of humour, as we have seen already: comedy presupposes humour, just as humour makes comedy a possibility. In our terms: writing is primarily, on a conceptual level, a form of pre-comic humour, which may or may not include in its discourse secondary elements of comic humour.

The conception of both humour and literary discourse as essentially *textualized* (that is to say reader-constituted) constructs generated from an initial ludic conflation of possible worlds invites us to consider the range of moves available to this newly authoritative *magister ludi*. Eco sees the aesthetic text as being 'like a multiple match played by different teams at a time, each of whom follows (or breaks) the rules of their own game' (*Theory* 271). The aesthetic text, in other words, is a way of interconnecting messages in order to produce a text that is characterized by the presence of *many* messages, on different levels and planes, their relationships organized by the contextual pressure of competing ambiguities and deviations. The deviation from the norms of any one game in Eco's multiple match will serve for the trained reader as a device putting into a different strategic perspective the deviations from the norms of the other games also simultaneously under way. The receiver's task in everyday, non-literary communication is to reduce the amount of information potentially carried by any given message in order to select the one contextually appropriate definitive interpretation. In the case of aesthetic messages 'which require the simultaneous grasping of multiple senses ... this informational quality of the message remains unreduced' (Eco, *Theory* 140). The aesthetic text, therefore, conventionally valued precisely for its formal control – and here we see the major chasm between Eco's and the formalist position – paradoxically tends to slide, just as language itself tends to do, but with intensified force, towards informational entropy, towards a hypothetical state of total statistical equiprobability. The verbal artefact, the well-wrought urn, reveals itself, in short, not just as a form of humour but as a form of entropic comedy, its highly polished surfaces distracting attention from its tendency to redissolve into the primeval entropic flux of language, into the semantic whirl of connotation, into wordlessness. 'In an extreme case,' writes Jurij Lotman, 'any word in poetic language may become a synonym for any other' (29). 'It is indeed difficult to avoid the conclusion,' writes Eco, 'that a work of art *communicates too much* and therefore *does not communicate at all*, simply existing as a magic spell that is radically impermeable to all semiotic approach' (*Theory* 270).

The postmodernist reader is far from allowing himself to be becharmed into critical immobility by this vision of entropy and paradox lurking below the shimmering and highly organized textual surface, however. Rather, like Maxwell's Demon, he industriously sets to work, assiduously sorting molecules, generating energy, reversing entropy. And as he works he laughs, for his work is play. Barthes, we remember, sees the essential difference between classical ('readerly') and modern ('writerly') texts in terms precisely of the increased element of play demanded of both author and reader. 'In readerly texts the signifiers march; in writerly texts they dance' (Hawkes, 114). The difference is one of degree rather than kind, however, for even the marching signifiers can be induced to dance by a sufficiently persuasive critic, as Barthes's own writerly analysis in *S/Z* of Balzac's readerly *Sarrasine* very amply demonstrates. In *The Pleasure of the Text* Barthes differentiates two kinds of pleasure involved in the writerly play of reading, a simple pleasure (*plaisir*) derived from the more straightforward processes of reading, and an orgasmic ecstasy (*jouissance*) derived precisely from a sense of breakdown, gap, interruption, when overt communicative purpose is suddenly subverted and breaks down, when 'the garment gapes,' as Barthes puts it: for 'Is not the most erotic portion of a body *where the garment gapes*?' (9). 'Ecstasy' is the writerly reader's reward for the

sense of loss, incongruity, crisis, entropy, precisely because of the
challenge to play along, go along with the joke, make a presence out
of an absence, become a co-producer rather than a passive consumer
of the text. Reading, in short, becomes a version of the type of game
that Caillois called *ilinx*; the reader becomes a willing actor in a
comedy of vertigo, a comedy of entropy.

The postmodernist reader celebrates with Barthes the death of the
author (*Image* 142) and the freedom of reading. Where meaning was
once determined, decided, that is to say closed off by the author as set
down in a complicated piece of 'work,' meaning is now opened up, set
free by the liberated play of a hedonistic reading. Some readers are
freer than others, of course. Wolfgang Iser, moving away from the
concept of the programmed realist reader, sees the reading process as
analogous to two people looking up at the night sky: the stars are the
same, he says, but one observer will see a plough where the other will
see a big dipper (282) – and we can extend the metaphor, for a third
would see a bear, a fourth a carriage with horses, and a fifth only
random twinklings of light. The reader, like the audience of any joke,
has the last word, it seems. Iser's point is that any one text is
infinitely richer than any of its individual realizations, but at least,
for him, though the interpretations may be different, the stars themselves are the same stars, and the originary point of reference and
authority is safely guaranteed: the reader is free to play, but only
under parental supervision. Iser's phenomenological reader better
exploits the humour of the literary text than does his brow-beaten
realist predecessor, whom all work and no play could very often make
a dull boy, but there is no hint of *ilinx*, no suggestion of vertigo, in the
Iserean reader's reconstruction of a text whose stability is underwritten by the solidity of the words upon the page. If the Iserean reader is
a humorist his humour is a form of the comedy of cosmos. The
productively playful reader suggested by a Barthes or a Derrida, by
contrast, is infinitely freer than Iser's reader, for the stars in the
poststructuralist sky are never the 'same,' never identical with themselves, but always point to a meaning that is never quite there: the
reader, it might seem, has at last achieved total freedom and complete
control, has ousted the repressive author and taken his place as
arbiter of meaning and as writer of the text. The beguiling oedipal
vision is only a vision, though, as it turns out, for even if the locus of
authority has been displaced from the author *and* from the words
upon the page, it does not on that account take up immediate and
untroubled residence with the reader either. The poststructuralist

reader, however *comparatively* free (s)he may be, can never be totally free. However unsubstantial the words upon the page may now be, however much they defer definition and postpone interpretive closure, they still constitute one pole of the dialectic out of which interpretation eventually arises, one pole of the interaction between text and receiver. The receiver's response, however idiosyncratic, cannot be entirely *cause*, for it is (however provisionally, playfully, humorously) also partly the *effect* of the text. The receiver not only makes the text (or joke) work, he is also made to make it work; but he can only be made to make it work if he chooses to make it work. This paradoxical, *Catch-22* interrelationship of freedom and determination, implicit in the semiotic account of the text as communicational act, has become a major focus of deconstructionist thought. The process of 'reading' a text, once conceived of as a practical matter of sticking in a thumb and pulling out a plum, deconstructs theoretically into a logical impossibility, a self-sustaining paradox. The thrust of poststructuralist thinking, in short, has been not wholly to eliminate authority, but to relocate it, and its new locus is precisely in paradox itself, the aporia and absent centre around which all deconstructionist thinking endlessly circles.

Paradox, as Gödel suggested, is of such a nature that it cannot be excluded from human thought, an insight that supports the whole edifice of deconstructionist thought. But one does not have to be a card-carrying deconstruction worker to be aware of the role of paradox as a keystone of twentieth-century modes of thinking. 'What happens in literary semiotics is but one version of a general situation which is gradually coming to be recognized as an inescapable feature of our ways of thinking about texts and signification,' as Jonathan Culler writes (*Pursuit* 39): namely the revelation of paradox as an inherent component of our concept of meaning. Twentieth-century mathematics and physics are strewn with glittering paradoxes; philosophy and logic no less so; and increasingly this situation is coming to be seen as less some unfortunate side-effect of our ways of thinking than a vitally necessary therapeutic function of the human mind. William Fry has suggested that paradox is essential especially to 'play, ritual, dreams, folklore, fantasy, art, drama, psychotherapy, and humor' (132): for any one of these discourses to function effectively, that is to say, the participants' awareness of their status as 'inauthentic' discourse is essential, an awareness of what Fry calls their 'metaphoric and paradoxic' nature (147), or what we are calling here an awareness of their common origin in a conflation of possible worlds.

This confrontation of worlds, as already argued, is always potentially humorous; in paradox the confrontation is intensified to its limit state. We began by characterizing the literary text as constituting a range of potentially actualizable humour texts as well, based on the notion of an incongruous conflation of possible worlds on each of the various planes of fictivity, metacommentary, metaphoricity, and ultimately language itself. The actualization of these multiple and multiply interwoven texts, both literary and humorous, it turns out on further examination, can be accomplished, however, only by means of a paradoxical procedure that itself constitutes a humour text and is thus susceptible to further actualization and so on in an infinite interpretive regress. Twentieth-century thinking moves asymptotically towards comedy, towards the comedy of entropy, and literature and literary criticism constitute one of the areas where this development has become most overt.

Part Three

TEXTS:
Narrative and Reading

6 The Comedy of Entropy: A Narrative Taxonomy

The truth is that nothing makes any difference, including that truth.

John Barth

So far we have been concerned almost entirely with arguments concerning the theoretical contexts and general conceptual reach of the comedy of entropy, the multiple ramifications of which we have now considered both in terms of a theory of modern and postmodern humour and in terms of modern and postmodern literary theory. We will now turn our attention in part 3, finally, to a third and quite different possibility of examining the systemic effects of entropic humour in twentieth-century literature, namely the 'hands-on' critical analysis of a set of narrative texts that illustrate the reach of the comedy of entropy as a mode both of writing and of reading. In order to emphasize the pervasiveness of the phenomenon in modern literature we will undertake a fairly full analysis of each of a dozen different narratives produced in three different linguistic and cultural environments over the last half-century or so – both the linguistic and chronological reach, however, could certainly be considerably extended. We turn, therefore, from theory to practice. But practice is never free of theory, and our practice here will be no exception, for our twelve texts will also be seen as illustrating three quite different *articulations* of entropic comedy. Before proceeding to the individual analyses, therefore, we must first look briefly at the theoretical underpinnings of the resulting taxonomy as suggested here, a taxonomy whose three major armatures can be classified as entropic satire, entropic irony, and entropic parody.

Schiller, in his essay on *Naive and Sentimental Poetry* (1795), saw modern, increasingly self-conscious writing as divided into three major modes, each characterized by a perceived disjunction between the real and the ideal. *Satire*, says Schiller, rejects the real as falling far short of the ideal; *elegy* largely ignores the real, choosing instead to mourn the loss of the ideal; the *idyll*, finally, projects a hypothetical world, whether past or future, where the real and the ideal coincide. Samuel Beckett's novel *Watt* (1953) might seem an unlikely place to look for a commentary on Schiller's text. As Watt enters Mr Knott's house, however, he encounters his departing predecessor, Arsène, who comments at length on many matters, including what he calls 'the laughs that strictly speaking are not laughs, but modes of ululation ... I mean the bitter, the hollow, and the mirthless.' These laughs correspond, Arsène continues, to

> successive excoriations of the understanding, and the passage from the one to the other is the passage from the lesser to the greater, from the lower to the higher, from the outer to the inner, from the matter to the form. The laugh that now is mirthless once was hollow, the laugh that once was hollow once was bitter. And the laugh that once was bitter? Eyewater, Mr Watt, eyewater ... The bitter laugh laughs at that which is not good, it is the ethical laugh. The hollow laugh laughs at that which is not true, it is the intellectual laugh. But the mirthless laugh is the dianoetic laugh ... It is the laugh of laughs, the *risus purus*, the laugh laughing at the laugh, the beholding, the saluting of the highest joke, in a word the laugh that laughs – silence please – at that which is unhappy.   (48)

Satire is the soil in which entropic humour as a literary mode may be seen as taking root. Satire may be a literary expression of either normative humour, the humour of order, or entropic humour, the humour of disorder. Even as a form of normative humour it tends by its nature to be aggressive and derisive. Its range, however, can encompass a less punitive, more didactic form of correction as well as more aggressive forms, what we might call benign or sympathetic satire, firmly but tolerantly anchored in its own value-system. As tolerance gives way to harshness, and the didactic urge to the punitive, so satire moves from the at least latently sympathetic to the more overtly derisive forms of expression, and the desire to correct and rehabilitate the erring object of attention is transformed gradually into the instinct of the healthy organism to expel a dangerous foreign body that potentially threatens the integrity and stability of the orderly system. At the more benign end of its spectrum satire is characterized by a firm belief in its own moral efficacy, by a confidence that what is broken can be mended, by a confidence that the real, in Schiller's terms, can indeed be brought closer to the distant ideal. As this confidence wanes, and even the most derisive attacks prove incapable of achieving what more benevolent approaches have already failed to achieve by kindly instruction, so satire slides over into its entropic mode, where disorder is acknowledged as triumphing over order, and didactic confidence gives way to a fascinated vision of maximum entropy, total disorder. Here we enter on the gradations of Beckett's ethical laugh, directed against 'that which is not good,' and at the blacker end of the scale we find, for example, Swift's advocacy of cannibalism in the *Modest Proposal* and Sade's revelling in the degradation of the human body.

'The hollow laugh laughs at that which is not true, it is the intellectual laugh.' If entropic satire focuses on disorder in terms of social relationships, entropic irony focuses on disorder in the human condition itself. The former is a comedy of observation, of seeing, as we might say, a vision of the disruption and breakdown of social and moral conventions; the latter is a comedy of knowing, or rather a comedy of ignorance, a Socratic, ironic, knowing that we can never know anything. In Schillerean terms, the gap between the real and the ideal widens to the point where the real ceases, in Beckett's terms, to be true anymore, ceases, that is to say, to be reconcilable to the lost ideal. Irony, as we have seen, whether normative or entropic, is a disjunctive structure, just as satire is: irony says one thing and insinuates that it means something else; satire says that one thing *should* be something else. Normative satire aims at the elimination of the difference between its two terms, what *is* and what *should be*, while entropic satire accepts and even seems to rejoice in the difference. Normative irony, however, like entropic irony, already exists only by virtue of the difference. (To this extent, it could be suggested that irony is more 'naturally' an entropic mode than satire is.) Normative irony metamorphoses into entropic irony not as a result of the discursive difference per se, then, but rather as a result of the context in which the difference is situated. Normative irony exists as a trope, a 'figure of speech,' within a larger universe of discourse in which its difference, its otherness, is a tolerated and even a valued irritant, a controlled uncertainty, a vaccination, as one might say, against a more general undermining of the host system. In entropic irony the

roles of host and guest (or parasite) are reversed, irony as trope metamorphoses into irony as mode, and the uncertainty once held under
control by discursive norms invades and subverts the entire system.

Entropic irony, however, typically manifests itself less through the
whimsical, quizzical, sceptical, but still more or less kindly tones we
tend to associate with normative irony than through the grotesque
and the absurd. Seeing the grotesque as a submode of irony, even if
specifically only of entropic irony, may seem paradoxical, but it is a
paradox that is at the heart of entropic comedy. Genetically, as
Northrop Frye has shown, irony is the weapon of the wily underdog,
the *eiron* of Greek comedy who counters the exaggerations of the
boastful *alazon* by the inverse strategy of sly understatement. Irony
thus tends naturally to be a finely honed instrument, a rapier rather
than a bludgeon. The grotesque, by contrast, operates precisely by
exaggeration rather than by understatement, by brutal surprise rather
than by subtle insinuation. Irony tends towards the intellectual and
rational, the grotesque towards the emotional and irrational. Irony is
genetically self-confident; the grotesque is 'the artistic expression of
that estrangement and alienation which grips mankind when belief
in a perfect and protective natural order is weakened or destroyed'
(Kayser, 188). The grotesque always emphasizes the unresolved clash
of incompatibles, and it is this primary (diegetic) incongruity in the
very nature of the grotesque compounded by the secondary (extradiegetic) incongruity of combining the natural exaggeration of the grotesque and the natural understatement of irony that motivates the simultaneous horror and exhilaration we may typically experience
when we read, say, Kafka's *Metamorphosis* or Beckett's hilarious
accounts of human misery. The grotesque is a submode of entropic
irony essentially to the extent that the grotesque undermines the autonomy of the real – Kafka's Gregor Samsa who *really* turns into a
monstrous vermin, Beckett's Nagg and Nell who *really* live in garbage cans – and by extension undermines the validity of the epistemological guarantee implied by the very notion of a linkage between
real and ideal. The absurd, the second submode of entropic irony,
continues the process and registers the disappearance of the ideal
altogether. All that is left of the Schillerean play of real and ideal is
the gap in the centre, the yawn of the absurd, and Arsène's appropriately hollow and elegiac laugh.

Schiller's triad of satire, elegy, and idyll, though based on the potentially tragic difference between the real, what is, and the ideal,
what should be, is essentially an optimistic and idealistic one, as we

might expect from the context in which Schiller was writing: his satire is confidently ameliorative, his elegy acknowledges at least the existence of the no longer accessible ideal, his idyll envisages at least the possibility of an imaginative, poetic union between the sundered realms. Arsène's vision is both entropic and comic. Each of Arsène's laughs is a 'mode of ululation,' representing as a triad an ascending series of 'successive excoriations of the understanding, ... from the lesser to the greater, from the outer to the inner, from the matter to the form.' The third and highest term in his taxonomy of ululation is the 'mirthless laugh,' the dianoetic laugh. The 'dianoetic,' in Arsène's terms, is a thinking *through* or *beyond* the merely noetic, the intellectual; the dianoetic laugh is metalaughter, a comedy of discourse, a breaking out of or through the intellectual frame that leads to the absurd. 'It is the laugh of laughs, the *risus purus*, the laugh laughing at the laugh, the beholding, the saluting of the highest joke.' It is, in our terms, the mode of entropic parody.

Parody is genetically a form of commentary, etymologically a *parodia*, a counter-song, a song sung 'against' or 'beside' another. It thus represents a third form of disjunction, a third term continuing the disjunctive series begun by satire and irony. In the entropic spectrum, satire focuses, in Schillerean terms, on the deficiencies of the real; irony focuses on the absence of the ideal; parody focuses on the very idea of a relationship between the two. Insofar as we have earlier defined humour as essentially focusing on the relationship between possible worlds, parody is the most 'naturally' humorous of the three entropic modes. Though it is the most pronouncedly humorous, however, the difference is again one of degree rather than of kind. All three modes of entropic comedy are humorous modes, but parody is the one that most overtly reflects on its own operation. As suggested in an earlier chapter, however, it should be clear that the very notion of entropic humour must always include a degree of reflexivity, and that to this extent all entropic humour always gravitates towards the parodic end of its range. In our spectrum of humour, as earlier outlined (see figure 1), it was suggested that just as the self-confident humour of order has two major articulations, that of sympathetic and that of derisive humour, so the humour of entropy also has two major articulations: at the less obviously 'humorous' end of the entropic range we find the savagely anomic humour of a Sade or Swift, where humour is evoked but simultaneously inhibited; at the more obviously 'humorous' end we have the overtly parodic humour of a Nabokov or Borges, where humour is evoked but reflexively interrogated. Entropic satire corresponds to the first of these, entropic parody to the second. Entropic irony, Janus faced, forms a bridge between the two extremes, its grotesque aspect facing in one direction towards satire, its absurd aspect turned in the other towards parody (and cf. Frye, 223–39, here, as well as Hutcheon, *Theory* 50–68).

Entropic parody is postabsurd, takes the absurd for granted. If entropic satire is a comedy of human relationships and entropic irony a comedy of human inability to know, entropic parody is a comedy of comedy itself. Entropic humour, in other words, which 'begins' with a satiric savagery that threatens to choke humour altogether, 'ends' with parodic humour about humour itself. Parodic metahumour finds its literary expression in the highly polished reflexivity of, for example, Borges's *Ficciones*, Nabokov's *Pale Fire*, Robbe-Grillet's *Maison de rendez-vous*, Calvino's *Cosmicomiche*, Handke's *Die Hornissen*. These are indeed postabsurd acknowledgments of the 'highest joke,' but their laughter is not simply one of passive acknowledgment and resigned acquiescence. Rather it is an active laughter of collaboration and connivance, of keeping up the joke. The 'blacker' extreme of entropic satire constitutes a rejection of order, an inverted reflection of ameliorative satire's rejection of disorder; the metahumorous extreme of entropic parody constitutes a celebration of disorder, an inverted reflection of sympathetic humour's celebration of order.

Arsène characterizes his highest mode of ululation as the 'mirthless' laugh and as marking the transition 'from the matter to the form.' Arsène himself, however, a character in a character's world, views the affair from the side of matter rather than form, fails to penetrate from the level of story to the level of discourse, where the *risus purus* is actualized rather than hypothesized. Entropic parody is a mode of 'ululation' only for its *characters*, who have no way of knowing that their world is parodically discoursed – just as none of us would ever know if we were living in a world where everything was reversed. On the level of discourse entropic parody is a mode of celebration rather than ululation, but in order to appreciate that, the observer has to be situated *on* the level of discourse – this is by no means unusual, of course, for any slapstick farce (from the audience's point of view) always teeters on the brink of turning into unadulterated nightmare from the point of view of the characters whose world we regard as farcical. Metahumour in its full parodic sense is a play with paradox, delighting in the construction of gratuitous, iridescent counterworlds of flaunted fictivity; it is self-deconstructive in the sense that it is marked by joyful affirmation even though what it

affirms (in terms of 'matter' rather than 'form') is disorder and nothingness. It is in these structurations of uncertainty that we find
support for the notion that the spectrum of humour is inscribed on a
Möbius strip, circling back on itself until the celebration of entropy
becomes a paradoxical celebration of order, cosmos regained, but
through the looking-glass, and in terms of 'form' rather than 'matter,'
discourse rather than story. 'Denn solange wir noch Geschichten
erzählen, leben wir,' as the artist Amsel puts it in Günter Grass's
novel *Hundejahre*, and 'solange uns Geschichten noch zu unterhal-
ten vermögen, vermag keine Hölle uns unterhaltsam sein' (641) / 'As
long as we're telling stories, we're alive,' and 'as long as stories have
power to entertain us, no hell can divert us' (*Dog Years* 536). It is no
longer the matter of the stories that counts, any more than it was the
matter that counted for Scheherazade; what matters is to keep on
talking. Entropic parody is a comedy of talking, saying, narrating,
discoursing. It is a Nietzschean tightrope act over the abyss of the
absurd, a response to Zarathustra's challenge to learn to laugh. Parody
and paradox are the mode of being of these narcissistic anti-worlds,
and in their play with uncertainty and entropy they emphasize precisely form, craft, structuration. Anomic humour, the humour of
disorientation and abandoned norms, moves towards metahumour,
the humour of parodic reorientation and parodied norms. Ululation
metamorphoses into celebration. 'To become conscious of what is
horrifying and to laugh at it,' as Ionesco wrote, echoing Zarathustra,
'is to become master of that which is horrifying' (quoted in Esslin,
158). Or to put it another way, as Valéry is reported to have said once,
Sisyphus goes on rolling his stone, but at least he ends up with a re-
markable set of muscles.

Entropic comedy has three major literary modes, then, satire,
irony, and parody. Which is not at all to say that satire, irony, and
parody are always entropic – each of them has a spectrum of possibilities ranging from the normative to the entropic. Each of the entropic
modes, moreover, has its own expressive range too. If normative
satire, for example, is above all else purposefully engaged, entropic
satire ranges, as we might say, from the purposelessly engaged to the
metasatirically disengaged. In its engaged form the emphasis of entropic satire is on the observed object, that is to say social relationships. In its disengaged form the emphasis is on the observing subject
(though still within the realm of story rather than on the level of
discourse). To this extent entropic satire, as already suggested, is a
comedy of seeing, observation, evaluation, axiology. In the case of

irony a similar gradation exists from the purposeful engagement of normative irony as an enrichment of discourse through non-purposeful engagement for its own sake to meta-ironic disengagement. Irony is primarily concerned with the controlled duplicity of meaning; to this extent entropic irony is a comedy of interpretation, a comedy of hermeneutics and epistemology. In the case of parody there is again the progression from sympathetic or derisive, but in either event purposeful engagement, through engagement for its own sake, to metaparody. Parody is concerned with intertextuality, with the relationship between texts; entropic parody is a comedy of narration, discourse, structuration, fiction, making. In each of the three modes, that is, there is a potential range from the referential to the reflexive, the engaged to the disengaged, the apocalyptic to the metacomic – though we would naturally tend to expect satire to favour one end of this range and parody the other.

Finally we may observe the relationship between the three modes of entropic comedy in terms of narrative levels. Satire essentially concerns the affairs of characters who interact within a 'real' story-world. We may well be given a superior bird's-eye view of this world, but the emphasis remains on story rather than discourse. Irony concerns the affairs of characters who try and fail to discover the rules of the game according to which their story-world is discoursed. Here the emphasis is on the relationship between story and discourse, but from 'underneath,' as characters 'look up.' Parody shifts the emphasis to narrative levels, to the process of constructing (and being constructed by) discourses. The relationship is now that between discourse and story, from 'above,' moving theoretically at least in the direction of 'pure' discourse, untrammelled by story, recalling again Flaubert's desire someday to be able to write a book about 'nothing.' Satire has to do with the relationship between characters and the 'real' world they inhabit; irony and parody have to do with inter-world relations. Satire is homodiegetic, irony and parody are heterodiegetic in their emphasis. Entropic satire has two basic forms, what we might call the extroverted or explosive and the introverted or implosive vision, respectively: in the former we share with a focalizing protagonist the vision of a disordered society, in the latter the emphasis shifts from the society observed to the observing subject, social anomie becoming the background for psychological anomie, characterized by disorientation and isolation. We might conveniently diagram this double interaction or relationship (R) between character (C) and society (S) as being

$$R = C \rightarrow S$$

in the case of extroverted satire, and

$$R = C \leftarrow S$$

the case of introverted satire. Using the same notation for the relationship between character and the narrative instance (N) that constitutes the character and his (its) world, entropic irony can likewise be diagrammed as

$$R = C \rightarrow N$$

and parody as

$$R = C \leftarrow N.$$

In entropic irony, that is to say, the focus is on the protagonist C's investigation of the meaning-giving instance N that constitutes his world; in entropic parody the focus is on the *constructed* reality of all narrated worlds, including the multifarious versions of what we regularly persuade ourselves to be the definitively 'real' world we ourselves unproblematically inhabit. Moreover, if we revert briefly to the notational system introduced in the discussion of possible worlds in the last chapter, we can observe that just as the relationship (R) between story, text, and narration is

$$R = (Narration(Text(Story))),$$

so the relationship between satire, irony, and parody in the economy of entropic comedy is

$$R = (Parody(Irony(Satire))).$$

We may further observe that since realist writing, as we have seen, typically privileges the diegetic level of story, while modernist and postmodernist writing favour irony and parody respectively, we duly obtain the relationship (to be read as suggestive rather than prescriptive, of course)

$$R = (Postmodernism(Modernism(Realism)))$$

– which in its turn, as we have also suggested, might be rewritten as

$$R = (Humour(Play(Work))).$$

Robert Scholes, honing Ockham's razor, has recently refurbished a salutary warning for the literary critic in observing that often 'what

begins as clarification ends as nonsense, producing categories so exclusive or inclusive that they bring all attempts at systematic thinking about literature into disrepute' (*Semiotics* 17). The usefulness of
literary systems at all levels for the literary critic – as opposed to the
practitioner of literary theory per se – as Scholes goes on to suggest,
will not be found in elaborate taxonomies, but rather is more likely to
be derived from a small number of their more basic and powerful
concepts, ingeniously applied. The proof of the critical pudding,
moreover, is notoriously in the eating, and over the next three chapters we will look at the interpretive implications of entropic comedy
as they emerge from a consideration of some selected modern and
postmodern narratives. The modes of entropic comedy, as introduced
above, will not be considered as being in any way rigid or prescriptive.
The texts will be read not with a view to proving that they *are*
entropic satires or parodies in hard-edged generic terms, but rather in
order to explore to what extent they can defensibly be read as *functioning* predominantly in terms of one or other of the postulated
entropic modes.

Two obvious questions – or rather, two aspects of the same question – immediately arise with regard to the texts we shall be examining. First of all, why these particular texts rather than any others?
Secondly, assuming that entropic comedy is indeed a function of lost
norms, *whose* loss of norms makes the text (partially or wholly)
entropic? With regard to the first question, it must immediately be
freely admitted that there is inevitably a good deal of the arbitrary
about the choice. No doubt many other texts exist that would have
served equally well or even better to make the point. My failure to
deal with these texts instead is certainly partly the result of ignorance, partly the result of personal likes and dislikes. In one sense,
however, these limitations are not unduly debilitating, for the aim is
not to present an encyclopedic or even systematic survey of the global
reach of entropic comedy, even in twentieth-century fiction, but
rather to illustrate its major modes of functioning on the basis of
selected texts from more than one national literature. This ambition
immediately brings up the second question, of course, for how do I
know that the satiric or ironic or parodic elements of the selected
texts are functioning entropically rather than otherwise? Where, if
anywhere, is the decisive and dominant locus of entropic comedy?
Primarily in the author's personality and/or practice? In purely formal and structural characteristics of the 'text itself'? In the reader's
(that is, *my*) reaction? What role especially does the reader's personal,

and perhaps even highly idiosyncratic, sense of humour play as a complicating factor?

Some of the theoretical aspects of these questions have already been looked at in our last chapter. It will be the task of the remaining chapters to attempt answers in 'practical' terms in the case of the individual texts examined. But while the answers may possibly turn out to be practical, they will certainly not be definitive, for in any investigation of literary humour the wary critic is more than ever else aware to what extent the reading of texts is essentially a process of negotiated settlement, agreement to disagree. Authors, texts, and readers alike, in the case of the texts looked at here, are all products (and producers) of the same cultural and social forces that shape what might without excessive melodrama be called our Age of Entropy. Knowing, however, is inextricably involved with showing: as the semioticians consistently warn us, the role of the reader in constructing meaning, though far from unproblematical, is crucial. To quote Robert Scholes again: 'As semiotic interpreters we are not free to *make* meaning, but we are free to *find* it by following the various semantic, syntactic, and pragmatic paths that lead away from the words of the text. That is, we can't bring just any meanings to the text, but we can bring all the meanings we can link to the text by means of an interpretive code. And, above all, we can generate meaning by situating this text among the actual and possible texts to which it can be related' (*Semiotics* 30).

André Gide's *Counterfeiters* (*Les faux-monnayeurs*, 1925) and Thomas Mann's *Felix Krull* (1954) are only two of many twentieth-century works to make the point that the literary text is always to a degree a confidence trick. Modern literary theory has amply demonstrated that the literary critic is equally well qualified to bear the title of counterfeiter and confidence trickster. However responsible, however conscientious and answerable the critic's performance may be, he remains and must remain precisely a performer. His performance is always, by its very nature, a more or less convincingly constructed act of rhetorical *persuasion*, whose design is not primarily the objective revelation of some hitherto concealed or obscured ontological truth, but rather the demonstration of the rhetorical validity of his own reading. 'Every decoding,' as David Lodge's jet-propelled poststructuralist Morris Zapp succinctly puts it, 'is another encoding' (*Small World* 25). Including this one.

7 Entropic Satire:
The Observation of Anomie

Die Krone der Schöpfung, das Schwein, der Mensch

Gottfried Benn

The glory of creation, man, the swine

All traditional definitions of satire – which is to say of *normative* satire – stress its ameliorative intent: satire exposes human vices and follies to ridicule or scorn with the avowed or implicit intention of correcting them. The correction is assumed to be of at least potential benefit both to society and to the deviant individuals whose aberrant behaviour is pilloried: it is both social and moral in intent. To the traditional satirist there are true versions and false versions of reality, that is to say, and the norms separating them are stable and dependable and authoritative. The satire may be generous and even kindly in tone, such as Pope's *Rape of the Lock*, Fielding's treatment of Parson Adams in *Joseph Andrews*, or Dickens's treatment of Micawber in *David Copperfield*; or it may be unrelentingly grim, as in Huxley's *Brave New World* or Orwell's *Animal Farm* or *Nineteen Eighty-Four*. Whatever his register, however, the traditional satirist is a 'guardian of ideals. The best satire, that which is surest in tone, is that which is surest in its values' (Pollard, 3).

Traditional, normative satire has three clearly distinguishable moments: what we might call the *deictic* moment, pointing to and identifying the wrong to be righted, the vice to be corrected, the folly to be laughed into line; the *apodeictic* moment, the at least implied process of necessary correction, righting, re-education; and the *apotropaic* moment, the warding off of the potential threat to order and the normal previously identified. Entropic satire, by contrast, wholly lacking the prescriptive authority with which normative satire is unproblematically imbued, and lacking also any confidence or belief in the regulative power of moral or social norms, abandons both the apodeictic and apotropaic functions of normative satire and concentrates all its energies on the purely deictic gesture of identification and demonstration. If traditional satire is normative and ameliorative, entropic satire is anomic: all versions of reality are merely fictional constructs, no principle is necessarily truer than any other (Schulz, *Black Humor* 17), and, as Todd Andrews puts it in John Barth's *Floating Opera*, 'nothing has intrinsic value' (218). Where normative satire typically focuses on a particular individual or group of individuals considered eccentric to the social norm, entropic satire typically focuses not on a corrigible part but on the incorrigible whole. Entropic satire has to do with what Durkheim called social anomie: a 'lawless' (*anomos*) state of society where normative, rule-oriented, authoritative, prescribed standards of conduct and belief have irreparably broken down. Normative satire is judicial, regulative, prescriptive: the narrator implicitly reaches into the world of his characters in an effort to reorientate that potentially disordered world or explicitly instructs the narratee as to how to do so. Entropic satire is merely descriptive, observational, revelatory, apocalyptic, voyeuristic. The entropic narrator limits himself to recording: if the reader is capable of seeing even implicit possibilities of correction it is the reader's affair; the narrator limits himself to revelation. The normative satirist defuses a disturbing question by providing a reassuring answer; the entropic satirist limits himself to posing the question in as exacerbated a form as possible and then leaving it provocatively and disturbingly open. Normative satire sees a job to be done and does it; entropic satire by its nature is metasatiric, including itself among the objects of its attack. To quote Barth's *Foating Opera* again: 'To realize that nothing makes any final difference is overwhelming; but if one goes no farther and becomes a saint, a cynic, or a suicide on principle, one hasn't reasoned completely. The truth is that nothing makes any difference, including that truth' (246).

Relating the Unspeakable: Céline's *Voyage*

Louis-Ferdinand Céline's *Voyage au bout de la nuit* (1932; *Journey to the End of the Night*) is as thoroughgoing an example of entropic satire as we are likely to find. Ferdinand Bardamu, a cynical young medical student in Paris in the early days of the First World War, is in the middle of a peroration denouncing the iniquity of war when a platoon of soldiers marches past. Without even pausing to finish his denunciation Bardamu on an impulse leaps from his chair and runs after them to enlist, to go see for himself 'si c'est ainsi' (18) / 'if that's the way it is' (5). Predictably, like any of his picaresque predecessors, Bardamu discovers that war is indeed hell, as he had suspected, and is very soon devoting all his energies to escaping from it. Terror-stricken, he is sent back to Paris to recover from a wound, where an apparent nervous breakdown saves him from being returned to the army. But a couple of unsatisfactory love affairs and a growing disgust for the hypocrisy and cant of the civilians he meets impel him to escape as quickly from society at peace as he had from society at war, and he determines to head for Africa. On the long, hot voyage to Africa he inadvertently manages to become the focus for the concentrated rancour of all the other passengers on the boat and escapes lynching only by theatrically rehearsing the chauvinistic and hypocritical cant he is attempting to escape.

Africa, the land of escape and refuge, turns out to be a nightmare, 'la guerre en douce' (167) / 'a quiet war' (108). The corruption, viciousness, and venality of the colonial system is paralleled by the sheer brute weight of nature. Crushing heat, torrential rain, mosquitoes, termites, snakes, the terrifying noises of the jungle night, solitude, and finally fever drive Bardamu to desert the jungle outpost he mans on behalf of the 'Société Pordurière.' Apparently helpful natives carry him, delirious with fever, through the jungle for several days to a coastal town, where their philanthropy is unmasked: they sell Bardamu to the master of an ocean-going galley. The anachronous galley's mysterious business never emerges, but one morning Bardamu awakes to find himself staring at the New York skyline (237/159). If Africa was characterized by the chaotic proliferation of nature, America, as represented by 'la ville lunatique' (255) / 'the lunatic city' (171), 'raide à faire peur' (237) / 'terrifyingly stiff' (159), is stamped by the dehumanization of a system devoted entirely to the service of the great god Dollar (248/166). After Kafkaesque encounters in the endless corridors of the 'Laugh Calvin Hotel' and the gigantic 'caverne fécale' (251) / 'fecal cavern' (169) under the streets of New York, after working on Chaplinesque assembly lines in the Ford plant in Detroit, after falling in love in his own fashion with Molly, the inevitable whore with the heart of gold, Bardamu is seized once more by his mania for running away (293/197) and returns once more to Paris.

Bardamu's picaresque adventures, which take some 300 pages to recount, take up almost exactly half of the text. During the second half the adventures are in a distinctly lower key, as Bardamu, now a licensed physician, goes into practice as an accepted if always rather marginal member of the society he had once so violently rejected. His first practice is in Rancy, a dingy suburb of Paris. The name is overtly suggestive of the rottenness and corruption that Bardamu has found everywhere he has already been, and the name is apt. Poverty, ignorance, rapacity, brutality, inhumanity, hypocrisy, disease, and death are almost unrelieved in Rancy, and eventually Bardamu, after falling into a fever as he had once done in Africa, can take no more and attempts yet again to escape: early one morning he simply walks out on his practice and disappears (438/299).

Meanwhile, a second story-line has been growing in importance, one concerning an old acquaintance of Bardamu's, one Robinson Léon. Robinson is a drifter and a malcontent who eventually becomes involved in a grotesque murder attempt: he accepts a commission to get rid of an inconvenient mother-in-law, booby-traps a rabbit hutch to explode in her face, but bungles the job and succeeds only in blinding himself instead. To hush up the affair the daughter-in-law and her husband, with Bardamu's connivance, quietly ship both the would-be victim and the would-be murderer off to distant Toulouse, where the two collaborate for some time as caretakers of a collection of mummies in the crypt of a local church. In time Robinson recovers his sight, wearies of his custodial duties, belatedly finishes the job of murdering the old lady, and becomes embroiled in a torrid love affair. Bardamu has in the interim managed to find a new position as chief doctor of a lunatic asylum in another suburb of Paris. He is shortly joined there by Robinson, who has quickly grown tired of the violent affections of his Madelon. She follows him, however, there is a violent altercation, and, in spite of Bardamu's efforts to reconcile the two, Robinson eventually goads Madelon to the point where she fatally shoots him. Dawn is breaking and tugs are peacefully towing their barges along the river as Bardamu walks home by the Seine after seeing to the police formalities. Would he, when the time came, he muses, have the strength 'pour aller crever bien magnifiquement un jour, comme Léon' (630 / 'to go and die magnificently one day, like Léon' (433)?

De loin, le remorqueur a sifflé; son appel a passé le pont, encore une arche, une autre, l'écluse, un autre pont, loin, plus loin ... Il appelait

vers lui toutes les péniches du fleuve toutes, et la ville entière, et le
ciel et la campagne et nous, tout qu'il emmenait, la Seine aussi, tout,
qu'on n'en parle plus.   (631–2)

Far in the distance the tugboat whistled; its call passed the bridge,
one more arch, then another, the lock, another bridge, farther and
farther ... It was summoning all the barges on the river, every last
one, and the whole city and the sky and the countryside, and
ourselves, to carry us away, the Seine too, everything – let's say no
more about it.   (435)

Like Simplicius, like Candide, Bardamu begins his journey with the
experience of war, and the lesson it teaches him is that life is a series
of variations on disorder, that your fellow man will kill you if you
give him half a chance, and that the only hope for survival is never to
stop being afraid (26/10). Bardamu's memories of the war are typically
of terrified groups of men blundering through the darkness, without
maps, in unknown country, with only the light of an occasional
burning village to show the way, and under the orders of a gang of
vicious lunatics bent as much on their own death as on that of
everybody who came in contact with them, be it friend or foe (51/26).
Above all, the war teaches Bardamu during his very first days as a
soldier, man is meat. Before his eyes his commanding officer and a
dispatch runner are hurled by an exploding shell into a grotesque,
obscene embrace:

Ils s'embrassaient tous les deux pour le moment et pour toujours,
mais le cavalier n'avait plus sa tête, rien qu'une ouverture au-dessus
du cou, avec du sang dedans qui mijotait en glouglous comme de la
confiture dans la marmite. Le colonel avait son ventre ouvert, il en
faisait une sale grimace.   (28–9)

They were embracing each other for the moment and for all eternity,
but the cavalryman's head was gone, all he had was an opening at
the top of the neck, with blood in it bubbling and glugging like jam
in a kettle. The colonel's belly was wide open, and he was making a
nasty face about it.   (12)

Bardamu spends only some three months as a soldier before being
invalided out and as first-person narrator takes only some fifty pages,

about one-twelfth of the narrative as a whole, to relate his wartime experiences. The war, however, becomes the metaphor that underlies all of Bardamu's journey to the end of night, for open warfare is only the official recognition of the never-ending tooth-and-nail conflict that underlies all human interaction in his vision of things. War simply gives orgiastic expression to the murderous impulses only provisionally restrained beneath the innocuous façade of the man in the street, alias *homo homini lupus*. Hundreds of people will wish you dead in a single day, people waiting behind you in line, for example, people who don't have an apartment when you do, your children who can't wait for you to get out of the way (153/99). War if anything is more honest than peace, since at least it does not hypocritically disguise the snarl of hatred as a polite smile.

Hypocrisy is what most infuriates Bardamu during his recuperation in Paris, where a wave of patriotic enthusiasm for the boys in uniform is the latest social rage, especially among those who run no risk of being asked to join them and who stand to make a lot of money out of the whole affair. As one who would be in neither of these camps, Bardamu feels differently: whenever the talk came around to France and heroism 'je pensais irrésistiblement à mes tripes' (72) / 'I instantly thought of my guts' (42). The rhetoric of patriotism is founded on a combination of stupidity, viciousness, greed, and hypocrisy, and this conjunction is wholly appropriate, for these are the same cardinal virtues upon which the entire social system is constructed. Bardamu continually rediscovers this fundamental truth in Paris, in Africa, in America, and throughout his years in Rancy. The barely suppressed killer-instinct is as obvious in the casual torture of a caged pig by a crowd of strollers in Rancy (369/249) as it is in the self-destructive mutual hostility of the colonists in Africa: 'les rares énergies qui échappaient au paludisme, à la soif, au soleil, se consumaient en haines si mordantes, si insistantes, que beaucoup de colons finissaient par en crever sur place, empoisonnés d'eux-mêmes, comme des scorpions' (166) / 'The little energy that hadn't been sapped by malaria, thirst, and the heat was consumed by hatred so fierce and deep seated that it wasn't uncommon for these colonials to drop dead on the spot, poisoned by themselves like scorpions' (107).

Throughout his narrative Bardamu displays his instinctive sympathy and fellow-feeling for the poverty-stricken lower classes, 'les pauvres' – not that this ever endeared him to his patients, most of whom despised and resented him precisely because he did not charge as much for his services as did competing doctors. The poor are trapped in a system that slowly sucks them dry, squeezes them to death, uses them as lifeless tools for serving assembly lines, generating wealth of which they enjoy no part, fighting wars for causes that will ensure that the system remains unchanged. The system ensures that the poor become even more brutish, vicious, and demoralized than nature has made them, ensures that they will continue to victimize themselves, too stupid to realize what is happening, like the mother who prefers to let her haemorrhaging daughter bleed to death at home rather than have her admitted to a hospital where the fact of her unwanted pregnancy might become public knowledge (334/224). The system ensures that the poor will have their own alternative currency, 'les mensonges, ces monnaies du pauvre' (510) / 'lies, the currency of the poor' (349).

If civilization is rotten, nature offers no Rousseauistic alternative. If society is anomic, nature is a living metaphor for entropy, 'avec ses bourbiers qui n'en finissent pas, ses maisons où les gens n'y sont jamais et ses chemins qui ne vont nulle part' (23) / 'those endless fields of mud, those houses where nobody's ever home, those roads that don't go anywhere' (8). Nature above all else means the process of decomposition, dissolution, decay, death. Images of deliquescence and amorphousness abound: the grotesque 'bubbling and glugging' of the headless messenger, the all-pervasive mud of Flanders, the maggots transforming the colonists in Africa into 'sacs à larves' (153) / 'bags of worms' (98), their 'melting' into the jungle, the fatally haemorrhaging girl 'bubbling and glugging' between the legs like the messenger, whose message is all too clear. 'C'est quelque chose de toujours vrai un corps' (345) / 'A body always tells the truth' (233), and the truth it tells is rehearsed with morbid relish by Bardamu: 'ce n'est rien après tout que de la pourriture en suspens' (536) / 'it is nothing but suspended putrefaction' (367). Our proudest accomplishments are none the less based on this irrefutable truth, just as the skyscrapers of Bardamu's surrealistic New York rise from the foundation of the Bosch-like 'fecal cavern' and its 'travailleurs rectaux' (251) / 'rectal toilers' (169). Dante-Bardamu's visit to the underworld of the labouring shades is not without its difficulties – 'On discernait mal les figures à cause de la fumée' (251) / 'The smoke made it hard to distinguish the faces' (169) – but he has no difficulty in locating his Virgil, for, as he had discovered on his foraging expeditions during the war, 'ce qui guide encore le mieux, c'est l'odeur de la merde' (52) / 'the best guide of all is the smell of shit' (28).

Man is meat that rots and stinks. The only lasting truth is death, and life is only a fictional evasion of that realization, even if we manage to forget this fact most of the time. Mother Henrouille, the old lady whom Robinson eventually kills, is one who is able to ignore the inevitability. She vigorously plies her underground trade as a guide to the collection of 500-year-old corpses as if she herself were a sales representative of death, not forgetting to remind visitors that a tip would not be out of place, as she thumps the bellies of her charges to display their drumlike qualities (488/335). Even Mme Henrouille's ability to make the dead work for their living does not exempt her from the necessity to pay her own dues, however: Robinson's second attempt belatedly succeeds in sending her to join the labouring shades herself, flinging her headlong down the 'petit escalier si mince et si traître' (491) / 'the treacherous narrow stairs' (336) upon which her living had depended. Sooner or later we all have to follow Mother Henrouille, for the real enemy is time itself (365/247).

'La nature est une chose effrayante'(76) / 'Nature is a terrifying thing' (45), and one of the areas where our vulnerability is most obvious, as Bardamu sees it, is constituted by all aspects of sexual relationships. The grotesque embrace of the colonel and the messenger of death is a first implication of the relationship of sex and death, echoed later, as we have noticed, by the fatally haemorrhaging young woman. One of Bardamu's first discoveries after his return to Paris from the front lines is the link between war, money, and sex, a link characterized for Bardamu by a basic viciousness. The killer instinct, the aggressor's need to find a victim, on which society is founded is focused for Bardamu on the female genitals: 'La guerre, sans conteste, porte aux ovaires' (119) / 'Unquestionably, war goes straight to their ovaries' (75). Heroes must at all costs be found, created, manufactured, and sent into battle to die for *la Patrie*, the economy, and the sexual satisfaction of their female admirers. The most overt example of this killer instinct is embodied in the schoolmistress on the voyage to Africa who attempts to make sure that Bardamu is lynched: 'Scène de haut carnage, dont ses ovaires fripés pressentaient un réveil. Ça valait un viol par gorille' (155) / 'A scene of high carnage, from which her weary ovaries promised themselves an awakening. As good as being raped by a gorilla' (100). Bardamu talks himself out of the awkward situation fairly easily by shamelessly flattering the vanity of the military – 'Tant que le militaire ne tue pas, c'est un enfant' (158) / 'As long as a soldier isn't killing, he's a child and easily amused' (103) – and treating them afterwards to a man-to-man round of drinks and patriotic rhetoric. 'Seulement les femelles du bord nous suivaient des yeux, silencieuses et graduellement déçues' / 'But the females, silent and increasingly disappointed, kept their eyes on us,' prominent among them the schoolteacher, 'la hyène' (160) / 'the hyena' (104).

Bardamu the medical student views the world, somewhat self-consciously, as a card-carrying anarchist and absurdist should. The world is nothing more than the sick joke of 'un Dieu qui compte les minutes et les sous, un Dieu désespéré, sensuel et grognon comme un cochon' (17) / 'a god who counts minutes and pennies, a desperate sensual god who grunts like a pig' (4). For the twenty-year-old student this is little more than adolescent rhetoric in the vein of a Lautréamont. Twenty-odd years later, as he watches dawn break over the Seine the morning after Robinson's murder, the rhetoric would be less colourful, but his general view of things remains unchanged. It has in fact been succinctly phrased by Robinson in the outburst that finally provokes Madelon to shoot him: 'Tout absolument ... Eh bien, c'est tout, qui me répugne et qui me dégoûte à présent!' (618) / 'Everything, absolutely everything disgusts me and turns my stomach right now!' (425). It is Robinson's overwhelming disgust with everything, himself included, that drives him to his bizarre act of suicide – for even though it is Madelon's finger that pulls the trigger, Robinson carefully and methodically manoeuvres her into the position where, half crazed, she sees no other way out. His taunting of her is reminiscent of Bardamu's earlier action in slapping her across the face just to see how she would react, just as his final declaration of an all-embracing disgust is anticipated twenty-odd years earlier in Bardamu's physical reaction on seeing the regimental butchers at work shortly after he witnesses the death of the colonel and the dispatch runner: 'j'ai dû céder à une immense envie de vomir, et pas qu'un peu, jusqu'à l'évanouissement' (32) / 'I was overcome by an enormous urge to vomit, which I did so hard that I passed out' (15).

Robinson functions throughout as a *Doppelgänger* for Bardamu, a hypostasized narrative alter ego who evokes a markedly ambiguous response. They first meet as soldiers one night during the war, Robinson having deserted his regiment with the intention of giving himself up to the Germans (59/33). Robinson turns up again in Paris (142/91), and turns out later to have been Bardamu's predecessor in the African jungle outpost as well, which he also deserts just before Bardamu (who will desert it in his turn) arrives. Bardamu is convinced that he will encounter him again in America and that this time Robinson will have made good. 'C'était un resolu lui, au moins! Un brave! ... Il possédait peut-être un moyen pour acquérir cette certitude, cette tranquillité qui me faisait à moi tellement défaut ...' (263) / 'He was determined, at least! Courageous! ... Maybe he knew some way of acquiring the certainty, the peace of mind, in which I was so sadly lacking' (176–7). When they in fact do meet in America, Robinson turns out not to have been at all successful, nor does he do any better subsequently in Paris when he unexpectedly turns up there once again too (378/257). Bardamu is at once slightly contemptuous of him and fascinated by him – the latter all the more so when Robinson tells him of his plan to help kill the old lady. 'Décidément d'avoir suivi dans la nuit Robinson jusque-là où nous en étions, j'avais quand même appris des choses' (390) / 'I had definitely learned a thing or two by following Robinson in the night so far' (266). He none the less makes several attempts to avoid ever having to meet Robinson again, but instead becomes more and more deeply involved in his fate, first as regards the attempted murder, then the fatal affair with Madelon. During the final months, when they are living together at the asylum where Bardamu works, Robinson becomes more and more withdrawn, estranged, wrapped in 'forgetfulness and silence all around' (388) / 'avec de l'oubli déjà, du silence tout autour' (565). Bardamu makes some initial attempt to reconcile the two of them, then, as he realizes his inability to alter the course of events, becomes a fascinated observer. The end of the narrative, with its images of the breaking dawn, the shadows of the night yielding before the clarity of the new day, the river flowing peacefully under one arch after another, and so on, can very easily be read as an affirmation, in spite of everything, of life over death, a restatement of Valéry's 'Cimetière marin' with its freshening wind of hope and confidence. This is patently a misreading, however, because what is affirmed for Bardamu, with the force of a revelation, is precisely not a way of *living* in spite of the absurdity of life but a way of *dying* in spite of the absurdity of life. Rather than meekly giving in to the atrocious inevitability of death and dying like a dumb beast, 'sottement' (227) / 'stupidly' (152), Robinson dies 'bien magnifiquement' (630) / 'magnificently' (433), on his own terms. Neither waiting for death nor choosing to die by his own hand, Robinson, by successfully engineering his own destruction in a macabre game with the unfortunate Madelon, effectively thumbs his nose at death. 'De loin, le remorqueur a sifflé' (631) / 'Far in the distance the tugboat whistled' (435) Bardamu begins the last paragraph of his narrative, which ends in silence – 'qu'on n'en parle plus' (632) / 'let's say no more about it'

(435) – and white space. Bardamu has followed Robinson's lead on other occasions; as to whether or how he may respond to the final signal from the pilot we have only silence to play with.

Up to Robinson's final gesture of washing his hands of the whole thing, Bardamu's only concern has been survival at all costs in a world plainly out to destroy him. His main weapons for ensuring this end have been fear, cowardice, and mendacity: 'on n'est jamais assez craintif' (150) / 'One can never be too afraid' (96). To all the blandishments of military honour, martial valour, and patriotic glory, Bardamu, as a professed and professing coward, has the definitive rejoinder: 'Il n'y a que la vie qui compte' (88) / 'The only thing that counts is life' (54). As to the alleged virtue of truth as opposed to the immediate advantages of lies, our entire life is merely a lie, for the only real truth of life is death, and the only real choice is between lies on the one hand and death on the other (256/173). Within the greater lie lesser lies are not only permissible, they are inevitable and unavoidable if we are not to capitulate hopelessly to the single great and overriding truth which is death. 'La vérité c'est pas mangeable' (461) / 'Truth is inedible' (315). Some lies are less effective than others, if only because they have become assimilated as part of the pernicious system that the individual must at least try to resist – patriotism, for example, or religion, or, most overrated of all, love. 'L'amour, c'est l'infini mis à la portée des caniches' (17) / 'Love is the infinite placed within the reach of poodles' (4). Bardamu does not revise his opinion as a result of a succession of love affairs – Lola, Musyne, Molly, Tania, Sophie. Molly, the American prostitute who supports him for a time in Detroit, comes closest to rousing any sort of lasting affection in him – one of the very few almost tender passages in his narrative refers to his continuing love for her 'à ma manière' (301) / 'in my own way' (203). It was not enough to interrupt his odyssey more than momentarily, however, and for the rest love is simply a more or less tolerable method of forgetting the limitations of your putrefying body for a brief moment (109/68), a more or less pleasurable series of 'distractions du derrière' (596) / 'distractions of the rear end' (410). Indulged in any more seriously, as Robinson's entanglement with Madelon demonstrates, love simply becomes one more way of getting killed.

There are a very few other instances, other than his muted affection for Molly, which might be read as suggesting that perhaps, after all, there are occasional gleams of faint light in the enveloping darkness, some prospect of faint hope that humankind might after all be capable of redemptive actions, if only in isolated individual cases so rare as to be negligible. There is the sergeant, Alcide, who voluntarily spends extra years in the steaming jungle outpost in order to finance the education in France of his little niece (208/138); there is Bardamu's mother, whom he remembers with affection (222/148); there is the child Bébert in Paris, whom he is unable to save from a lingering and fatal illness (309/209). Any hint of a possible hope for a possible future is drowned utterly in the brute reality of the world as it is, as envisioned by Bardamu.

Bardamu's journey is a voyage into disorder, a voyage that, if we take the epigraph from the 'Song of the Swiss Guards' at face value, is portrayed as representative: 'Notre vie est un voyage / Dans l'hiver et dans la Nuit, / Nous cherchons notre passage / Dans le Ciel où rien ne luit' / 'Our life is a journey / Through winter and night, / We look for our way / In a sky without light.' Though the primary thrust of the narrative is clearly satirical, a horrified denunciation of things for being as they are, there is also a constant insistence that reality must be *seen* to be as it is, must be *understood* in its true unvarnished colors. Bardamu sets out to *see* 'if that's the way it is' (5) – 'voir si c'est ainsi' (18) – to experience reality on his own body. The enormity of life cannot be taught, it can only be learned: 'Faut comprendre!' (347) / 'You have to understand!' (235). Bardamu may indeed be an outsider, a misfit, sickened by his obsessive 'désir d'en savoir toujours davantage' (300) / 'wanting to know more and more' (202), but perhaps that is the whole point: 'C'est peut-être ça qu'on cherche à travers la vie, rien que cela, le plus grand chagrin possible pour devenir soi-même avant de mourir' (300) / 'Maybe that's what we look for all our lives, the worst possible grief, to make us truly ourselves before we die' (203).

Understanding is a question of norms, a question of obtaining an evaluative viewpoint, a point of perspective. Bardamu both suffers from and diligently ensures his own isolation: 'C'est cela l'exil, l'étranger, cette inexorable observation de l'existence telle qu'elle est vraiment' (274) / 'That's what exile, a foreign country, is, inexorable perception of reality as it really is' (184). What his understanding shows Bardamu is an entropic world, emblematized by the voyage to Africa: 'Dans cette stabilité désespérante de chaleur, tout le contenu humain du navire s'est coagulé dans une massive ivrognerie' (149) / 'In that despondent changeless heat the entire human content of the ship congealed into massive drunkenness' (95), a cosmic boredom that 'recouvre la mer, et le bateau, et les cieux' (156) / 'fills the sea, the ship, and the heavens' (100). In this retort tube of human society norms of everyday behaviour, constrained by the habits of social intercourse, dissolve, and atavistic blood-lusts triumphantly surface and search out an appropriate victim. The struggle to keep disorder at bay on the social level is paralleled by the struggle on the level of the physical body:

> L'ordure, elle, ne cherche ni à durer, ni à croître. Ici, sur ce point, nous sommes bien plus malheureux que la merde, cet enragement à persévérer dans notre état constitue l'incroyable torture ... Ce corps à nous, travesti de molécules agitées et banales, tout le temps se révolte contre cette farce atroce de durer. Elles veulent aller se perdre nos molécules, au plus vite, parmi l'univers ces mignonnes!   (427)

> Feces on the other hand make no attempt to endure or to grow. On this score we are far more unfortunate than shit; our frenzy to persist in our present state – that's the unconscionable torture – This body of ours, this disguise put on by common jumping molecules, is in constant revolt against the abominable farce of having to endure. Our molecules, the little dears, want to get lost in the universe as fast as they can!   (291)

It is this double aspect of entropy, social and physical, that sums up for Bardamu what is most truly human (525/359).

The stubborn rage for the preservation of some semblance of order in spite of this universal deliquescence is what leads to that state of madness – as Baryton, the director of the asylum, phrases it – characteristic of 'ceux que torture la marotte de la civilisation' (527) / 'those who are tortured by their obsession with civilization' (361). We should probably have little enough hesitation in assigning Bardamu, and Robinson as well, to this category. We should have to add Baryton himself, who from being a self-confident and jovial deliverer of orations on a variety of subjects begins quite suddenly to tend towards interminable digressions, lack of interest in the affairs of the establishment, and an abrupt desire to travel (550/377). He departs precipitately for England, sends a postcard from Finland months later, and is heard from no more. Then there is Parapine, Bardamu's old professor and a distinguished medical researcher, who in the course of twenty years' research on typhoid fever has examined so many contradictory theories that he is entirely incapable of forming a lucid opinion on anything any more. Among so many possibilities reason, in the last analysis, forbids us to choose, he eventually concludes (362/245), echoing *Bouvard et Pécuchet*, and lapses into near-total silence, a silence that he interrupts only after Robinson's death.

Bardamu and Robinson, Baryton and Parapine, are all escapists, each in his own way. Robinson, Baryton, and Parapine all escape into silence, each in his own way. Bardamu the narrator presents the reader with a series of alternatives during the course of the narrative, in fact, possible routes that Bardamu the protagonist might or might not have chosen to take. Each of these characters represents, so to speak, a synecdochic variation of Bardamu himself, as do other characters as well. There is, first of all and most obviously, Robinson, whose cowardice and anxiety to desert at all costs establishes him as an alter ego of Bardamu's at their very first meeting. (That meeting takes place in the suggestively named Noirceur-sur-la-Lys, 'ville de tisserands' (53) / 'a city of weavers' (28), *noirceur* ironically evoking not only the 'blackness' of the real night and the heinousness of the metaphorical night in which they meet but also the stain on the 'whiteness' of *le lys*, the unsullied lilies of France. By making the townspeople weavers the text parodically refers to its own work of construction.) Robinson, as we have seen, will function throughout as the explorer of uncharted territories, Crusoe to Bardamu's Friday. Less obviously, perhaps, there is Princhard, the one-time teacher turned thief in order to be cashiered from the army, who says openly and in public what Bardamu says only to himself. Princhard is an intellectual, and the dark glasses he affects (89/54) are not enough to protect him. After a particularly energetic denunciation of the system, in terms identical to those of Bardamu, he disappears and is never heard of again. There is Branledore, more circumspect than Princhard, who has perfected the double trick of being continually hospitalized and still considered a hero as a result of his carefully orchestrated patriotic outbursts. Much later, in Rancy, there is Mother Henrouille, who is so afraid of being assassinated that she refuses to let anybody, even her own son, into her gloomy apartment at the end of her daughter-in-law's garden, and rarely leaves it herself – as it turns out, of course, she is absolutely right to be so afraid. Parapine's and Baryton's separate flights at the asylum complete the series – and are relativized in their turn by the communicative difficulties of the tongue-tied comic policeman Gustave Mandamour (582/400).

Bardamu's own attempts at escape, as we have seen, are numerous: first his physical travels, then his attempted escape into observation rather than participation. His final escape is into narrative. Narrative is a protest against silence, and silence, as Scheherazade knew, is the voice of death, quiescence and acquiescence, entropy. Bardamu's journey, which is not his alone, takes place 'dans la nuit, là, dans le silence où nous étions perdus' (63) / 'in the darkness and the enveloping silence' (36). In the face of this ultimate silence, words are merely a pathetically futile gesture: 'Donc, on ne se méfie jamais assez des mots, c'est ma conclusion. Mais d'abord que je raconte les choses ... ' (611) / 'I conclude that we're never suspicious enough of words. But now let me tell you what happened ...' (420).

Narratives in the end are futile in the face of the great silence out of which they come – 'Moi, j'avais jamais rien dit' (15) / 'I'd never said a word' (3) – and into which – 'qu'on n'en parle plus' (632) / 'Let's say no more about it' (435) – they inevitably fade. It is equally futile to imagine, in the world of Bardamu, that by merely pointing to the evils and injustices in a world where God is very clearly dead and the devil, unaccountably, very much alive anything will change for the better, however slightly. Unlike normative satire, firm in its ameliorative will to change the world, entropic satire aims only at exposure, not at correction. Entropic satire is a comedy of *seeing*: how we may subsequently choose as readers to deploy our newly shaped understanding of the world as a result of our reading is entirely our own private affair and remains external to the world of the narrative. Bardamu's narrative does not aim at changing the world, it aims only at portraying it in a particular light, and what Bardamu claims for his narrated journey is true of his narrative journey as well: 'Voyager, c'est bien utile, ça fait travailler l'imagination' ([11]) / 'Travel is useful, it exercises the imagination' ([v]). Its 'usefulness' resides in the fact that as long as our imagination is at work we can picture things differently, and as long as we can picture things differently, we are in control of them, even if only fictively. This is the principle on which all forms of humour work, including entropic humour. It is a principle of integration, a reshaping of the world to *my* particular and instinctive conception of what constitutes order. Even entropic humour, that is to say, is thus implicitly, in spite of itself, a form of ordering activity, but by its nature it is inevitably a parodic, self-deconstructive form. The humour in Bardamu's narrative is very largely the result of the new perspective, the new way of seeing events and their relationships that Robinson's manner of dying abruptly makes available to him. Robinson's death functions as the punch line that retrospectively makes the *whole* joke, not just the punch line itself, comic. It carries

for Bardamu the force of a spontaneous work of art, a controlled, anti-
entropic shaping of an amorphous inevitability. As such it is at once
pathetically futile as a gesture and at the same time a parodic victory,
the only kind available, of order over disorder. It is prefigured in
Bardamu's narrative by Alcide's meticulous drilling in the African
jungle of native soldiers lacking boots, uniforms, and weapons, but
carrying out intricate parade-ground manoeuvres anyway (196/129).
Its parodic achievement of order is ironically relativized by
Bardamu's labours to bring order into the classification of body vermin in New York (242/163) and by the meticulous care with which
Robinson's death is regularized by the scrupulous police report describing it (629/433). It functions finally as a parodic *mise en abyme*
of the narrative itself as an act of ordering.

The portentous title of Céline's book, together with the invitation
extended by the epigraph to interpret the whole thing allegorically,
can be read as an ironic intertextual reference to those picaresque narratives of the sixteenth and seventeenth centuries where the hero,
after experiencing all the foulness and baseness of life here below,
retires to a desert island to prepare himself for the heavenly reward
that will retrospectively make sense of all his earthly tribulations.
Beckett's 'bitter laugh' is all Bardamu can count on to make 'sense' of
his own particular foray into the heart of darkness. His narrative is
obsessive in the unrelenting savagery of its attack on the human
condition, in its vehemence, its one-sidedness, its almost manic
exaggeration. There are plenty of grotesque episodes that may provoke the reader's laughter, but the comic response will be as anxiety-
ridden and inhibited as it is when we read the blacker pages of Swift's
or Sade's or Lautréamont's jaundiced humour. Though we may laugh
at it, Bardamu's world is essentially no laughing matter. It is an appalled vision of man's inhumanity to man and the precariousness of
human existence. The entropic humorist does not set out to reassure
us; he sets out to open our carefully closed eyes. 'La grande défaite, en
tout, c'est d'oublier ... et de crever sans comprendre jamais jusqu'à
quel point les hommes sont vaches' (38) / 'The biggest defeat of all is
to forget ... and to die without ever realizing just how much people are
bastards' (18).

The Cannibal Machine: Heller's *Catch-22*

Not that having your eyes open is much guarantee of anything, of
course, especially of escape. There's a catch, as Joseph Heller points

out:

> There was only one catch and that was Catch-22, which specified
> that a concern for one's own safety in the face of dangers that were
> real and immediate was the process of a rational mind. Orr was crazy
> and could be grounded. All he had to do was ask; and as soon as he
> did, he would no longer be crazy and would have to fly more mis-
> sions ... Yossarian was moved very deeply by the absolute simplicity
> of this clause of Catch-22 and let out a respectful whistle.
>   'That's some catch, that Catch-22' he observed.
>   'It's the best there is,' Doc Daneeka agreed.   (47)

The eponymous catch of Heller's *Catch-22* (1961) has clauses for
other contingencies too, for in its simplest, most direct form Catch-
22 'says they have a right to do anything we can't stop them from
doing' (416). 'They' are the machine, the system, impregnable, omnipresent, self-perpetuating, inescapable; 'we' are the individuals without whom as a whole the machine could not possibly function, but
who as discrete units of its machinery merely constitute a single
potentially defective item in the whole ensemble, an item of absolutely no intrinsic individual value, an item replaceable instantly and
at will by any one of an unlimited reservoir of alternatives. Heller's
theme, man against the machine, the individual against the dehumanizing system, is one that has been exploited with great regularity
over the last century or so; Heller's contribution is to present the
'spinning reasonableness' (47) of the cannibal machine in terms of
spinning comic unreasonableness.

The plot – insofar as one is justified in speaking of one at all –
involves the lives and, increasingly, the deaths of the men of an
American bomber squadron stationed off the Italian coast during the
latter part of the Second World War. Heller's narrative, presented by
an external, impersonal narrator and very largely focalized through
the experience of one central character, Yossarian, portrays a world
completely out of control. Like Céline, Heller chooses war as the
tone-setting metaphor, but where Céline uses Bardamu's wartime
experiences as a springboard for the portrayal of a diseased and self-
destructive society, Heller stays with the war metaphor throughout:
the war is equated with, rather than seen as an aspect of modern
industrial society. Where Céline at an early stage presents the reader
with the physical horror of war in the embrace of the dead colonel and
the headless messenger, however, Heller reserves the full force of the

corresponding death of Snowden until the final pages of the narrative – where its punch-line effect also corresponds to that of Robinson's death. Céline's humour is very overtly grim from the beginning, and we could characterize it very roughly as evoking something like shocked gasps rather than laughter. Heller's humour, by contrast, though in the end result no less grim than Céline's, is far less overtly so: the promotional extracts from reviews quoted on the preliminary pages of the paperback edition favour adjectives like 'hilarious,' 'exhilarating,' and 'uproarious.' Heller's war, no less than Céline's, portrays a *mundus perversus*, a world in disarray, and we are led into its deepening coils laughing helplessly.

The focus of the narrative's (and the reader's) attention throughout is Yossarian, who emerges from a bas-relief frieze of dozens of supporting characters. There is Dunbar, 'one of the finest, least dedicated men in the whole world' (14), who 'was working hard at increasing his life span. He did it by cultivating boredom. Dunbar was working so hard at increasing his life span that Yossarian thought he was dead' (9). There is Chief White Halfoat, an Indian from Oklahoma, 'who, for occult reasons of his own, had made up his mind to die of pneumonia' (44) There is Major Major: 'Even among men lacking all distinction he inevitably stood out as a man lacking more distinction than all the rest' (85). There is Nately, who 'got on well with his brothers and sisters, and ... did not hate his mother and father, even though they had both been very good to him' (255). There is Doc Daneeka, who 'was Yossarian's friend and would do just about nothing in his power to help him' (29). All of the subsidiary characters, of whom the above are a random sampling, are in fact less characters in any realized sense than they are elements of an animated setting, no more real (and in their way no less real) than the physical setting on the Mediterranean island of Pianosa. As we are informed in a preliminary statement: 'The island of Pianosa lies in the Mediterranean Sea eight miles south of Elba. It is very small and obviously could not accommodate all of the actions described. Like the setting of this novel, the characters, too, are fictitious' ([6]). Characters and setting alike are bas-relief, as regards both the referential world of everyday reality and the fictional world of the narrative, partly localizable and recognizable, partly figments of the narrative imagination. The plot similarly is less importantly a linear progression of events linked by the logic of cause and effect, complication and resolution, than a narrative reflection, or series of variations, on an unchanging *situation*, namely Yossarian's attempt, continually reiterated, to escape from the war, the 'plot' (49) that all too palpably threatens to destroy him. To this extent we can characterize *Catch-22* – like Kafka's *Prozess*, as we shall see later on – as a comedy of entropic indecision, a comedy of stasis.

The primary obstacle to Yossarian's salvation is the bomber squadron's commanding officer, Colonel Cathcart, who 'had courage and never hesitated to voluteer his men for any target available' (57). Cathcart's ambition is to rise from colonel to general by the quickest route, and his modus operandi is to attract favourable attention from above by raising continually the number of bombing missions required of his men. The number rises from twenty-five to eighty before Yossarian, having flown seventy-one already, refuses, risking summary court-martial, to fly any more. Captain John Yossarian, lead bombardier, Yo-Yo to his friends, is no hero who gallantly rises on behalf of the oppressed against an iniquitous system, however. He is in fact, like Bardamu, a convinced and professing coward: fear becomes second nature to him on the mission over Avignon, where Snowden, the young radio-gunner, literally 'lost his guts' (230). After that mission Yossarian 'climbed down the few steps of his plane naked, in a state of utter shock, with Snowden smeared abundantly all over his bare heels and toes, knees, arms and fingers' (267). Yossarian's first major move to escape from the machine takes place in the wake of Snowden's death, for he swears never to wear a uniform again, presenting General Dreedle with the problem of where to pin the decoration he has been awarded when he attends parade dressed only in moccasins (223). The protest fizzles out, and Yossarian flies more than thirty further missions, but never forgetting the 'secret' he has learned from Snowden: 'It was easy to read the message in his entrails. Man was matter, that was Snowden's secret. Drop him out a window and he'll fall. Set fire to him and he'll burn. Bury him and he'll rot like other kinds of garbage. The spirit gone, man is garbage. That was Snowden's secret. Ripeness was all' (450). Yossarian's only ambition from this point on is 'to live forever or die in the attempt, and his only mission each time he went up was to come down alive' (30). He is far from being the only one who has such an ambition. Orr, Dobbs, Hungry Joe, Dunbar, Flume, Doc Daneeka, Danby, all are like men 'who had grown frozen with horror once and had never come completely unthawed' (35). Yossarian is simply the one who owns up to his consuming fear most openly; and to that extent, as Dr Stubbs puts it, 'That crazy bastard may be the only sane one left' (114).

The individual as individual is non-existent for the faceless machine manifested by the oracular pronouncements designated 'Catch-
22.' The 'individual' has identity only as a minimal term in the
deployment of 'military quantities' (222), a physical unit that is 'filed'
(10) and occasionally misfiled, like the 'bald and pedantic cetologist
from the zoology department at Harvard who had been shanghaied
ruthlessly into the Medical Corps by a faulty anode in an IBM machine' (15). 'Let's give him a total and knock him out. Then we can do
what we want with him' (441), suggests an anaesthesia-happy surgeon in the military hospital after Yossarian has been near-fatally
wounded, and this scenario summarizes the optimum relationship
between the system and the individual – except, of course, from the
latter's point of view, which, however, represents only a trivial objection. Not that the system can be called uncaring, however, for each
and every individual death, disappearance, or other calamity is carefully registered and an appropriate personal letter dispatched to the
next of kin. Doc Daneeka's wife is the recipient of one of these:
'"Dear Mrs., Mr., Miss, or Mr. and Mrs. Daneeka: Words cannot
express the deep personal grief I experienced when your husband, son,
father or brother was killed, wounded or reported missing in action"'
(354). Doc Daneeka has in fact suffered no such fate except officially.
Though safely on the ground when the plane whose passenger list
erroneously included his name crashed, his continued survival constitutes a totally unnecessary administrative problem in the face of
the contradictory documentary evidence. 'Records attesting to his
death were pullulating like insect eggs and verifying each other beyond all contention' (353), and despite Doc Daneeka's increasingly
insubordinate attempts to demonstrate the contrary the case is
closed. Colonel Korn lets it be known 'that he would have Doc
Daneeka cremated on the spot if he ever showed up at Group Head-
quarters' (353). Doc Daneeka, in short, has an attitude problem.
Lieutenant Scheisskopf is a much more enthusiastically committed
officer, whose area of specialization is parades: 'He considered every
means of improvement, even nailing the twelve men in each rank to a
long two-by-four beam of seasoned oak to keep them in line. The plan
was not feasible, for making a ninety-degree turn would have been
impossible without nickel-alloy swivels inserted in the small of every
man's back, and Lieutenant Scheisskopf was not sanguine at all about
obtaining that many nickel-alloy swivels from Quartermaster or en-
listing the co-operation of the surgeons at the hospital' (74–5). With
commitment like this Scheisskopf rises rapidly to colonel and –

though admittedly as the fortunate result of a misinterpreted memo – eventually to general in command of the whole theatre of operations. Only two men are more powerful than he is in the end: Milo the mess officer and a mail clerk named Wintergreen, who, however, is 'not only a mail clerk, but ... has access to a mimeograph machine' (311).

The ostensible enemy – Hitler, as one might think, Fascism, Mussolini – is rarely mentioned, and this is understandable, for the ostensible enemy is not the real enemy any more than it was for Bardamu. The real enemy for General Peckem, for example, who is in command of Special Services, is General Dreedle, in command of combat activities (332), and their private war ceases only when Scheisskopf is inadvertently promoted over both their heads. In more general terms the real enemy is people with ideals, principles, moral commitments (like Clevinger, Nately, or the Chaplain) or just people who strongly prefer living to dying (like Dunbar or Yossarian). In the widest terms of all, the real enemy is people who don't pay their bills. In these terms the enemy is certainly not the Germans, as Milo explains to Yossarian: 'Sure, we're at war with them. But the Germans are also members in good standing of the syndicate. ... Maybe they did start the war, and maybe they are killing millions of people, but they pay their bills a lot more promptly than some allies of ours I could name' (262–3).

If the organized lunacy of the military establishment is one face of the system, the other is Milo's syndicate. Milo, a man blessed with 'a simple, sincere face that was incapable of subtlety or guile, an honest, frank face' (65), rises from mess officer to founder of a syndicate in which 'everybody has a share' (257). 'Everybody' is to be taken literally, for eventually 'Milo was not only the Vice-Shah of Oran, as it turned out, but also the Caliph of Baghdad, the Imam of Damascus, and the Sheikh of Araby. Milo was the corn god and the rice god in backward regions where crude gods were still worshiped by ignorant and superstitious people, and deep inside the jungles of Africa, he intimated with becoming modesty, large graven images of his mustached face could be found overlooking primitive stone altars red with human blood' (244). Milo's frank and honest face is the face of international monopoly capitalism, capitalism red in tooth and claw, capitalism for which world war is just a minor though profitable subsidiary. Milo's reach transcends the petty and superficial squabbles of the combatants. He contracts with the American military authorities to bomb a German-held bridge and with the German military authorities to defend the same bridge with anti-aircraft fire.

'His fee for attacking the bridge for America was the total cost of the operation plus six per cent, and his fee from Germany for defending the bridge was the same cost-plus-six agreement augmented by a merit bonus of a thousand dollars for every American plane he shot down' (261). He lands a contract from the Germans to bomb and strafe his own men and does so conscientiously. This time, however, Milo has gone too far. 'Bombing his own men and planes was more than even the most phlegmatic observer could stomach ... High-ranking government officials poured in to investigate ... Decent people everywhere were affronted, and Milo was all washed up until he opened his books to the public and disclosed the tremendous profit he had made' (266). Milo plays the game and plays it by the rules: 'Milo was by nature opposed to any innovation that threatened to disrupt the normal course of affairs' (118), was a staunch defender of 'the historic right of free men to pay as much as they had to for the things they needed in order to survive' (377), and was always very scrupulous about carrying out his business deals in plain honest English – most especially with people who didn't understand a word of English (68).

The only stable principle in the world of Catch-22 is the principle of relativity. 'There were many principles in which Clevinger believed passionately. He was crazy' (17) – and he doesn't last long. Saner people like Colonel Cathcart and Milo, winners rather than losers, believe equally passionately, but less absolutely: Colonel Cathcart believed in 'browbeating everyone he wasn't afraid of' (216), for example; Milo 'that it was never a sin to charge as much as the traffic would bear' (66); both are firm believers in that clause of Catch-22 which asserts that the strong can do anything the weak can't stop them from doing. It's all a question of where you're standing. 'The technique of protective rationalization' (372), as the chaplain realizes, 'in a moment of divine intuition,' is the key to success: 'It was almost no trick at all, he saw, to turn vice into virtue and slander into truth, impotence into abstinence, arrogance into humility, plunder into philanthropy, thievery into honor, blasphemy into wisdom, brutality into patriotism, and sadism into justice. Anybody could do it; it required no brains at all. It simply required no character' (372). The chaplain's realization comes in the wake of the first white lie he has ever, as a man of God, permitted himself. The chaplain's God was a God of wisdom and justice, however, 'an immortal, omnipotent, omniscient, humane, universal, anthropomorphic, English-speaking, Anglo-Saxon, pro-American God' (293), and his faith is beginning to waver. In the world of Catch-22 God works in such mysterious ways that in fact, as Yossarian observes, 'there's nothing so mysterious about it. He's not working at all. He's playing. Or else He's forgotten all about us' (184). However, as Yossarian also observes, there is room for religious freedom: 'You don't believe in the God you want to, and I won't believe in the God I want to' (185). Believed in or not, God is by definition on our side, and his pseudo-symbolic representative on the American side is Major — de Coverley, 'a splendid, awe-inspiring, grave old man with a massive leonine head and an angry shock of wild white hair that raged like a blizzard around his stern, patriarchal face'(135). Major — de Coverley, whose first name is no more utterable than that of Yahweh himself, is always among the first wave of American soldiers marching into the latest liberated Italian town, sitting regally in a commandeered jeep, seeming 'eternally indestructible as he sat there surrounded by danger' (136). His duties, however, are earthy: when not pitching horseshoes, he devotes himself to kidnapping Italian labourers and arranging for the supply of prostitutes for the officers and men. Eventually – shades of Zarathustra – 'he seems to have disappeared' (253). Major de Coverley's counterpart is the 'diabolical' (250) and nameless old man, who, 'like Satan himself' (138), jumps on to the major's jeep in Rome and blinds him in one eye with a flower flung at close range. This 'evil and debauched ugly old man' (247) supervises a Roman brothel, makes disparaging remarks about America, and, unlike the idealistic Nately's staunchly establishment father, who 'believed in honor and knew the answer to everything,' this Mephistophelean old man 'believed in nothing and had only questions' (250). He is the archetypal spirit of cynical relativism, as he himself gleefully boasts to Nately: 'I was a fascist when Mussolini was on top, and I am an anti-fascist now that he has been deposed. I was fanatically pro-German when the Germans were here to protect us against the Americans, and now that the Americans are here to protect us against the Germans I am fanatically pro-American' (251). His complete lack of principles and his unscrupulous opportunism may or may not, as Nately reproaches him, be shameful; what is more to the point, as he reminds his accuser, is that he is a hundred and seven years old (252). No principle is worth suffering for; certainly no principle is worth dying for. The supreme virtue, at all costs – one that by its very nature is inevitably and always relative – is the simple fact (as it is for Bardamu and Yossarian) of survival.

The world of Heller's narrative is an entropic one, where all clear outlines blur. Reality and unreality intermingle as easily as they do in the half-real, half-imaginary island of the narrative's setting. Hungry Joe's screaming nightmare in which Huple's cat is sitting on his face turns into a waking reality in which Huple's cat *is* sitting on his face. Captain Flume is so terrified his tentmate will slit his throat that he tries never to fall asleep: 'Actually, Captain Flume slept like a log most nights and merely *dreamed* he was awake. So convincing were these dreams of lying awake that he awoke from them each morning in complete exhaustion and fell right back to sleep' (58). 'So many monstrous events were occurring,' the chaplain reflects, 'that he was no longer positive which events *were* monstrous and which *were* really taking place' (287). 'Are you sure you didn't imagine the whole thing?' Hungry Joe inquires of Yossarian after the latter has been attacked by Nately's whore, then, remembering that he himself has been an eye-witness: 'Maybe I imagined the whole thing too' (407). What we *think* exists can be just as dangerous as what really exists. Yossarian realizes eventually that there is no such thing as Catch-22: 'Catch-22 did not exist, he was positive of that, but it made no difference. What did matter was that everyone thought it existed, and that was much worse, for there was no object or text to ridicule or refute, to accuse, criticize, attack, amend, hate, revile, spit at, rip to shreds, trample upon or burn up' (418). The real is indistinguishable from the unreal, the true from the false, the sane from the insane, order from chaos – or rather the poles have become reversed, and the unreal, the false, and the insane have become the norm, producing 'a world boiling in chaos in which everything was in proper order' (148). 'There was no way of really knowing anything,' the chaplain reflects, 'not even that there was no way of really knowing anything' (274).

Individuality is lost, faces blur. In a dying world – 'Of course you're dying. We're all dying. Where the hell else do you think you're heading?' (187) – whether a grieving family talks to their own dying son or some other family's dying son, for example, is a trivial distinction. In one of the funniest sequences of the book Yossarian unwillingly sits in for such a grieving family's dying boy, though staunchly denying his 'father's' impression that his name is Giuseppe rather than Yossarian. But as the mother says, 'What difference does it make? ... He's dying' (190–1). The 'dead man in Yossarian's tent' is a real presence even if Yossarian sleeps alone – we're all dead men, it's just a question of time until it becomes indisputable. This one's name, a painful pun, was Mudd. 'Mudd was the unknown soldier who had never had a chance, for that was the only thing anyone ever did

know about all the unknown soldiers – they never had a chance'
(112). Nameless, motionless, indistinguishable, interchangeable, the
'soldier in white' is the ideal citizen of this republic of death:

> The soldier in white was encased from head to toe in plaster and
> gauze. He had two useless legs and two useless arms ... the two
> strange legs hoisted from the hips, the two strange arms anchored up
> perpendicularly, all four limbs pinioned strangely in air by lead
> weights suspended darkly above him that never moved. Sewn into
> the bandages over the insides of both elbows were zippered lips
> through which he was fed clear fluid from a clear jar. A silent zinc
> pipe rose from the cement on his groin and was coupled to a slim
> rubber hose that carried waste from his kidneys and dripped it
> efficiently into a clear, stoppered jar on the floor. When the jar on the
> floor was full, the jar feeding his elbow was empty, and the two were
> simply switched quickly so that stuff could drip back into him. All
> they ever really saw of the soldier in white was a frayed black hole
> over his mouth.   (10)

The soldier in white is a 'bright reminder' of a 'nauseating truth'
(172): what *is* certain is death, and at best we have only some very
limited choice in the manner of its coming. Yossarian's preference is
to remain permanently in hospital, where there was 'a much health-
ier death rate' (170). Inside the hospital, at least, people

> didn't explode into blood and clotted matter. They didn't drown or
> get struck by lightening, mangled by machinery or crushed in land-
> slides. They didn't get shot to death in hold-ups, strangled to death
> in rapes, stabbed to death in saloons, bludgeoned to death with axes
> by parents or children, or die summarily by some other act of God ...
> People didn't stick their heads into ovens with the gas on, jump in
> front of subway trains or come plummeting like lead weights out of
> hotel windows with a *whoosh!*, accelerating at the rate of sixteen
> feet per second to land with a hideous *plop!* on the sidewalk and die
> disgustingly there in public like an alpaca sack full of hairy straw-
> berry ice cream, bleeding, pink toes awry.   (170–1)

Yossarian has been permanently marked, has been forced to open his
eyes to what we mostly prefer to forget, by his encounter with death
in the plane over Avignon, when he had ripped open Snowden's flak
suit in an attempt to help him and 'heard himself scream wildly as

Snowden's insides slithered down to the floor in a soggy pile and just kept dripping out' (449). 'His teeth were chattering in horror. He forced himself to look again. Here was God's plenty, all right, he thought bitterly as he stared – liver, lungs, kidneys, ribs, stomach and bits of the stewed tomatoes Snowden had eaten that day for lunch. Yossarian hated stewed tomatoes and rurned away dizzily and began to vomit, clutching his burning throat' (449). Heller's narrative, like Céline's, and for all the comicry, is an excoriation of the human condition *tout court*, once again with war as the central metaphor. In the end, in the long run, we don't have a chance. Yossarian knows it: 'Death was irreversible, he suspected, and he began to think he was going to lose' (355). If the enemy didn't succeed in managing to kill him, after all, he would manage all on his own: 'There were billions of conscientious body cells oxidating away day and night like dumb animals at their complicated job of keeping him alive and healthy, and every one was a potential traitor and foe' (177). Yossarian eventually attempts to break out of the futile closed circle of Catch-22 by simply running away, but some things cannot be run away from, and one of them is death, personified for Yossarian in the end by Nately's whore with her bone-handled kitchen knife. In the inevitable heat-death of the universe 'even the vast, burning, dazzling, majestic sun was in a state of progressive decay that would eventually destroy the earth too. There were no miracles' (293), and the fate of the universe is the fate of the individual too. The Supreme Being who was putatively responsible for a universe like this, Yossarian concludes, could only have a 'warped, evil, scatological mind' (184). The world created by this non-existent God is absurd; the world created by man is diabolical. And there is nothing new or surprising about this: 'Rome was destroyed,' the taunting old man reminds Nately, 'Greece was destroyed, Persia was destroyed, Spain was destroyed ... How much longer do you really think your own country will last?' (249). History, once again, as for Bardamu, is no untroubled linear progression, no spiral towards a transcendent meaning. History is a meaningless circle, a series of *déjà vu* situations where truly 'One dying boy is just as good as any other, or just as bad' (187).

Towards the end of the narrative Yossarian goes absent without leave and walks through 'the eternal city.' The eternal city is Rome, but also, in a surrealistic sequence demonstrating the everyday brutality of the strong and the everyday suffering of the weak, the eternal city is history itself, not the city of life, but the city of death, trapped in a never-ending cycle of aggression and victimization, a never-ending war of the strong against those unable to defend themselves. Yossarian witnesses a series of commonplace atrocities – beatings, muggings, thefts, a man 'beating a dog with a stick like the man who was beating the horse with a whip in Raskolnikov's dream' (424). 'The night was filled with horrors, and he thought he knew how Christ must have felt as he walked through the world, like a psychiatrist through a ward full of nuts, like a victim through a prison full of thieves' (424). Yossarian is no saviour, however, and no hero, and he offers no help to any of the victims: what, after all, would be the point? Only the particulars of the situation would be slightly changed; the situation itself is static and unchangeable. For every victim saved there are hundreds more to take his place, and every victim, given half a chance, happily turns aggressor himself. Yossarian's vision is a vision of anomie, a vision of a society gone rotten: 'When you added them all up and then subtracted, you might be left with only the children, and perhaps with Albert Einstein and an old violinist or sculptor somewhere. Yossarian walked in lonely torture' (422).

Still, the fact that you *might* be left with the children – Bardamu makes the same concession – is at least something. Perhaps there was a stand one could make after all. 'Someone had to do something sometime. Every victim was a culprit, every culprit a victim, and somebody had to stand up sometime to try to break the lousy chain of inherited habit that was imperiling them all' (414). This is the other side of Milo's declaration that everybody has a share: the system, like the syndicate, continues to exist only because we *are* the system. Following on this visionary experience, Yossarian decides simply to opt out of the system, even though it is against his own best interests. After his refusal to fly further missions a cynical deal has eventually been worked out, to prevent demoralization among the other men: instead of being court-martialled, Yossarian will be treated as a hero, decorated, and, most important, sent home to the United States, the very goal he has been trying to achieve all along. Though Yossarian initially accepts the deal with enthusiasm, he later changes his mind and decides to desert instead. Our reading of this decision plays a large part in our interpretation of the narrative as a whole.

Yossarian makes two major decisions towards the end of the narrative, the first to refuse to fly any further missions, the second, after his visionary experience in Rome, to desert to Sweden. The first decision concerns only his own survival and safety; the second has the appearance of being broader in scope, of being a gesture not only on his own behalf but on behalf of the weak, the powerless, the oppressed. 'I'm not running *away* from my responsibilities. I'm running *to* them,' Yossarian declares to Danby, who is trying to dissuade him. Danby points out that it is almost a geographical impossibility to get from Pianosa to Sweden undetected: 'Hell, Danby, I know that. But at least I'll be trying. There's a young kid in Rome whose life I'd like to save if I can find her, so it isn't all selfish, is it?' (462). The reader, in other words, is presented with a traditional happy ending, complete with inspirational moral message: the coward turns hero and embarks on a task he knows to be impossible because he has realized that what really counts is to stand firmly by your principles and speak out for what is right, regardless of the consequences. Yossarian's gesture, in this reading, is heroic and reverses the entire thrust of the narrative so far. In fact, what we have been reading as entropic satire all along suddenly, at the very last moment, metamorphoses before our eyes into a satire that for all its outlandishness is quite clearly normative and ameliorative: society, the world, the entire universe is admittedly in appalling condition, but as long as we remember personal responsibility and love, the message runs, the gates of hell will not prevail against us. How seriously *can* we afford to take Yossarian's flight into responsibility, though?

'Somebody had to stand up sometime' (414). The ambition is similar to the chaplain's feeling that the phenomenon of *déjà vu*, the 'weird, occult sensation of having experienced the identical situation before in some prior time or existence ... the subtle, recurring confusion between illusion and reality' (209), must somehow be susceptible to harnessing: 'He endeavored to trap and nourish the impression in order to predict, and perhaps even control, what incident would occur next, but the afflatus melted away unproductively, as he had known beforehand it would' (209). Insight by itself is not enough; some point of leverage must be found from which to exert 'control,' and the question becomes whether this point exists or not. The chaplain himself never manages to find it, and neither do Clevinger, Danby, Major Major, or Dunbar, all of whom at some point also have reformers' ambitions. Does Yossarian? His decision not to fly any further missions after Nately is killed over Spezia (401) is only the latest in a series of refusals to co-operate. Yossarian, in fact, continually refuses to fly further missions every time Colonel Cathcart raises the number – and each time the attempted insurrection comes to nothing. There is no particular reason why his latest refusal should be any more effective or lasting than any one of the previous ones. After his deeply disturbing vision of disorder in the eternal city, Yossarian may seem to have acquired a new resolve – but, firstly, he has had other such deeply disturbing experiences, most notably Snowden's death, and, secondly, he is in fact far from being resolved after Rome. He even announces his intention simply to stay in hospital and 'vegetate ... and let other people make their decisions.' 'You must make decisions,' Major Danby argues with him. 'A person can't live like a vegetable.' To which Yossarian replies simply: 'Why not?' (456).

Why not is because if you do you have no hope at all, and the system, the syndicate, Catch-22 burgeons all the more luxuriantly:

> 'Then there is no hope for us, is there?'
> 'No hope.'
> 'No hope at all, is there?'
> 'No, no hope at all.'   (458)

Staying put means no hope; running away is impossible. 'Sweden was out of reach, too far away' (318), Yossarian had long since concluded. What is needed is a miracle – and on cue a miracle is provided. 'Footsteps exploded in the corridor suddenly and the chaplain, shouting at the top of his voice, came bursting into the room with the electrifying news about Orr' (458). Orr, the chaplain has just discovered, has just been 'washed ashore' in Sweden many weeks after he was shot down in the sea off the Italian coast. 'It's a miracle, I tell you! A miracle! I believe in God again. I really do,' the chaplain exults. Yossarian goes one better: Orr was not washed up at all, 'he *rowed* there ... he planned it that way' (458). Either way it's a miracle, as far as the chaplain is concerned; even if Orr planned it 'it's still a miracle, a miracle of human intelligence and endurance' (458). If Orr could do it, Yossarian exults, so could he: 'There is hope, after all ... Even Clevinger [who had disappeared without trace during an aerial dogfight] might be alive somewhere inside that cloud of his, hiding inside until it's safe to come out' (459). In the world of miracle anything is possible, especially the impossible; and if the world of miracle – that alternative, ideal world where things that *should* happen *do* happen – refuses to manifest itself, it becomes necessary to invent it.

Before Orr's miraculous escape the chaplain had been unable to believe in miracles, though he desperately wanted to be able to believe. 'There were no miracles ... and the chaplain, who had conscience and character, would have yielded to reason and relinquished his belief in the God of his fathers ... had it not been for such successive mystic phenomena as the naked man in the tree at that poor sergeant's funeral weeks before and the cryptic, haunting, encouraging promise of the prophet Flume in the forest only that afternoon: *Tell them I'll be back when winter comes'* (293–4). The reader, of course, knows these 'mystic phenomena' for what they are. The naked man is Yossarian, no angel of the Lord; and 'the prophet Flume' merely hopes that if he hides in the woods until winter his tormentor, Chief White Halfoat, will have died of pneumonia as *he* promised to do. There *are* no miracles. The murderous system remains invincible and unchangeable, and the only escape is an invented one, an escape into the sustaining fiction of the miracle of Orr, the alternative world of that wished-for *or*.

'You're an intelligent person of great moral character who has taken a very courageous stand' remarks Colonel Korn to Yossarian of his refusal to fly further missions. 'I'm an intelligent person with no moral character at all, so I'm in an ideal position to appreciate it' (432). Yossarian's final flight *can* be read as a heroic gesture of defiance against the monolithic system on the part of one brave man; but if we focus our attention on the level of discourse rather than story, the level of the narrator rather than the character, we too are in an ideal position to appreciate that the narration undercuts and retracts the satisfyingly traditional happy ending, with its individual triumph of the good man, bloody but unbowed, who eventually refuses to be pushed around any further, puts his foot down, and says No.

Our attention has been drawn to sustaining fictions at various points throughout the narrative. We first encounter Yossarian as an army censor who invents little games to break the monotony: in one letter he will delete all modifiers, in another all articles, in another everything but articles or the salutation, and so on (8). Dunbar attempts to increase his life span, as we have seen, by cultivating boredom (9). In an attempt to avoid flying a mission over Bologna Yossarian alters the map to have it show Bologna as already taken (123). Colonel Cathcart 'lived by his wits in an unstable, arithmetical world of black eyes and feathers in his cap, of overwhelming imaginary triumphs and catastrophic imaginary defeats' (193). Orr constructs a mechanical version of such fictive worlds, tinkering with the faucet that feeds gasoline into the stove he built during his spare time: 'He worked without pause, taking the faucet apart, spreading all the tiny pieces out carefully, counting and then studying each one interminably as though he had never seen anything remotely similar before, and then reassembling the whole small apparatus, over and over and over and over again, with no loss of patience or interest, no sign of fatigue, no indication of ever concluding' (23). The entire Catch-22 system is a gigantic structure of interrelated fictional worlds: some merely more overtly so than the others, as in the case of 'the open-air movie theater in which, for the daily amusement of the dying, ignorant armies clashed by night on a collapsible screen' (26).

This, of course, is as much a self-reflective description of *Catch-22* the narrative as it is of the Catch-22 system. Heller's narrator is a showman who spreads before us in a comedian's patter an absurd and appalling world of viciousness, hypocrisy, and stupidity, and leaves us to draw whatever conclusions we may choose (or not choose) to draw. Where Céline's grim comedy only barely reveals its comic face, Heller's is obstreperously comic from the beginning, the frequently hilarious humour never completely absent even in the most appalling episodes. Céline's narrator, Bardamu, begins his narrative in a fairly conventional realistic vein, the older Bardamu looking back with grim humour on the experiences of the younger; in the second part of his narrative Bardamu, by emphasizing the parallel (or rather synec-dochic) experiences of other characters, expands his criticism overtly from the particular to the general. Heller's narrator, nameless, external to the action, omniscient and omnipotent like a narrative God, stands aloof from the action from the beginning, just setting it in motion and letting it run, so to speak. Bardamu is to a fairly large extent a believable character in realist terms; the world of *Catch-22* is more a Bosch-like or Brueghel-like portrayal of hell, orchestrated for animated cartoon characters – even Yossarian never really becomes a fully rounded character. One result of this presentation is that *Catch-22* tends naturally towards parody, becoming overtly so only at the very end in the opposing and self-erasing readings of Yossarian's flight with which we are provided by the narrator. The narrative style throughout, however, can be read as pointing towards the paradoxical self-erasure of Yossarian's flight (including in such details as Yossarian's nickname, since the flight of a yoyo always involves an immediate, 'self-erasing' retraction!). The characters are loosely ar-ranged as good guys, bad guys, and supporting cast. The action is largely a series of interlinking one-liner situations, one result being a cumulative effect of informational overkill, with contours emerging from the confusion only gradually. Contradiction of various kinds is a staple device throughout, especially in the form of the reversed cliché, which can, of course, be read as an oblique commentary on the system of values that generated the cliché in the first place. The manipulation of time, however, is probably the most striking disorientational device for most readers: the 'dead man in Yossarian's tent' (18), for example, is introduced long before the reader has any way of knowing what is involved; Yossarian's 'standing in formation stark naked' (104) is casually referred to in passing long before we are told what led him to do so. One past event referred to constantly is Snowden's death, the details of which are not revealed in full, however, until a dozen pages from the end. The disjunction is occasionally extreme enough to include the impossible: Appleby reports to Major Major, for example, well before the latter actually arrives on Pianosa (110). The phantasmagoric effect is heightened throughout by pervasive employment of a wide variety of standard but wholly inappropriate comic devices and routines. Heller's narrative style, in short, is the appropriately prestidigitatory stylistic equivalent of the double-talk and bafflegab of the system itself, as exemplified in Milo's various carefully incomprehensible explanations of his multifarious financial doings. No more than Milo's, Heller's explanations are not designed to explain anything. No more than Céline's, Heller's narrative does not favour rational answers and comfortable solutions; as entropic satire, its concern is with uncomfortable questions, the questions we would rather not have to ask at all – at any rate outside of sustaining fictions.

The Authority of Satire: Grass's *Die Blechtrommel*

This privileging of uncomfortable questions at the expense of comfortable answers is also a central characteristic of Günter Grass's novel *Die Blechtrommel* (1959; *The Tin Drum*), the consideration of which brings us a step further in our discussion of the range of entropic satire in that this work not only combines the savagery of Céline and the comicry of Heller but also overtly emphasizes that central element of self-parody latent in all entropic humour. Oskar Matzerath, Grass's first-person narrator, is a thirty-year-old inmate of a lunatic asylum at the time of writing his autobiography (as he informs us in his opening sentence), and his account is filled with incidents that can only be characterized as fantastic. As a three-year-old aficionado of the tin drum of the book's title, Oskar, according to his own account, decides to have nothing more to do with the world of grown-ups, especially those who threaten to take his drum away.

To achieve this end the three-year-old flings himself headlong down the cellar stairs, suffering no ill effects other than the desired one of curtailing his growth: for the next eighteen years, until his son (who is probably in fact his brother) knocks him (or perhaps doesn't) into the open grave of his recently deceased father (who may in fact not be his father at all), Oskar retains the stature of a three-year-old. A midget who refuses adamantly ever to be parted from his drum, Oskar has the supplementary gift of a miraculous voice that enables him to smash glass at will with a well-directed scream. The unrelenting savagery of Bardamu's denunciation of human affairs may occasionally give even his more hard-boiled readers pause; the narrator of *Catch-22* frequently disorientates his readers with his relentless comicry; Oskar's readers, by contrast, can never afford to take *anything* he says at face value. Where Bardamu's narrative may ostentatiously reject social and conventional norms that the reader might well prefer to have retained, it still, at least, displays one *narrative* norm: Bardamu's denunciation is self-consistent. His vision may be appalling, but his account of it contains few narrative surprises or inconsistencies. Heller's narrator, even though his narrative style is radically different from Bardamu's, is ultimately equally consistent and reliable. Perhaps the most salient feature of Oskar's narration, however, is its own (successful) attempt to undermine and relativize everything it presents.

Why did three-year-old Oskar, born clairvoyant and clairaudient, according to his own account, decide to opt out of grown-up society? Born in 1924, Oskar completes his narrative in 1954, the intervening thirty years having seen the incubation, the triumph, and the publicly acknowledged defeat of Nazism in Germany. Oskar begins his account in 1899, in fact, for 'niemand sollte sein Leben beschreiben, der nicht die Geduld aufbringt, vor dem Datieren der eigenen Existenz wenigstens der Hälfte seiner Grosseltern zu gedenken' (11) / 'no one ought to tell the story of his life who hasn't the patience to say a word or two about at least half of his grandparents before plunging into his own existence' (17). Not all his readers, Oskar clearly implies, would have either the patience or the desire in the Germany of 1954 to put their memory to such a test – or if they did it is very possible that the resulting account would be just as strange a blend of fact and fiction, *Dichtung und Wahrheit*, as Oskar's own determinedly garbled and ostentatiously unbelievable version of how things really were in the Central Europe of his time. If Bardamu's version of life in France between 1914 and the mid-thirties achieves its force because of his refusal to disguise his disgust, Oskar's account of life in Danzig and Germany before, during, and after the Second World War achieves its satirical thrust precisely because of its relentless obliquity, because of the elaborate care with which fact is disguised as fiction and fiction presented as unassailable fact.

Grass's novel, Oskar's narrative, is divided into three books, the satirical thrust focused respectively on the period before, during, and after the war. Oskar, like Grass, grows up in the Free City of Danzig, the focus of German-Polish tensions over many years. These tensions are presented, typically obliquely, in the account of Josef Koljaiczek, Oskar's grandfather, and his brief involvement as an advocate of the Polish cause: Koljaiczek is dismissed from his job as a sawmill worker for painting a fence red and white, the Polish national colours, and reiterates the chromatic theme (one reflected in the colours of Oskar's drum) by sending the whitewashed mill up in flames (19/27). The entire First World War merits only a reference to the changing design of postage stamps; the depression of 1923 passes by in a subordinate clause. Oskar's first day at school, where he listens to the 'barbaric voices' of his class-mates, is described in rather more detail, and in greater detail still the apparently innocuous beating of carpets in the communal courtyard, which, 'laut Hausordnung' (77) / 'as the house regulations decreed' (96–7), took place twice a week:

> Hundert Hausfrauen trugen Teppichleichen aus den Häusern, hoben dabei nackte runde Arme, bewahrten ihr Kopfhaar und dessen Frisuren in kurz geknoteten Kopftüchern, warfen die Teppiche über die Klopfstangen, griffen zu geflochtenen Teppichklopfern und sprengten mit trockenen Schlägen die Enge der Höfe.   (77)

> With a great display of bare arms a hundred housewives, their hair tied up in kerchiefs, emerged from the houses carrying carpet corpses, threw the victims over the rack, seized their plaited carpet beaters and filled the air with thunder.   (97)

In this idyllic scene of domestic industry, cleanliness, communal spirit, and *Ordnung*, only the word *Teppichleichen* 'carpet corpses' suggests an element of sublimated aggression, but it is sharply though again obliquely highlighted when in the same courtyard a group of children, under the leadership of one Susi Kater, trap Oskar and force him to drink down a nauseating brew whose recipe includes brickdust, spit, live frogs, and assorted flavours of urine. It is 1932, and every Thursday Oskar's mother punctually betrays her German husband, Matzerath, with her Polish lover, Jan Bronski. In the wake of drinking Susi Kater's brew Oskar utilizes the destructive powers of his miraculous voice to smash every window in the façade of the Municipal Theatre: 'Der Kasten zeigte mit seiner Kuppel eine verteufelte Ähnlichkeit mit einer unvernünftig vergrösserten, klassizistischen Kaffeemühle,' writes Oskar. 'Mich ärgerte dieser Bau, von dessen säulenflankierten Foyerfenstern eine absackende und immer mehr rot auftragende Nachmittagssonne nicht lassen wollte' (83) / 'This box with a dome on it looked very much like a monstrously blown-up neoclassical coffee mill ... The building annoyed me, especially the column-flanked windows of the lobby, sparkling in the rays of a sagging afternoon sun which kept mixing more and more red in its palette' (104).

The rise to power of the Nazi party is relegated to the inconsequential background in Oskar's account: Oskar prefers to talk about his suddenly increased contact with the theatre as an institution around 1933. First there is his defenestration of the Municipal Theatre, then a public performance of Tom Thumb, an open-air Wagner recital as a result of which Oskar's mother takes to 'domesticating' Wagner on the living-room piano (91/113), a visit to the circus, a visit to a Nazi rally. The picture of Beethoven over the piano is quietly joined by that of 'der ähnlich finster blickende Hitler' (93) / 'Hitler's equally gloomy countenance' (115). Meanwhile, little by little, Matzerath the greengrocer is piecing together his new uniform. 'Wenn ich mich recht erinnere' (93) / 'If I remember right' (116), as Oskar offhandedly phrases it,

> begann er mit der Parteimütze, die er gerne, auch bei sonnigem Wetter mit unterm Kinn scheuerndem Sturmriemen trug. Eine Zeitlang zog er weisse Oberhemden mit schwarzer Krawatte zu dieser Mütze an oder eine Windjacke mit Armbinde. Als er das erste braune Hemd kaufte, wollte er eine Woche später auch die kackbraunen Reithosen und Stiefel erstehen. Mama war dagegen, und es dauerte abermals Wochen, bis Matzerath endgültig in Kluft war.   (93)

> he began with the cap, which he liked to wear even in fine weather with the 'storm strap' in place, scraping his chin. For a time he wore a white shirt and black tie with the cap, or else a leather jacket with black armband. Then he bought his first brown shirt and only a week later he wanted the shit-brown riding breeches and high boots.

Mama was opposed to these acquisitions and several weeks passed
before Matzerath's uniform was complete.   (116)

The way in which the lower-middle-class society of which Oskar is
part pieces together its acceptance of Nazism just as Matzerath puts
together his uniform, starting with the cap signifying adherence to a
political ideal and ending with the shit-brown boots that soon will be
kicking in the windows of Jewish-owned shop-fronts, is choreo-
graphed with consummate technical and comic skill by Grass. The
heroic ideals are domesticated, in easy arrangements, just as Oskar's
mother domesticates Wagner between her furtive and obsessive visits
to Jan Bronski. German Idealism, canonized and revered, represented
by the heroics of Wagnerian tenors, by the demonic eyebrows of
Beethoven, by the Olympian serenity of the adulated poet-prince
Goethe, is ground down and churned out nightly in the coffee mill of
the culture industry, to form a fertile humus for that same Idealism's
latest and perverted offshoot – which also comfortably accommo-
dates the latent atavistic savagery of an apparently well-ordered bourgeois society. The difference between the heroic façade and the grimy
underpinnings is demonstrated perhaps most clearly in the episode of
the Nazi rally, which takes place in front of an immaculate and
imposing rostrum with its serried ranks of swastika banners, flags,
pennants, standards, and assorted uniforms. Distrustful of this highly
polished symmetry, Oskar, as he tells us, prefers to examine the back-
side of the rostrum, for 'wer jemals eine Tribüne von hinten anschaute, recht anschaute, wird von Stund an gezeichnet und somit
gegen jegliche Zauberei, die in dieser oder jener Form auf Tribünen
zelebriert wird, gefeit sein' (96) / 'Everyone who has ever taken a good
look at a rostrum from behind will be immunized ipso facto against
any magic practised in any form whatsoever on rostrums' (119). A
Jonah in the whale's belly (99/122), a Tom Thumb, a tiny resistance
fighter, Oskar disrupts the gleaming symmetry of the martial platform from underneath by undermining the military rhythms above
with the rhythms of the Charleston and Viennese waltzes from below, and the political rally, to the fury of its organizers, degenerates
into a *gemütlich* open-air dance.

Throughout the first book of the novel, covering the period from
1899 to 1938, Oskar's distorted refraction of German society, by
continually peripheralizing the major political happenings of the
time and sharply highlighting eccentric, insignificant, and frequently
grotesque details instead of the overall picture, strips away the façade

of respectability and reticence veiling the rise of Nazism in Germany. Grass's satirical thrust, for all the obliqueness of its application via Oskar, is quite clear: Nazism was not at all some kind of demonic hero-frenzy of the German psyche, some kind of almost supernatural eruption of evil incarnate, horrifying indeed, but in its excess fascinating and even grandiose. Rather it was the co-ordinated channelling on a huge scale of the petty viciousness, the petty hypocrisies, the petty greed and frustration and spite and boredom of very ordinary people, leading painfully ordinary lives until presented with a clearly defined and universally agreed upon focus for their concerted discontent and resentment. The holocaust came about not in spite of but because of the ordinary man in the street, and when it came about it involved little or no disruption of the existing system of values. Stormtrooper Meyn, for example, is unable to be present when his comrades, during the *Kristallnacht* of November 1938, kick in the windows of Jewish shop-fronts, burn down the synagogue, and terrorize Jewish citizens: quite properly, Meyn has been expelled in disgrace from the SA for cruelty to animals.

One question will have become obvious by now, however, and must be dealt with: namely, to what extent, if at all, this account need be, or even can be, read as *entropic* satire. It is fairly obviously satire, as most readers would presumably agree, but surely, many readers would say, it is precisely normative, ameliorative satire? Surely it differs from Bardamu's wholesale denunciation of human affairs and human nature in that it not only mercilessly exposes folly and vice but also, insistently even, demonstrates something of what went wrong in the fabric of society and in so doing at least implicitly warns its readers against ever permitting a recurrence? Surely this objection is supported by Günter Grass's own well-known and well-publicized political activity on behalf of the Social Democratic Party in Germany since the sixties and his determined onslaughts on public figures tainted by Nazi associations in the past? If *Die Blechtrommel* ended with its account of the pre-war years, and if that account came only from the pen of Günter Grass, the determined battler against hypocrisy and cant, then the objection just raised probably could not be answered, and the book would have to be classified as a well-intentioned if stylistically outlandish satire designed, as normative satire always is, to reject a threat to values held to be worth defending. Neither of these conditions is met, however: first, Oskar's account does go on to embrace the war years and the post-war years as well, and secondly, more important, it *is* precisely Oskar's account rather than Grass's alleged account that we are interested in dealing with here.

This distinction is far from being merely a legalistic formalist quibble. For Oskar the resistance fighter quickly acquires other and more disturbing traits as well. It emerges that his disruption of the Nazi rally may have had less heroic motives, after all, for Oskar goes on to relate that he was so pleased with the success of this little trick that he repeated it frequently over the next few weeks, breaking up further rallies not only of the Nazis but also of the Socialists and the Conservatives, not to mention the boy scouts, the vegetarians, and the Young Polish Fresh Air Movement (100/124). From being apparently a pint-sized freedom fighter and defender of humanity's cause, Oskar (always according to his own account) becomes an aimless destroyer, a rejecter not just of Nazism, but apparently of all causes. Never reluctant to supply the gullible reader with possible interpretive parallels, Oskar mentions at various points his dual intellectual heritage. After rejecting the public school system Oskar undertakes his own education by close reading of two books whose pages, for simplicity's sake, he has torn out and shuffled to make a single new volume, Goethe's *Elective Affinities* and a volume promisingly entitled *Rasputin and Women*. He notes at several points his family similarity to the Christ-child; uses the name Jesus during his days as leader of a gang of juvenile delinquents; much later informs a nurse whom he is unsuccessfully attempting to rape that his name is Satan; claims two fathers, one German and one Polish; and finally acknowledges in Nietzschean vein that he subsumes not only Apollo but Dionysus as well. Critics have pointed to the fact that Hitler, who shared with Oskar his lower-middle-class origins, his blue eyes, and his status as 'artist,' was also known to his intimates as 'der Trommler' / 'the drummer' and, like Oskar, referred to himself as the saviour of his people. Critics have also noticed that certain activities of Oskar's go so far as to constitute an allegory of the rise and fall of Nazism: his involvement in the death of his Polish father, Bronski, coincides with the German invasion of Poland in 1939; his self-reported sexual conquest of his cousin Maria coincides with the invasion of France in 1940; his again self-reported campaign on the shaky virtue of Lina Greff coincides with the Russian campaign of 1941; his amorous conquest of the Italian midget Roswitha Raguna begins under the sign of the *Anschluss* with Italy in 1938, and his involvement in her death very literally coincides with the invasion of Normandy in 1944, as Roswitha reaches the coffee urn simultaneously with a Canadian shell; finally, his involvement in the death of his German father, Matzerath, coincides with the fall of Germany in 1945.

From being predominantly an apparently uninvolved observer before the outbreak of war, in other words, Oskar apparently becomes a participant, and as such implicated in guilt, during the war. His participation, however, is impossible to categorize in realistic terms: there are first of all the grotesque 'facts' of his continued three-year-old's stature and his glass-demolishing scream (which he eventually redeploys as a nightclub act for the amusement of the troops); there is secondly the continued obliqueness and indirection of the account offered by the narrating Oskar, which repeatedly makes clear that it should not be taken at face value, while still exploiting the reader's natural impulse to believe a first-person narrator. What is focused on in the second book of the novel, indeed, is less the specific details of guilt than the fact of guilt itself, and Oskar's account of his own involvement, though more ostentatiously flamboyant, may well be no more fictional than many an answer to the question 'What did you do in the war, daddy?'

The complete unreliability of Oskar's account emerges particularly clearly in his description of the last time he saw Jan Bronski, whom he claims as his father. After being hauled out of the burning Polish Post Office, which the Germans have been shelling, Bronski is taken away in an ss staff car, waving forlornly to Oskar as he disappears – to his death, as we later find out. Oskar his next chapter as follows:

> Soeben las ich den zuletzt geschriebenen Absatz noch einmal durch. Wenn ich auch nicht zufrieden bin, sollte es um so mehr Oskars · Feder sein, denn ihr ist es gelungen, knapp, zusammenfassend, dann und wann im Sinne einer bewusst knapp zusammenfassenden Abhandlung zu übertreiben, wenn nicht zu lügen.   (200)

> I have just reread the last paragraph. I am not too well satisfied, but Oskar's pen ought to be, for writing tersely and succinctly, it has managed, as terse, succinct accounts sometimes do, to exaggerate, if not to lie.   (246)

Claiming his own intention to stick to the unvarnished truth, Oskar determines to outwit his less than straightforward pen and admits to three distortions of fact in the previous account. First of all, the hand of cards that Bronski, half mad with terror, had insisted on playing as the German shells demolished the building was not, Oskar now admits, a grand hand, as he had claimed before, but a diamond hand without twos. Secondly, he himself had not only taken with him his new tin drum, but an old one as well. And thirdly, 'ferner bleibt noch zu ergänzen' / 'it should be added,' as they were being dragged out of the Post Office Oskar had run with his drums to the advancing ss-men, crying and pointing accusingly at Bronski as a Polish *Unmensch* who had dragged an innocent German child into mortal danger. Oskar admits in his revised version of the incident that this was shameful behaviour, but points to the mitigating factor that as a result he had at least succeeded in protecting his drum from any damage – and moreover:

> wie jedermann halte ich mir an Tagen, da mich ein unhöfliches und durch nichts aus dem Zimmer zu weisendes Schuldgefühl in die Kisten meines Anstaltbettes drückt, meine Unwissenheit zugute, die damals in Mode kam und noch heute manchem als flottes Hütchen zu Gesicht steht.   (201)

> Like everyone else, on days when an importunate feeling of guilt, which nothing can dispel, crushes me into the pillows of my hospital bed, I tend to make allowances for my ignorance – the ignorance that came into style in those years and is still worn by many even today like a jaunty and becoming little hat.   (248)

The satirical thrust at carefully cultivated ignorance beforehand and amnesia afterwards is skilfully performed. It also reveals Oskar as a monster, however, and totally undermines his credibility as a satirist – how can we find ourselves nodding approvingly at the satirical swipes of so utterly callous a murderer? Indeed, by his own account, he is no less than a double parricide, for he later openly relates the way in which he connives in his 'other' father's death. As Russian troops hold the family at gunpoint in the burning Danzig of 1945 Oskar obligingly hands Matzerath his discarded Nazi party badge, which Matzerath, terrified, slips into his mouth and foolishly attempts to swallow. Oskar had thoughtfully opened the pin, however, and an equally thoughtful Kalmuck can prevent Matzerath from choking to death only by emptying an entire magazine of machine-gun ammunition into him. 'Man kann jetzt sagen, das hätte ich nicht tun sollen. Man kann aber auch sagen: Matzerath hätte nicht zuzugreifen brauchen' (327) / 'One could say I shouldn't have done that. But one could say too that Matzerath needn't have taken hold of it' (393).

One can in fact say what one wants, and our reality is more a product of these conflicting claims than it is of any ontologically stable original fact. Oskar's account also accuses him of murdering his mother, which seems highly dubious on the evidence given, and even of murdering both his greatuncle and his grandfather as well, which is patently false. Fact and fiction become interwoven in a web too tight and too complicated to disentangle. Reality is a construct whose power resides in its persuasiveness rather than in its adherence to what 'really happened.' What really happened, if it ever happened, is best forgotten, and this is exactly what West German society sets about doing in the third book of the novel, covering the immediate post-war years. And Oskar, whose role was initially that of clear-eyed observer and then involved pseudomythological implication in guilt, now acquires a third role, that of a grotesque normalization, attempting to become a part of that grown-up society he had vowed as a clairvoyant infant never to join. At Matzerath's funeral Oskar throws his drum into the open grave and begins to grow. At the same moment he is struck on the head by a stone flung by his four-year-old son (who may not be his son) and pitches headlong into the grave of his father (who may not be his father). History has spoken. Oskar, like the West Germany of the *Wirtschaftswunder*, the economic miracle of the immediate post-war years, arises from the grave and grows rapidly, the expensive suits he is soon able to afford elegantly concealing the misshapen hump he has now also acquired during his socially inspired growth. Oskar's new wealth is honestly come by, for in post-war Germany Oskar has become a practitioner of the arts, a constructor of alternative worlds, a reshaper of reality – an activity that in the new Germany finds numerous enthusiastic adherents. His first artistic endeavours are on the more functional side: he apprentices himself to a gravestone carver. Later he takes up modelling for a painter named Raskolnikoff. He is persuaded to take up his drum again and becomes a recording star. He performs in a nightclub, drumming up memories for clients who are thoughtfully provided with sliced onions to facilitate weeping. The proprietor of this establishment for properly regulated remorse is one Schmuh, and 'Schmuhs Lächeln glich dem Lächeln auf einer Kopie, die man nach der Kopie der vermutlich echten Mona Lisa gemalt hatte' (437) /

'Schmuh's smile was like the smile on a copy of a copy of the supposedly authentic Mona Lisa' (524). Not only do guilt and tears find their proper and authorized outlet; anger and aggression do too. There is Oskar's landlord, Zeidler, who gives vent to his feelings by regularly smashing liqueur glasses with great violence – before carefully sweeping up the remains. There is Schmuh, who enjoys nothing as much as shooting sparrows, but never shoots more than his self-imposed quota of a dozen a day, and sheds bitter therapeutic tears over those he has just allowed himself to shoot. The odd similarity of post-war Germany to pre-war Germany and its carpet-thrashing squadrons of housewives is not lost on Oskar. Victor Weluhn is one who experiences this meticulous regard for order and tidy-mindedness. Having escaped a Nazi execution squad in Danzig in 1939 he is pursued conscientiously by his would-be executioners, who attempt to complete their interrupted duties in 1954: an order is an order, as one of them explains, duty is duty, and he's just doing his job like everyone else.

'Plus ça change, plus c'est la même chose' clearly sums up the satirical thrust of the third book, already anticipated in Oskar's earlier musing on the ambiguity of the German title of the Polish national anthem, 'Noch ist Polen nicht verloren' / 'Poland is not yet lost.' The ambiguity resides in the question 'Lost to whom?'

> Während man hierzulande das Land der Polen mit der Seele sucht – halb mit Chopin, halb mit Revanche im Herzen – während sie hier die erste bis zur vierten Teilung verwerfen und die fünfte Teilung Polens schon planen, während sie mit Air France nach Warschau fliegen, und an jener Stelle bedauernd ein Kränzchen hinterlegen, wo einst das Getto stand, während man von hier aus das Land der Polen mit Raketen suchen wird, suche ich Polen auf meiner Trommel und trommle: Verloren, noch nicht verloren, schon wieder verloren, an wen verloren, bald verloren, bereits verloren, Polen verloren, alles verloren, noch ist Polen nicht verloren.   (86)

> While hereabouts they seek the land of Poland with their souls – their hearts full half of Chopin, half of revenge – while they condemn the first to fourth partitions of Poland and plan the fifth already, while they are flying Air France to Warsaw and laying remorseful wreaths on the spot where the ghetto once stood, while they are getting ready to seek the land of Poland with rockets, I

search for Poland on my drum and drum: Lost, not yet lost, lost
again, lost to whom, soon lost, already lost, Poland lost, all is lost,
Poland is not yet lost.   ([107–8])

This bitter lament is expressed in a tone that may well strike the
reader as more overtly sincere than many of Oskar's pronouncements
mentioned so far. It is one of a number of places in the text, in fact,
that point to Oskar's view of history and of human existence as
totally random, arbitrary, undirected, indifferent – and unchangeable,
whether by satire or otherwise. The disturbances over the first half of
the twentieth century, for all the impressiveness of their immediate
scope, constitute no more than one more episode in the interminable
continuing war we call history. Critics – especially John Reddick –
have drawn our attention to a number of such passages, all in one way
or another illustrating the bleakness and hopelessness of Oskar's
existential vision. He dreams at one stage that he is riding on a giant
merry-go-round with 4000 children whose death he has just heard of;
all of them, including Oskar, want to get off, but the merry-go-round
is operated by a smiling God the Father, who merely inserts another
coin in the slot for his own amusement. Life is no Hegelian spiral
towards some ultimate meaning that will retrospectively put everything else in its proper focus; life is simply an eternal and eternally
meaningless round. The same inescapable and pointless circularity
recurs in the image of the eels caught after the battle of the Skagerrak,
eels grown fat on sailors grown fat on eating eels. We find the same
bleakness of vision in the episode of the fisherman using a horse's
head on a clothes-line as bait for eels, a head so completely covered by
scavenging gulls that it seems white rather than black and seems to
scream rather than neigh (123/152). We find it in the account of
Matzerath's death, which fails to disturb the endeavours of the ants
carrying off the sugar from a split sack, 'denn jener aus dem
geplatzten Sack rieselnde Zucker hatte ... nichts von seiner Süsse
verloren' (328) / 'for the sugar that trickled out of the burst sack had
lost none of its sweetness' (395). We find it in the house of cards
Bronski builds with infinite care during the shelling of the Polish Post
Office, a metaphor for all human endeavour – including the bombard-
ment that destroys it and the account that describes the bombard-
ment – its very inception acknowledging the inevitability of its own
disintegration. We find it most consistently of all in the figure of the
Schwarze Köchin, 'black cook,' the wicked witch of a children's
rhyme who appears continually to Oskar throughout his account in

an ever-growing variety of disguises and who comes to dominate the closing pages of the novel. The *Schwarze Köchin*, for Oskar, represents everything we have to fear; and in the closing pages of his narrative what we have to fear is precisely everything. 'Immer war sie schon da ... Fragt Oskar nicht, wer sie ist! Er hat keine Worte mehr ... Schwarz war die Köchin hinter mir immer schon. / Dass sie mir nun auch entgegenkommt, schwarz' (493) / 'She had always been there ... Don't ask Oscar who she is! Words fail him ... Black, she was always behind me. / Now she is facing me too, black' (588–9). Thus ends Oscar's story. Only silence follows. Words fail him.

Oskar's final confession (or profession) of terror is impressive and highly effective. It is also – if only partly – fake, for it is quite clear that Oskar is at least partly *playing* at being terror-stricken, just as earlier he had played at revealing his 'guilt.' While *Die Blechtrommel* is patently a satire – and its satirical effect is attested to by the several dozen legal actions launched against its author by readers who felt personally addressed by it – it is equally patently also a parody. The satirical thrust is thus constantly undermined and indeed reflected back at the text itself. We may see this strategy at work in the deployment of other artist figures in the narrative, each of whom serves as a commentary on the artistic endeavours both of Oskar, drummer, screamer, and autobiographer, and of Grass himself. There is Gortfried von Vittlar, aesthete and dresser of shop-windows, whose only ambition is to be famous. There is Greff the greengrocer and admirer of boy scouts who builds what Oskar calls a drumming machine, namely a scaffold counterweighted with potatoes, on which he duly hangs himself – a one-time-only performance, as Oskar does not fail to point out. There is Klepp the clarinettist, who abandons monarchism for Marxism, and Marxism for spaghetti. There is Bebra, the Italian midget and acrobat, who warns Oskar to make quite sure above all else always to be on the winning side, 'immer auf der Tribüne zu sitzen und niemals vor der Tribüne zu stehen' (92) / 'always to be sitting on the rostrum and never to be standing out in front of it' (114). Finally there is Lankes, who turns from shooting nuns during the war to painting them after the war.

The artist, for Grass, at least, occupies no privileged place outside of the society he depicts; he is involved and implicated in the picture he paints. Above all else, art is concerned with making sense, and in Oskar's world (whatever about Grass's) the only sense is in the relativization of all sense-making activity. Nothing is fixed, nothing is certain. Among the various artist figures who reflect Oskar in the novel the closest to him in spirit is his keeper in the asylum, Bruno, who collects pieces of thrown-away string and knots them into complicated figures. As Bruno himself puts it later, however, he remains restless and dissatisfied: 'was ich rechts knüpfe, löse ich links auf, was meine Linke bildet, zertrümmert meine geballte Rechte' (352) / 'what I knot with my right hand I undo with my left, what my left hand creates my right fist shatters' (424). Bruno's creations, like Jan Bronski's house of cards, like Oskar's narrative itself, are fugitive entities whose ultimate end is silence. Whether the reader in the real world is in some way capable of deploying the energy released by these fugitive entities to the amelioration of that world; whether Günter Grass, citizen of the real world, may or may not have so intended the reader to act; these are concerns of importance, no doubt, to the reader, to the author, and to the real world. They are certainly no concern of Oskar's.

On Making No Difference: Camus's *L'étranger*

Bardamu's satirical vision focuses on a hopelessly corrupt society, and the discursive tone is unsparing, though with a comic overtone largely dependent upon the implied preposterous irreversibility of that corruption. Heller's narrator's vision is focused on a hopelessly lunatic society, and the discursive tone, though implicitly grim, is itself appropriately lunatic, reflecting the charateristic element of disproportion in the mores of that society. Oskar's satirical vision uncovers a hopelessly hypocritical society, and the discursive tone is essentially parodic, aptly reflecting both the double-speak of that society and the inclusion of the account itself among the targets of its own satire. All three are illustrations of what we may call entropic satire in its extroverted mode. In each, though in quite different ways, the narrative portrays a state of affairs envisioned as irreparably entropic by an observing subject. The observer is affected to varying degrees by the narrative reality he presents, but in each case it is clear that the narrative emphasis is primarily on the satirized reality rather than on the observer. This is most obviously so in the case of *Catch-22*, where the narrator is an external narrative voice; it is less so in the case of Céline's *Voyage*, where the protagonist Bardamu is part of the reality satirized by the narrator Bardamu; it is least obviously so in *Die Blechtrommel*, where Oskar the narrator ostentatiously demonstrates the reader's inability to arrive at a dependable view either of the nature of Oskar's involvement as character in the narrative reality presented or of the nature of his motives as narrator. Though there is an overt target of satire present in each case, that target becomes increasingly evanescent as the element of deconstructive parody progressively increases and with it the relocation of emphasis from the object observed to the observing subject.

'I swear that too great a lucidity is a disease, a true, full-fledged disease' (93), writes the nameless narrator of Dostoyevsky's *Notes from Underground* (1864), a text with a considerable claim to be regarded as the ancestor of a numerous progeny of entropic comedies, both satiric and ironic, whose focus is precisely on the observing subject rather than the observed reality. In the case of entropic satire in this introverted rather than extroverted mode the corruption, lunacy, and hypocrisy of the observed reality are taken for granted, and the emphasis is shifted to the effect on the endangered observer and the nature of his reaction. 'Obviously, in order to act, one must be fully satisfied and free of all misgivings beforehand. But take me: how can I ever be sure? Where will I find the primary reason for action, the justification for it? Where am I to look for it?' the Underground Man expostulates (103). 'In the end,' he concludes, echoing the decision reached by a fictional compatriot, Goncharov's Oblomov, some years earlier, 'it's best to do nothing at all!' (120). Their joint conclusion would be dramatically echoed again three-quarters of a century later by the protagonist of what is arguably the most striking twentieth-century example of entropic satire in its introverted, observer-oriented form, Albert Camus's *L'étranger* (1942; *The Outsider*).

Meursault, the eponymous 'stranger,' whose first name we never discover, seems to be a relatively ordinary sort of man who takes pleasure in ordinary things like swimming and eating at cafés. He has no particular difficulty in making friends, and is not unhappy with his position as an office-worker in the port of Algiers. His mother's death in an old-people's home does not seem to affect him unduly: his mother was old, and her death not unexpected. Shortly after attending her funeral he spends a day on the beach with some friends and during the course of it kills an Arab, pumping four extra bullets into the body for good measure. His only defence during his trial is that the murder took place 'à cause du soleil' (158) / 'because of the sun' (103). As the narrative ends he is in the death cell, waiting for his execution.

Meursault's attempt to attribute the murder to the heat of the sun only succeeds in causing laughter in the courtroom. But in a way the murder of the Arab is the lesser of two charges against which he is unable to mount a convincing defence. The greater crime, at least in the argument of the prosecuting counsel, is his unfeeling treatment of his mother and his indifferent reaction to her death: Meursault, argues the prosecution, put his mother into an old-age home in order to be rid of her; after her death he calmly smoked cigarettes and drank coffee in the presence of her dead body, and could not even remember her age; the very day after her death he went swimming and sunbathing and later went to the cinema and eventually to bed with a girl he happened to meet on the beach. A man capable of such heartless insensitivity, the prosecution concludes, is quite simply a moral monster capable of any enormity, a menace to society, and deserving of no clemency.

Even allowing for the courtroom rhetoric, we find much evidence in Meursault's first-person narration to support the case for the prosecution. Indifference is the hallmark of Meursault's character as it emerges from his own account. A handful of examples can stand for many. He does not deny that his mother's death left him unmoved: 'Sans doute, j'aimais bien maman, mais cela ne voulait rien dire' (102) / 'Certainly I'd been quite fond of mother – but really that didn't mean anything' (69). Marie, his girl-friend, suggests they should get married: 'J'ai dit que cela m'était égal ... que cela n'avait aucune importance' (69) / 'I said it was all the same to me ... it had no importance really' (48). Did he love her? 'Cela ne signifiait rien mais ... sans doute je ne l'aimais pas' (69) / 'That meant next to nothing – but I supposed I didn't' (48). Would he have agreed as readily to marry somebody else, then? 'Naturellement' (70) / 'Of course' (48). He agrees to write a scabrous letter on behalf of his next-door neighbour, one Raymond, insulting the latter's mistress, not because he has any feeling at all for either of them, but simply 'parce que je n'avais pas de raison de ne pas le contenter' (54) / 'I'd no reason not to satisfy him' (40). When Raymond subsequently gives his mistress a savage beating Meursault agrees to testify in his defence that she had provoked such treatment, not because he knows this to be the case, but simply because 'cela m'était égal' (62)/ 'it was all the same to me' (45). He turns down a promotion and a move to Paris because 'dans le fond cela m'était égal' (68) / 'basically it was all the same to me' (48). On trial for his life, he occasionally feels that perhaps he should say something in his own defence – 'Mais réflexion faite, je n'avait rien à dire' (152) / 'But on second thoughts I found I had nothing to say' (99). Meursault's silence and his indifference derive quite naturally, and without any theatricality, from his casually stated conviction that 'tout le monde sait que la vie ne vaut pas la peine d'être vécue' (173) / 'everybody knows life isn't worth living' (112).

It is this massive and all-embracing indifference that makes Meursault the moral monster he is in the prosecutor's eyes. Never once, the prosecutor observes to the jury, had Meursault displayed any emotion during his trial or shown any sign that he had any regrets. This is an accurate enough summary, Meursault agrees. What is past is past, as far as he is concerned, and there is simply no point in wasting time on regrets, whether for the murder of the Arab or the death of his mother or anything else. In principle all feelings are pointless, all personal relationships of purely pragmatic interest, without anything about them of lasting value. While this stamps him as soulless, inhuman, monstrous, and an intolerable threat to the stability of society itself in the eyes of the prosecutor, however, for Meursault himself it is an attitude so self-explanatory that it needs no discussion or justification. Indeed, as far as Meursault is concerned, few things, if any, warrant the trouble of discussion, for discussion involves interpretation, and one interpretation is basically as pointless as any other in a world where phenomena exist not in a pattern of meaningful relationship to each other but as discrete and random bits and pieces of experiential data. Meursault is more surprised at the vehemence of the prosecutor's condemnation of his act than he is at his interpretation of its meaning, and his sole attempt at justifying his action remains to blame it on the sun.

L'étranger differs markedly from the texts we have looked at so far in that it is not at all satirical in any overt, traditional way. There is no evidence at all of a focused, directed satire, that is to say – nor are we presented with a general panorama of a world gone mad, as we are, say, in Catch-22. Meursault's account, however, is satirical in an unfocused rather than a focused sense, in that what we are presented with, without any fanfare or hysteria, is a world that, though seemingly ordinary, quite simply does not make any sense at all. Or, more accurately, we are shown the effect on one man of the dead weight of a world where nothing matters or makes any difference any more. The oppressive sun becomes the appropriate symbol of this brute weight, much as the African jungle was for Bardamu, and the appropriate response is a state of perpetual daze. Meursault's mother's funeral takes place under the blinding glare of a sun that makes everything shimmer in its crushing heat. 'L'éclat du ciel était insoutenable' (29) / 'The dazzling sun was unbearable' (25), melting the tar on the road into a black mud through which Meursault trudges wearily after his mother's corpse, dazed, blinded, just as he had been the night before in the silence of the dazzlingly illuminated mortuary. His weariness, which he frequently refers to, is the link between the death of his mother at the beginning and the death of the nameless Arab at the end of the first part of his narrative. As he sets out for the beach on the fateful day it is again in a state of utter fatigue, with the sun once again beating down 'comme une gifle' (77) / 'like a fist' (53). The encounter with the Arab takes place with Meursault in an almost trancelike state and has the symmetrical structure of a dance, in this case literally a dance of death. The Arab, with his friends, has been following Raymond for several days – the girl Raymond had insulted and beaten up was his sister. On the beach 'le soleil tombait presque d'aplomb sur le sable et son éclat sur la mer était insoutenable ... Je ne pensais à rien parce que j'étais à moitié endormi par ce soleil sur ma tête nue' (85) / 'The sun was blazing down almost vertically on the sand, and the glare on the water was unbearable ... I wasn't thinking of anything because I was half asleep from the sun beating down on my bare head' (58). Meursault takes no part in the first confrontation: Raymond and another friend have a brief scuffle with the Arab and one of his friends before Raymond receives a superficial knife wound and the Arabs withdraw. The second encounter occurs later – 'le soleil était maintenant écrasant' (89) / 'the sun was crushingly hot now' (60) – when Raymond, now armed with a revolver, and Meursault confront the two Arabs again. This time, 'au coeur du silence et de la chaleur' (90) / 'surrounded by the silence and the heat' (61), Meursault uncharacteristically takes the initiative and insists that Raymond fight his man fairly while he, Meursault, covers the other with the gun. As Raymond hands him the revolver it flashes in the sun. 'J'ai pensé à ce moment qu'on pouvait tirer ou ne pas tirer' (91) / 'It crossed my mind that one might fire or not fire' (62), but suddenly the two Arabs slip quietly away again. The final confrontation involves only Meursault and the Arab, in the scorching heat of 'le même soleil que le jour où j'avais enterré maman' (94) / 'the same sun as on the day I buried my mother' (63). When the Arab pulls a knife, in what appears to be merely a warning gesture, the sun on the steel is like 'une longue lame étincelante qui m'atteignait au front' (94) / 'a long thin blade that transfixed my forehead' (64), like a 'glaive éclatant' (94), a 'dazzling sword' (64), like an 'épée brûlante' (95), a 'searing rapier' (64). Everything begins to reel and sway as 'le ciel s'ouvrait sur toute son étendue pour laisser pleuvoir du feu' (95) / 'the sky opened from end to end and rained sheets of fire' (64). When his finger tightens on the trigger it is the sun he shoots as much as the Arab, the sun as ultimate threat in the person of the Arab as immediate threat. 'J'ai secoué la sueur et le soleil' (95) / 'I shook away the sweat and the sun' (64). When Meursault is questioned later as to why he fired four more times into the Arab's dead body he obstinately refuses to give any answer, remembering once more the red glow of the beach and the sun smashing down on his bare head (106/71).

Meursault's narrative recounts the slow growth of an awareness, a movement from confusion to clarity and understanding. But this staple form of the *Bildungsroman* tradition, traditionally operating to privilege the notion of order and integration, is here subverted into privileging the notion of disorder and disintegration. Meursault's moment of insight comes in the closing pages of his narrative and serves to illuminate for him with blinding clarity in the light of his own impending death what had failed to emerge for him previously from the death either of his mother or of the nameless Arab. The insight is a crushingly simple one, and it is the same insight regulating the behaviour of Bardamu and Yossarian: death is all there is. Throughout his life he had functioned as if nothing mattered, as if nothing had any intrinsic importance, but he must look on the face of his own individual death before it becomes incontestably clear just *why* nothing matters: 'Du fond de mon avenir, pendant toute cette vie absurde que j'avais menée, un souffle obscur remontait vers moi à travers des années qui n'étaient pas encore venues et ce souffle égalisait sur son passage tout ce qu'on me proposait alors dans les années pas plus réelles que je vivais' (183) / 'From the depths of my future, my whole absurd life long, a lazy breeze had been blowing towards me across the years that were yet to come, and on its way that breeze had levelled out all the things people tried to foist on me in the equally unreal years I then was living through' (118). This is the insight he had already caught an inadequate glimpse of in the wrinkled faces and nodding heads of the old people who had come to pay his mother their last respects and who sat immobile and in silence in the blinding light of the mortuary chapel. 'Je les voyais comme je n'ai jamais vu personne et pas un détail de leurs visages ou de leurs habits ne m'échappait. Pourtant je ne les entendais pas et j'avais peine à croire à leur réalité ... J'ai eu un moment l'impression ridicule qu'ils étaient là pour me juger' (18–19) / 'Never in my life had I seen anyone so clearly as I saw these people; not a detail of their clothes or features escaped me. And yet I couldn't hear them, and it was hard to believe they really existed ... For a moment I had the ridiculous impression that they had come to sit in judgement on me' (19–20). This moment of close, even fascinated attention to the outside world is again quite uncharacteristic of Meursault, for he behaves for the most part as if separated from his surroundings by some sort of impenetrable screen or barrier that prevents him from ever quite making contact.

His account begins with a confusion: 'Aujourd'hui, maman est morte. Ou peut-être hier, je ne sais pas' (9) / 'Mother died today. Or, maybe, yesterday; I can't be sure' (13). Disturbed and delayed perception characterizes the entire account of his mother's funeral. He doesn't listen to what the director of the home is telling him. The concierge's remarks on the necessity for rapid burial in such a hot climate make an impact on him only later, when the concierge is talking about something quite different. He remembers the concierge bringing him coffee, but not what happens after that. The funeral itself passes in a blur. He is belatedly struck by random details, such as the pervasive hum of insects. None of these details is particularly striking in itself, but together they paint a picture of a man asleep or in a daze – a man who, like Josef K. in Kafka's *Prozess*, may one day be called upon to wake up. During his vigil Meursault at one point starts groggily awake to find one of the old men staring at him, 'Comme s'il n'attendait que mon réveil. Puis j'ai encore dormi' (21) / 'as if he had only been waiting for me to wake. Then I fell asleep again' (21). Throughout his trial he similarly seems to 'forget' that he *is* on trial. After his first interrogation by the examining magistrate he is about to shake hands until he 'remembers' that perhaps he should not since he has killed somebody. It takes him by surprise that he had never really realized before that the point of putting someone in prison is to deprive them of their freedom. He is 'astonished' when he suddenly realizes that the courtroom audience, which he had up to that point registered only vaguely, turns out to contain in fact many people with whom he is closely connected.

Meursault lacks the ability to reach out and touch other people, to establish contact with them, to communicate. The visiting hour in the prison constitutes the appropriate image of this lack: a huge room with prisoners on one side, visitors on the other, and between them two long grilles separated by eight or ten metres of empty space. Some people manage to converse well enough across this barrier, but for Meursault the gap is not merely physical. Above all he wishes not to become involved in explanations. After his mother's death he avoids eating at his usual café, because they would have asked him questions about the funeral. After Raymond is wounded by the Arab Meursault avoids having to give his other friends any explanation, because he can see no point in doing so. During his hearings he readily admits to being taciturn and uncommunicative: 'C'est que je n'ai jamais grand-chose à dire. Alors je me tais' (104) / 'I rarely have anything much to say. So I keep quiet' (70). His own silence is reflected in the silence of a world that also does not have anything much to say, the silence of the mortuary, of the beach just before the murder, of the prison late at night. Communication is simply a noisy form of silence, to which Meursault typically reacts with 'une sorte d'étourdissement' (115) / 'a sort of dizziness' (76). His trial, with the prosecution and defence alternately explaining and counter-explaining his behaviour, is the culmination of this noisy silence: 'tout devenait comme une eau incolore où je trouvais le vertige' (160) / 'everything was dissolving into a watery haze and making me dizzy' (104).

Meursault's reluctance to enter into contact with others is clearly in some sense a form of escape. So is his excessive love of sleep, which is a leitmotif of his account up to the murder of the Arab, the result of a perpetual weariness and fatigue. In prison he eventually manages to sleep up to eighteen hours a day, leaving only six to kill, as he says himself. Even before going to prison, killing time was a major preoccupation: he fills an entire Sunday with simply staring into the street from his window and smoking cigarettes. Work, even though he has difficulty in getting up in the mornings, and the trivial details of the daily routine are a welcome escape. His room is a haven: after his mother leaves the apartment for the old-age home he collects everything he needs into his bedroom and lives from then on in that one room. He develops a similar liking for his prison cell, as opposed to the raucous visiting room. Even the murder of the Arab is the result of an attempt to escape, to escape everything all at once by once and for all obliterating it. From the very beginning he is simultaneously aware that there can be no real escape, as emerges from his comment on a remark of the district nurse at his mother's funeral, a remark about the effects of walking in the sun: 'Elle m'a dit: "Si on va doucement, on risque une insolation. Mais si on va trop vite, on est en transpiration et dans l'église on attrape un chaud et froid." Elle avait raison. Il n'y avait pas d'issue' (30) / 'What she said was: "If one goes too slowly, there's the risk of a heat-stroke. But if one goes too fast one perspires, and the cold air in the church gives one a chill."

She was right. There was no way out' (26). Months later, in his prison cell, he remembers the nurse and her remark and repeats: 'Non, il n'y avait pas d'issue' (126) / 'No, there was no way out' (83). And yet, even after he is sentenced to the death penalty we still find him ruminating on what he very well knows to be the non-existent chances of escape: 'savoir si l'inévitable peut avoir une issue' (165) / 'to find out if the inevitable can leave any way out' (107). It takes the outburst of pent-up anger released by what he sees as the chaplain's facile belief in a self-evident redemptive meaning to life to make him realize that the only way one can escape is not backwards but forwards. Hope is simply an impediment to the acceptance of reality; the only way out – as the narrator of *Catch-22* might put it – is the acceptance that there is no way out.

Meursault's world is an entropic one, an in-different world where nothing matters, a world where stasis reigns and norms lose all validity. The comedy, an uneasy comedy, more subliminal than overt, arises from the narrator Meursault's account of the character Meursault's stumbling efforts to come to grips with this one basic given, which throughout seems simultaneously to be within and yet beyond his reach. He is continually ill at ease with conventions of behaviour, for example. 'Naturally' he would marry any other woman just as easily, he tells Marie. 'Naturally,' he says he does not believe in God, even though a polite evasion would clearly be immensely to his advantage as far as his trial is concerned. Rather than feeling any regret for the murder he has committed, he likewise admits publicly only to a certain feeling of boredom with the whole affair. Nor will he allow his defence counsel to draw a veil of polite sentiment over his lack of any show of grief at his mother's funeral. By sticking to his private version of what is natural, obvious, and true Meursault manages to become his own most effective accuser, because his views are not ones that society at large can afford to share. Meursault is no rebel, no social revolutionary, however. He is concerned that his employer will think he has used his own mother's death to get an extra free day off work, and excuses himself for the nuisance as not being his fault, any more than it is his fault if people break his employer's rule of no personal telephone calls in the office. He works hard and well, to the extent that his employer wants to promote him to the Paris office. It is not that Meursault does not *want* to fit in or that he even consciously objects to a society found to be hypocritical and deceitful; it is rather that he *cannot* fit in. He is in fact tolerant to the degree that he fully understands the prosecution's case against him, just as he understands the old man Salamano's mistreatment of his dog or Raymond's mistreatment of his mistress. His tolerance is in fact his undoing, for a society can continue to exist only if it characterizes certain practices as acceptable and certain others as unacceptable – though the degree of acceptability of the same set of actions can of course vary very widely both from one society to another and in the same society at different times, such as in times of war as opposed to times of peace.

Ironically, it is because he *does* intervene, quite uncharacteristically, to prevent Raymond from shooting the Arab in the first place, insisting on a fair fight by socially accepted rules, with himself as referee, that he becomes a murderer, since his reason for taking the gun from Raymond in the first place is to ensure fair play. Indicatively, he devises three separate and successive sets of rules ensuring this 'fair play,' the first requiring that the Arab say something before being shot, the second that he draw his knife first, and the third that there be no shooting at all, but that Raymond should fight him hand to hand. With the revolver in his hand, however, Meursault reflects that in the long run it simply boils down to the physical act of either pulling the trigger or not pulling it, however many rules of fair play are drawn up. When he finally shoots the Arab himself it is in accordance with his own second rule of fair play (since the Arab draws his knife), but it is also quite clear that the rules have in fact nothing at all to do with the whole affair. For all the intricate choreography of the almost ceremonial killing of the victim, in the end his death is the result of pure chance.

Chance is the arch-enemy of order, and ultimately all social systems depend on its regulation. The arbitrary must be incorporated in an order capable of invalidating it. The reaction of the religiously minded examining magistrate when Meursault declares himself a non-believer is indignation: How can there be any meaning to life without a belief in a meaning-giving God? Meursault replies that it really has nothing to do with him, but what for Meursault is tolerance, or indifference, is enough to categorize him for the prosecutor as an intolerable menace to the very fabric of an ordered society; for if the Meursaults cannot be stamped out, then society, sooner or later, will be forced to face the possibility that 'aucune de ses certitudes ne valait un cheveu de femme' (182) / 'none of their certainties was worth one strand of a woman's hair' (118). In a world where nothing matters nothing changes, and all courses of action are equally neutral, equally pointless, equally uninterpretable. The elaborate staging of the Arab's death is the formal equivalent of this story of moral and hermeneutic stasis. In three successive versions of the encounter the Arab wins the first, evades the issue in the second, and is killed in the third, while Meursault himself merely observes in the first, intervenes to regulate the second, and kills in the third. These are possible alternative outcomes, in possible alternative worlds, and any one means no more or no less than either of the others. Any one of them could have been the end of the affair, only one of them is, and this fact is without moral value. Meursault's relationship to his mother is likewise paralleled by the encounter during the prison interview scene of the unnamed young prisoner and his mother who find nothing at all to say to each other until the young man's parting words, 'Au revoir, maman.' Other possibilities of relationships are presented in the apparent affection of the old man Thomas Pérez for Meursault's mother, Raymond's abuse of his mistress, Meursault's own indifferent relationship to Marie, and the old man Salamano's love-hate relationship with his dog. Salamano has only abuse for his mangy old dog for years until the dog gets lost, whereupon he goes to pieces. Here too are possible worlds, with a variety of alternative relationships displayed, as it were, for the window-shopper to choose from: Meursault's gaze, however, registers little meaningful distinction, perceives little reason for preferring one mode of existence to any of the others. This impassivity is itself paralleled in the lapidary gaze of the group of Arabs who watch Meursault and Raymond, totally without emotion: 'Ils nous regardaient en silence, mais à leur manière, ni plus ni moins que si nous étions des pierres ou des arbres morts' (79) / 'They were staring at us silently, in their own fashion, as if we were stones or dead trees' (54). Their fashion is, of course, his fashion of seeing things too: in killing the Arab, Meursault in a manner of speaking both behaves consistently and commits a form of displaced suicide.

These narrative reflections and refractions are indicative of the importance of observation in the structure of Camus's text. Not only is Meursault on trial by judge and jury; Meursault the character is throughout on trial, under observation in a series of narrative experiments conducted by Meursault the narrator. The observation motif is mirrored too in the story – Meursault himself, initially at least, is quite interested in watching his own trial, never having seen one before (128/84). There are the journalists, with their blasé air of ironic indifference (132/86), and among them especially the young man in the grey suit who rather than writing lays down his pen and simply stares at Meursault: 'j'ai eu l'impression bizarre d'être regardé par moi-même' (132) / 'I had the odd impression of being scrutinized by myself' (87) – one of the reasons, perhaps, the narrator goes on, why he was unable to follow what was going on with any attention. (Camus, we may remember, was a journalist himself at the time he wrote *L'étranger*.) When Meursault returns to the courtroom to hear the jury's verdict and his death sentence, he notices that the young journalist has averted his gaze. As he awaits execution he further remembers hearing that his father had once witnessed a public execution and spent the remainder of the morning at home being sick: 'à l'idée d'être le spectateur qui vient voir et qui pourra vomir après, un flot de joie empoisonée me montait au coeur' (168) / 'the mere thought of being an onlooker who comes to see the show, and can go home and vomit afterwards, flooded my mind with a wild, absurd exultation' (109). After the idea of escape is abandoned, Meursault's narrative ends with the observation that the appropriate and not unsatisfactory end to his life would be to have 'beaucoup de spectateurs le jour de mon exécution et qu'ils m'accueillent avec des cris de haine' (186) / 'a huge crowd of spectators on the day of my execution and that they should greet me with howls of execration' (120).

While in prison, Meursault finds under his mattress an old scrap of newspaper containing part of the story of a man who leaves home to make his fortune and returns to his family twenty-five years later without revealing his identity, only to be murdered for his money by his mother and sister. Meursault develops a fascination for this bizarre little story and reads it to himself over and over again, concluding eventually that the man 'l'avait un peu mérité et qu'il ne faut jamais jouer' (125) / 'deserved it to some extent – one shouldn't try to play games' (82). While this may indeed be the opinion of the character Meursault, it is scarcely adhered to by the narrator – that is to say, Meursault after as opposed to Meursault before his final illumination. (We find very much the same relationship with regard to games, incidentally, in another outsider's narrative in Hesse's *Der Steppenwolf*.) Only a page later Meursault the narrator relates that Meursault the character one day, after five months in prison, looked at his reflection in his tin dish: 'Il m'a semblé que mon image restait sérieuse alors même que j'essayais de lui sourire. Je l'ai agitée devant moi. J'ai souri et elle a gardé le même air sévère et triste' (126) / 'It seemed to me that my reflection remained serious even when I tried to smile at it. I moved it about in front of me. I smiled and it retained the same sad and serious expression' (83). Repeating the experiment, Meursault suddenly realizes that the sound he has been vaguely aware of for days is the sound of his own voice.

In any narrative recounting a *Bildungserlebnis*, a progress from confusion to clarity, there is always an element of at least potential humour, as the narrator, who knows the appropriate context, puts the character, who operates in varying stages of ignorance of the appropriate context, through a variety of experiences and experiments that the character is going to misunderstand and misinterpret. First-person narratives can exploit this humour potential particularly effectively by confusion of the narrated I-then and the narrating I-now. Camus's text achieves this end inter alia by juxtaposing passages where narrator and character are clearly separated by extended periods of time and passages of a journal-like character where narrator and character are much closer together both in terms of time and in terms of psychological reactions. While most of *L'étranger* is written in the first of these narrative modes, there are sufficient examples of the latter to introduce doubt in the reader's mind as to the exact relationship of the narrating voice (which we will certainly be tempted to rely upon as an arbiter of truth) and the character (whose misunderstandings and confusions we are unlikely to be unduly surprised by). The opening paragraph indeed leads us to expect a journal, a day-to-day presentation of events – the narrator's mother has just died. The second paragraph follows with a series of future tenses, as the narrator plans his journey to attend the funeral. The third paragraph, however, recounts in the past tense the events presented in the second paragraph as planned future events, and thereafter the past tense – more accurately, the *passé composé* – becomes and remains the narrative norm. Every so often, however, a reference to present time recurs to discomfit the reader afresh: 'c'est aujourd'hui samedi' (33) / 'today is Saturday' (27); 'aujourd'hui j'ai beaucoup travaillé' (43) / 'I was very busy today' (33); 'hier c'était samedi' (57) / 'yesterday was Saturday' (41). The reader, in other words, is impelled by narrative sleight of hand to shuttle backwards and forwards between the narrated first person and the narrating first person and thus to share in the confusion of the former as well as the detached observation of the latter. (Kafka achieves a similar end by different means in *Der Prozess*, as we shall see further on.)

The comedy in *L'étranger* is elusive – and many readers would no doubt deny that it is there at all. It resides, however, on the one hand in the character Meursault's inability to relate the discrete phenomena he perceives to any explanatory, meaning-giving context, and on the other in the fact that when the narrator Meursault eventually provides the narrative frame that allows *us* to see the character's reactions in an explanatory context, the context ordering the whole turns out to be based on a vision not of order but of entropy. Meursault throughout has difficulty in interpreting (that is to say, contextualizing) discrete events; the reader in turn has difficulty in interpreting or contextualizing this failure; and the explanatory 'punch line,' when it arrives, legitimizes rather than corrects the failure to discover meaning. The reader is continually faced with situations where he or she is uncertain as to the appropriate degree of 'seriousness' with which to interpret an interpretive failure on Meursault's part, such as the old people at his mother's wake who nod continually, leaving him unsure whether they are greeting him or just nodding off, or the Sunday strollers passing by under his window who 'm'ont fait des signes' (39, 40) / 'made signs to me' (31, 32) that, however, remain impenetrable. Meursault as character continually concludes that events to which the reader would probably be inclined to attribute significance mean nothing at all, such as whether he loves Marie or wants to marry her, or whether the Arab should live or die. Occasionally he devotes what seems like quite unnecessary attention to an apparently totally insignificant detail, as when he deduces from the movements of the nurse's arms that she is knitting (18/19). And on one occasion he is cast in the role of explicator himself in a comic *mise en abyme*, when he goes to the cinema with his friend Emmanuel, who never understands what's going on and has to have it all explained to him (57/41).

Other than concluding that nothing means anything at all, Meursault has one interpretation of events that recurs with some regularity, and that is to find them ridiculous. The trial and the interrogations are 'un jeu' (100) / 'a game' (67), the crime itself ridiculous (129/85). He finds his own lack of interest in defending himself ridiculous and especially his own claim that the sun was to blame (158/103). He also finds his own defence counsel's arguments ridiculous (159/104), just as he does the notion that he will actually be killed as a result of the sentence (167/108), just as he had found it ridiculous that the old people at the wake might somehow be sitting in judgment on him (19/20). The imposing mechanism of law and order *is* there to judge him, but it is no less ridiculous, since law and order themselves are merely comic fictions. On the other hand, none of it matters anyway, and this is the most ridiculous thing of all. Guilty or not, everybody is condemned anyway. The chaplain, for example, so confident of the redemptive power of his faith: 'Lui aussi, on le condamnerait. Qu'importait si, accusé de meurtre, il était exécuté pour n'avoir pas pleuré à l'enterrement de sa mère?' (184) / 'He would be condemned too one day. And what would it matter if after having been accused of murder he was executed for not weeping at his mother's funeral?' (119). One truth is as valid as the other – and as invalid. 'Voilà l'image de ce procès. Tout est vrai et rien n'est vrai!' (141) / 'That's typical of this trial. Everything is true and nothing is true' (92). Meursault's entropic vision of a world where nothing makes any difference whatsoever clearly points towards our next mode, that of entropic irony, where we find strong family relationships between *L'étranger* and such texts as Kafka's *Prozess* and Sartre's *Nausée*. While Josef K. and Roquentin are both in their different ways obsessed by the search for a putative meaning in the world they inhabit and by the simultaneous unattainability of any verifiable knowledge about it, however, the emphasis in Meursault's world is quite different. *L'étranger* is entropic satire rather than entropic irony in that Meursault is less obsessed by the assumed meaning or senselessness of an indifferent world than he is quite simply stunned, dazed by the dead weight of a world gone silent, a world that is beyond the reach of satire, where nothing is more or less important than anything else, and where any attempted gesture whether of self-assertion or self-defence is not just futile but quite simply ridiculous.

8 Entropic Irony: Information and Interpretation

Stat rosa pristina nomine, nomina nuda tenemus.

Umberto Eco

The original rose exists only as a name, mere names are all we have.

Entropic satire, then, is concerned with the (entropic) reactions of characters to the (entropic) story-world in which they exist: Bardamu is appalled by the senseless savagery of the world of which he is part, Yossarian vainly attempts to find a point of purchase in a lunatic world of which he too is a part, Oskar as character vainly and hypocritically shapes and reshapes his own world of hypocrisy and cant, and Meursault is quite simply mesmerized by the appalling, lunatic, hypocritical, and essentially *pointless* world that eventually – as he always knew it would – crushes him as casually as he himself might casually have stepped on an ant. It is typical of these worlds of entropic satire that they remain entirely unchanged, totally impassive to any impact, ameliorative or otherwise, on the part of the characters who play out their parts in them.

As argued already in chapter 6, this relationship of character and story-world, for all the possible vagaries of narrative technique involved, is essentially an entirely 'normal,' entirely realist one – even when that relationship may operate within a text like *Die Blechtrommel*, which in other ways has a good deal more in common with postmodernism than with realism. In our next category of the comedy of entropy, that classified as entropic irony, the relationship between the character and his world is an entirely different one, one where the emphasis is far less on the 'realist' relationship between character and *story*-world than on the 'modernist' relationship between character and *discourse*-world, between the character, that is, as a narrated entity and the narrative instance that shapes that character's being. If entropic satire, to repeat, is essentially concerned with the observation of anomie, entropic irony is essentially concerned with information and its interpretation. This is true in different ways of all four of the representative texts we will examine in this chapter, all of which are concerned with the essential duplicity of meaning, but perhaps it is most immediately and startlingly true of Kafka's *Der Prozess* (1925; *The Trial*), to which we will turn first.

Narration and Knowledge: Kafka's *Der Prozess*

Josef K., thirty years old, holder of a good job in a bank in an unnamed city reminiscent of turn-of-the-century Prague, and not aware of having committed any crime, wakes up one morning to find himself under arrest. He is indeed free to carry on with his normal routine, but he is under arrest none the less. He is never informed what his offence has been or what sort of court or code of law he has come up against, but his guilt is clearly assumed. Casual acquaintances seem to be much more aware of the existence of this court than he is, but even its officials, when he succeeds in questioning them, are incapable of grasping its subtleties or perhaps even its essence. But perhaps these officials, though clearly functionaries of considerable importance, are after all simply too low down in the hierarchy to have any real information, for the high judges are so very remote that even their existence is not entirely certain. Summoned to an interrogation in a squalid suburb, Josef K. indignantly denounces the sham, hypocrisy, and illogicality of so iniquitous and so foolish a system, and then sets out energetically to prove himself innocent of whatever it is that he is being accused of. He spends an entire year looking for people who may be able to help him, such as his fellow lodger, a Fräulein Bürstner (whom he casually attempts to seduce while telling her of his arrest), his landlady, or a washerwoman whom he believes to be associated in some capacity with the court. Initially full of self-confidence, K. gradually becomes increasingly demoralized. With the help of his uncle, who moves into town to help him, he succeeds in locating a reputedly powerful advocate named Huld, but while his uncle is arguing K.'s case with the lawyer K. himself slips out of the room to make love to the lawyer's nurse, Leni. A business associate points him towards a painter named Titorelli, who is allegedly the official portrait painter for the court. Titorelli explains at great length the three possible outcomes of K.'s trial: a definite acquittal, which, however, is unheard of; an ostensible acquittal, which does not prevent its recipient from possible re-arrest even before he leaves the courtroom; and an indefinite postponement, which simply leaves things exactly as they are. (Not surprisingly, perhaps, Titorelli's paintings, as far as K. can see, all look exactly the same.) K. abandons Titorelli, attempts to dismiss Huld, thinks about submitting a private plea on his own behalf though there is no evidence that such a plea would ever be read by anybody, and discusses his case with a ruined businessman named Block, who has also been arrested, who maintains a whole stable of advocates all working away busily on his behalf, and whose case is none the less hopelessly bogged down, just as it has been for the last several years. In the cathedral of the unnamed city, where business affairs have taken K., he is addressed from the pulpit by a priest who claims to be a prison chaplain and officer of the court, and who informs K. that his trial is going very badly for him and that he has completely misunderstood the entire nature of the proceedings. The priest recounts a parable about a 'man from the country' who comes to the door of the Law seeking admission, only to be informed by a door-keeper that he cannot be admitted at the moment. For many years the man sits before the Law, more and more feebly trying to persuade the door-keeper to admit him. Finally his strength is exhausted, and as he lies dying he asks the door-keeper why, since the door is always open, nobody else has sought admission to the Law in all these years. The door-keeper replies that that door had been intended solely for the man from the country – and now he (the door-keeper) was going to close it. Exactly one year after his initial arrest K. is visited by two further emissaries of the court, two plump and well-dressed men in top hats who lead him away unresisting. With great politeness they prepare his execution. At the last moment a window in a nearby house flies open, and a figure leans far out with arms outstretched, possibly to offer some help, possibly without any relevance whatsoever. At any rate it is too late. The knife is already embedded and twisted for good measure in K.'s heart, and his executioners are watching with polite interest as he dies, 'wie ein Hund' / 'like a dog.'

'Jemand musste Josef K. verleumdet haben, denn ohne dass er etwas Böses getan hätte, wurde er eines Morgens verhaftet' (7) / 'Somebody must have been telling lies about Josef K., for without his having done anything wrong he was arrested one morning' (1). In the opening sentence of *Der Prozess* we are faced as readers with an exacerbated version of the predicament that faces any reader of any fictional text: we are challenged to begin determining a reading, to make a decision. The challenge is an aggressive one in this case. Who is the someone who 'must' have been telling lies? Who says he (or she) must have been lying? What sort of lies? What sort of 'wrong' has Josef K. allegedly not done? Why does he not enjoy a full surname? What sort of arrest is involved? All our initial, tentative answers must remain provisional, any attempt at an interpretive decision must be deferred as we read on, assuming that further information will enable us to fill in the gaps so rapidly opened under our feet by the opening statement, the opening act of narration. For all our information, all our knowledge of this textual world, is dependent upon this narrating voice who (or which) is, we hope, master of the knowledge we assume will be imparted to us in due course. Etymology, after all, supports this assumption: to narrate, *narrare*, is possible because the speaker is *gnarus*, a knowing one, and *gnoscere*, *gignoskein*, 'to know' is to be master of the communicative situation, to be an authority who narrates what he knows. This etymologically untroubled linkage of knowledge and narration as cause and effect, origin and presence, is undermined, however, not only by our first sentence but by the very first word. 'Jemand,' 'somebody,' is a narrative presence marking an epistemological absence – the narrator 'knows' it was somebody if only because the verb *verleumden*, 'to tell lies about,' must have a grammatical subject, but he allegedly does not know or is unwilling for some reason to admit that he knows who that somebody was. This opening play with concealment and revelation is merely the first example of a technique massively employed throughout the narrative, namely a deconstructive giving of information with one hand and taking it back with the other.

But who is this information giver? It is by now a commonplace of Kafka criticism that the narrating voice in *Der Prozess*, as in many other Kafka texts, is close to, but not identical with, the voice of the character Josef K.'s own consciousness. Early critics – the text was published in fragmentary form in 1925 after Kafka's death – were seduced by this apparent closeness of the narrator and the main character into assuming that the perspectives were identical – and indeed throughout much of the text it is quite impossible to distinguish them conclusively. Nevertheless, there are also several points in the text – although different readers may not be able to reach agreement as to which points they are, exactly – where the narrating voice does rather more obviously step back and align itself, even if only fleetingly, with the position of an observer rather than that of an observed. Concentrating on the level of story tends to focus our attention unwaveringly on the observed, while a consideration of discourse clearly shifts our focus rather to the observer and the relationship between the observing subject and the observed object. From the beginning the text itself is full of watchers observing Josef K. The old lady across the street who is watching him through the window as he lies in bed in the very opening paragraph is soon joined by an old man and then by a young man, all of whom simply observe K. as he is arrested. This is their only function as characters. Once their observations are terminated they leave the text and are never seen again. Their places are soon filled by a whole series of others, however: the spectators at K.'s interrogation, the girls as he talks to Titorelli the painter, the priest in the cathedral, the executioners as he dies. Sometimes, however, it is K. himself who is the observer. The most notable occurrence of this is in the fifth chapter, 'Der Prügler' / 'The Whipper,' where K. watches, in a room he had thought to be merely a *Rumpelkammer* or lumber-room, as a man clad in black leather brutally whips the two warders involved in K.'s initial arrest in consequence of a complaint that K. has allegedly made about their behaviour on that occasion. As the alleged plaintiff, K. is thus in a transferred or synecdochic sense the whipper, but he simultaneously wonders uneasily if the whip really hurts as much as it seems to do, and is later made to reflect that 'so wäre es einfacher gewesen, K. hätte sich selbst ausgezogen und dem Prügler als Ersatz für die Wächter angeboten' (67) / 'it would have been simpler to take off his own clothes and offer himself to the whipper as a substitute for the warders' (88). In this crucial scene the narrative self-consciously refers to its own central structural principle, as K. is identified simultaneously as whipper, whipped, and observer. K. as observer, that is, projects himself into two separate and complementary roles at once as winner and loser, active and passive, subject and object. K. in other words is playing with a decision, or perhaps it would be more accurate to say that a decision is playing with him. He eventually cuts the knot by refusing to make the decision and simply slams the door. But the knot refuses to stay cut: next day he opens the door to the lumber-room again, 'wie aus Gewohnheit' (68) / 'as if out of habit' (89), and is faced with exactly the same scene, unchanged by any passage of time. Again he responds by slamming the door, but as if realizing his inability to escape from the potentially endlessly recurring situation by mere postponement he now erases it: 'Räumt doch endlich die

Rumpelkammer aus!' he cries, almost in tears, to the bank attendants. 'Wir versinken ja im Schmutz!' (68) / 'Clear the lumber-room
out, can't you? ... We're smothering in dirt' (90).

Josef K.'s momentary play with the hypothetical possibility of
being either whipper or whipped is a reflection of the text's play with
the polar opposites of domination and defeat, as seen also in various
other active/passive groupings: arrestors/arrested, seducers/seduced,
advisers/advised, door-keeper/suppliant, executioners/executed. In
the world of the story Josef K. balances whipper against whipped. In
the world of discourse the narrator balances K. the master against K.
the victim – as, for example, during the first interrogation, where K. is
shown as pendulating wildly between total domination of the situation and utter defeat. In the world of narration as opposed to text, to
go one step further, the implied author has the narrator now identify
with K., whether victorious or defeated, now back off for impartial
observation of the defeats or victories. Behind the implied author we
may, if we wish, catch glimpses of the real author, Franz Kafka
himself, as he identifies now with this textual possibility, now with
that, simultaneously spider and fly, spinning and trapped at the
centre of his webwork of language, a perennial observer slamming
one lumber-room door after another on his own interrogation, but
never coming to the final door since in an infinite series the final
term by definition endlessly recedes. Kafka's texts – and *Der Prozess*
is no exception – always appear to be searching desperately for an
elusive answer, but they never find it precisely because they do not
set out to find it; they set out only to search for it. Kafka's thematiza-
tion of the essentially abyssed structuration of narrative as the structural principle of his individual texts provides him with a refractive
technique, a series of prisms continually rebreaking and restating, a
series of superimposed filters providing a play of contrastive colora-
tions and effects. Viewed in this light Kafka's texts in general, and
Der Prozess in particular, constitute a theatre of alternatives, a narrative palimpsest formed by the process of erasure and reinscription of
hypothetical structures of possibility, an indefinitely extensible series of narrative paradigms that in the never-arriving end, like the
painter Titorelli's landscapes, are in one sense all exactly the same.
For all their surface multiplicity, 'die Schrift ist unveränderlich und
die Meinungen sind oft nur ein Ausdruck der Verzweiflung darüber
(158) / 'what is written is unalterable, and commentaries are often
simply an expression of despair with regard to it' (217), as the priest
tells Josef K. in his explication of the parable. The structure of *Der*

Prozess, indeed, is essentially paradigmatic rather than syntagmatic, implying a reading that is primarily vertical or metaphoric, as one reads lyric poetry, rather than horizontal or metonymic, as one reads traditional realist narrative fiction, characterized as it is by cause-and-effect motivation.

From this perspective, attempts to establish the correct chapter-order – for the traditional order is disputed – are essentially irrelevant, as is the fact that *Der Prozess*, like several other Kafkan texts, is unfinished. It would alter nothing if it had been finished. *Der Prozess* indeed has a final chapter, but the series of hypothetical scenarios bracketed between Josef K.'s awakening and his execution is infinitely extendable, a latter-day demonstration of Zeno's proof of the impossibility of motion. Nor should K.'s execution be regarded as in any way a definitive end, a final decision, an Archimedean point of privileged knowledge. Chronologically it is the final chapter of the narrative; structurally it is one more slamming of the lumber-room door. Josef K. will appear again as the protagonist of *Das Schloss* (*The Castle*). Kafka's texts, in short, generate a potentially infinite series of possible worlds, signifying nothing except the impossibility of exhausting the series. We set out each time with Kafka's questers in search of knowledge, and each time we – and they – must make do with narration. Paradoxically, we – and they – fail not because we are given too little information, but because we are provided with too much, an entropic superfluity of unorganizable information resulting in cognitive short-circuit. The obvious distinction is that for the characters who inhabit the world of story this situation is a tragic one, while for the observer attuned to the world of discourse the result is comedy. Kafka called only one of his texts *Die Verwandlung* (*The Metamorphosis*), but this would be a singularly appropriate overall title for his oeuvre as a whole, combining as it does the notion of ontological metamorphosis and theatrical scene-change. Kafka's oeuvre – and *Der Prozess* most especially – is a theatre of metamorphosis. Even more so, since nothing changes – 'Die Schrift ist unveränderlich' / 'what is written is unalterable' – it is simultaneously a comedy of stasis, a comedy whose central ludic mechanism is located precisely in the interstice between discourse and story, observer and observed, narration and knowledge.

Like Gregor Samsa in *Die Verwandlung*, who wakes up one morning to find himself transformed into a 'monstrous vermin,' Josef K., too, wakes up one morning to find himself transformed, changed like Gregor into something 'ungeheuer' / 'monstrous,' something that is no longer part of the familiar everyday world where it once belonged. Josef K. has been made strange, defamiliarized, 'arrested.' We do not actually witness his arrest. The first sentence seems to suggest that it has already taken place, but this suggestion is effectively retracted by the next three sentences, which show Josef K. in a frozen moment of time characterized primarily by an absence, a perceived lack – 'Die Köchin der Frau Grubach ... kam diesmal nicht' (7) / 'Frau Grubach's cook ... did not come this time' (1) – and by his being a specimen under the microscope for the observation of 'die alte Frau, die ihm gegenüber wohnte und die ihn mit einer an ihr ganz ungewöhnlichen Neugierde beobachtete' (7) / 'the old lady who lived opposite him and who was watching him with a curiosity quite unusual for her' (1). Nothing has yet happened. Josef K. is made to set his own 'trial' in motion by ringing the bell. 'Sofort klopfte es und ein Mann, den er in dieser Wohnung noch niemals gesehen hatte, trat ein' (7) / 'There was a knock on the door immediately, and a man whom he had never yet seen in that house entered' (1). The first words we witness Josef K. speaking are 'Wer sind Sie?' / 'Who are you?' directed to the man who turns out to be called Franz, Franz who is a 'Wächter,' a 'warder' who will watch over Josef K., and who is a parodic representative in the world of story of that other Franz who operates vicariously in a different world, the textual world of the implied author. Not only does K. not know who Franz is; he has difficulty in proving who he himself is – beyond producing his bicycle licence. 'War es eine Komödie, so wollte er mitspielen' (9) / 'If it was a comedy, he was going to play along' (5).

It *is* a comedy, but this fact is soon lost on Josef K. Ostentatiously observed by three officials, three clerks from the bank, and the three watchers from across the street, he is pointedly advised to collect himself: 'Denken Sie weniger an uns und an das, was mit Ihnen geschehen wird, denken Sie lieber mehr an sich' (14) / 'Think less of us and of what's going to happen to you, think more about yourself instead' (12). K., however, is too self-confident at this stage to be self-conscious and soon feels completely in control of the situation: 'Er spielte mit ihnen' (16) / 'He was playing with them' (14), as the narrator puts it, playing himself with Josef K. K.'s self-esteem suffers only a very minor setback when at the end of this episode he realizes that his conversation with the three bank clerks has prevented him from noticing the three officials leaving, just as earlier his dealings with the latter had prevented him from noticing the bank clerks in the first place. 'Viel Geistesgegenwart bewies das nicht' (18) / 'That did not show much presence of mind' (16), K. reflects, or the narrator observes, or both. K.'s next trial is the encounter with his fellow lodger, Fräulein Bürstner, which takes place in her bedroom. Once again the scenario is that of a contest, a game of victory or defeat in sexual terms, and at its conclusion K., having subdued Fräulein Bürstner with a long kiss, this time returns to his bed satisfied that the victory is his. The reader is less sure, since K.'s sexual 'victory' can just as easily be read as having been carefully orchestrated by the presumed victim herself. The high point of K.'s' 'seduction' is his narration of the course of his first interview with the officials, a retelling revealingly skewed by K.'s playing the role of the interrogating officer in his impromptu staging of the scene for Fräulein Bürstner's benefit – 'Ich bin der Aufseher' (25) / 'I am the inspector' (27) – while unaccountably 'forgetting' the role of the arrested K. 'Ja, ich vergesse mich. Die wichtigste Person' (25) / 'Why, I'm forgetting myself. The most important person' (27). As K.'s imitated shout of 'Josef K.!' shatters the silence, an irritated knocking from the room next door indicates that his cry has awakened a certain 'Hauptmann' Lanz – the title means 'captain,' but is also a play on 'the most important person.' K. himself, however, returns satisfied to his room and 'schlief sehr bald ein' (27) / 'very quickly fell asleep' (30). Thus ends the first chapter.

The next three chapters are characterized throughout by the same dialectic of apparent victory and apparent defeat, perceived superiority versus perceived inferiority. K. completely cows his interrogators during the so-called 'first interrogation' – which is really rather the third round in an ongoing interrogation. On his attempt to repeat his triumph a week later, however, he is thwarted by the discovery that no sitting has been scheduled. He is partly compensated for this setback by another apparent quick sexual victory over a washerwoman whom he perceives as being intimately connected with his tormentors, only to have her literally snatched from his grasp by a 'student,' one Berthold. 'K. sah ein, dass das die erste zweifellose Niederlage war, die er von diesen Leuten erfahren hatte' (46) / 'K. recognized that this was the first unequivocal defeat that he had received from these people' (58). Translated abruptly to the world of the court offices, K. arrogantly demonstrates his perceived superiority over a group of fellow defendants before being overcome by 'ein wenig Schwindel' (53) / 'a slight dizziness' (67) – 'Schwindel,' however, connoting 'swindle' as well as 'dizziness.' Leaving abruptly, K. adjusts his rumpled appearance with the help of a pocket mirror and 'lief dann die Treppe hinunter, so frisch und in so langen Sprüngen, dass er von diesem Umschwung fast Angst bekam' (57) / 'leapt down the stairs so buoyantly and with such long strides that he became almost afraid of his own reaction' (73). Chapter 4 finds him attempting to consolidate his earlier 'victory' over Fräulein Bürstner, but instead of the hoped-for passive victim he is this time confronted and his efforts decisively scotched by a forbidding Fräulein Montag, a Monday-morning 'friend' of Fräulein Bürstner.

We have already looked at the fifth chapter 'Der Prügler' / 'The Whipper,' in some detail, and have seen that it too functions as a 'pocket mirror' in which Josef K. can adjust his appearance. It demonstrates for K. – if he had the eyes to see it – the indecisiveness of his accumulated gains and losses. 'Ich bin es!' / 'It's me!' he cries to some bank attendants who approach as he slams the lumber-room door, 'es schreit nur ein Hund auf dem Hof' (66) / 'it's just a dog howling in the courtyard' (87). As K. watches from his window the reflection of the moon in the windows across the street,

> es quälte ihn, dass es ihm nicht gelungen war, das Prügeln zu ver-hindern, aber es war nicht seine Schuld, dass es nicht gelungen war, hätte Franz nicht geschrien – gewiss, es musste sehr weh getan haben, aber in einem entscheidenden Augenblick muss man sich beherrschen – hätte er nicht geschrien, so hätte K., wenigstens sehr wahrscheinlich, noch ein Mittel gefunden, den Prügler zu überreden. (66–7)

> he was deeply disappointed that he had not succeeded in preventing the whipping, but it was not his fault that he had not succeeded; if Franz had not shrieked – it must certainly have been very painful, but in a decisive moment one must control oneself – if he had not shrieked, then K., in all probability at least, would have found some means of persuading the whipper.

> (88)

This pivotal episode, the fifth of ten chapters, foreshadows Josef K.'s own execution down to the details of the moonlight, the windows, the executioners who watch the 'Entscheidung' (165) / 'decisive moment' (229), and his dying words, 'Wie ein Hund' (165) / 'Like a dog!' (229). If the text's implied author wanted to, he could certainly – or 'in all probability at least' – find a way to avert or at least postpone K.'s execution. But would there be any point? From the lumber-room scene on K.'s behaviour is characteristically 'müde und gedankenlos' (68) / 'tired and vacant' (90), and the remaining chapters, with the exception of the last, become increasingly prolix as the game scenarios of the earlier chapters give way to endless roundabout discussions in which an overwhelming excess of information deconstructs as an entropic absence of knowledge.

On the level of story, the level of Josef K.'s experience, the reader from now on shares K.'s hopelessness, while accompanying him sympathetically in his futile attempts to achieve some sort of clarity. On the level of discourse K.'s doomed efforts are distanced by a variety of narrative stratagems. K.'s 'Onkel Karl, ein kleiner Grundbesitzer vom Lande' (68) / 'Uncle Karl, a small land owner from the country' (91), or, as K. calls him, 'das Gespenst vom Lande' (69) / 'the ghost from the country' (92), materializes in chapter 6, his epithet of 'Grundbesitzer' connoting one who possesses 'reasons' for his actions and the doubled reference to his country origins pointing forward to the man from the country in the priest's parable who comes to gain entry to the Law. Uncle Karl, having heard of K.'s plight, is determined to expedite his affairs by resolute action and adroit use of professional connections, an attempt that is scuttled, however, by K.'s irresolution and maladroit efforts to exert an oblique influence himself through Leni, the advocate's maid. 'Je ruhiger ich bin, desto besser ist es für den Ausgang' (71) / 'The quieter I am, the better it will be in the end' (94) is now K.'s motto; his uncle, by contrast, continues the energetic line of attack that had been Josef K.'s in the earlier chapters. 'Deine Gleichgültigkeit bringt mich um den Verstand' (73) / 'Your indifference is driving me insane' (97), he upbraids the now increasingly passive K. This 'Onkel Karl,' in fact, who later metamorphoses without explanation into 'Albert K.' (78/100), functions as a discursive synecdoche for that side of K.'s nature which still believes that there is still some point in continuing the obviously uneven contest. The reverse synecdoche is presented in chapter 8, where K., during a momentary revival of confidence, is contrasted with the crawling and cowering merchant Block, who treats his own defence lawyer with all the dread of one facing his executioner. 'Dieses Kapitel wurde nicht vollendet' (144) / 'This chapter was not completed' (196) reads the editorial note at the end of chapter 8, a revelation concealing the endlessly extensible nature of the text. The two ostensible information givers of these chapters, the advocate Huld and the painter Titorelli, whose 'explanations' occupy the very long chapter 7, describe endless circles around the very absence of any explanation, never making any statement without simultaneously retracting it or qualifying it into meaninglessness. 'War es Trost oder Verzweiflung, was der Advokat erreichen wollte? K. wusste es nicht' (92) / 'Was it reassurance or despair that the lawyer was aiming at? K. did not know' (125). In similar vein, at the conclusion – or temporary conclusion – of Titorelli's lengthy explanations, when he finds that the artist's studio is itself actually part of the law courts, 'K. erschrak nicht so sehr darüber, dass er auch hier Gerichtskanzleien gefunden hatte, er erschrak hauptsächlich über sich, über seine Unwissenheit in Gerichtssachen' (121) / 'K. was startled not so much because there were Law Offices here too; he was chiefly startled by himself, by his own ignorance of the affairs of the Court' (164). K.'s bafflement is ironized by the discourse when he is made to buy several of Titorelli's heathscapes, each indistinguishable from all the others.

If the early chapters dealing with the possibility of achieving a decisive and privileged Archimedean point of external vantage are summarized and deconstructed in the relativity of chapter 5, 'Der Prügler' / 'The Whipper,' the later chapters thematizing indeterminacy are summarized and deconstructed in the relativity of chapter 9, 'Im Dom' / 'In the Cathedral.' As the whipper chapter provides a *mise en abyme* of the text's discursive method or narrative expression, so the cathedral chapter provides a *mise en abyme* of the story or narrative content in the parable of the 'Mann vom Lande,' the 'man from the country' who attempts with great perseverance but complete lack of success to gain entry to 'das Gesetz' / 'the Law.' 'Das Gesetz,' however, that which is 'set down' (*setzen*), that which is fixed, is as much subject to infinite regression as 'das Gericht' / 'the Court,' that which enunciates a final decision (*richten*), for Josef K. and the man from the country share the same crime, ignorance of the law, just as they are condemned to the same unappealable sentence, which is to remain ignorant of the law. Their search for the law is endlessly and irrevocably futile, for the law *is* to remain in ignorance of the law. Josef K. and his mirror image, the man from the country, are wholly innocent of all guilt in that they act in complete accord with this law of universal ignorance, but to be thus innocent is to partake of ineradicable guilt. Franz the warder knows this: 'Sieh, Willem, er gibt zu, er kenne das Gesetz nicht, und behauptet gleichzeitig, schuldlos zu sein' (11) / 'See, Willem, he admits that he doesn't know the law and claims at the same time to be innocent' (6–7). The final chapter, 'Ende' / 'The End,' portrays K. awaiting his executioners in a scene that parodically draws attention to its own theatricality

(162/223). As he walks to his death K. is grateful, and the narrator reports the fact in tagged direct monologue, 'dass man es mir überlassen hat, mir selbst das Notwendige zu sagen' (164) / 'that it has been left up to me to say what is necessary to myself' (226). 'Alle drei zogen nun in vollem Einverständnis über eine Brücke im Mondschein' (164) / 'All three now made their way in complete harmony across a bridge in the moonlight' (226) – a perfect scene of harmonious reconciliation, as it might appear. K.'s moment of insight, long postponed, is apparently now at last at hand:

> K. wusste jetzt genau, dass es seine Pflicht gewesen wäre, das Messer, als es von Hand zu Hand über ihm schwebte, selbst zu fassen und sich einzubohren. Aber er tat es nicht ... Vollständig konnte er sich nicht bewähren, alle Arbeit den Behörden nicht abnehmen, die Verantwortung für diesen letzten Fehler trug der, der ihm den Rest der dazu nötigen Kraft versagt hatte.   (165)

> K. realized quite clearly that his duty was supposed to be to seize the knife as it passed from hand to hand over him and stab himself. But he did not do so ... He could not completely rise to the occasion, could not relieve the authorities of all their tasks; the responsibility for this last failure lay with him who had refused him the remnant of necessary strength.   (228)

As K.'s glimpse of his own narrator exposes the theatricality of the hypothetical happy ending, all his doubts revive, and he dies, as he must, 'wie ein Hund' / 'like a dog,' watching his executioners watching him and his 'Entscheidung' (165) – the word connotes not only 'decision' or 'decisive moment,' but also an 'unsheathing.' The final decision, this 'unsheathing' of the butcher's knife, is not one determined by Josef K., but one that determines and terminates his futile search by abruptly cutting it short: an arbitrary end, at an arbitrary point, imposed from without. 'Es war, als sollte die Scham ihn überleben' (165) / 'It was as if the shame must outlive him' (229), reflects the text as K. dies – and there is no reason why it should not in the text's own terms, for K. has made no headway at all.

In the earlier chapters of *Der Prozess* the narrative voice throughout parodically balances victory and defeat in a continuing celebration of relativity. The later chapters explore the possibilities of indeterminacy as both an epistemological and a narrative problem. The element of discursive play, alerting the reader to the dual world of the narrative, is present throughout. The play with narrative distance begins with the first sentence and continues throughout the narrative. The dialectic of concealment and revelation is carried by such minute qualifications as that involved in the assertion that Frau Grubach's room after the arrest looks 'fast genau' (8) / 'almost exactly' (2) the same as it did the day before, or the observation that Franz 'sah K. mit einem langen, wahrscheinlich bedeutungsvollen, aber unverständlichen Blick an' (10) / 'gave K. a long, probably significant, but incomprehensible look' (6). There is parodic play with psychiatry's predilection for the unconscious mind, not only in the lumber-room episode but also in the 'unnützen Kram' (47) / 'useless rubbish' (60) of the attics where the court offices are housed. The central structural principle of *mise en abyme* is continually referred to and foregrounded. Other than the whipper scene and the parable in the cathedral there are K.'s own account of his arrest ostensibly for Fräulein Bürstner's benefit, K.'s encounter with the caretaker's son at the door of the building he himself lives in, the filthy pictures in the law books at the first interrogation, Titorelli's heathscapes, K.'s piecemeal examination of the picture in the cathedral (150/205), as well as the observers throughout and the continually recurring framing device of doors and windows, each one always an entrance into a possible new reality, a possible new way of seeing things. Above all there is the constant play on various levels of identity: Josef K.'s 'Wer sind Sie?' (7) / 'Who are you?' (1) addressed to Franz; the thrice-repeated cry 'Josef K.' (first from the supervisor of the warders, then from K. himself for Fräulein Bürstner's benefit, then from the priest in the cathedral); K.'s Uncle Karl who metamorphoses into Albert K.; K.'s 'Ich bin es' / 'It's me!' after the lumber-room scene; K.'s unprovoked inquiry of the merchant Block 'Ist das Ihr wirklicher Name?' (123) / 'Is that your real name?' (168), paralleling the earlier information that Titorelli's name is only a pseudonym (100/136). Finally, of course, there is the pervasive play with the reader, who is continually invited – whether intentionally or not is irrelevant – to resolve the narrative dilemmas in terms of Kafka's own biography, to which the text provides numerous references. *Der Prozess*, indeed, is centrally concerned with the play of questions rather than the provision of answers, and its central preoccupation is the self-undermining construction of the double bind, the impasse, the aporia: it is useless to go on talking, to continue searching for alternative solutions, new explanations, and yet going on talking is in the end the only way of postponing the admission of that uselessness.

K.'s infinitely repeatable encounters with the enigma of the court and the trial (and likewise K.'s encounters with the castle in *Das Schloss*) are characterized by a process of degeneration: beginning typically in a position of critical detachment and perceived superiority, K. slides time and again into confusion and eventually exhaustion and sleep. Language and communication repeatedly break down, yielding to cybernetic noise, informational entropy, communicational silence. The confrontation is overtly agonistic, gamelike: the trial is an hypostasized hermeneutic seduction, inviting and repelling penetration, characterized (like the castle in the later narrative) by multiple entrances and impregnable defences, provoking interpretive decisions on both Josef K.'s and the reader's part that immediately deconstruct in endless regression into the necessity for further interpretive decisions. Kafka's comedy is a discourse of disorientation and, insofar as they reveal fissures carefully concealed in our workaday notions of our own linguistic and hermeneutic competence, Kafka's texts (of which *Der Prozess* is certainly a typical example) explore an epistemological dilemma that has come to be central in contemporary critical thought. Kant, Husserl, Freud, Einstein, and Heisenberg have in turn drawn our attention to relativity and indeterminacy as basic constraints of hermeneutic performance, while Nietzsche and Heidegger, Derrida and Barthes alike have taught us to be wary of our traditionally assumed abilities as controllers rather than creatures of language. Kafka's texts, structured around a central vacuum simultaneously demanding and rejecting interpretation, thematize this moment of undecidability both in language and in the hermeneutic 'process.' Kafka's protagonists, like Josef K., are typically interpreters themselves of undecipherable 'texts,' and we as readers are offered the opportunity to observe not just their efforts but our own efforts to emulate them as well.

In the theatre of alternatives staged by Kafka's text, narration is simultaneously exorcism, therapy, prophylaxis, and parody. The obligation to *decide* is the central necessity and the central impossibility in this comedy of dilemma, and different observational aims determine different readings: the character Josef K. must decide how to act (or react), the reader must decide how to interpret and make sense of the text, the writer must decide among the multiple seductions of language, language that is the only guarantor of the link between narration and knowledge. The narrator, we remember, is *gnarus* by derivation, one who knows. Liddell and Scott's *Greek Lexicon* offers three areas of meaning for the root verb *gignoskein*: its primary meaning is 'to know, by the senses,' as Josef K. comes to know; its secondary meaning is 'to decide, to form an opinion,' a process whose impossibility is memorialized in the Kafkan text; its tertiary meaning, as sensible to the writer Kafka as to any of his fictional scapegoats, is 'to condemn.' Kafka's entire fictional universe can be read as an extended play on this single lexical entry, sustained by the forces linking decision and condemnation, narration and knowledge.

A Discourse on Absence: Sartre's *La nausée*

Like Josef K., Antoine Roquentin is 'arrested' one day too, stopped in his tracks by a sudden and problematic awareness: absent-mindedly picking up a stone on the beach to throw into the sea, as he had no doubt done hundreds of times before, he abruptly stops short, hesitates, drops the stone, and leaves, much to the amusement of a nearby group of watching children. Something, he reflects later, had suddenly 'disgusted' him, though he can no longer be sure whether it was the sea or the stone or something else entirely.

La nausée (*Nausea*), Jean-Paul Sartre's first novel, appeared in 1938, when Sartre was thirty-three, had finished his studies in philosophy at French and German universities, and had spent some time teaching at Le Havre, the model for the Bouville of the novel. *L'être et le néant* (*Being and Nothingness*), his first major philosophical work, appeared in 1943, and represents a systematic working out of the existential dilemma that had preoccupied Roquentin five years earlier. One obvious and predictable result of this sequence is that *La nausée* has traditionally been seen as very much a 'philosophical' novel, to be read with great earnestness for its insights into humankind's existential plight. As in the case of Kafka, though, there is a clearly identifiable streak of humour (as more than one critic has already observed) running through the text as well, and it is this apparent incongruity that most obviously prompts the present reading of *La nausée* as an example of entropic irony.

The theme of *La nausée*, as suggested by the title, is disgust: disgust with life, with self, with existence. The basic reason for this revulsion, paradoxically, is not any lack, but rather an over-plenitude, precisely the total *freedom* of existence, its total independence of the observing eye. The relationship between the unadulterated existence of the concrete object and the sense-making vision of the observing eye is the central concept of phenomenological thought, of which Sartre is an outstanding practitioner. For the phenomenologist 'existence' precedes 'essence,' the concrete object is logically prior to its intellectually apprehended nature. Raw existence, in other words, is transformed into essence, into systematic relationships, by an interpretive process of organization and rationalization, and these relationships are canonized by being assigned names. For the idealist and rationalist tradition the converse is true, a general Idea – such as Hegel's teleological view of history – being held to be central to human being and logically prior to the merely random and discrete data of existence. Existentialism is one very powerful strand of phenomenological thought that recoils from such rationalist ideology and its implicit devaluation of the particularity of individual human experience. Its heritage, as William Barrett has shown in his classic study *Irrational Man* (1958), goes back at least as far as the pre-Socratic philosophers of ancient Greece and was revived most notably in modern times by Pascal in the seventeenth century, the Romantic movement of the nineteenth century, and the strain of thought more narrowly labelled existentialist that achieved celebrity in France immediately after the Second World War. For the existentialist there is no grand, supernal Ideal that will make sense of everything; there is only reality, and reality in turn is only what each unique individual personally knows and experiences.

Roquentin's problem, stated in its simplest terms, is the same as Meursault's: there is absolutely no logical justification for existence. While Meursault accepts this without drama as a given, however, and acts (or fails to act) accordingly, Roquentin – whose name means 'dotard' or 'greybeard' – is obsessed by this originary absence. Only gradually, indeed, did Roquentin achieve celebrity among the critics as the protagonist of a sort of parody of Descartes's *Discourse on Method*; early readers of *La nausée* regarded him as merely abnormal, diseased, psychotic, a marginal phenomenon best ignored by reasonable people. His psychosis seemed to be evidenced by his frequent sense of dissociation from his own body, his obsession with details rather than whole patterns, his occasional fantasies bordering on hallucination, all potentially pathological in origin, as critics observed. All of these symptoms are traceable to the distinction upon which Roquentin's crisis hinges, the distinction, namely, between existence and essence. The essence of any object is everything about it that permits us to recognize it in its individuality; that is to say, the set of its phenomenological, accidental attributes. Its existence, by contrast, is simply the fact that it *is*. For Roquentin, essences begin to become progressively more volatile, more transparent, more overtly *fictive,* until eventually, in the famous climactic encounter where he sits staring in transfixed disgust at the root of a chestnut tree, he becomes fully aware of reality as pure existence – a horrifying reduction. Existence stripped down is disgusting, nauseating, terrible, because it demonstrates the complete dispensability of the observing eye, the shaping subject, demonstrates that there can be no rational explanation as to why it is the way it is rather than something entirely different. Why, after all, Roquentin asks himself, should we *not* have a third eye in the middle of our forehead or one of our cheeks? Why should we *not* wake up one morning (à la Gregor Samsa) and find our tongue, for example, transformed into a scrabbling centipede inside our mouth? Why should a harmless-looking tram-seat *not* abruptly metamorphose into an equally harmless-looking dead donkey? Existence per se is arbitrary, meaningless, absurd – and ultimately comic.

Roquentin's crisis and his survival of it are narrated in diary form. He is a historian as the account opens, writing away on a long-term project on the life of the Marquis de Rollebon, an eighteenth-century politician of somewhat dubious character and a native of the town of Bouville. Roquentin has been carrying on his research in Bouville ('mudville') for three years, following six years of extended travels in Central Europe, North Africa, and the Far East. He is thirty years old, has no financial problems, lives in a hotel room, has a fine head of red hair and an estranged mistress, Anny, who lives in Paris. The diary account opens in January 1932 and covers approximately a month, during the course of which Roquentin weathers his crisis and decides to abandon his historical research in order to write a novel instead.

Roquentin's diary, that is to say, documents first an apparent loss of control, then an apparent regaining of control. As historian (and one-time amateur archaeologist), he is of necessity routinely involved in the gathering, sifting, and organizing of material; as traveller in space and time his work is a matter of mapping, co-ordinates, measurement, control. An early symptom of his crisis is the growing erosion of his belief in his own ability to complete the biography of Rollebon on which he has been working for a good ten years. The broad outline of the project is clear: Rollebon fled France for Russia at the outbreak of the French Revolution, became a secret agent of the czar, was imprisoned on charges of treason on his return to France, and died before being brought to trial. Roquentin is initially fascinated by Rollebon's enigmatic career, but the historian's impulse to unearth the true facts behind the historical image of the man rapidly gives way during the period documented in the diary to a galloping inability to exercise control in the sifting of a plethora of conflicting accounts of the man. Eyewitness accounts even of his physical appearance are irreconcilably various. The more information becomes available, the more evanescent the figure to which it refers becomes. Roquentin eventually abandons history altogether when he concludes that behind the apparently ordered and meaningful pattern of the recorded past 'il n'y a rien' (137) / 'there is nothing' (96). Unrecorded time, whether past or present, dissolves into a featureless blur. 'Le passé n'existait pas' (137) / 'The past did not exist' (96). History, recorded time, is a fixative, as art is, but unlike art it refuses to acknowledge its own fictivity.

Roquentin's perception of objects during his crisis parallels his new insight into the workings of historiography. Just as we believe we are talking about the past when we are really talking about our own (or some historian's) *view* of the past, so we normally tend to assume, unproblematically, that we are dealing directly with objects 'themselves' when we are really dealing with our own perception of what they 'are,' which is to say, what they are *for*, what they *mean* in terms of the particular frame of reference in which we happen to be operating. A pebble found on the beach by children playing at skipping stones on the water is 'for' throwing in the sea as long as it has the right physical characteristics; lacking these characteristics it is rejected, ceases to exist in terms of the particular fiction we are busily imposing on the world around us. Roquentin's (comic) apocalypse on the beach involves the astonished and horrified awareness that the stone *does* exist, exists not just in spite of us, but worse, independently of us. 'Le galet était plat, sec sur tout un côté, humide et boueux sur l'autre. Je le tenais par les bords, avec les doigts très écartés, pour éviter de me salir' (12) / 'The stone was flat and dry, especially on one side, damp and muddy on the other. I held it by the edges with my fingers wide apart so as not to get them dirty' (2).

It is not going to be quite so easy to avoid contamination by the newly liberated objects, however, as Roquentin soon discovers. A Sorcerer's Apprentice, Roquentin has inadvertently torn the veil of fictivity, of discretion, that confines the objects to their orderly and inconspicuous roles and discovers them to be revolting – in both senses. Trapped in a world of metamorphosis and unpredictable flux, Roquentin can only watch in horrified fascination as a finger transforms itself under his gaze into a worm, a hand into a crab, a tram-seat into a dead donkey. Their ability to metamorphose is essentially an indication of their deliquescence, their refusal to be pinned down, named, reliably classified.

> Les choses se sont délivrés de leurs noms. Elles sont là, grotesques, têtues, géantes et ça parait imbécile de les appeler des banquettes ou de dire quoi que ce soit sur elles: je suis au milieu des Choses, les in-nommables. Seul, sans mots, sans défenses, elles m'environnent, sous moi, derrière moi, au-dessus de moi. Elles n'exigent rien, elles ne s'imposent pas: elles sont là.   (177)

> Things are divorced from their names. They are there, grotesque, headstrong, gigantic and it seems ridiculous to call them seats or say anything at all about them: I am in the midst of things, nameless things. Alone, without words, defenceless, they surround me, are beneath me, behind me, above me. They demand nothing, they don't impose themselves: they arethere.   (125)

Since there is no law, norm, or logic governing its superfluous exis-tence, anything can turn into anything else, cause and effect lose their hierarchical relationship. Animate can become inanimate or the reverse; the human and the inhuman are randomly interchangeable. One's own body, à la Bosch, is included in this all-embracing flux: 'la Chose, c'est moi' (141) / 'I am the Thing' (98). Roquentin has diffi-culty in recognizing his own reflection in the mirror as anything more than 'la chose grise' (31) / 'the grey thing' (16). Not that objects are always subject to this process of transformation: there is no more reason why they should be so than the contrary. Even untransformed, however, they are still objects of horror, imbued with an extraordi-nary density and presence. His pipe, a beer glass, a fork, a pair of braces, a knife, the root of a tree, each in turn impresses him with its strangeness, its unfamiliarity, its unstated but powerful threat. These miscellaneous objects, indeed, *expose* themselves to Roquentin, who is just as fascinated and disgusted and frightened as the little girl in the park whom he watches being victimized by an exhibitionist, obscene, indecent, disruptive of all civilized order. Roquentin's vis-ceral reaction is the recurrent and eventually all-enveloping nausea he first experiences on the beach as he holds the fatal stone: 'C'était une espèce d'écoeurment douceâtre ... Et cela venait du galet, j'en suis sûr, cela passait du galet dans mes mains. Oui, c'est cela, c'est bien cela: une sorte de nausée dans les mains' (24) / 'It was a sort of sweetish sickness ... It came from the stone, I'm sure of it, it passed from the stone to my hand. Yes, that's it, that's just it – a sort of nausea in the hands' (10–11).

Roquentin's role is that of the disaffected intellectual, the lonely outsider who watches himself and others with more or less tolerant disdain. In the process his world – momentarily at least – begins to fall to pieces, lose all cohesion. At the opposite end of the scale from Roquentin are the 'salauds,' as he calls them, the 'stupid bastards' who plod placidly through a reassuringly commonplace day-to-day existence without ever having the thought occur to them that there is anything problematic about their way of perceiving what they consider to be reality. The *salauds* are those who no longer are capable of distinguishing the carefully cultivated fiction they live from reality itself, who elevate notions of duty, rights, privileges, morality, and normality into an unassailable principle of self-evident order. The historian Roquentin finds himself forced to the conclusion that the past is non-existent, irrecoverable; the *salauds*, however, alias the good people of Bouville, well-dressed representatives of bourgeois solidity and self-importance, sacralize and solidify their past into 'experience' – not to mention statues and portrait galleries, churches and town halls – explaining the present always in terms not of what is but of what has been. The *salauds* memorialize their vision, turn it into the hardness of statues, the unchanging stare of a portrait. The Bouville library is guarded by the statue of one of the most revered sons of the town, Gustave Impétraz, one-time school inspector and now a 'géant de bronze' (47), a 'bronze giant' (28). Little old ladies walking their dogs can do so secure in the knowledge that all is well, for 'les saintes idées, les bonnes idées qu'elles tiennent de leurs pères, elles n'ont plus de responsabilité de les défendre; un homme de bronze s'en est fait le gardien' (47) / 'they no longer have the responsibility of standing up for their Christian ideals, the high ideals which they get from their fathers; a man of bronze has made himself their guardian' (28). Olivier Blévigne, one-time member of parliament and founder of an influential club devoted to the preservation of public order, stares masterfully out of his richly framed portrait in the municipal gallery, another giant among men – to Roquentin's irrational delight the giant turns out to have been less than five feet tall: 'Admirable puissance de l'art' (134) / 'Admirable power of art' (93). The *salauds* are those who no longer feel the need to look for answers, because they have forgotten that the questions exist.

Ils ont la preuve, cent fois par jour, que tout se fait par mécanisme, que le monde obéit à des lois fixes et immuables. Les corps abandonnés dans le vide tombent tous à la même vitesse, le jardin public est fermé tous les jours à seize heures en hiver, à dix-huit heures en été, le plomb fond à 335°, le dernier tramway part de l'Hôtel de Ville à vingt-trois heures cinq.   (221)

They have proof, a hundred times a day, that everything happens mechanically, that the world obeys fixed, unchangeable laws. In a vacuum all bodies fall at the same rate of speed, the public park is closed a 4 p.m. in winter, at 6 p.m. in summer, lead melts at 335 degrees centigrade, the last streetcar leaves the Hotel de Ville at 11.05 p.m.   (158)

'Ils n'ont pas peur, ils se sentent chez eux' (221) / 'They aren't afraid, they feel at home' (158), Roquentin reflects as he looks down Zarathustra-like on Bouville from a nearby hill shortly before he leaves for good. 'Cependant, la grande nature vague s'est glissée dans leur ville, elle s'est infiltrée, partout, dans leur maison, dans leur bureaux, en eux-mêmes' (221) / 'And all this time, great, vague nature has slipped into their city, it has infiltrated everywhere, in their house, in their office, in themselves' (158). Bouville is a city built on mud, but the secret of typical *salaud* self-confidence is the ability to ignore what is staring them in the face. Roquentin has lost this gift and as a result has fear for his constant companion, as do the few other alienated outsiders he encounters in Bouville, such as M. Achille, 'crazy as a loon' (66), who sits in a corner of a bar 'waiting for his own nausea or something of that sort' (65). Recognition of a fellow sufferer constitutes no bond, however: 'Il doit bien savoir que nous ne pouvons rien l'un pour l'autre. Les familles sont dans leurs maisons, au milieu de leurs souvenirs. Et nous voici, deux épaves sans mémoire' (97) / 'He must know that we can do nothing for one another. The families are in their houses, in the midst of their memories. And here we are, two wanderers, without memory' (65). This insight is borne out in the case of the two outsiders with whom Roquentin comes most closely in contact, the so-called Autodidact and Anny, his estranged lover.

The Autodidact – or Self-Taught Man, as the English translation styles him – is a bailiff's clerk and a self-taught humanist, who has spent all his free hours for the last seven years in the public library in a heroic attempt to read *everything* that has been written, continuing the grand tradition of those other ambitious clerks, Bouvard and

Pécuchet. The autodidact is a synthesis of every variety of humanism known, as Roquentin grimly reflects on one occasion, and to this extent is no more than a caricature of the *salauds* and their trust in predigested thinking. Roquentin discovers his method of procedure in his attempt to acquire an encyclopaedic education: he is reading alphabetically by author, regardless of subject-matter, through the entire library and after seven years has reached the letter *L* by the time Roquentin writes his diary. The autodidact's rage for order suffers from a fatal flaw, however. He has little confidence in his own attempts at mastery of the body of received wisdom and no confidence at all in his own insights, for 'si c'était vrai, quelqu'un l'aurait déjà pensé' (156) / 'If it were true, someone would already have thought of it' (109). He is a collector of other people's ideas, 'right answers,' but remains uneasily aware that they *are* precisely other people's ideas and answers; to this extent he remains an outsider and a potentially tragic figure in spite of his comic role. The autodidact preaches love and understanding and suffers from bad breath. His pathetic attempt to move from the abstract to the concrete in matters of love leads to immediate disaster: discovered shyly stroking the hand of a pimply, grinning schoolboy, he is violently ejected with a bloodied nose from his beloved library and warned never to come back.

Anny, with whom Roquentin had been in love six years ago, suddenly resurfaces and summons him to Paris for a consultation of allegedly vital importance. Where Rollebon had previously been Roquentin's avowed only reason for living, Anny now takes over that role; even a single night with her, he thinks, would cure him of his fear for good and all. Anny has her own problems, however, and her own attempted solutions – which do not necessarily include Roquentin. All of her solutions might be described as elaborate fictions of control of one sort or another, fragile barriers against reality of the same nature as the autodidact's alphabetical library shelves. At one stage she had always travelled with a large trunk full of shawls, turbans, Japanese masks, pictures, carpets, and the like, with which she would elaborately decorate any room she occupied, even if only overnight. For many years she had cultivated the notion of 'moments parfaits' (200), perfect moments, whose nature she defines for Roquentin: 'il fallait d'abord être plongé dans quelque chose d'exceptionnel et sentir qu'on y mettait de l'ordre' (208) / 'First you had to be plunged into something exceptional and feel as though you were putting it in order' (148). The first time she had kissed him, for example, she had been sitting in a patch of nettles, and her overcoming of the intense discomfort had been far more than mere stoicism: 'Il ne suffisait pas de ne pas marquer ma souffrance: il fallait ne pas souffrir' (209) / 'It wasn't enough not to show my suffering: it was necessary not to suffer' (149). She has meanwhile become an actress, one who can occasionally create such perfect moments for an audience, but she herself has lost all faith in them. Roquentin had been quick to assume that M. Achille and he, though fellow outsiders, could not help each other in any way; in Anny's case he is almost equally quick to assume that together they could overcome their alienation and their fears. Anny simply laughs at him, however. For her he has always been a yardstick of bourgeois well-adjustedness: 'comme le mètre de platine qu'on conserve quelque part à Paris ou aux environs' (193) / 'like that platinum wire they keep in Paris or somewhere in the neighbourhood' (137). She casually takes leave of him and departs for foreign climes in the company of a rich admirer. Roquentin returns crestfallen to Bouville.

Roquentin sees Anny's quest for the perfect moment as similar to his own search for 'adventures,' and both as 'en somme ... une sorte d'oeuvre d'art' (208) / 'in fact ... a sort of work of art' (148). Art has two faces in *La nausée*. On the one hand we have the unreflected humility and respect of the *petits bourgeois* whom Roquentin watches in the Bouville art gallery, hushed and solemn as in a cathedral, timidly bent on improving their minds by dutiful if uncomprehending adulation of what they are assured is 'great art,' celebrating the deeds of great men. Against this function of art as a soporific there is the central notion of art as a fixative, an ordering process imposed on the random flux of existence. *La nausée* is centrally concerned with transformation: the transformation of meaninglessness into meaning, with all the potential for absurdity, tragedy, and comedy that this entails. The world of the *salauds*, of course, is in one sense an extremely successful application of this principle of control and order. In fact, it is *too* successful, in that it has taken over its creators and induced them to forget its fictivity: the *salauds* have *become* their roles, become characters in their own fiction, abandoned discourse for story. Roquentin rejects this bourgeois serious-mindedness just as he rejects history:

> je commence à croire qu'on ne peut jamais rien prouver. Ce sont des
> hypothèses honnêtes et qui rendent compte des faits: mais je sens si
> bien qu'elles viennent de moi, qu'elles sont tout simplement une
> manière d'unifier mes connaissances ... J'ai l'impression de faire un

travail de pure imagination. Encore suis-je bien sûr que des person-
nages de roman auraient l'air plus vrais, seraient, en tout cas, plus
plaisants.

(28)

I am beginning to believe that nothing can ever be proved. These are
honest hypotheses which take the facts into account: but I sense so
definitely that they come from me, and that they are simply a way of
unifying my own knowledge ... I have the feeling of doing a work of
pure imagination. And I am certain that the characters in a novel
would have a more genuine appearance, or, in any case, would be
more agreeable.

(13–14)

It is precisely fiction that Roquentin discovers in the end of his
account as the answer to his crisis: he would write a book, he exclaims with unprecedented enthusiasm on the last page of his journal: 'Un livre. Un roman. Et il y aurait des gens qui liraient ce roman
... et ils penseraient à ma vie ... comme à quelque chose de précieux et
d'à moitié légendaire' (248) / 'A book. A novel. And there would be
people who would read this book ... and they would think about my
life ... as something precious and almost legendary' (178). Fiction is
the answer after all, but it must be a fiction that acknowledges its
own fictivity, flaunts its own futility, its Kantian purposiveness without purpose. Its sole point would be to exist as a gesture of defiance
against existence, to counter the vague, viscous, disgusting morass of
life with a hard, pure, disinterested perfection of form: 'Une histoire,
par exemple, comme il ne peut en arriver, une aventure. Il faudrait
qu'elle soit belle et dure comme de l'acier et qu'elle fasse honte aux
gens de leur existence' (247) / 'A story, for example, something that
could never happen, an adventure. It would have to be beautiful and
hard as steel and make people ashamed of their existence' (178).

Roquentin's journal is partly a working out of day-to-day problems,
partly a reconstruction of the processes that led to such problems: 'Je
n'écris plus mon livre sur Rollebon; c'est fini ... Il était trois heures.
J'étais assis à ma table ...' (135) / 'I'm not writing my book on
Rollebon any more; it's finished, ... It was three o'clock. I was sitting
at my table' (94). The opening, undated entry reads: 'Le mieux serait
d'écrire les événements au jour le jour. Tenir un journal pour y voir
clair' (11) / 'The best thing would be to write down events from day to
day. Keep a diary to see clearly ...' (1). Only a few pages later he is
already less confident of being able to carry out the project quite so
simply: 'C'est curieux: je viens de remplir dix pages et je n'ai pas dit la

vérité – du moins pas toute la vérité ... J'admire comme on peut mentir en mettant la raison de son côté' (22) / 'This is odd: I have just filled up ten pages and I haven't told the truth – at least, not the whole truth ... I admire the way we can lie, putting reason on our side' (9). As the journal progresses he begins to consider abandoning his historical research in favour of a novel about Rollebon: 'après tout, qu'est-ce qui m'empêche d'écrire un roman sur sa vie?' (88) / 'after all, why shouldn't I write a novel on his life?' (59). Eventually writing becomes both a necessity – 'La vérité, c'est que je ne peux pas lâcher ma plume' (241) / 'The truth is that I can't put down my pen' (173) – and a possible answer. Not an answer that would make living day to day any easier, but one that retrospectively might help to put things in perspective. The diary is undertaken in the belief that writing can bring clarity to the present and the future; it concludes with the insight that it may possibly shed some light on the past – not the 'real' past, which is over and done with and 'non-existent,' but a created, shaped past subject to the laws of narrative logic. Not to live, but to write: 'pour que l'événement le plus banal devienne une aventure, il faut et il suffit qu'on se mette à le *raconter*' (61) / 'for the most banal event to become an adventure, you must (and this is enough) begin to *recount* it' (39). 'Quand on vit, il n'arrive rien' (62) / 'Nothing happens while you live' (39). Life is just a series of discrete, disconnected, more or less random events. 'Ça, c'est vivre. Mais quand on raconte la vie, tout change' (63) / 'That's living. But everything changes when you *tell* about life' (39), and what in reality was so much noise becomes radiant with meaning:

> 'Il faisait nuit, la rue était déserte.' La phrase est jeté négligemment, elle a l'air superflue; mais nous ne nous y laissons prendre et nous la mettons de côté: c'est un renseignement dont nous comprendrons la valeur par la suite. Et nous avons le sentiment que le héros a vécu tous les détails de cette nuit comme des annonciations, comme des promesses, ou même qu'il vivait seulement ceux qui étaient des promesses, aveugle et sourd pour tout ce qui n'annonçait pas l'aventure.
>
> (63)

> 'It was night, the street was deserted.' The phrase is cast out negligently, it seems superfluous; but we do not let ourselves be caught and we put it aside: this is a piece of information whose value we shall subsequently appreciate. And we feel that the hero has lived all the details of this night like annunciations, promises, or even that he

lived only those that were promises, blind and deaf to all that did not
herald adventure.   (40)

As Roquentin reaches his final insight and the final paragraph of his
journal the narrative abruptly adopts precisely this overtly 'significant' tone:

> La nuit tombe. Au premier étage de l'hôtel Printania deux fenêtres
> viennent de s'éclairer. Le chantier de la Nouvelle Gare sent forte-
> ment le bois humide: demain il pleuvra sur Bouville.   (248)

> Night falls. On the second floor of the Hotel Printania two windows
> have just lighted up. The building-yard of the New Station smells
> strongly of damp wood: tomorrow it will rain in Bouville.   (178)

The overtone of parody, latent throughout the narrative, is hard to
overlook in the final pages. Roquentin's insight that art is the answer
to the ills of life uneasily recalls a whole series of nineteenth- and
twentieth-century *Künstlerromane*, most notably, of course, Proust's
A la recherche du temps perdu. Proust's hero, Marcel, is prompted by
a piece of music (Vinteuil's septet) to conceive of art as an answer to
the emptiness of life and sets out to attempt that answer himself in
the final pages of the novel. Roquentin is similarly inspired by a piece
of music, in his case a scratched gramophone record of a blues rendi-
tion to a saxophone accompaniment of a song whose most striking
passage is: 'Some of these days / You'll miss me, honey!' The song
becomes the only guaranteed barrier against the attacks of nausea and
a model in its 'hardness' and 'purity' for the projected novel. The
quite unexpectedly upbeat ending oddly recalls the ending of Céline's
Voyage; the suddenly illuminated windows likewise recall the ending
of Kafka's *Prozess*. The neurasthenic intellectual's apocalyptic visions of tram-seats metamorphosing into dead donkeys and the like
frequently have a decidedly parodic and self-deflationary ring to them
– critics have noted the parodic similarity of Roquentin's 'extase
horrible' (184) / 'horrible ecstasy' (131) under the chestnut tree to
Moses's encounter with the burning bush. Roquentin is perhaps not
even as much of a genuine (and interesting) outsider as he would like
to think. He is capable of genuine compassion for people (Lucie, the
chambermaid, who has been abandoned by her lover, for example, or
the unfortunate autodidact), even love, as in the case of Anny – who
for her part considers him to be a good bourgeois in spite of himself.

Even the more tragic figures have a certain parodic twist to them: Anny, the middle-aged actress stepping forlornly into a train en route to a fate worse than death, a life of luxury bereft of privileged moments; the autodidact expelled bleeding from his bibliographical paradise.

The relationship between Roquentin and the autodidact, indeed, is one whose nature is particularly ambivalent from the very beginning. The differences between them are very apparent, as we have already seen. The similarities and interconnections are less obvious, but certainly, teasingly, there – such details, for example, as when Roquentin challenges the autodidact to demonstrate his alleged love for humankind by telling him what colour of hair the girl at the table beside him has, paralleled by Anny's later demand that Roquentin demonstrate his alleged love for her by telling her (without looking) what colour her hair is. The autodidact's almost maniacal regard for the written word finds an oblique correlative in Roquentin's decision to become a writer. By the end of his account, of course, Roquentin *is* an 'autodidact,' one who has literally taught himself. The suspicion easily arises that the whole role of the autodidact serves as a parodic counterpart and deflation of Roquentin's role as intellectual, a Sancho Panza to the latter's Quijote, a Wagner to his Faust – as in the scene, for example, where the autodidact surprises Roquentin, as he fondly supposes, purging his prose of involuntary alexandrines.

The autodidact is introduced as follows: 'Ce matin, à la bibliothèque, quand l'Autodidacte est venu me dire bonjour, j'ai mis dix secondes à le reconnaître. Je voyais un visage inconnu, à peine un visage' (16) / 'This morning in the library, when the Self-Taught Man came to say good morning to me, it took me ten seconds to recognize him. I saw an unknown face, barely a face' (4). A footnote informs us that we are talking about one 'Ogier P ..., dont il sera souvent question dans ce journal. C'était un clerc d'huissier. Roquentin avait fait sa connaissance en 1930 à la bibliothèque de Bouville' (16n) / 'Ogier P ..., who will be often mentioned in this journal. He was a bailiff's clerk. Roquentin met him in 1930 in the Bouville library' (4n). None of the other characters is introduced with such editorial meticulousness – which none the less does not stretch to including the full surname. Roquentin never talks to anyone, he writes at one point – for 'l'Autodidacte ne compte pas' (19) / 'the Self-Taught Man doesn't count' (6). 'Avec l'Autodidacte, on n'est jamais deux qu'en apparence' (110) / 'with the Self-Taught Man, you only appear to be two' (75). Roquentin shows him photographs from his travels, to which the autodidact responds that if ever *he* went on a voyage he would want to make careful notes about his own character before starting since he has heard that it is not unusual for such travellers to return changed beyond recognition. The autodidact yearns for adventure; Roquentin dispiritedly feels that in spite of his own travels everything he knows has come from books. The autodidact has no appreciation of art. 'Au fond,' Roquentin reflects, 'il est aussi seul que moi; personne ne se soucie de lui. Seulement il ne se rend compte de sa solitude' (171) / 'At heart he is as lonely as I am: no one cares about him. Only he doesn't realize his solitude' (121). Finally he is forced to recognize his solitude when he is expelled from the library – which takes place on Roquentin's final visit to the library as well, his last day in Bouville, and which Roquentin watches with fascination. 'L'Autodidacte n'avait pas l'air surpris. Il devait y avoir des années qu'il s'attendait à ce dénouement' (231) / 'The Self-Taught Man did not look surprised. He must have been expecting this for years' (166). As he makes his final preparations for departure Roquentin thinks of him: 'L'Autodidacte erre dans la ville' (237) / 'The Self-Taught Man is wandering through the city' (170). 'Peut-être qu'il va se tuer' (238) / 'Maybe he is going to kill himself' (171).

The autodidact, in short, is partly a realistic character, partly a parodic foil for Roquentin – a relationship comparable to that of Josef K. and the two warders, Franz and Willem. The journal itself enjoys a similarly ambivalent status. It is preceded by an 'Avertissement des Editeurs' / 'Editors' Note' informing the reader that the following notebooks were found among the papers of one Antoine Roquentin and published here without alteration. Found by whom? Where has Roquentin gone? Why did he leave his diary behind? If left in Bouville, is the autodidact perhaps the editor – or one of the editors? Is it true that nothing has been altered? Is this really a diary, or is it in fact – à la Proust – the novel that Roquentin sets out to write in its closing pages? The whole editorial apparatus, so conscientious for the first few pages, quickly disappears entirely with a final footnote where 'les éditeurs' have become 'l'éditeur' (26). Roquentin quite often employs overtly novelistic techniques in his alleged journal – as in the case of the autodidact's expulsion, for example. The end result is an ambiguity as to the status of the text we have just read. As Roquentin himself writes of his efforts to come to grips with Rollebon (whose journal *he* is working on in the library at Bouville), 'ce qui manque dans tous ces témoinages, c'est la fermeté, la consistance. Ils ne se contredisent pas, non, mais ils ne s'accordent pas non plus' (27)

/ 'What is lacking in all this testimony is firmness and consistency. They do not contradict each other, neither do they agree with each other' (13).

An editor's task is the imposition of order and consistency on the materials at hand. Our editors begin with a single, undated entry, for which they claim 'good reasons' for assigning to the beginning of January 1932, though without explaining what exactly these good reasons may be. This undated entry contains several blanks where words were allegedly missing or illegible – one of the latter may be '"forcer" ou "forger"' (11) / '"force" or "forge"' (2), we notice. The next entry is very exactly dated, 'Lundi 29 janvier 1932' (but the diligent critic discovers on consulting a calendar that 29 January 1932 was actually a Friday rather than a Monday); the following entry has a partial date, 'Mardi 30 janvier'; while all subsequent entries are headed only by the day of the week or references to the time of day. While it is in all cases possible to establish the exact date by cross-checking, the 'editors' obviously did not feel the necessity to do so.

At several points in his account Roquentin comes back to the distinction between living and writing, disorganization and organization – or, to put it in narratological terms, story and discourse. Living is a featureless flux: 'Les jours s'ajoutent aux jours sans rime ni raison, c'est une addition interminable et monotone' (62) / 'Days are tacked on to days without rhyme or reason, an interminable, monotonous addition' (39). 'Ça, c'est vivre. Mais quand on raconte la vie, tout change; seulement c'est un changement que personne ne remarque: la preuve c'est qu'on parle d'histoires vraies. Comme s'il pouvait y avoir des histoires vraies; les événements se produisent dans un sens et nous les racontons en sens inverse' (63) / 'That's living. But everything changes when you tell about life; it's a change no one notices: the proof is that people talk about true stories. As if there could possibly be true stories; things happen one way and we tell about them in the opposite sense' (39). *La nausée* too is no 'true story,' it is a narration, and as such an arrangement of information on the part of a narrator. The diary format invites the reader to ignore the narrator, but we do so at our own risk. Roquentin's 'arrest,' we recall, comes about as the result of his sudden inability to play the game – literally: the stone will not skip any more, refuses its role as plaything, becomes 'stonier,' as if in response to Shklovsky. This is Roquentin the character, however; by the end of the novel (for in the end that is clearly what it is) Roquentin the character is well on his way to becoming Roquentin the narrator. Indeed, he has been there all along, and his ability to play the game of narrative is in no doubt at all.

'C'est une farce!' (158) / 'It's a comedy!' (111), Roquentin exclaims to himself, looking around a restaurant full of *bons bourgeois* suffused with solemn self-importance. *La nausée* is likewise full of concepts with an air of solemn self-importance, demanding to be treated accordingly – being and nothingness, existence and essence, contingency and freedom, nausea and anguish. That it is also a brilliant comic novel would no doubt have seemed unthinkable to its early readers, just as Kafka's comedy lay dormant for decades under obscuring layers of scholarly exegesis. The central element of its comedy is the notion of self-deception, the absurdity of seriousness in the face of the fact that all our most hallowed systems of coming to grips with the world around us are fictions pure and simple – 'coins,' as Nietzsche puts it, 'which have their obverse effaced and now are no longer of account as coins but merely as metal' ('On Truth' 174). Much of the comedy consists of straightforward satire of the puffed-up bourgeoisie, parading in their Sunday best outside the church, memorializing themselves in oil-paints and bronze, blissfully convinced of their own centrality and indispensability. There are comic figures like M. Fasquelle, who lapses into suspended animation as soon as his café closes; Françoise the *patronne*, who does not interrupt her professional commentary on the latest aperitifs while engaging in her weekly sexual encounter with Roquentin; and a number of more or less grotesque overheard conversations faithfully 'transcribed' by Roquentin. There is the autodidact and his trust in the alphabet, and directly related to this there is, above all, Roquentin's undermining of his own predicament – and his solution to it. His initial encounter with the stone is specifically a cause for merriment for the watching children, and almost all of the other situations inducing attacks of nausea continue to have a marked comic potential. His failure to recognize his own face in the mirror, the *patron*'s mauve braces, the Bosch-like centipede-tongue, the supplementary eyes, the dead donkey in the tram, or Roquentin himself standing Cassandra-like on the hill overlooking Bouville: all of these conform to the definition of entropic humour advanced earlier in that humorous experience is evoked while humorous pleasure is (at least initially) inhibited by the context of reception. All of existence *borders* on the comic for Roquentin, is 'vaguement comique' (180) / 'vaguely comic' (128) – and so are all attempts to come to grips with it, including his own. 'Le mot d'Absurdité naît à présent sous ma plume' (181) / 'The word absurdity is coming to life under my pen' (129), and all one can do is play with it. Roquentin tries to kick some of the bark off the root of the chestnut tree, the root of his nausea, but not with any rational intention in mind: 'pour rien, pour défi, pour faire apparaître sur le cuir tanné le rose absurde d'une éraflure: pour *jouer* avec l'absurdité du monde' (183) / 'For no reason at all, out of defiance, to make the bare pink appear absurd on the tanned leather: to *play* with the absurdity of the world' (130).

Essentially Roquentin's central realization is that we can know nothing and say nothing about existential reality other than that it exists. Any attempt at explaining its purpose or motivation can only be fictional, for to explain is to order and reality is not orderable other than fictively. Chance reigns supreme – 'L'essentiel c'est la contingence' (184) / 'The essential thing is contingency' (131) – and our notions of order are merely attempts to forget this central principle of all existence, including our own. 'Tout existant naît sans raison, se prolonge par faiblesse et meurt par rencontre' (188) / 'Every existing thing is born without reason, prolongs itself out of weakness and dies by chance' (133). Existence, characterized throughout in terms of amorphousness, vagueness, viscosity, deliquescence, is an 'ignoble marmelade' (189), an 'ignoble mess' (134), an entropic morass that simply absorbs all attempts to comprehend it, a mindless jungle that inevitably swallows up all attempts to establish an outpost of order, a 'profusion d'êtres sans origine' (187) / 'profusion of beings without origin' (133), an 'immense ennui' (190) / 'immense weariness' (134). The semblance of what we too lazily assume to be normality is maintained only by virtue of inertia, not in consequence of any normative principle. At any moment it may suddenly prove no longer susceptible of our traditional notions of the self-evident – as when the stone on the beach *refuses* to play the game any longer: 'je ne me rappelais pas bien au juste ce qu'il refusait d'être. Mais je n'avais pas oublié sa résistance passive' (183) / 'I can't remember exactly just what it was that the stone refused to be. But I had not forgotten its passive resistence' (130). Roquentin knows that he knows more than the *salauds*, but he also knows that what he knows is nothing, for that is precisely what is behind the 'unnameable' things, 'les Choses, les innommables' (177), among whose number we are all counted. This is the reason for the impassive stare of the trees, the 'smile' on the face of the garden during Roquentin's encounter with the chestnut tree. 'Le sourire des arbres, du massif de laurier, ça *voulait dire* quelque chose; c'était ça le véritable secret de l'existence' (190) / 'The smile of the trees, of the laurel, *meant* something; that was the real secret of existence' (135), and the secret is its fundamental absurdity and inexplainability: 'Cette racine ... existait dans la mesure où je ne pouvais pas l'expliquer' (182) / 'This root ... existed to the extent that I could not explain it' (129). Life is a game one can only lose – only the *salauds* believe in their power to win. That fact once acknowledged, however, the way is clear to respond with a game of one's own. He will still lose, Roquentin knows, but at least there will have been some possibility, in spite of everything, that 'on peut justifier son existence ... Un tout petit peu' (247) / 'you can justify your existence ... Just a little' (177).

Roquentin is a historian who becomes a novelist; Sartre was a novelist who became a philosopher and rejected Roquentin's solution for one of political engagement – which for Roquentin is still merely part of the world of the *salauds*. *La nausée* is centrally about the failure of explanations, the futility of principled positions. Roquentin's insight utterly marginalizes the individual: we are simply *not* important, merely aleatory marginalia, gratuitous, totally unnecessary. But the universe we are part of is equally gratuitous and pointless: instead of meaning anything, it simply exists, *is*, absurdly, obscenely, superfluously. It is an illogical universe, a universe where freedom of choice is total and totally meaningless. Any course of action is as meaningful, which is to say bereft of all meaning, as any other: entropy is complete. Josef K.'s world is ruled by uncomprehended and apparently irrational laws – but as far as Josef K. is concerned they are still laws. Roquentin's world is closer to Bardamu's vision of anarchy, with that vision transposed, as critics have pointed out before, from the social to the metaphysical plane. (The epigraph – omitted in the English translation – is taken from Céline: 'C'est un garçon sans importance collective, c'est tout juste un individu' (7) / 'He's a fellow without collective importance, he's merely an individual.') Josef K.'s world is deterministic in the sense that it is, or seems to be, governed by systems of meaning and organization over which K. believes he has no power. Roquentin's world is appalling in its total *lack* of determination, its treacherous offer of complete and total freedom. *Der Prozess* and *La nausée* are two sides of the same coin, and Todd Andrews's dictum is as applicable to the one as to the other: in their vision of reality nothing has intrinsic value, and no 'truth' advanced to explain that reality makes any difference whatsoever.

Explanatory Positions: Beckett's *Watt*

There is surely no other modern narrative that offers so many and such complete explanations of reality as Samuel Beckett's *Watt*, written during the early forties, published only in 1953. Watt's quest, it seems, is precisely for meaning, wholeness, and coherence, and he is already engaged in this archetypal search when we first meet him, en route to the locus of ultimate enlightenment, travelling, in other words (by tram, then train), through the Irish countryside to the house of one Mr Knott. The story is entirely 'of the coming to / of the being at / of the going from / Knott's habitat' (249): Watt (first name no longer known) arrives at Mr Knott's house, spends two years there as a servant (the first on the ground floor, the second on the first floor), and quietly departs again, again by train. *Watt* positively bristles with episodes, incidents, objects, and relationships that look as if they certainly *should* be highly significant, and the reader is subjected to constant temptation to read the whole as a complicated allegory of some sort; unaccountably, though, nothing turns out to mean very much, if anything. As far as one can tell, of course. And that's the point.

Watt's 'quest,' like that of Josef K., is rooted in the everyday and the ordinary: the chimneys of Mr Knott's house can be seen rising out of the trees just beyond the railway station. Unlike Josef K., or Gregor Samsa, or Roquentin, there is no sense of 'arrest' in Watt's case, no sudden awakening. He is already under way when we catch our first glimpse of him 'in the failing light' (7) through the combined eyes of three evening strollers: a tram stops, there is a brief altercation, and the tram moves on, 'disclosing on the pavement, motionless, a solitary figure, lit less and less by the receding lights, until it was scarcely to be distinguished from the dim wall behind it. Tetty was not sure whether it was a man or a woman. Mr Hackett was not sure that it was not a parcel, a carpet for example, or a roll of tarpaulin, wrapped up in dark paper and tied about the middle with a cord' (16). Watt has no very prepossessing appearance – 'Like a sewer-pipe, said Mrs Nixon' (18) – one of a breed later described as 'big bony shabby seedy haggard knockkneed men, with rotten teeth and big red noses, the result of too much solitude' (58). His past is obscure. He may occasionally be seen in the streets wearing only one shoe, but he is 'a university man, of course' (23). He is not without his likes and dislikes, for 'if there were two things that Watt disliked, one was the moon, and the other was the sun' (33), the avoidance of both involving protracted periods of lying face down in any convenient ditch. Not that this is much better, for 'if there were two things that Watt loathed, one was the earth, and the other was the sky' (36).

Watt has one sovereign way of coming to grips with this abominated reality, and that is to explain it – conclusively, and without the possibility of error. Arriving at Mr Knott's house, for example, Watt at first finds both the front door and the back door locked, then, on trying them both again, finds the back door open after all. 'Watt was surprised to find the back door, so lately locked, now open. Two explanations of this occurred to him. The first was this, ... that the back door, when he had found it locked, had not been locked, but open. And the second was this, that the back door, when he had found it locked, had in effect been locked, but had subsequently been opened, from within, or without, by some person, while he Watt had been employed in going, to and fro, from the back door to the front door, and from the front door to the back door' (36). This enumeration certainly contains the answer to the question – conclusively, and without the possibility of error. Only the final step remains to be taken, and that is the choice of the first explanation or the second.

> Of these two explanations Watt thought he preferred the latter, as being the more beautiful. For if someone had opened the back door, from within, or without, would not he Watt have seen a light, or heard a sound? Or had the door been unlocked, from within, in the dark, by some person perfectly familiar with the premises, and wearing carpet slippers, or in his stockinged feet? Or, from without, by some person so skilful on his legs, that his footfalls made no sound? Or had a sound been made, a light shown, and Watt not heard the one nor seen the other?
>
> The result of this was that Watt never knew how he got into Mr Knott's house. He knew that he got in by the back door, but he was never to know, never, never to know, how the back door came to be opened. (37)

The situation is paradigmatic of Watt's dilemma throughout the narrative: however apparently slight or trivial or however important the problem involved, Watt will subject it to an utterly exhaustive explanatory enumeration that will certainly include the correct solution to the problem but that none the less will end with Watt's confusion and the one available certainty, namely 'never to know, never, never to know,' except purely by chance, and even then subject to further exhaustive analysis. By summoning up *all* the logical possibilities of combination and permutation of the constituent factors of any given problem, Watt reduces the situation to order – for if something is merely part of a series, after all, it is unproblematically localizable and explainable, subject only, of course, to the final decision as to which of the available solutions is to be canonized as the definitive answer. Pending that decision each of the possible permutations is a possible sense-conferring system; each is potentially the 'truth.'

Very occasionally the truth may even manifest itself. Watt on one occasion finds solace in the face of present problems in the memory of a distant summer night when a much younger Watt in a different ditch heard 'the three frogs croaking Krak!, Krek!, and Krik!, at one, nine, seventeen, twenty-five, etc., and at one, six, eleven, sixteen, etc., and at one, four, seven, ten, etc., respectively' (136) and relives that distant chorus (reprinted in full in the text) with Krak!, Krek!, and Krik! singing their separate songs until, gloriously, they come together again, though separated since beat one, in beat 121, after sixteen Kraks, twenty-five Kreks, and forty-one Kriks. Such perfection is achieved only rarely, however, and, as in this particular case, has relatively limited possibilities of application in the intractable world we live in. Watt, however, pays little or no attention to that outside world other than in theory – a stone experimentally hurled at him by one Lady McCann of somewhat dubious virtue, for example, succeeds in knocking off his bowler hat, but Watt, typically, and 'faithful to his rule, took no more notice of this aggression than if it had been an accident' (32), and merely sets himself, 'after one or two false starts, again in motion' (32).

Even the voices that speak to Watt, unheard by others, are regulated by mathematical logic, for 'sometimes they sang and cried and murmured, and sometimes they sang and stated and murmured, and sometimes they sang and cried and stated and murmured, all together' (29). Sometimes the voices sing as a mixed choir, intoning texts such as 'Fifty-two point two eight five seven one four two eight five seven one four ... ' (34), or 'Fifty-one point one four two eight five seven one four two eight five seven one ...' (35). Mr Knott's eating arrangements suggest twelve possible constellations of circumstances to Watt, minutely different, meticulously recorded (89–90). The disposal of his leavings, possibly by feeding them to a dog specially kept for the purpose, leads to seven bravura pages of speculation as to the possible existence of such dog or dogs and the possible circumstances of its or their owner or owners (94–100). Watt's brief amorous interlude with Mrs Gorman, the fishwoman, is less than wholly satisfactory, for in view of their several common and separate physical debilities sometimes 'no fewer than two, or three, or four, or five, or six, or seven, or eight, or nine, or ten, or eleven, or even twelve, or even thirteen changes of position were found necessary, before the time came for Mrs Gorman to take her leave' (141).

Nor indeed is Watt alone in his attempt to subdue the world by lisping in numbers. Arsène, his immediate predecessor but one in Mr Knott's employ (and whose lucubrations on 'the laughs that strictly speaking are not laughs, but modes of ululation' we have glanced at elsewhere), is equally given to such all-inclusive explanation. The 'poor old lousy old earth,' Arsène notes in passing, is 'an excrement,' or to be more precise, 'my earth and my father's and my mother's and my father's father's and my mother's mother's and my father's mother's and my mother's father's and my father's mother's father's,' and so on down to 'other people's ... fathers' fathers' fathers' and mothers' mothers' mothers'. An excrement' (46–47). A servant girl is described 'quietly eating onions and peppermints turn and turn about,' or more specifically, in Arsène's terms, 'I mean first an onion, then a peppermint, then another onion, then another peppermint, then another onion,' etc., etc. (51). And so on. Arthur too, Watt's immediate successor in Mr Knott's employ, places much emphasis on the truths of mathematics as well, describing inter alia the conundrum facing the members of a committee who attempt the apparently innocuous manoeuvre of exchanging meaningful glances, 'for though in theory only twenty looks are necessary, every man looking four times, yet in practice this number is seldom sufficient, on account of the multitude of looks that go astray' (175). We are duly regaled with four pages of these 'looks that go astray' before Arthur demonstrates over two further pages the most efficient way for the committee to look at itself and 'with the minimum number of looks, that is to say x squared minus x looks if there are x members of the committee, and y squared minus y if there are y' (180). Mr Knott himself, as he appears to Watt at any rate, is characterized by behaviour that seems to aim at exhausting all available possibilities. In his room, for example, Mr Knott 'moved, to and fro, from the door to the window, from the window to the door; from the window to the door, from the door to the window; from the fire to the bed, from the bed to the fire; from the bed to the fire, from the fire to the bed; from the door to the fire ...' (204). Mr Knott, moreover, inexplicably, continually changes his furniture around: 'Thus it was not rare to find, on the Sunday, the tallboy on its feet by the fire, and the dressing-table on its head by the bed, and the night-stool on its face by the door, and the washhand-stand on its back by the window; and, on the Monday, the tallboy on its back by the bed, and the dressing-table on its face by the door ... ' (205), and so on for nineteen days, down to the Friday fortnight.

Watt's perceptions of Knott occupy much of the narrative. Mr Knott, the master, is constantly attended by two servants, one on the ground floor, one on the first floor, each servant spending one year on each floor before finally departing and making way for a new ground-floor servant. Thus Arsène leaves when Watt arrives, Vincent when Arthur arrives, Watt when Micks arrives. In the midst of this constant change Knott remains, a still centre for 'these two men for ever about Mr Knott in tireless assiduity turning' (61), 'eternally turning about Mr Knott in tireless love' (62). The first book ends with the sun rising on Watt's first day, 'the day without precedent at last' (64), in Mr Knott's house. The second book opens with the observation that 'Watt had no direct dealings with Mr Knott, at this period. Not that Watt was ever to have direct dealings with Mr Knott, for he was not' (67). Watt sees him from time to time, from a distance, muses continually on the circumstances that surround him and the reason for them, without being 'so foolish as to suppose that this was the real reason ... This was merely the reason offered to the understanding' (68). And the understanding has much to occupy it: the stairs, for example, from the ground floor to the first floor, 'that were never the same and of which even the number of steps seemed to vary, from day to day, and from night to morning' (83). Or Mr Knott's big round bed, the circuit of which his head, and his feet, complete in twelve months (207). Or Mr Knott's hours of rising and retiring: 'For on Monday, Tuesday and Friday he rose at eleven and retired at seven, and on Wednesday and Saturday he rose at nine and retired at eight, and on Sunday he did not rise at all, nor at all retire. Until Watt realised that between Mr Knott risen and Mr Knott retired there was so to speak nothing to choose' (86). Or Mr Knott's food, a sufficient quantity of which was prepared and cooked on Saturday night to carry him through the week, whereby all manners of food and drink 'too numerous to mention' (87) were well mixed in a pot, boiled for four hours, and served cold. Watt 'knew, as though he had been told, that the receipt of this dish had never varied' (88), and 'tears of mental fatigue' would drop from his brow into the pot as, 'stripped to the waist, and plying with both hands the great iron rod' (88), he mixed his master's meal for all seasons.

Watt gradually reaches the conclusion 'that nothing could be added to Mr Knott's establishment, and from it nothing taken away, but that as it was now, so it had been in the beginning, and so it would remain to the end, in all essential respects, any significant presence, at any time, and here all presence was significant, even though it was impossible to say of what' (131). Mr Knott himself, occasionally glimpsed, 'was seldom the same figure, from one glance to the next' (147), but always different in shape, size, colouring, and gait. Mr Knott is a fixity, but a 'fixity of mystery' (199), a sameness characterized by difference, metamorphosis in stasis, the manifestation of a 'pre-established arbitrary' (134). Mr Knott is entirely self-sufficient in that he needs nothing 'except, one, not to need, and, two, a witness to his not needing' (202). And needing nothing but this, Mr Knott 'of himself knew nothing. And so he needed to be witnessed. Not that he might know, no, but that he might not cease' (203).

Watt's self-imposed task as witness is to know Knott, but inevitably he must end as he does – and as Josef K. does – knowing not. Knott is knot, no, not to kno(w), naught, nought, not-nought, Not (German 'need'), and not-Not. Watt needs to know, to wot, needs Knott to know what, to know Watt. Watt and Knott are question and answer, centre and circle, circle and centre. Knott's 'answers' are not-answers, non-answers, noise, silence. They exist in the first place only insofar as they are hypothetical answers to hypothetical questions, all the possible answers to all the possible questions, a knot of possibilities. Knott is a *deus absconditus* and a patent absurdity, a joke. 'But what kind of witness was Watt, weak now of eye, hard of hearing, and with even the more intimate senses greatly below par?' (203). Watt remains 'in particular ignorance' of Mr Knott, because of 'on the one hand the exiguity of the material propounded to his senses, and on the other the decay of these' (199). Watt eventually simply gives up, abandons his efforts to sum up his knowledge or lack of knowledge once and for all, 'tired, so very tired, by all he had told already, tired of adding, tired of subtracting to and from the same old things the same old things' (212). The relationship of Watt and Knott eventually becomes 'unspeakable' (85), incommunicable. 'Do not come down the ladder, Ifor, I haf taken it away' (44).

Watt's testimony, in consequence, is not always as crystal clear as one might wish. His account of his second year in Mr Knott's employ, for example, is told to the narrator in a series of private languages or codes constructed by a process of progressive deformation of everyday English, involving a series of inversions and rearrangements of letters in words, words in sentences, and sentences in periods. There are eight of these variegated inversions, practised by a Watt who now also walks backwards and dresses backwards and is the inmate of an institution whose precise nature is never discussed. The first inversion, the least complex, laments that 'Now till up, little seen so oh, little heard so oh ... Ears, eyes, failing now also' (164). The third, where the sentences in the period are inverted: 'Of nought. To the source. To the teacher. To the temple. To him I brought. This emptied heart. These emptied hands ... My little rejected to have him. My little to learn him forgot. Abandoned my little to find him' (166). The fourth: 'Deen did taw? Tonk. Tog da taw? Tonk. Luf puk saw? Hap! Deen did tub? Ton sparp. Tog da tub? Ton wonk' (166), which with normal word order restored reads, 'Wat did need? Knot. Wat ad got? Knot. Was kup ful? Pah! But did need? Praps not. But ad got? Know not.' The seventh, transliterated, sees both Watt and Knott 'dum, num, blin. Knot look at wat? No. Wat look at knot? No. Wat talk to knot? No. Knot talk to wat? No ... Niks, niks, niks' (168). The eighth and final inversion depends on a method so totally arbitrary and random that the narrator can 'recall no example of this manner' (169), though eventually, he adds, even in this case 'I grew used to these sounds, and then I understood as well as ever, that is to say fully one half of what won its way past my tympan. For my own hearing now began to fail, though my myopia remained stationary. My purely mental faculties on the other hand, the faculties properly so called of ? ? ? ? ? were if possible more vigorous than ever' (169).

Studies of *Watt*, understandably preoccupied with the relationship of Watt and Knott, have by and large devoted surprisingly little attention to the narrator of that encounter – whose name, as he informs us, is Sam (153). We only very gradually become aware of Sam's presence. The narrative is introduced by what appears to be an omniscient and anonymous narrating voice, which recounts the meeting of Mr Hackett and his friends the Nixons on a park bench in the evening light, Watt's journey to Mr Knott's house, and Arsène's 'short statement' (39) of twenty-four pages. Shortly after the opening of Book II there is an ambiguous reference to there being 'no light for Watt' and 'none for his mouthpiece,' though 'there may be light for others' (69). A little later the difficulties of dealing with 'delicate questions' concerning Watt's 'pursuit of meaning, in this indifference to meaning' are discovered as being at least partly the result of 'the obscurity of Watt's communications, ... the material conditions in which these communications were made ... the scant aptitude to receive of him to whom they were proposed,' and 'the scant aptitude to give of him to whom they were committed' (75). Soon the narrator is referring more overtly to himself as 'one' – 'one is sometimes tempted to wonder, with reference to two or even three incidents related by Watt as separate and distinct, if they were not in reality the same incident, variously interpreted' (78) – and even to 'Watt's revelation, to me' (79). The account of Watt's adventures is abruptly described as one where the difference between various episodes is allegedly 'so nice as with advantage to be neglected, in a synopsis of this kind' (80). The narrator momentarily confuses his character – 'This refusal, by Knott, I beg your pardon, by Watt ... ' (115) – speculates independently on the nature of Mr Knott – 'But what conception have I of Mr Knott? None' (120) – and finally declares that 'if Watt had not known this, ... then I should never have known it.... For all that I know on the subject of Mr Knott ... and on the subject of Watt ... came from Watt, and from Watt alone. And if I do not appear to know very much on the subject ... it is because Watt did not know a great deal on these subjects, or did not care to tell' (125). And furthermore, Watt, as it immediately thereafter transpires, 'made no secret of this, in his conversations with me, that many things described as happening, in Mr Knott's house ... perhaps never happened at all, or quite differently, and that many things described as being or rather as not being, for these were the more important, perhaps were not, or rather were all the time ... And this does not mean either that I may not have left out some of the things that Watt told me, or foisted in others that Watt never told me, though I was most careful to note down all at the time, in my little notebook' (126). By this time the reader is, or should be, uncomfortably aware that this particular literary game is very evidently being played, as far as he is concerned, with a twisted cue on a cloth untrue and that the billiard balls are highly elliptical indeed.

Book II ends with the completion of Watt's first year, and 'it was about this time that Watt was transferred to another pavilion, leaving me behind in the old pavilion. We consequently met, and conversed, less than formerly' (151). All of Watt's (alleged) account so far, it now emerges, has apparently been relayed to 'Sam' (153), while both were the inmates of an institution bearing all the marks of a lunatic asylum. Sam's presence becomes very overt indeed in what follows in

Book III, allegedly conveyed to him by Watt as they march face to face around the asylum grounds, each in his 'pretty uniform' (160), Watt backwards, Sam forwards, the hands of each on the shoulders of the other, occasionally grinding birds' nests and their eggs 'into fragments, under our feet, with peculiar satisfaction, at the appropriate season, of the year' (155), or feeding a plump young rat 'to its mother, or its father, or its brother, or its sister, or to some less fortunate relative. It was on these occasions, we agreed, after an exchange of views, that we came nearest to God' (156). Watt's account from now on, we are told, is characterized by 'scant regard for grammar, for syntax, for pronunciation, for enunciation' (156), in the form of the peculiar inversion techniques already noticed. That anyone would ever again speak in a voice '*at once* so rapid and so low, is hard to believe ... Of this impetuous murmur much fell in vain on my imperfect hearing and understanding, and much by the rushing wind was carried away, and lost for ever' (156). A 'singular' (158) account, indeed, as Sam observes, going on to describe himself looking about for a hole in the fence, 'like a mad creature' (158). Looking at Watt, covered in blood from his backwards careering, Sam observes, 'suddenly I felt as though I were standing before a great mirror' (159), and 'from the hidden pavilions, his and mine, ... the issuing smokes by the wind were blown, now far apart, but now together, mingled to vanish' (213).

Sam's claim that he knows all he knows on the subject of Watt only from what Watt himself has told him is of course untenable: witness the opening and closing conversations, both of them concerning Watt, both of them duly presented by the narrator, and both taking place in Watt's absence. The more closely one looks at Sam's contribution to the whole, the more endemic uncertainty becomes to the whole. Not indeed that it *is* a whole, for Sam leaves some dozen gaps in his narrative, marked by question marks (29, 32, 85, etc.), apparently where the right word failed to occur to him. Eight pages of material are given as 'Addenda': 'Only fatigue and disgust prevented its incorporation' (245). Sam clearly has his likes and dislikes too, is clearly delighted with the comma – 'Watt saw, in the grate, of the range, the ashes grey' (37) – while the semicolon, for example – 'How hideous is the semi-colon' (158) – fails to find his favour. Sam finds his way to Watt in the latter part of the narrative through a hole in the high fence surrounding his 'pavilion,' 'Watt likewise finding a similar hole in the high fence surrounding *his* pavilion,' and the two converse in their fashion in the long 'couloir' (160) between these two long, parallel fences – but not before Sam (Watt forgotten) treats us to several pages of speculation as to how the two holes could have come about: 'For where was the boar, where the bull, capable, after bursting a hole in the first fence, of bursting a second, exactly similar, in the second?' (160). How many of the other lengthy monologues of a mathematico-logical cast, attributed directly or indirectly to Watt, or Arsène, or Arthur, and how much of the alleged behaviour of Knott, are in fact Sam's contribution, pure and simple? Is Watt's missing first name Sam? Are Watt *and* Knott *and* Sam the sam(e)? With Sam's voice the guarantor of narrative order, how can we ever know?

This, of course, once again, is the whole overt point of the narrative: 'I tell you nothing is known, cried Mr Nixon. Nothing' (21). Watt is described as continually searching for (and finding) signs of what he presumes to be some explainable meaning, but all of these turn out to be like the visit of the piano-tuners, the Galls, 'incidents that is to say of great formal brilliance and indeterminable purport' (74). Much time is devoted to analysing the possibility or necessity of a bell, for example, in the room of Erskine, Watt's immediate successor; the search for the bell involves a preliminary search for a key. And indeed 'there was a bell in Erskine's room, but it was broken'(128). There is also a picture, containing a circle and a dot, which after much rumination Watt concludes 'was perhaps this, a circle and a centre not its centre in search of a centre and its circle respectively, in boundless space, in endless time' (129). This discovery moves Watt to tears – but the picture, we are told much later, 'yielded nothing further. On the contrary, as time passed, its significance diminished' (208). The failure of each and every apparent sign fails to deter Watt, who continues 'to enquire into what they meant, oh not what they really meant, his character was not so peculiar as all that, but into what they might be induced to mean, with the help of a little patience, a little ingenuity' (75). 'But to elicit something from nothing requires a certain skill and Watt was not always successful, in his efforts to do so' (77), for 'Watt's imagination had never been a lively one' (83). The same is scarcely true of Sam, who summarizes Watt's achievements by the end of his first year in these terms:

> What had he learnt? Nothing.
> What did he know of Mr Knott? Nothing.
> Of his anxiety to improve, of his anxiety to understand, of his anxiety to get well, what remained? Nothing.
> But was not that something?   (148)

Making his way to the railway station on departing Mr Knott's house, Watt sees in the distance a figure striding along, also towards the station, but notices that the figure never draws any nearer. 'Pressing forward all this time, with no abatement of its foundering precipitation, towards the station, it had made no more headway, than if it had been a millstone' (227). Abruptly the figure disappears. Here Watt – like Josef K. in the episode with the whipper – is presented with a *mise en abyme* of his own endeavours, all his 'useless wisdom so dearly won' (62) amounting in the end to nothing at all. In the end, all the explanations, Watt's and Sam's alike, provide not information but merely endless enumeration, noise, entropy, stasis. But that is no reason to desist from producing them, as long as we remain resolutely aware of their provisionality, their fictivity. There are no 'real' answers: the only answers we have are the questions we have. In Sam's case his questions amount to *Watt*.

'Personally of course I regret everything' (46), Arsène assures us, before going on to discuss in detail 'all the laughs that strictly speaking are not laughs' (48). *Watt* is a rich repository of the latter, crammed with grotesques and grotesqueries, of whom the ill-fated Lynch family is a bravura example. The Lynch family attempts to impose a mathematical grid on the flux of existence in a more practical sense than any evoked by Watt or Sam. Their noble ambition – or at any rate Sam's noble ambition for them – is to reach, as a family, a total combined age of a thousand years.

> There was Tom Lynch, widower, aged eighty-five years, confined to his bed with constant undiagnosed pains in the caecum, and his three surviving boys Joe, aged sixty-five years, a rheumatic cripple, and Jim, aged sixty-four years, a hunchbacked inebriate, and Bill, widower, aged sixty-three years, greatly hampered in his movements by the loss of both legs as the result of a slip, followed by a fall, and his only surviving daughter May Sharpe, widow, aged sixty-two years, in full possession of all her faculties with the exception of that of vision. Then there was Joe's wife née Doyly-Byrne, aged sixty-five years, a sufferer from Parkinson's palsy but otherwise very fit and well, and Jim's wife Kate née Sharpe aged sixty-four years, covered all over with running sores of an unidentified nature but otherwise fit and well.   (101)

The enumeration proceeds through an increasingly hilarious series of almost all the ills to which the flesh is heir, ending with the two little boys, Pat and Larry, 'aged four and three respectively, and little Pat was rickety with little arms and legs like sticks and a big head like a balloon and a big belly like another, and so was little Larry' (103). 'Five generations, twenty-eight souls, nine hundred and eighty years, such was the proud record of the Lynch family, when Watt entered Mr Knott's service' (103–4). Sam goes on to demonstrate mathematically that the Lynch millennium was at that point only eight and a half months out of reach if all were spared till then, but, not surprisingly perhaps, 'all were not spared' (104), as documented in another six pages of progressive and multifarious decay of the unfortunate Lynch dynasty, a living (or rather, dying) monument to entropy. The accomplishment of the Lynch millennium is hampered by more than the vagaries of nature, however. Sam's addition is faulty, for the total family age actually amounts to only 978 rather than 980 years, which means that the projected figure of eight and a half months is also wrong. Sam indeed is well aware of this, advising in a footnote that 'the figures given here are incorrect. The consequent calculations are therefore doubly erroneous' (104). This assumes that Sam *is* responsible for the footnotes as well as the text, of course, and if he is not, then *our* calculations are 'doubly erroneous' too. The metafictional aspect of *Watt*, the parody of *all* explanatory positions, including fictional ones, is nowhere more overt than in the account of the Lynch millennium. In another footnote Sam takes care of possible objections to the fact that one of the Lynch ladies is a 'bleeder' by observing that 'Haemophilia is, like enlargment of the prostate, an exclusively male disorder. But not in this work' (102).

The element of parody is present throughout, of course, continually reinforced by the endless enumerations and permutations favoured by Sam. Ultimately what is parodied is the whole notion of interpretation, be it Watt's of Knott, Sam's of Watt, or the reader's of Sam and *Watt*. *Watt* is a shaggy-dog story of the same kind as Arthur's story of the Irish 'autochthon' Nackybal, who can allegedly extract cube-roots in his head – a mathematical feat causing the investigatory committee members to attempt unsuccessfully, as we have seen, to look at each other in amazement. (Nowhere in his writings is Beckett closer to Flann O'Brien than here.) The essence of the shaggy-dog story is its refusal to come to the point – Arthur loses interest in *his* narrative after twenty-six pages and simply breaks off. The point of *Watt*, from the beginning, is that there *is* no point to come to in the first place. *Watt* is a 'funambulistic stagger' (31), where nothing happens, several times. 'No symbols where none intended'

(254), the last line of the Addenda drily advises us, but we are continually provided with 'symbols' that have a weighty air of being 'intended': Watt's resemblance to Christ (159), for example, or Sam's frequent use of biblical phraseology with reference to both Watt and Knott. *Watt* begins in the 'failing light' (7), ends in 'the early morning light' (246), but the glorious dawn admired by the three employees of the state railway system is just as spurious as Bardamu's. 'And they say there is no God, said Mr Case. All three laughed heartily at this extravagance' (246). Whereupon the three 'stayed a little while, Mr Case and Mr Nolan looking at Mr Gorman, and Mr Gorman looking straight before him, at nothing in particular' (246). *Watt* is an epistemological parody, Watt an anti-Faust: Faust's joyful 'die Erde hat mich wieder' / 'I am life's again' becomes for Watt 'die Merde hat mich wieder' (250), where Faust's affirmation of *die Erde* 'the earth, life' is transmuted into an earthy acknowledgment only of the same old *merde.* The reader throughout may well share Watt's dilemma listening to the 'little voice' in his head: 'Watt never knew quite what to make of this particular little voice, whether it was joking, or whether it was serious' (91). The thrust of the narrative throughout is that the distinction is a spurious one. Towards the end, recovering from a blow to the head, Watt hears the little voice (or another like it) singing 'fragments of a part: / ... *von Klippe zu Klippe geworfen* / *Endlos ins ... hinab*' (239). The lines are Hölderlin's – 'flung from crag to crag / Endlessly down into ...' – and the missing word is *Ungewisse* 'the uncertain.' Uncertainty is inevitable, but unpredictable, marked by absence rather than presence. Uncertainty is precisely uncertain; we can count on it, reckon with it, as Sam demonstrates, but we can never be sure of it. Watt's blow to the head, knocking him out, comes from an abruptly opening door in a waiting-room where he has spent the entire night waiting in total darkness for the morning train; no symbols where none intended, of course, but in Watt's world this is completely par for the course. The parodic reference to Kafka's man from the country is apparent; like Kafka's people, Watt is under way to nowhere in particular, just under way, first sighted descending from a tram, last seen boarding a train. Like the figure he sights on the way to the station, like Achilles chasing Zeno's tortoise, Watt spends his days assiduously getting nowhere with enormous expenditure of effort, in pursuit of a quarry whose very nature is defined by its essential elusiveness. The narrative, in the end, tells us nothing, *says* nothing. Watt and Sam together have merely – 'But was not that something?' – 'turned, little by little, a disturbance into words, ...

made a pillow of old words, for a head' (117). The rest is a noisy silence.

Reading for the Plot: Pynchon's *Lot 49*

The narrator of *Der Prozess* presents a world impossible to interpret; the world of *La nausée* is one whose interpretation is meaningless since it is itself meaningless; in *Watt* the uninterpretability of the world is played with, subjected to permutations of pointlessness. In Thomas Pynchon's *The Crying of Lot 49* (1965), our last example of entropic irony, the emphasis shifts towards the element of plots and plotting – and consequently provides us with a transition to our final category of the comedy of entropy, that of entropic parody.

Oedipa Maas, the focal character of *Lot 49*, is closer in spirit to Josef K. than to Watt or Roquentin. Like Josef K., like Roquentin, Oedipa is arrested too – arrested in her case in the comfortably anodyne routine of southern Californian suburban housewifery by a letter informing her that she has been named executor of the estate of her one-time lover, 'one Pierce Inverarity, a California real estate mogul who had once lost two million dollars in his spare time but still had assets numerous and tangled enough to make the job of sorting it all out more than honorary' (1). Much more, as it turns out, for not only are Inverarity's holdings apparently vast and complexly interlinked, they are also apparently – or, at any rate, possibly – deeply and ambiguously involved in a massive conspiracy that seems to have undermined the entire fabric of American society. Oedipa, marked already by her name as a latter-day reflex of the archetypal investigator and solver of riddles of Western civilization, gradually allows herself to be drawn into attempting to get to the bottom of it all – only to find that there apparently *is* no bottom.

Oedipa's quest for solid ground and the meaning of Pierce Inverarity's legacy takes place against the backdrop of a comic-book America of the early sixties, a *Catch-22* in mufti, as represented by the lunatic world of southern California. (The 'Lot 49' of the title is in one sense a particular lot of postage stamps in a philatelists' auction; in another it is this America itself, the legacy of that key event in Californian and American history, the gold-rush year of 1849.) This America is a Waste Land, populated by grotesques. Oedipa's psychotherapist, Dr Hilarius, phones his patient at three in the morning, reversing the usual cliché, to persuade her to take part in an amusing little experiment on the effects of LSD on suburban housewives, turns

out to have worked on experimentally induced insanity in Buchen-
wald during the war – his specialty was pulling faces, one of them at
least with 'an effective radius of a hundred yards' (100) – and eventually goes hopelessly insane himself under the impression that he is
being pursued by avenging Zionists disguised as local policemen. Her
'trusted family lawyer' (8) makes occasional desultory attempts to
seduce her but is really interested only in destroying the TV lawyer
Perry Mason by undermining his credibility, to which end he has
spent years elaborating a rough draft of 'The Profession v. Perry
Mason, A Not-so-hypothetical Indictment' (8–9). Her husband,
Wendell ('Mucho') Maas, suffers regular crises of conscience about his
professions – first as a used-car salesman, then as a disc jockey – and
can console himself only by risking statutory rape charges with
underaged 'chicks' before he discovers true happiness in LSD and
millennial visions of 'this big, God, maybe a couple hundred million
chorus saying "rich, chocolaty goodness" together, and it would all be
the same voice' (106). Metzger, her co-executor of Inverarity's will
and one-time child movie star, has a casual affair with Oedipa before
even more casually deserting her, running off with yet another underaged chick. John Nefastis, who explains entropy to her, also hospita-
bly suggests casual sex in front of the TV, preferably during the news.
'I like to do it while they talk about Viet Nam, but China is best of all'
(79). In a gay bar she encounters a member of a group that calls itself
Inamorati Anonymous (IA for short), professes isolation as the supreme virtue, and religiously renounces love in any shape or form,
'hetero, homo, bi, dog or cat, car, every kind there is' (85). Oedipa, by
now deep in the coils of the labyrinthine conspiracy she thinks she
may have discovered, is briefly overcome by despair, then 'entered
the city again, the infected city' (86).

Oedipa's America is a dead world of Tupperware parties and
Muzak, freeways and advertising hype, drugs and booze, affluent
boredom and disregarded poverty, entrepreneurs pushing specials on
ready-to-wear Nazi uniforms in teenage sizes: 'This is America, you
live in it, you let it happen' (112). With no grail hero in sight who
might redeem the waste land, this is a terminally sick society, characterized by all the most vicious excesses of rampant capitalism, by
isolation, lack of communication, absence of relationship, dehumanization, paranoia and psychosis, pervasive waste of both materials and
lives, sterility and entropy. This is a culture that breeds isolates like
the Inamorati Anonymous, dedicated to non-participation, with-
drawal. In a bar called The Scope – which has a strictly electronic

music policy – Oedipa and Metzger encounter a member of the Peter
Pinguid Society, which commemorates the hero of the first military
confrontation (in 1863) between America and Russia, who also turns
out, however, to have been a convinced opponent of industrial capitalism – 'Didn't it lead, inevitably, to Marxism?' (33). In a Mexican
greasy spoon she encounters one Jesús Arrabal, a member of the CIA –
which stands, however, for the 'Conjuración de los Insurgentes Anar-
quistas' (88), the 'Coalition of Anarchist Insurgents.' In a washroom
she finds an advertisement, complete with box number, for the AC-DC,
otherwise the Alameda County Death Cult. 'Once a month they were
to choose some victim from among the innocent, the virtuous, the
socially integrated and well-adjusted, using him sexually, then sacri-
ficing him. Oedipa did not copy the number' (90). Just below the
plastic-coated surface of the consumer society there exists a whole
spectrum of dropouts, extremists, apocalyptic revolutionaries of one
stripe or another. Moreover, they all seem to communicate by way of
an alternative postal system known as WASTE, whose letterboxes are
the green waste receptacles dotted throughout the city.

Oedipa's first inkling of the (apparent) existence of this apparent
organization comes in the form of a misprint on an envelope, advising
users of the mails to report all obscene mail to their 'potsmaster' (30).
In a washroom, again, she finds a symbol that turns out to be,
apparently, a muted post-horn (34). 'So began, for Oedipa, the languid,
sinister blooming of The Tristero' (36). Gradually the newly sensi-
tized Oedipa begins to piece together clues to the existence and the
nature of an extraordinary organization – the Tristero – that may even
have been in continuous existence since the fourteenth century,
when it came into being in complex political circumstances as a
subversive terrorist group dedicated to the overthrow of the European
postal monopoly of the Thurn and Taxis family, adopting as its
symbol a muted post-horn. Around the middle of the nineteenth
century (1849, perhaps?) it appeared in the United States, ambushing
and slaughtering the messengers of the Pony Express and Wells Fargo,
waylaying them disguised as Indians or as mounted outlaws dressed
entirely in the obligatory black. And apparently, Oedipa realizes, it
still exists even in the 1960s in California, where, as the WASTE
system, it serves as a channel of communication for society's assorted
rejects, the disaffected. Physical violence has now given way to textual subversion and postage-stamp forgery, the WASTE stamps being
exactly like those of the U.S. Mail except for some tiny, barely detect-
able flaw in the design. WASTE, it further turns out, is in fact an

acronym for 'We Await Silent Tristero's Empire,' and is also known as DEATH, for 'Don't Ever Antagonize The Horn.' The association's founding father was apparently one Hernando Joaquín de Tristero y Calavera – *calavera*, 'coincidentally,' means 'skull' in Spanish, linking with the DEATH acronym, we may notice. 'Perhaps a madman, perhaps an honest rebel, according to some only a con artist' (119), Tristero had styled himself 'El Desheredado,' 'The Disinherited' and dressed his followers in black to symbolize their adherence to 'the only thing that truly belonged to them in their exile: the night' (120).

Some of Oedipa's information comes from rather unlikely sources. The first reference to the name Tristero, for example, occurs in a play called *The Courier's Tragedy*, a seventeenth-century work by one Richard Wharfinger, but it does not occur in all editions of the play, even when an edition not containing it is a straight reprint of one that allegedly does. Oddly enough, the actor who speaks the line in question commits suicide shortly after. Oddly enough, both the theatre where the play is performed and the bookstore that provides Oedipa with her copy of the text are owned by Pierce Inverarity, it turns out – and the professor of English literature who explicates the textual history for her is employed at a university endowed by Inverarity's estate. Oddly enough, a scene in Wharfinger's decidedly gruesome play about dead men's bones ground up to make ink is strangely reminiscent of one of Inverarity's own business undertakings involving dead men's bones transferred from Italy to an ornamental lake in one of his housing developments for the amusement of scuba enthusiasts. Oddly enough, Wharfinger's play seems to be all about communication and the lack of it. Oddly enough, the clues occur only sparingly in the beginning, then, as Oedipa tries to ignore them, in an enormous flood of unwanted information that seems to blanket all of southern California.

Lot 49 is centrally concerned with information systems and information channels, of which dozens figure in the plot – phones, TVs, radios, movies, phonograph records, audio tapes, mobile news units, postal systems, stamps, letters, acronyms, graffiti, books, plays, seminars, auctions, psychoanalytic sessions, and hallucinations, not to mention planes, boats, submarines, and scuba-diving equipment as well as the omnipresent automobile and the ubiquitous freeway. Oedipa's quest centres on the processing, the interpretation, the sorting out of this mass of information, and the interim conclusion to be drawn as the story pauses on the last page (to gather breath, as it were – for the word 'End' in no way indicates a conclusion) is – as in *Watt* –

that too much information is simply another form of entropy. Like a real-life Maxwell's Demon, Oedipa gamely attempts the job of 'sorting it all out' (1) in her effort to bring some apparent order into the legacy of Pierce Inverarity, 'to bring the estate into pulsing stelliferous Meaning' (58). She would organize 'the scatter of business interests that had survived Inverarity. She would give them order, she would create constellations' (65), she promises herself, only to realize in the end her total inability to sort reality from fantasy, real clues from hallucination, information from noise. Oedipa becomes involved in a situation that initially seems to promise not just information but communication, even Revelation of some higher or deeper meaning, but the result is a progressive undermining of her understanding of the situation, a progressive self-destruction of the interpretive process. The situation explodes in her face, as it were, as out of control as the broken aerosol can of hair-spray hurtling around the motel bathroom propelled by the escaping gas (the word *gas*, we may remember, being originally coined on *chaos*). 'The can knew where it was going, she sensed, or something fast enough, God or a digital machine, might have computed in advance the complex web of its travel; but she wasn't fast enough' (23).

Oedipa knocks over the aerosol can while she is attempting to control the outcome of the game of 'Strip Botticelli' she and her fellow executor Metzger are playing by muffling herself drunkenly in endless layers of clothing. Her attempts to strip away the layers of (possible) meaning around the Tristero partake of the same interplay of concealment and revelation. 'No symbols where none intended,' the narrator of *Watt* had warned; Oedipa's problem is to find some way of deciding what is intention (but whose?) and what is not. From an initial sense that 'there were revelations in progress all around her' (28), she reaches the point where revelations (but of what?) 'Now seemed to come crowding in exponentially, as if the more she collected the more would come to her, until everything she saw, smelled, dreamed, remembered, would somehow come to be woven into The Tristero' (58). Paranoia confers a lucidity all its own on the *disjecta membra* of reality – but where is the point of leverage allowing one to decide what is paranoia and what not? Oedipa's problem is to decide which one of several possible plots she is operating in as character, a decision by definition impossible. She is enmeshed, in other words, in what John Fowles, referring to *The Magus*, called a godgame (for a discussion of which see Wilson, 'Godgames and Labyrinths'). Which 'signals' really are signals? Is the fact that the bulk of Inverarity's holdings are located in a town called San Narciso significant or not? And if so, of what? What of the fact that she 'chooses' a motel called 'Echo Courts'? Oedipa 'felt exposed, finessed, put down' (3) by the obligation to execute the will. To how great an extent is this intuition true? To how great an extent is the whole Tristero business 'magic, anonymous and malignant, visited on her from outside and for no reason at all' (11)? Or is it indeed true that, like Wharfinger's play, the whole affair just 'doesn't mean anything' (54)? 'With coincidences blossoming these days wherever she looked, she had nothing but a sound, a word, Trystero, to hold them together' (80). As Driblette, the director of Wharfinger's play, warns her, 'You could waste your life that way and never touch the truth' (56). Her mirror holds no reflection (26), and, as in the Strip Botticelli game where she has to guess the outcome of a movie, 'she had no way to tell how long the movie had to run' (20). Faced with one more clue, maybe vital, maybe trivial, 'she looked around, spooked at the sunlight pouring in all the windows, as if she had been trapped at the center of some intricate crystal, and said, "My God"' (67).

In the end Oedipa is hopelessly trapped, a fly in a web, enmeshed in an intersection of texts she is powerless to disentangle. Long before the whole Tristero affair ever begins, however, Oedipa is already trapped – and originally sees Pierce Inverarity as the knight in shining armour who will deliver her. Before she met Inverarity, the narrative suggests, it was as if she were cut off from the real world by some kind of invisible barrier, encapsulated in a fairy-tale princess's tower, 'prisoner among the pines and salt fogs' (10). 'There had hung the sense of buffering, insulation, she had noticed the absence of an intensity, as if watching a movie, just perceptibly out of focus, that the projectionist refused to fix' (10). When Pierce turns out not to be her Prince Charming after all, Oedipa realizes that she is still a prisoner in her tower, that 'the tower is everywhere and the knight of deliverance no proof against its magic' (11). Lacking any 'apparatus except gut fear and female cunning to examine this formless magic, to understand how it works, how to measure its field strength, count its lines of force' (11), Oedipa drifts aimlessly, drifts finally into a desultory marriage with the self-centred Mucho Maas and 'a fat deckful of days which seemed (wouldn't she be the first to admit it?) more or less identical' (2), a sameness of Tupperware parties and supermarket Muzak. She is not immediately jolted out of this Briar Rose sleep by a long-distance call in the middle of the night from Inverarity, who addresses her in a variety of comic music-hall voices, but with no identifiable message before hanging up. 'Silence, positive and thorough, fell' (3), until a year later, when the jolt arrives in the form of the letter announcing his death and her nomination as executor of his legacy. 'Oedipa stood in the middle of the living room, stared at by the greenish eye of the TV tube, spoke the name of God, tried to feel as drunk as possible. But this did not work' (1).

At one point during her brief affair with Inverarity, Oedipa had been fascinated and saddened by a painting she had found in a gallery in Mexico City: 'a number of frail girls with heart-shaped faces, huge eyes, spun-gold hair, prisoners in the top room of a circular tower, embroidering a kind of tapestry which spilled out the slit windows and into a void, seeking hopelessly to fill the void: for all the other buildings and creatures, all the waves, ships and forests of the earth were contained in this tapestry, and the tapestry was the world' (10). Oedipa reads the painting as confirmation that there can be no escape from her own personal prison tower, but her interpretation, obviously, can just as easily (too easily?) be stood on its head: escape lies not in languishing for the shining saviour who never comes but precisely in the attempt, hopeless or not, to fill the void yourself. The Tristero enigma appears to offer Oedipa just the opportunity to discover or create a surrogate world and imbue it with meaning, to eliminate the fatal absence of intensity in her comfortably moribund existence. 'Under the symbol she'd copied off the latrine wall of The Scope into her memo book, she wrote *Shall I project a world?* If not project then at least flash some arrow on the dome to skitter among constellations and trace out your Dragon, Whale, Southern Cross. Anything might help' (59). Oedipa, after initial hesitation, becomes her own knight of deliverance, 'so like the private eye in any long-ago radio drama, believing all you needed was grit, resourcefulness, exemption from hidebound cops' rules, to solve any great mystery' (91), and just as any private investigator worth the name sooner or later suffers cruel punishment Oedipa soon seems to be coming to grief too. 'They knew her pressure points, and the ganglia of her optimism, and one by one, pinch by precision pinch, they were immobilizing her' (91–2). But who are 'they'? Are they real, or is she imagining them? And to this pair of alternatives she is eventually forced to add a second symmetrical pair, 'hanging like balanced mobiles right and left' (136): are 'they' and the whole Tristero enigma just a vengeful (or pedagogical?) hoax on Inverarity's part – or is she merely imagining *that*?

> Either way, they'll call it paranoia. They. Either you have stumbled indeed ... onto a secret richness and concealed density of dream; onto

a network by which X number of Americans are truly communicating whilst reserving their lies, recitations of routine, arid betrayals of spiritual poverty, for the official government delivery system; maybe even onto a real alternative to the exitlessness, to the absence of surprise to life, that harrows the head of everybody American you know, and you too, sweetie. Or you are hallucinating it. Or a plot has been mounted against you, so expensive and elaborate, involving items like the forging of stamps and ancient books, constant surveillance of your movements, planting of post horn images all over San Francisco, bribing of librarians, hiring of professional actors and Pierce Inverarity only knows what-all besides, all financed out of the estate in a way either too secret or too involved for your non-legal mind to know about even though you are co-executor, so labyrinthine that it must have meaning beyond just a practical joke. Or you are fantasying some such plot, in which case you are a nut, Oedipa, out of your skull.   (128)

'This, oh God, was the void. There was nobody who could help her. Nobody in the world' (128). The final turn of the screw comes when Inverarity's stamp collection is to be auctioned off, including the Tristero 'forgeries' as lot 49, and a mysterious bidder is announced who *may* be from Tristero, wanting to keep evidence of Tristero's existence out of unauthorized hands. Oedipa deliberately gets herself drunk and goes driving on the freeway in the dark, without lights, 'to see what would happen. But angels were watching' (132). Our last glimpse of Oedipa is in the auction room, trying to guess which of the potential buyers will turn out to be the man from Tristero, if there really is such a thing as Tristero. 'An assistant closed the heavy door on the lobby windows and the sun. She heard a lock snap shut; the sound echoed a moment. Passerine [the auctioneer] spread his arms in a gesture that seemed to belong to the priesthood of some remote culture; perhaps to a descending angel. The auctioneer cleared his throat. Oedipa settled back, to await the crying of lot 49' (138).

In the end, Oedipa fails, as she must, to establish the truth about the reality she inhabits. That reality is America, and Pynchon's novel is frequently read primarily as a flamboyant satire for that reason. Such a reading is entirely defensible, for a central concern is indeed the nature of the reality America. Another central concern, however, and one prompting a reading as entropic irony rather than satire, is the impasse in which Oedipa finds herself, both as an isolate within that society and as a quester for an alternative reality that would somehow serve to validate, to redeem the reality America. That there is a (quasi)religious dimension to her quest is made evident (albeit ambivalently) by the narrative. America is the Waste Land, awaiting delivery, awaiting the regenerative Word, 'the cry that might abolish the night' (87). As Oedipa first drives into San Narciso (on a Sunday), the streets, seen from a slope, resemble nothing so much as a printed circuit, demonstrating the same 'hieroglyphic sense of concealed meaning,' in 'an odd, religious instant' where 'a revelation ... trembled just past the threshold of her understanding' (13), 'some immediacy, ... some promise of hierophany' (18). Oedipa's relation to the Truth, however, if such there be, remains at that level, one of never quite touching. Epileptics, Oedipa reflects, learn to recognize the signals announcing their seizures, and afterwards all that is remembered is 'this secular announcement, and never what is revealed during the attack' (69). Would it be the same with her? she wonders, 'left with only compiled memories of clues, announcements, intimations, but never the central truth itself, which must somehow each time be too bright for her memory to hold; which must always blaze out, destroying its own message irreversibly, leaving an overexposed blank when the ordinary world came back' (69).

Oedipa's voyage to the end of the night reveals no Transcendental Signified, only a superabundance of ambiguous signifiers. The most ambiguous of these is the Tristero itself, which on one level is the realm of terror and evil and death, on another a realm of true communication at least potentially redeeming a trivialized and ruined society. Oedipa hears from one of her contacts about a seventeenth-century sect called the Scurvhamites, for whom 'Creation was a vast, intricate machine. But one part of it ... ran off the will of God, its prime mover. The rest ran off some opposite Principle, something blind, soulless; a brute automatism that led to eternal death' (116), a 'blind, automatic anti-God' (124). Tristero aptly symbolizes this diabolical Other – without which the divine plan, however, is incomplete. One of Inverarity's innumerable holdings, the Galactronics Branch of Yoyodyne (59), appears – in its name, at least – to suggest an oblique version of the same concept: it's not just love that makes the world or the galaxies go round, it's the power of the yoyo, yin-yang, day and night, good and evil, creating a perpetual-motion machine just like Maxwell's Demon. Is Inverarity himself exactly the principle opposed by Tristero – for Jesús Arrabal he is a capitalist 'miracle' (89), so perfectly does he embody its principles – or is he in fact the inventor of Tristero? One of his names for himself is The Shadow (3).

Like Mr Knott, or like Klamm in Kafka's *Castle*, Inverarity is at the
centre of everything, and like Knott and Klamm he is a shape-shifter,
a chameleon, not to be pinned down, a man without qualities – and
America is his legacy (134). Critics have toiled mightily with Inverarity, seeing in his name suggestions of Professor Moriarty, arch-crimi-
nal to Oedipa's Holmes, of 'inverse rarity' (a stamp prized by collec-
tors precisely because it is not a genuine stamp but a forgery), of both
truth ('in verarity') and untruth ('*inverarity*'); critics have even
pointed out that John Knox's birthplace in Scotland was near the
town of Inverarity. Oedipa is no more successful in 'piercing' to the
heart of Inverarity, the heart of ambiguity. Oedipa is no saviour, of
Thebes or anywhere else, no Perceval to redeem the Waste Land. At
worst the only (unregenerative) Word she discovers is the NADA, 'nothing' writ large, that terrified her husband Mucho (whose used-car lot
was a member of the National Automobile Dealers' Association). At
best all she finds are questions, either/or formulations: 'Behind the
hieroglyphic streets there would either be a transcendental meaning,
or only the earth' (136). Her ambiguous revelations generate no order,
only indeterminacy, incompletion, postponement. The quest fails as
it must fail, just as Josef K. fails. Whether she has really discovered a
Plot, redemptive or destructive, or just assembled a collection of
random coincidences, meaningless accidents, chance occurrences,
'clues' in endless regression point only to other 'clues,' progressively
more meaningless. The picture – if there *is* a picture – remains always
just out of focus, too blurred for recognition, but too recognizable to
ignore.

The reader, in turn, is left with little option but to plod along in
Oedipa's footsteps. As the Yoyodyne example just mentioned suggests, there is for the reader as well as for Oedipa a generous admix-
ture of clues whose main purpose is to point to other clues rather
than to some fixed central meaning, leaving the reader too to 'project
a world' (59), 'create constellations' (65). What is the reader to make
of Mucho Maas's 'enigmatic' whistling of '"I Want to Kiss Your
Feet," a new recording by Sick Dick and the Volkswagens' (12) – alias
the Beatles' 'I Want to Hold Your Hand,' of course – in the light of the
death of one of Wharfinger's characters after kissing the (poisoned)
feet of a statue of none other than 'Saint Narcissus, Bishop of Jerusa-
lem' (45)? Oedipa never even notices *this* 'clue,' but the narrative
invitation to 'project a world' ensures that the reader will. Or what
about the fact that Mucho, in a world soon to be full of muted horns,
is accused by his program director of being 'too horny' (6)? Why does

he work for a radio station called KCUF? The characters' names are outrageous, of course, even more so than in Beckett's Watt/Knott games. We meet Manny di Presso, Genghis Cohen, Stanley Koteks as well as Dr Hilarius, Mr Thoth (a nod at Thoth, the Egyptian god of speech, letters, communication), and Mucho Maas. For the most part these are comic-book names for comic-book characters, but often with teasing hints built in for the industrious critic: Mucho Maas, for example, is 'mucho más,' 'much more' in Spanish, and Mucho not only becomes 'much more' indeed under the influence of LSD – 'He enters a staff meeting and the room is suddenly full of people, you know?' (104) – he begins his career moreover on a used car 'lot,' where he is terrified by a sign saying 'nada,' 'nothing.' *Maas*, 'incidentally,' also means 'mesh' or 'loophole' in Dutch – and Oedipa not only finds some of her information on the Tristero in 'an ambiguous footnote in Motley's *Rise of the Dutch Republic*' (119), she also eagerly searches for loopholes and ends up entrapped in the mesh, like her classical namesake who seeks truth only to his own undoing. We may also remember the submarine in the movie Oedipa watches with Metzger: it too is searching for a loophole, a gate, in a 'gigantic net' (19) hung to keep submarines out. And so on. Mucho at one point interviews Oedipa for radio in his mobile broadcasting unit, giving her name as 'Mrs. Edna Mosh,' thereby allowing, as he claims himself, 'for the distortion on these rigs, and then when they put it on tape' (104). Mucho's is not the only rig where allowance has to be made for distortion, as the reader gradually discovers.

Pynchon, as almost all his critics point out at some point or other, is an expert at blending the suggestively sinister and the overtly playful. Oedipa seeks the meaning of Inverarity's legacy; the reader seeks the meaning of her quest, the book. Oedipa stumbles into a labyrinth, into a performance in which she is not at all sure what her role is; so do we. The more Oedipa finds out – thinks she finds out – about the Tristero, the more open the possibilities of interpretation become, for Oedipa and the reader alike. Maxwell's Demon, the tiny hypothetical sorter who by sorting out the 'hot' molecules from the 'cool' could theoretically create a perpetual-motion machine (62), clearly plays an emblematic role in *Lot 49* on all levels. Oedipa is the most obvious sorter in the text, and one who does, in a sense, create a perpetual-motion machine for herself, ending up becalmed in a situation so symmetrically balanced between alternatives that no redemptive solution is possible any longer. The reader runs the risk of ending up in Oedipa's shoes, with the difference that what for Oedipa is reality for the reader is a fiction: Oedipa is becharmed, the reader merely charmed. Pierce Inverarity too has his 'demonic' aspect, for just as Maxwell's Demon in a sense is no more than a graceful metaphor linking the two entirely different worlds of heat engines and information flow, Pierce Inverarity is the link between the two entirely different worlds of what we usually call order and disorder, the two faces of the reality we inhabit, whether we call it America or not. Pynchon's narrator, finally, discreet and entirely unobtrusive, is yet another manifestation of the demon sorter, guardian at the doorway of communication, expediting 'hot' and 'cool' molecules of information, generating a fictional perpetual-motion machine whose effect is that of the hypnotist's gold watch dangled seductively to and fro before the eyes of the willing subject. Realizing that Maxwell's Demon is at the heart of the matter, however, is to realize that the heart of the matter is entropy. What joins the world of thermodynamics to the world of information theory, as we have seen before, is precisely the concept of entropy, itself a metaphor. 'The Demon makes the metaphor not only verbally graceful, but also objectively true' (77).

Objectivity is in the eye of the beholder, however. Oedipa's informant on entropy is a lunatic inventor named John Nefastis, who has constructed an 'actual' working model of Maxwell's theory, a machine worthy of Flann O'Brien's *Third Policeman*. The box is fitted up with two pistons, and all you have to do to move the pistons and generate thermodynamic energy is watch the picture of James Clerk Maxwell pasted on the outside and concentrate on one of the cylinders. The demon will handle the rest, using the psychic energy provided. In theory. Oedipa fails to make the machine work – but Pynchon succeeds brilliantly in activating his. In so doing he points the way to our third and final category of the comedy of entropy, entropic parody, where such perpetual-motion machines are commonplace, running flawlessly and friction-free on polished bearings of narrative artifice.

9   Entropic Parody:
The Structuration of Uncertainty

Mirror on mirror mirrored is all the show.

Yeats

In one sense, clearly, narrative always borders on parody. All narrative, by definition, is narrated, is the product of a narrator, and the narrator always has the choice of telling the story differently. Or rather, the narrator always *had* the choice of producing different versions, for the words we read on the page might seem to have put an end to the matter and fixed the text once and for all. This is only partly true, however, for even though the words on the page do indeed represent a final choice taken, they also represent as well the sum of all the other choices *not* taken, ghostly reminders of what might have been. Most of the time, of course, we are completely unaware – *choose* to remain unaware – that this choice has been made and simply accept the monological narrative presented to us for our consumption as if it were the only possible version, the *true* version, of 'what really happened.'

In one very obvious sense, too, all narrative always is a matter of manipulating characters. One of the most common devices that demonstrate this fact is the flashforward (or prolepsis, to use Genette's term) to a narrative future that the character, for his or her part, cannot possibly yet know: 'Little did he know as he uttered these words that years later he would come to regret them so bitterly.' Most of the time, of course, we do not regard such a narrative manoeuvre as being in any way *parodic* – rather we merely register it more or less unthinkingly as a perfectly standard narrative device. On occasion, however, our attention is drawn so forcibly to the artifice involved that we have little choice but to register the artifice itself as being a major component of the narrrative statement. One of the most striking and effective examples of this is the opening sentence of García Márquez's *Cien años de soledad* (1967; *One Hundred Years of Solitude*), where the narrator is immediately and ostentatiously shown to be in possession of information that is of necessity completely beyond the character's reach: 'Muchos años después, frente al pelotón de fusilamiento, el coronel Aureliano Buendía había de recordar aquella tarde remota en que su padre lo llevó a conocer el hielo' (9) / 'Many years later, as he faced the firing squad, Colonel Aureliano Buendía was to remember that distant afternoon when his father took him to discover ice' (11). We sense parody, in other words, as soon as the element of reflexivity becomes ostentatious, as soon as the telling of the tale becomes ostentatiously more important than the tale told, as soon as the narrator steps forward and steals the limelight usually – or at any rate, usually in *realist* texts – reserved for the characters. A 'normal' example of prolepsis is unlikely to strike us as being either 'unfair' to the character or a joke at the reader's expense, but in the case of García Márquez's bravura example both of these suspicions are probably near to the surface.

If the opening of García Márquez's novel only hints at its comic potential, Flann O'Brien's *At Swim-Two-Birds* (1939) employs deliberate confusion of narrative levels to high comic effect. The narrator, a determinedly drunken Irish student, sets out to write a novel about a man named Trellis, an unpleasant character who owns a public house in Dublin and, like the narrator, spends most of his time in bed. Trellis in turn sets out to write a novel himself, creates a heroine of surpassing beauty and virtue, and, à la Pygmalion, unable to resist his own handiwork, ravishes her. He also creates himself a son, Orlick Trellis, a soft-spoken man in his middle years who, as it turns out, strongly disapproves of such behaviour. Trellis senior is a man of limited imagination, however, and to save himself unnecessary mental fatigue in creating secondary characters arranges to employ temporarily in that capacity a bunch of cowpokes from the works of a popular author of westerns. Trellis's fate is sealed when he ill-advisedly refuses to pay these hired characters a decent living wage, and since he spends so much of his time asleep in his bed they have ample time to plot their revenge. They are assisted in this endeavour by the outraged heroine (who, unknown to Trellis, has meanwhile fallen in love with and married one of them), by various characters from Irish myth and legend, and by Orlick, who becomes the key to the whole undertaking. Orlick is an author too, it turns out, and with enthusiastic assistance from his aggrieved associates he in turn sets out to write a narrative in which Trellis is scheduled to come to a very bad end indeed. All three narratives come to an abrupt end themselves, with nothing decided on any level, when the highest-ranking narrator, the drunken student, receives his Bachelor of Arts degree and moves on, presumably, to better things.

Trellis, writing a narrative about characters who are writing a narrative about him, is caught up in the self-reflective universe of entropic parody – or rather, he is caught up in *one* of the possible worlds of entropic parody. A brief recapitulation of the nature of the various modes of entropic comedy may be helpful at this point, before introducing a further distinction.

In entropic satire, then, to repeat, the emphasis is on the relationship of characters and the social world they live in. Satire, moreover, is essentially a realist mode of writing (and reading), and its characters and their world alike are essentially portrayed as being real rather than fictional, a true reflection of the real world inhabited by author and reader. Entropic irony has to do with the relationship of characters to the meaning of the world they inhabit, as they read that meaning. Irony, as opposed to satire, is essentially a modernist mode of writing, reflecting in its turn its authors' and readers' preoccupations with the nature of meaning and the nature of knowledge. In entropic satire characters look at the world around them; in entropic irony they look 'up,' from the discoursed world of which they are inescapably a part, at the world 'above' them, the world of discourse. Entropic parody, finally, has to do precisely with the discoursing of worlds, and the characters become increasingly less important as the question of the structuration of their world becomes increasingly foregrounded. Entropic satire is a comedy of anomie; entropic irony is a comedy of epistemology; entropic parody is a comedy of narration.

We may further distinguish three different submodes of entropic parody. In the first, the emphasis is on the ludic manipulation of characters by the sovereign narrator, and the examples just discussed from García Márquez and Flann O'Brien clearly operate in this mode. This mode – which we might call *character-based* – is obviously closely related to entropic irony, but whereas in the latter the reader's attention is focused on the character (Oedipa Maas, for example) looking 'up,' in the case of this first submode of entropic parody our attention is focused rather on the element of narrative play in the construction of the character's world, or, as we might say, on the narrator looking 'down.' The second submode of entropic parody is *reader-based* rather than character-based, and our attention as readers is focused on *ourselves* and our efforts to play competently the narrative game whose rules we are allowed to learn only as we play, only as the narrator allows us to learn. In reader-based entropic parody, in other words, the reader plays out on the discursive level the role that is played in the mode of entropic irony on the level of story by the character. The third mode of entropic parody, finally, is *language-based*, and our attention as readers is focused less on the game that the narrator chooses to make us play than on the game that reader and narrator alike have no option but to play and whose rules are the always unstable rules of language itself, a narrative in which we all function as characters.

Traditional parody is normative parody and is parodic of *something*, of some target text, just as traditional satire is normative satire and satirical of something that it aims to change. *Don Quijote* takes as its target a whole generation of tales of chivalry, *Ulysses* takes aim at the *Odyssey*, *Doktor Faustus* measures itself against *Faust*, however different their reasons for doing so may be. Entropic parody, by contrast, like entropic satire, is *disengaged*, needs no target, or, rather, is parodic only of itself, which is to say of the endeavour of narrative itself. Entropic parody, that is to say, is essentially a postmodernist mode of writing. Jean-François Lyotard has characterized the postmodern condition as being defined by 'incredulity towards metanarratives' (xxiv), the shattering of belief in systems of all kinds that lay claim to the authoritative discourse of truth. In place of such a belief in the authority of a single central and verifiably true explanation, a single legitimation of the reality we inhabit, postmodernist thinking invents new realities, new *possible* explanations, the possibility of whose existence is more interesting than their claim to truth. These multiple 'narratives of delegitimation,' as Lyotard calls them, are overtly provisional, overtly fictive, and overtly less concerned with explaining 'reality' than with explaining themselves. To this extent entropic parody is emblematic of postmodernism.

Our neatly defined categories of character-based, reader-based, and language-based modes of entropic parody are, of course, only explanatory fictions too. All narrative texts involve characters, readers, and language, after all, and the threefold categorization is obviously far more a matter of theory than practice. Rather than indulging in any futile attempt to isolate 'pure' examples of the three submodes, therefore, let us turn at this point to some exemplary entropic parodies in which to examine their interplay.

The Narrator as Despot: Robbe-Grillet's *La maison*

In realist narratives characters are more important than events – what interests the reader essentially is what happens to *them*, rather than what *happens* to them. Judged by this criterion Alain Robbe-Grillet's *La maison de rendez-vous* (1965; translated under the same title) is certainly anything but a realist text. In La *maison* the characters are little more than tokens or counters to be moved like pieces in a board game, acquiring any importance they may have not from any innate individual value but only from their relative position on the board. Little more than a 'simple armature en fil de fer' (148), a 'simple wire armature' (104), a character may easily become fused or confused with another – like the girl named Kim, who is frequently confused with another girl 'dont le prénom peut-être s'écrit également Kim, et se prononce de façon très voisine, le différence ne pouvant être sensible qu'à une oreille chinoise' (118–19) / 'whose name may also be written Kim, and is pronounced quite similarly, the difference imperceptible except to a Chinese ear' (82). The triangular rip in the oilcloth cushion of a rickshaw or a discarded Chinese magazine in the gutter is as important as the interchangeable characters – 'tous les Chinois ont la même figure' (110) / 'all Chinese look alike' (75) – or indeed the interchangeable situations, as it turns out. *La maison* is a narrative not about characters or story or stories but about the *generation* of characters and stories, the essentially arbitrary *structuration* of discourse out of uncertainty.

It is possible to reconstruct a relatively coherent – and distinctly sensational – story: Lauren, a young woman who has come to Hong Kong to marry a Dutch businessman, Georges Marchat, is completely demoralized by the news of his suicide and becomes an inmate of a deluxe brothel, the 'maison de rendez-vous' of the title, operated by one Lady Ava. There she encounters Ralph Johnson, an American drug dealer, who becomes infatuated with her. In order to afford her increasingly expensive favours he attempts to borrow a very large sum of money from an eccentric millionaire, Edouard Manneret, and when Manneret refuses to co-operate Johnson kills him. Rather than making good his escape, he returns to the brothel to speak to Lauren one last time, only to walk into a trap. The police are waiting as he enters her bedroom, and Lauren watches impassively as he is arrested.

To attempt such a reconstruction of the story, however, is to fall oneself into the precise trap set by the text – to search for a unitary meaning – and on closer scrutiny the putative 'real' story we have extracted from the baroque ornamentation of the text quickly begins to unravel under our gaze. 'Lauren,' for example, is referred to on some occasions as 'Lauren,' on others as 'Loraine,' on yet others as 'Laureen,' and while the reference in all cases *seems* to be to the same woman we can never be quite sure. Marchat, similarly, metamorphoses into Marchant and Marchand. Lady Ava seems 'actually' to be called Eve, or perhaps Eva. The American, Johnson, is described at an early stage as not being an American at all, but actually 'de nationalité anglaise et baron' (46) / 'English and a baron' (27), but this correction is then ignored throughout and he is continually referred to as American after all. There are various works of sculpture described as being by such 'noms célèbres' (185) / 'famous names' (133) as 'Edouard Manneret, R. Jonestone, G. Marchand, etc.,' while 'Jonestone' is later described as being a playwright, and Manneret as being a writer. Objects and locations suffer from the same instability. Lady Ava's sofa, for example, is described as yellow (30/15), then as 'un canapé de velours rouge – ou plutôt de velours jaune' (37), a 'red velvet – or rather yellow velvet – couch' (20), becomes red after all (46/27, 62/39), then yellow again (63/40), becomes almost immediately afterwards 'à bandes jaunes et rouges' (63) / 'red-and-yellow striped' (40), then 'aux couleurs indéfinies' (83) / 'varicolored' (55), and finally, as if tired of this relentless metamorphosis, 'sans couleur' (184) / 'colorless' (132). The apartment of the murdered Manneret shows a similar indecision as to its exact location, being placed sequentially on the second floor (70/45), the fifth (118/81), either the third or the fifth (126/87), and finally, no doubt following the rising tension, on the seventh (209/150). The apartment, moreover, seems sometimes to be located immediately over Lady Ava's drawing-room, but at others to be in another building entirely. Manneret's death, too, is not left to chance. It seems at first to be due to poison, but this presentation of it turns out to be only a theatrical performance put on in Lady Ava's establishment for the entertainment of her guests (73/48). Some time later he is violently killed in his own apartment, his neck broken by a single crunch of the jaws of a savage black dog (159/112). Nothing daunted, he dies again some time later, an unknown assailant stabbing him with a poisoned Chinese stiletto (175/125), and once again a little later still, this time assassinated by the Communists (202/145). Finally, to make assurance multiply sure, he is fatally shot 'cinq fois de suite' (211) / 'five times in a row' (152) by the desperate Johnson. The unfortunate Manneret, obviously, never had a chance.

Now, clearly, this is a splendid example of character-based entropic parody. To an even greater extent than in *At Swim-Two-Birds*, the characters of *La maison* obviously have no say in their own narrative destiny, but are subjected to a whole series of such destinies, to be endured at the whim of an extravagantly despotic narrator. This despotism becomes apparent as early as the epigraph of the novel – or rather, as early as the epigraphs, for there are two. The first advises the reader that 'ce roman ne peut, en aucune manière, être considéré comme un document sur la vie dans le territoire anglais de Hong-Kong. Toute resemblance, de décor ou de situations, avec celui-ci ne serait que l'effet du hasard, objectif ou non' (7) / 'this novel cannot, in any way, be considered as a document about life in the British Territory of Hong Kong. Any resemblance to the latter in setting or situations is merely the effect of chance, objective or not' (iii). The second, however, observes that 'si quelque lecteur, habitué des escales d'Extrême-Orient, venait à penser que les lieux décrits ici ne sont pas conformes à la réalité, l'auteur, qui y a lui-même passé la plus grande partie de sa vie, lui conseillerait d'y revenir voir et de regarder mieux: les choses changent vite sous ces climats' (9) / 'should any reader familiar with Oriental ports suppose that the places described below are not congruent with reality, the author, who has spent most of his life there, suggests that he return for another, closer look: things change fast in such climes' (iv).

Things certainly move fast as soon as the narrator gets into his stride. The narrative opens with his admission, or rather profession: 'La chair des femmes a toujours occupé, sans doute, une grande place dans mes rêves' (11) / 'Women's flesh has always played, no doubt, a great part in my dreams' (1). He goes on to imagine a variety of sadistic possibilities involving women's flesh, leather whips, iron manacles, dog collars, and the like. 'Souvent je m'attarde à contempler quelque jeune femme qui danse, dans un bal' (12) / 'Often I linger to stare at some young woman dancing, at a party' (2). Within a paragraph he is talking not about 'some' indefinite young woman at whom he 'often' stares, but about a specific young woman whom he *is* watching at the moment of narration dancing with 'son danseur, haute silhouette noire, comme en retrait' (12) / 'her partner, a tall, dark, almost recessive figure' (2). Abruptly she is obscured from his ostensibly lascivious gaze by two people who 's'avancent et masquent bientôt la scène, une haute silhouette en smoking sombre, à qui un

gros homme au teint rouge parle de ses voyages' (13) / 'step forward
and soon conceal the scene, a tall figure in a dark tuxedo listening to a
fat, red-faced man talking about his travels' (2). Abruptly the narrator
begins a fresh train of thought: 'Tout le monde connaît Hong-Kong, sa
rade, ses jonques, ses sampans, les buildings de Kowloon, et l'étroite
robe à jupe entravée, fendue sur le côté jusqu'à la cuisse, dont sont
vêtues les eurasiennes, longues filles flexibles, moulées dans leur
fourreau de soie noire à petit col droit et sans manches' (13) / 'Everyone knows Hong Kong, its harbor, its junks, its sampans, the office
buildings of Kowloon, and the narrow hobble skirt, split up the side to
the thigh, worn by the Eurasian women, tall, supple girls, each in her
clinging black silk sleeveless sheath' (2), which crinkles into a sheaf
of tiny creases at the waist when 'la promeneuse' / 'the stroller,' who
's'est arrêtée' (13) / 'has stopped' (3) in front of a shop window, turns
to stare at 'la jeune femme de cire vêtue d'une robe identique en soie
blanche, ou bien son propre reflet dans la vitre' (14) / 'the wax girl
wearing an identical white silk dress, or else at her own reflection in
the glass' (3). The wax girl is holding on a leash a big black dog 'qui
marche devant elle' / 'walking in front of her,' and her stylish high-
heeled shoes have slender thongs criss-crossing her feet. 'Le corps
souple se tord, de droite et de gauche, pour essayer de se libérer des
minces liens de cuir qui enserrent les chevilles et les poignets; mais
c'est en vain, naturellement' (15) / 'The supple body twists from right
to left, attempting to free itself from the slender leather thongs which
bind ankles and wrists; but to no purpose, of course' (4), for the
movements her bonds permit are so limited that 'la danseuse paraît
maintenant tout à fait immobile' (15) / 'the dancer now seems quite
motionless' (4). The fat, red-faced man is still talking, but stops
'comme s'interrogeant sur cette attention qu'il croit fixée sur lui.
Devant la vitrine, la promeneuse en fourreau noir rencontre le regard
que réfléchit la paroi de glace' (16) / 'as though wondering about the
gaze he supposes fixed on himself. Strolling in front of the shopwin-
dow, the girl in the black sheath meets the glance reflected in the
plate glass' (4–5), but turns and continues walking, 'retenant au bout
de la laisse tendue son grand chien' (16) / 'holding on its taut leash the
big dog' (5).

   This rapid synopsis of the first five pages of the narrative is entirely
typical of the style of La maison. Some one of many anonymous
women ogled by the narrator at various times and places metamorphoses into a specific dancer at a specific place and time; some one of
many anonymous women who wear black silk dresses metamor-

phoses into a specific stroller; a wax mannequin in a shop window metamorphoses into a woman struggling to free herself from her bonds; the struggling captive metamorphoses into the dancer; the red-faced man's glance metamorphoses into the reflected glance of the strolling woman in the black dress; the stuffed dog of the mannequin in the white silk dress metamorphoses into the real dog with which the woman in the black silk dress now continues her walk. This is a completely fluid world, where nothing has any claim to constancy except metamorphosis. Groups of statuary come to life, events presented as real turn out to have been only descriptions of statuary or of a theatrical performance or of the illustrations in a magazine found in the gutter. Murdered men come back to life and are murdered all over again. Sofas change colour, and apartments cannot decide which floor of the building they belong on. Ultimately there is no reality. At one stage Lady Ava denies that she has ever been to China: 'le bordel de luxe, à Hong-Kong, c'est seulement une histoire qu'on lui a racontée ... "Tout ça, dit-elle, ce sont des histoires inventées par les voyageurs"' (186–7) / 'the fancy brothel, in Hong Kong, is merely a story people have told her ... "It's all stories," she says, "invented by travelers"' (134).

The reader, clearly, has only these stories 'invented by travellers' to go on too. Indeed, while the element of character-based entropic parody will be apparent by now, so obviously will be the element of reader-based parody. If the characters are shorn of all autonomy and manipulated ruthlessly, the reader in turn is caught up – from the conflicting epigraphs on – in a narrative game over which he or she has little or no control. Even the identity of the narrator himself remains unstable throughout. Introduced with comforting solidity by first-person pronouns in each of the first three sentences, the *je*, the subject, rapidly shows itself to be as fluid as everything else in this narrative, dissolving into a play of identification and difference that prevents the reader from ever being able to say with certainty who it is that speaks or writes. At several points the reader is tempted to identify the narrative voice with that of the fat red-faced man, at many others with that of the American, Johnson – while on other occasions both of these are referred to as 'he' as distinct from the narrative 'I.' There are points where the murdered Manneret seems in fact to be the narrator, and others where it seems more likely to be Marchat (or Marchant or Marchand, whichever), or Kim, the servant girl, or even one of the anonymous 'petits hommes désoeuvrés' (144) / 'unoccupied little men' (101) who spend their time idling in doorways waiting for the rain to stop or to begin. This is a narrative about possibilities. There is no single story, or meaning, or central narrative identity, but only potentially limitless, kaleidoscopic possibilities of combination. The setting is the Hong Kong of pulp fiction, real or unreal as preferred, depending on which of the epigraphs the reader chooses to regard as 'the truth.' The chronology is self-contradictory in many places, impossible in some. The content is a parody of mass-appeal pornographic kitsch, as well as of detective stories – and, of course, of reading. This is indeed a 'maison de rendez-vous,' an inter-section of possibilities, a narrative brothel where 'la belle esclave enchaînée, promise à de longs supplices, dans le secret, la solitude, et le loisir' (12) / 'the lovely captive chained there, doomed to long tortures, in secrecy, solitude, and at leisure' (2) is none other than the hapless reader.

To a certain extent, however, the narrator himself also plays the role of a distinctly hapless reader, and this is a particularly unsettling feature of *La maison*. We are, of course, accustomed to being uncer-tain ourselves as readers, since uncertainty is the very stuff of narra-tive, but we certainly expect the narrator to know what he is talking about, to be in control of the narrative situation. We have already examined something of the effect of an uncertain narrator in Kafka's *Prozess*. but even there the narrator seems to be experimenting with *alternatives*, seems to be capable of generating various possible narra-tives all centred on a common question to which they function as possible, tentative, experimental answers. In *La maison* the narrator – in many places, at least – does not project the same sense of being in control of the stories he narrates, of balancing one version of events against another. The narrator of *La maison* is frequently rather in the position occupied by Josef K., a disoriented observer bemusedly watching the various only partly understood stories as they unfold, as varicoloured as Lady Ava's sofa, as shifting as the floor on which Manneret allegedly lives. There are several points in the narrative where the narrator overtly makes an attempt to put things together in his own mind, to make sense of what seems to be happening. 'Sans doute cette scène a-t-elle eu lieu un autre soir; ou bien, si c'est aujourd'hui, elle se place en tout cas un peu plus tôt' (30) / 'Doubtless this scene has taken place another evening; or else, if it is today, it occurs, in any case, a little earlier' (15). 'Je crois avoir dit que Lady Ava donnait des représentations pour amateurs sur la scène du petit théâtre privé de la Villa Bleue. C'est sans doute de cette scène qu'il s'agit ici' (41) / 'I believe I have said that Lady Ava gave performances for habitués on the stage of the little private theater of the Blue Villa. It is probably this stage which is involved here' (23). At other points he seems possibly to be in control of the various episodes but to be uncertain as to the best order in which to assemble them. 'Cet épisode, déjà passé, n'a plus sa place ici' (158) / 'This episode, already past, no longer has its place here' (111). 'Si Manneret vient déjà d'être assassiné, cette scène se passe auparavant, de toute évidence' (182) / 'If Manneret has already just been murdered, this scene takes place earlier, of course' (130). He assembles strings of mutually contradictory adjectives as if either planning on deciding later which he would delete or unable to decide why one should take precedence over another in the first place: 'elle offre soudain vers lui son visage lisse au regard démesuré, consentant, révolté, soumis, vide, sans expression' (47) / 'she suddenly turns toward him her smooth face with its excessive, consenting, rebellious, submissive, blank, expressionless gaze' (27–8). Episodes are related in several versions, with minute or major differences, as if the narrator were attempting to come ever closer to some elusive true version of the events presented – or as if any one version was just as illusory as any other. Sometimes he apparently loses track in the labyrinth of competing narrative possibilities. The by now sorely tried reader may well be persuaded that he has not been following with sufficient attention when he comes across the section beginning with the words 'Ensuite, c'est la fumerie d'opium, déjà décrite' (195) / 'Afterward, there is the opium den, already described' (140), for example. But this readerly guilt is uncalled for, for no such scene has in fact been presented.

The manipulation of the reader, indeed, is just as important a feature of *La maison* as the manipulation of the characters or the ostensible uncertainty and confusion of the narrator. *La maison* is essentially about itself rather than about anything else, and the reader – like the narrator or any one of the characters – is ultimately only one of the pieces to be manipulated in this narrative game. From the beginning the element of narrative play is overtly present. Such details as the exact colour of Lady Ava's sofa, the precise location of Manneret's apartment, or the real cause of Manneret's death are clearly moves in the narrative game designed to tease and to test the reader. We are hardly surprised to be told eventually that Manneret lives in an 'immeuble au luxe ultra-moderne avec ses labyrinthes de glaces et ses parois escamotables' (169), an 'ultramodern luxury apartment building with its labyrinths of mirrors and its sliding panels' (120), for that is where we as readers have been all along too. This is only one of multiple *mises en abyme* in *La maison* that continually draw our readerly attention back to the only real given in this narrative, namely that it *is* just that, a narrative, a system of fictional discourse where nothing is real or fixed or immutable and everything is potentially unreal and different and negotiable. Lady Ava's sofa, the long dark corridors down which Kim flees, the sparkling fragments of a smashed champagne glass, the multiple references to other modes of fictional expression, not to mention the numerous 'factual' contradictions and uncertainties, are all indicators to the reader – as long as he or she is prepared to play – that play is the name of the game. Like any metafictional construct, *La maison* is ultimately a joke, and the joke is on the reader unless he accepts his role as part of it. The joke, of course, is all the more so on the earnest critic, for like any good joke – and like other texts of a similar metafictional orientation – *La maison* essentially resists sober explanation and critical exegesis.

One of the peripheral characters in *La maison* is 'le roi Boris' / 'King Boris,' who lives 'au-dessus' / 'upstairs.' King Boris plays no obvious role in the action of the narrative other than to provide a fictional authority figure, partly a parodic God angrily thumping with his cane on the floor, partly merely 'le fou qui habite au-dessus' (188) / 'the lunatic who lives upatairs' (135). He is variously identified with Manneret, 'le Vieux' (179) / 'the Old Man' (128), who is further variously identified as a painter and a writer, as well as being a millionaire who indulges in vampirism, necrophilia, and apparently cannibalism – the Japanese prostitute Kito allegedly ends her career, with Manneret's assistance, as one of the ingredients in an interesting specialized item of Chinese cuisine. The incident is typical of a narrative that is 'tout de suite excessive' (11) / 'excessive from the start' (1) and that revolves ultimately around the exercise of power. On the one hand there are the violent pornographic fantasies of the narrator; on the other there are the convoluted manipulations of the narrative that provide their stylistic analogue. On the one hand this *is* not pornography – it is a parody of pornographic writing. On the other hand, there is a sense in which one could say that this is not narrative either – it is a parody of narrative, a subversion of narrative writing. The two meet in the figure of Manneret, who acts *out* the narrator's erotic fantasies of power, acts *in* the narrator's narrative fantasies of power, and is overtly associated not only with King Boris but, as we have noticed earlier, with the narrator as well. Manneret is both the parodic perpetrator and the parodic victim of (narrative) violence, and his elaborate demise can be read as a parodic and elegantly structured form of self-destruction – which he, of course, parodically survives. The latent cartoon-like, comic-strip unreality of the narrated violence that we noticed earlier in the case of the Marquis de Sade – where again the key word is *excessive* – becomes ostentatious in Robbe-Grillet's text. The brutality of the quasi-pornography here is just as unreal as the reality of the world the characters inhabit, for this is not writing about reality, about real victims suffering real pains, it is writing about ostentatiously make-believe, hypothetical characters whose suffering is also ostentatiously make-believe and hypothetical. This is writing about power, but only to the extent that writing is power. It is writing about writing, a series of structurations of uncertainty, not with any real-world end in sight, but for its own sake.

The Blinding of the Reader: Handke's *Die Hornissen*

In a sense *La maison de rendez-vous* is most primarily about its own failure to tell a story. The same could with equal validity be said of Peter Handke's novel *Die Hornissen*, 'The Hornets,' which appeared in 1966, just one year later than *La maison*, and has not yet been translated into English. The reader has to wait for 236 pages before there is any apparent reference to the hornets of the title, and while such reticence is hardly a feature unique to Handke's text it is none the less symptomatic. The passage that looks as if it might be going to deal at last with the elusive hornets is in the form of a five-page-long section of narrative entitled 'Die Hornissen' / 'The Hornets,' the third last of sixty-seven such separate sections, varying from a few lines to some thirty pages in length, and each with its own separate title. As it turns out, however, even this section, in spite of its title, has in fact nothing to do with hornets anyway – but may indeed be read as having a lot to do with the text *called Die Hornissen*, being apparently a series of instructions to an actor (but who is the actor and who is the speaker?) as to the best way of getting his meaning across to an audience, an endeavour portrayed as doomed from the start. If the (realist) reader's problem in *La maison* is to disentangle the knotted skein of possible stories offered, the problem in *Die Hornissen* is more analogous to a jigsaw puzzle with the individual pieces tipped out of their box in a pile. Some of the pieces look right away as if they belong together, some may even be fitted together already, but we cannot be sure in either case that this apparent connection is more than pure – or at any rate, induced – chance. There is the additional problem that, while we normally have the comforting certainty as we look at the pieces of a jigsaw puzzle that however great the apparent confusion may be initially all of the pieces can be made to fit together in one coherent whole, in the case of *Die Hornissen* we will find no guarantee that this is true.

It is possible, as with *La maison*, to put together the bare bones of a 'central' story. A first-person narrator, who appears to be blind, recounts a variety of events out of his own childhood, though the order in which these events may have occurred is highly problematic. There is a brother, Matt, who drowns while still a boy; another brother, Hans, who runs away from home, possibly immediately after the death of the first; an unnamed sister, who grows up to become the landlady of a tavern in the small and remote Austrian village where all the action appears to take place; a brutish father, given to violent rages, eking out a hard living as a subsistence farmer; a nameless mother, who apparently dies while the children are still small and is quickly replaced by another nameless woman, referred to consistently as 'die Frau des Vaters' / 'the father's wife'; and there is the narrator himself, Gregor Benedikt, who seems to have gone blind or been blinded under unexplained circumstances – possibly in some way connected with the drowning of his brother, but there are also pervasive though oblique references to war in general and bombers in particular.

It could, of course, be objected that these discrete events do not constitute even the bare bones of a story, central or otherwise; rather they constitute merely a series of props around which a story – or several stories – could be constructed. And it will emerge that it is not just the relationships between these individual events that at least potentially shift and slide; the individual events themselves, as the multiple qualifications in even the bare-bones account offered above may suggest, are far from certain in their details. What a realist reader might well regard as the very basics of narrative good manners, in other words, are missing in *Die Hornissen* – and that is its very point. The same reader might well feel that this was true of *La maison* as well, of course, and to the degree that both texts are examples of entropic parody the parallel is perfectly justifiable and intuitively obvious. But there is clearly a qualitative difference involved too, for with Handke's text we move from what I am calling character-based to reader-based entropic parody. In *La maison* the narrative joke, so to speak, is primarily on the characters, whose existence is completely beyond their own control, immediately and radically alterable at the whim of a despotic narrator who has no time for the niceties of realist narrative convention; in *Die Hornissen* the joke is clearly primarily on the reader, forced continually to admit his or her embarrassing ignorance of just who – to quote a well-known limerick out of context – did what, and with what, and to whom. In an obvious sense, of course, both Robbe-Grillet's and Handke's texts share these qualities with even the most traditionally realist work of fiction; the distinction, ultimately, is a matter of degree rather than kind, for in any narrative – even if most obviously in the subgenre *called* jokes – the *what* is always less important than the *how*.

Handke's narrative joke, like most jokes, focuses on the relationship of narrating and reading, which is to say on the nature of discourse. The crux of the matter in *Die Hornissen* is certainly the figure of the narrator. From the very beginning our attention is drawn to the element of mediacy in the narrative: 'Damals, sagte mein Bruder, sei ich vor dem Ofen gesessen und hätte in das Feuer gestarrt' (7) / 'On that occasion, my brother said, I was sitting in front of the stove and staring into the fire.' The opening word, 'damals,' / 'on that occasion' or 'back then,' immediately introduces the temporal difference between what allegedly happened and the later narration of it, a theme that will reverberate throughout the narrative. The narrating 'ich' is introduced not as a narrative voice but as a narrated character, an element of his brother's earlier narration. The element of narrative uncertainty is more overtly marked in the German than in the English translation given here, owing to the strategic use of the optional subjunctives 'sei' and 'hätte,' which do not necessarily imply uncertainty but always admit it as a possibility. (Kafka employs the subjunctive to the same effect in the opening sentence of *Der Prozess*, we may remember.) The sense here can be caught to some extent by a translation such as 'my brother claimed' in English, but this would be to go too far in the other direction. Such narrative complexity is hardly unusual in the modern novel, of course (or the realist novel either, for that matter); but in *Die Hornissen*, once again, it is symptomatic of the central role that is played throughout by readerly uncertainty.

Handke's Gregor, indeed, is a more undependable – and more destabilizing – narrator than any we have encountered since Grass's Oskar. His name may well remind the diligent reader of that other Gregor who wakes one morning to find himself metamorphosed into a monstrous insect in Kafka's *Verwandlung*. His surname Benedikt (*benedictus*, 'the blessed one') may even be seen as obliquely invoking – again like *Die Verwandlung* – the memory of yet another Gregor, that 'holy sinner' of medieval legend, Gregorius, who is born of an incestuous union, marries his own mother, and eventually, after a life of penitence, becomes pope, thus doubly displacing his father, both as his mother's husband and as the Holy Father. This putative connection will almost inevitably lead the well-read reader to that other displacer of his father, Oedipus, who, of course, pays for his transgression by his blindness – and Gregor's own blindness is a leitmotif throughout. But the scholarly reader will also doubtless reflect that Homer, the archetypal narrative artist of the Western world, was also blind; or that Teiresias, the seer, was a seer precisely because he was blind, his lack of sight compensated for by his abundance of insight. And throughout there is the nagging suspicion that Gregor's alleged blindness may in fact ('in fact') be more symbolic than real, for the narrator, after all, is in a sense always both blind, writing for a reader he will never see, and invisible, perceptible to the reader ultimately only as a speaking voice. 'Wer blind ist, ist auch unsichtbar. In der fremden Mundart wird sowohl für einen, der blind ist, als auch für einen, der den andern nicht sichtbar ist, dasselbe Wort verwendet' (244) / 'He who is blind is also invisible. In the strange dialect the same word is used both for someone who is blind and for someone who is not visible to others.' The 'strange dialect,' in terms of the story, is Slovenian, spoken along the border regions of Handke's native Carinthia. In terms of the narrative discourse of *Die Hornissen* everything we read is in a 'strange dialect,' a dialect of disorientation in which we can never be sure of anything. '"Gregor Benedikt ist ein Lügner"'(114) / '"Gregor Benedikt is a liar,"' an anonymous hand scrawls on a wall. The disgruntled comment may or may not be true of Gregor the character; it is certainly true of Gregor the narrator, as Plato told us long ago.

Die Hornissen is a hermeneutic quagmire. The reader is generously supplied with narrative facts that have a temptingly solid appearance to them in isolation but melt away disconcertingly as soon as any extended attempt is undertaken to organize them into some sort of explanatory interpretive system. There are numerous episodes, for example, that are concerned to a greater or lesser extent with casual, unremarkable, everyday violence. A horse, plagued by a swarm of flies, panics when he is stung in the eye (47); the brothers torture a horsefly (48); a headless chicken careers around the barnyard, knocking its own just severed head off the chopping block in the process (69); a cat is brutally beaten to death (72); a dog almost dies of the heat in a parked car (107). All of these episodes are narrated in meticulous detail, some of them at considerable length. In some of them the invitation to read with symbolic overtones – violence on a larger, less routine scale, the war, the pervasive presence of death – is very overtly present. The section dealing with the killing of a pig is a good example, and merits closer inspection. The section in question (97–102) begins immediately after a reference to the drowned brother's grave-stone – 'Unser lieber Bruder Matthias Benedikt, ertrunken' (96) / 'Our dear brother Matthias Benedikt, drowned' – and opens with a long description of the scalding to death of a pig. The section is entitled 'Die Liturgie' / 'The Liturgy,' however, and metamorphoses halfway through into a partial description of the liturgy of the Mass: 'Sehet das Lamm Gottes, hatte der Priester gesagt, sehet, das hinwegnimmt' (98) / 'Behold the Lamb of God, the priest had said, behold, who taketh away.' The abbreviation of the liturgical formula 'das hinwegnimmt die Sünden der Welt' / 'who taketh away the sins of the world' turns Christ the Saviour into Christ the bringer of death, while the soteriological sacrificial lamb of salvation is all too realistically transformed into a squealing scalded pig. The section concludes with Gregor and his brother, as altar servers, reading out another liturgical text, the Stations of the Cross – but in Slovenian, 'die fremde Mundart' / 'the strange dialect,' from 'Je k smerti obsojen' / 'He is condemned to death' to 'bo u grob poloshen' (101–2) / 'he is laid in the tomb.' The liturgical reading itself concludes without transition with one brother asking the other if he has heard the noise of the bombers too: 'Ich hab's gehört, sagte ich. Was? fragt mein Vater. Den Omnibus, sage ich. Pünktlich um zehn, sagt mein Vater' (102) / 'I heard it, I said. What? asks my father. The bus, I say. Ten sharp, says my father.'

This passage is remarkably similar to Günter Grass's style in its use of ostentatiously 'unsuitable' parallels, its balancing of the reality of death against a myth of salvation, its pervasive background of war, and the pervasive indirection of its narrative presentation. There is a striking incongruity in the images used: both the drowned brother and the divine Lamb reflected in the scalded pig; the proper method of killing the pig – four men needed, one to hold each leg – reflected in the liturgy of the Mass; the sacrifice of Christ guaranteeing salvation, that of the pig ensuring a full larder, that of the brother underwriting the moment of narrative tension necessary to any good tale. The passage, in short, is ostentatiously overwritten – in the same way that Grass employs overwriting – to the point where it undercuts itself, displays its own artificiality, directs the reader's attention to the centrality of his or her own constructive and reconstructive efforts. The overt disruption of time levels in the final exchange of the passage is a further example of this overstated narrative self-conciousness: Gregor's 'Ich hab's gehört' / 'I heard it' is uttered by Gregor the boy, referring to the sound of the bombers – although even this much is strictly speaking an interpretive reading of the situation on my part, for the bombers are not referred to by name at any point in this section – while the father's 'Was?' is addressed to the adult Gregor, years later, and in an entirely different context. Or rather, in a chronologically different variation of the same context, for Gregor and his father are on their way to church again as they talk about the bus, and Gregor's reply that he has just heard the bus coming, moreover, links the death of the one brother with the disappearance of the second, for in a previous section Gregor has imagined his brother Hans returning home on just this bus. The father's non-committal 'Pünktlich um zehn' / 'Ten sharp' is an unreflected celebration of an unproblematic 'ordinary' world where things happen when and where and how they are supposed to happen; the narrative voice in Handke's text, however, is enmeshed in a world where nothing – whether we are talking about 'then' or 'now', 'here' or 'there,''blind' or 'seeing,' 'speaker' or 'listener' – has unconditional meaning in and of itself but acquires meaning only insofar as such meaning is underwritten by the text of which everything is part.

The father's satisfaction in the fact that the bus is running according to schedule is also an example of another motif that occurs throughout *Die Hornissen*, the motif of mapping. If the war is the pervasive reminder of disorder throughout, the various attempts on the narrator's part to establish some enclave of perfect order – in however small an area – are the other side of the coin. We are hardly surprised when these attempts at narrative triangulation on Gregor's part turn out to be no less ambiguous than were the attempts of those other narrative geometers, Oskar and Josef K. and Watt. The narrator, for instance, describes the days when he and his two brothers were still schoolboys:

> Das Schulhaus befand sich in der Ortschaft Übersee. Die Schule der näher gelegenen Ortschaft Öd war in dem Jahr zuvor abgebrannt. Aus diesem Grund mussten die unterrichtspflichtigen Kinder der Ortschaft Öd zum Unterricht in die Ortschaft Übersee gehen. Später, nachdem der Krieg auch über die Schule der Ortschaft Übersee

gekommen war, mussten die unterrichtspflichtigen Kinder der
Ortschaften Übersee und Öd in die Schule der Ortschaft Anhöh
gehen. Die Ortschaft Anhöh, die durch ihr Stadtrecht eine Stadt war,
befand sich südlich in einer Entfernung von soundsoviel Kilometern
zu der Ortschaft Übersee und in einer Entfernung von soundsoviel
Kilometern zu der Ortschaft Öd..Die Entfernung der Ortschaften
voneinander und ihre Lage haben sich im Laufe der Zeit nicht
verändert.   (37)

The schoolhouse was in the district of Übersee. The school in the
district of Öd, which was closer, had burned down the year before.
For this reason the school-age children of the district of Öd had to go
to school in the district of Übersee. Later, after the war had passed
over the school of the district of Übersee as well, the school-age
children of the districts of Übersee and Öd had to go to school in the
district of Anhöh. The district of Anhöh, which had the legal status
of a town, was situated to the south at a distance of so-and-so many
kilometres from the district of Übersee and at a distance of so-and-so
many kilometres from the district of Öd. The distance of the
districts from each other and their position have not changed in the
course of time.

We are certainly reminded of *Watt* here, and the effect is the same:
the more exact the attempted description, the less 'realistically' the
reality described is presented, and the more artificial – and foregrounded – the description inevitably becomes. Immediately following this section there is another entitled 'Die Namen der Geräusche' /
'The Names of the Sounds' where the narrator meticulously records
the names of various noises such as those of a curtain swaying in the
wind, a fire dying, sand thrown against a window-pane, the drumming of rain on a galvanized iron roof, the rustling of dry grass, the
clatter of a falling bicycle. The reader – or at any rate the realist reader
– once again is in an interpretive quandary: Are we to read the list of
sounds whose names are described in such detail as being in a progressive series of some sort? Is the noise of the bicycle falling, for example, the most significant of these noises since it is mentioned last,
or is it simply one more neutral term in a neutral series described
merely in the interests of maximum potential narrative order? Gregor
is described at considerable length in another place wheeling a bicycle through the village and for some reason incurring the displeas-
ure of several of the villagers while doing so. Is there a connection?

And is the bicycle also connected in some way with the death of the one brother or the flight of the other or even both – or neither? And so on.

Handke's text demands a reader who reads for the discourse rather than the story, the process of mapping rather than the area mapped, as another instance of this triangulation strategy makes clear in the description of a Sunday afternoon walk through the village. 'Der Zweite Kartenspieler, der ihm als erster auf der Strasse begegnet, wird nach seinem Vater Koch genannt, wiewohl er Zimmermann ist, weil sein verstorbener Vater vorzeiten ... ein Kellner war' (168) / 'The Second Cardplayer, who is the first one to meet him on the street, is called Cook after his father, even though he is a carpenter, since his late father once worked as a waiter.' Here the narrator openly pokes fun at his own endeavours to emulate Maxwell's Demon, to establish order on a reality that resists it. The description continues to hilarious effect, recalling Beckett's happy account of the unfortunate Lynch family, as the narrator meets individuals variously called equally inappropriate names, such as the doctor, called Idiot after the idiot son he fathered while drunk, the Second Teacher, who is always 'aus unerfindlichen Gründen Dritter Lehrer genannt' (171) / 'for inexplicable reasons called the Third Teacher,' the three sons of the Second Teacher, called A, B, and C, and the two sons of the veterinary surgeon, called 'Echt und Unecht' / 'True and False.' Here the whole process of nomination is comically undermined. Our nomination is arbitrary and provides us with only a spurious semblance of control, a map whose inaccuracy is a given.

In spite of his various exercises in descriptive exactitude, however, much of the narrator's attention is devoted to exploiting rather than reducing that element of uncertainty, especially when his own activities constitute the area to be mapped.

> Ich möchte mich verstecken. Ich gehe also weg und verstecke mich.
> Während ich weggehe, überlege ich, dass nicht ich gehe, sondern
> dass unter mir diese Füsse gehen, und dass nicht ich überlege,
> sondern dass mein Gehirn überlegt ... und was mein ist, nicht ich
> sein kann. Nicht ich kann es sein, der hier überlegt. Ich kann mich
> nicht verstecken.   (178)

> I would like to hide. So I go away and hide myself. While I'm going
> away I reflect that it is not I who am going but these feet under me
> that are going, and that it is not I who am reflecting but my brain

that is reflecting ... and what is mine cannot be me. It can't be me
that is reflecting here. I can't hide.

Why the narrator wants to hide in the first place is something we are
never told. Indeed, there seems to be much that we are not told, in
spite of the narrator's almost manic attention to detail in other
places, and frequently the narrator overtly draws our attention precisely to this point. 'Es ist etwas in der Beschreibung vergessen
worden. Nein. Es ist mit Absicht nicht erwähnt worden. Nein, es ist
vergessen worden. Nein. Ich weiss nicht, wovon' (85) / 'Something
has been forgotten in the description. No. It was deliberately not
mentioned. No, it was forgotten. No. I don't know what sort of ...'
Some four or five pages later it turns out that the forgotten item in the
description was 'only' a wasps' nest, but the ponderous artifice with
which this trifling omission is treated – it has a section all to itself,
'Der vergessene Gegenstand' (87) / 'The Forgotten Object' – clearly
can serve to alert us to the possibility that other items of potentially
much more importance, whatever they might be, may also have been
omitted.

The narrator's carefully cultivated distance from his narrative material is apparent throughout, and is necessarily paralleled by the
reader's inability to arrange the information with which he or she is
provided into a satisfactory story without ostentatious loose ends.
Much is made of Gregor's blindness, but there are constant disturbing
hints that this blindness may be just a fake, 'vielleicht nur erlogen'
(204) / 'perhaps just a pretence,' perhaps more a reference even to the
reader's blindness than to the narrator's. Very belated assistance
seems to be offered the increasingly groggy reader only half a dozen
pages from the end of the book in the second last section of the
narrative, which is called 'Die Entstehung der Geschichte' (241–6) /
'The Genesis of the Story' and placed immediately after the section
already discussed entitled 'Die Hornissen' / 'The Hornets.' This section helpfully informs us that the reason for the narrative contradictions and hesitations so far is that the narrator – 'wenn ihn die
Erinnerung nicht trügt' (241) / 'if his memory does not deceive him' –
has 'actually' been attempting all along, though we are not told why
exactly, to recall the contents of a book he has once read and now
very largely forgotten. 'Indessen zweifelt er nicht, dass er das Buch
vorzeiten gelesen hat; da er es also gelesen hat, kann er damals das
Augenlicht noch nicht verloren haben; ein Zweifel plagt ihn nur über
die Begebenheiten, die in dem Buch vor sich gegangen sind' (242)/ 'At

the same time he does not have any doubts that he did read the book at some stage in the past; and since he did read it he therefore cannot at that time have lost his sight already; he is assailed by doubts only as to the events that took place in the book.' He is allegedly intrigued by certain similarities between what happens to the narrator of the book he wishes to remember and what has happened in his own life.

The beleaguered reader of a realist bent might well decide at this point that Handke must have been the victim of either amazing clumsiness or sheer perversity or both in choosing to release this apparently vital piece of information as to how to read the book only at this ridiculously late point. This, however, would be to underestimate grievously the deviousness of Handke's text and its narrator and to walk into one of those narrative traps with which postmodern fiction is so liberally strewn. For there is no reason at all – in spite of the narrator's sudden adoption of the third person rather than the first to refer to his own alleged reading of the alleged text – to assume that this penultimate section has to be read as any more authoritative in any way than any other section in the narrative of which it also is a part. The narrator, indeed, by referring to himself in the third person throughout this section – and in no other – manages to throw yet another layer of obfuscation between himself and the events that he now claims have nothing to do with him anyway but only with some character in a narrative who is oddly similar to him in many ways, including his apparent or alleged blindness. (We also notice that through the adoption of the third person here a new narrator is effectively introduced, reducing the narrating Gregor to a character himself and suggesting an endless narrative regress.) In the final section he reverts to the first person in describing a scene where 'wieder ein anderes Mal' (246) / 'on still another occasion' he had seen – we note the verb – his brother crossing over the frozen crust of a snowbank, only his momentum and the regularity of his movements preventing him from breaking through.

> Er hat die Ordnung der Bewegungen gefunden, die ihn herausführt.
> Wenn er gerufen wird, darf er nicht halten oder Antwort geben. Als
> ich ihn rief, blieb er stehen. Als ich ihn anrief, brach er ein. Als er
> den linken Fuss herauszog, brach der rechte ein. Als er den rechten
> Fuss herauszog, brach der linke ein. Als er zu laufen anfing,
> brach er beidseits ein. Unter der Eisschicht ist der Schnee aus
> dichtem Staub.
>
> (247)

He found the order of movements that would bring him through. If he is called he must not stop or give any answer. When I called him he stopped. When I called to him he broke through. When he pulled out his left foot his right foot broke through. When he pulled out his right foot his left foot broke through. When he began to run he broke through with both feet. Under the crust of ice the snow is a thick powder.

These are the concluding words of the narrative, and we may well be struck by the sudden and disconcerting shifts of tenses. We may also be struck by the image of drowning, even though the crust of ice conceals only harmless deep snow rather than water. The story of Matt's drowning has already been told in exact detail in an early section (36–42), where the cause of the accident has been described as a game of schoolboy daring between the narrator's two brothers Hans and Matt, who challenge each other to swing on a rope over the river at a point where it flows through a ravine. Hans calls out to Matt (but we do not know why), the rope comes undone, and Matt falls into the river and drowns. There are some noteworthy details in this account. The section is called 'Die Ertrinkungsgeschichte' / 'The Story of the Drowning' rather than 'Die Ertrinkung' / 'The Drowning,' we notice. In spite of the meticulous detail, the point is made that the story is told 'aus zweiter Hand' (41) 'at second hand.' In a text where the chief characters' names are used extremely rarely the names of Matt and Hans are mentioned with striking frequency. There can be no doubt that Hans, if this story is true, must bear much of the responsibility for Matt's death, and Hans, as we know, disappears shortly afterwards. Gregor, who is innocent of any involvement in the whole affair, fantasizes Hans's return at various points in his narrative, but Hans never reappears.

But how innocent is Gregor really? There are some striking oddities in the ostensibly explanatory section 'Die Entstehung der Geschichte' / 'The Genesis of the Story' as well. The book the narrator has now allegedly been trying to recall, for example, is stated as dealing with only two brothers rather than three. We are surprised to discover this, for this is the first time it might occur to us that there might also only be two rather than three brothers in the book that *we* are reading.

Das Buch erzählt von zwei Brüdern, von denen später der eine, als er allein nach dem abgängigen zweiten sucht, erblindet; es wird aus der

Erzählung nicht ganz klar, durch welches Ereignis der Knabe erblindet; es wird nur mehrmals gesagt, dass ein Kriegszustand herrsche;
die näheren Angaben über das Unglück jedoch fehlen, oder er hat sie
vergessen.   (243)

The book tells of two brothers, of whom one later goes blind as he
searches for the second, who has gone missing; it does not become
quite clear from the story what causes the boy's blindness; it is
merely said several times that a state of war is in effect; more exact
details about the accident are missing, however, or he has forgotten
them.

What is the meaning of this sudden disappearance of one of the brothers? Are we to read the final pages of the narrative, perhaps, as some
kind of involuntary admission on Gregor's part that the responsibility
for his brother's drowning was in fact his and his alone? That the
apparently guilty brother who went missing had in fact never existed
in the first place? That the whole point of Gregor's narrative is to
write himself out of the story? That the point of his blindness is to
make him invisible? That Gregor, at least in his own eyes, is a
criminal hiding behind an apparently indecipherable text – which the
sophisticated reader, however, has now none the less triumphantly
deciphered?

While our naïve reader who gratefully accepts at face value the
helpful hints of 'The Genesis of the Story' is led astray in one way by
the text, however, our more sophisticated reader is no less thoroughly
sent on a similar if more interesting wild-goose chase. Unfortunately
for our sophisticated reader's efforts at literary detection it is not only
Hans as Gregor's presumed invention or Gregor as presumed malefac-
tor who is written out of the story. 'The Genesis of the Story' concludes with the blind man still waiting for his (single) brother to
return – but it is the brother who went missing that he is still waiting
for. It is the drowned brother, in other words, who in the end is
simply written out of the account altogether, literally goes missing –
together with any suspected possible crime. But then again, why
should we give this particular deletion any more credence than any of
the others? And perhaps there is another even better concealed crime
to be looked for? And so on. In the end this narrative is distinctly
reminiscent of the Cheshire Cat, and we too are left in the end with
little more than the grin.

'The Genesis of the Story' also suggests that Gregor (if that is really his name, for by now the reader is multiply uncertain) at one point suspects his father's second wife of some discreditable complicity in the whole affair (whatever 'the whole affair' was), suspects that 'es werde etwas vor ihm geheimgehalten' (243) / 'something is being kept hidden from him,' and 'sein Fragen wird mit deutlichen Lügen erwidert oder gar mit Schweigen übergangen' (244) / 'his questions are answered with obvious lies or even passed over in silence.' Whether or not we share Gregor's alleged suspicions of his stepmother, we certainly recognize ourselves in his alleged bafflement as amateur detective. We recognize ourselves too in the figure picking his way over the fragile frozen crust of the snow at the end of the narrative, threatened at every step with falling through, and making his position more hopeless the more he struggles. We recognize a parody of ourselves in the blustering rage of the narrator's father who cannot find his lost housekey – any more than we can find the key that will unlock the hidden secret of the narrative. The father's rage is brilliantly travestied by Handke's narrator – in the section 'Der Schlüssel' (117–19) / 'The Key' – by transposing his furiously incoherent ravings into indirect speech in an immaculately polished and imperturbable style reminiscent of the later Goethe. To the extent that we as readers choose to spend our time in such nostalgic searches for lost keys – to the extent, that is, that we attempt to privilege story over discourse, the *what* over the *how*, what 'really happened' over what is really happening – Handke's text likewise exposes and parodies our own earnest efforts as readers throughout, our naïve assumptions, preconceptions, expectations laid bare in a brilliant demonstration that the medium is indeed the message. We are given fair warning that Gregor Benedikt is a liar, and we ignore the warning at our own risk. But all narrators are liars, however scrupulously they may stick to the truth as they – and their authors and readers – see it. *Die Hornissen* is first and foremost about our ability to deal with those lies, and the real 'story' of the narrative is less what Gregor Benedikt did or did not do than what the reader does or does not do with Gregor's account. Handke's text, in the end, is most centrally about the act of reading itself, its blindnesses and insights, and the real protagonist is the reader.

The same, indeed, could be said with equal validity of a very considerable number of contemporary narratives in which the metafictional moment is primary. Metafiction, though far from being a creation of our own times, enjoying as it does a tradition reaching back to

Tristram Shandy and *Jacques le fataliste* (and *Don Quijote* before that), has become a privileged means of expression for a whole generation of writers – and has already been the subject of several excellent critical studies such as Patricia Waugh's *Metafiction* and Linda Hutcheon's *Narcissistic Narrative*. Such narratives employ a wide variety of strategies that share the constant that they are essentially disruptive of realist notions of plot, character development, and the centrality of an authoritative narrative voice speaking for the empirical author and conveying a monological meaning of the text at hand.

Many of these texts go to considerable lengths to put the reader – ostensibly, at any rate – in something resembling the position of authority once occupied by the sovereign author. Julio Cortázar's *Hopscotch* (*Rayuela*, 1963), for example, consists of 155 numbered chapters ranging in length from a sentence or two to some twenty pages. The narrative proper is preceded by a 'Table of Instructions' that advises the reader that 'in its own way, this book consists of many books, but two books above all' (5). The first of these books, the reader is informed, can be read by proceeding in a traditionally linear fashion as far as chapter 56, 'at the close of which there are three garish little stars which stand for the words *The End*. Consequently, the reader may ignore what follows with a clean conscience' (5). Since 'what follows' amounts to no less than ninety-eight chapters and a good two hundred pages of text, the reader is likely to want to carry on in spite of his clean conscience. He is advised, however, that the second 'book' contained in these pages should not be read in so simple-mindedly linear a fashion, but should commence with chapter 73 and then follow 'the sequence indicated at the end of each chapter. In case of confusion or forgetfulness, one need only consult the following list: 73–1–2–116–3–84–4–71–5– ...' (5) and so on. What at first sight seems a quite arbitrary order turns out on closer inspection to be merely a rereading of the linear 'first' novel from chapter 1 to chapter 56, interspersed with material in the recommended order from the 'Expendable Chapters' (363) numbered 57 to 155. But if this is the 'recommended' order, why the arbitrary order of the 'extra' chapters? Why not an order like, say, 57–1–2–58–3–59–4–60–5, etc.? At the same time, why the scrupulously detailed instructions for the proper incorporation of this material that is arranged in such an arbitrary fashion? Or are the instructions so scrupulous, after all? Chapter 55, for example, disappears without trace, and without explanation, in the suggested second reading. The final chapter in the recommended second series is chapter 131, but this chapter ends by sending the reader to chapter 58, which ends by sending the reader to chapter 131, and so on endlessly. The narrative cannot, in fact, be finished according to the untrustworthy instructions with which we are so helpfully provided.

One would hazard a guess that most readers, on their first reading of Cortázar's text, will simply read straight through from chapter 1 to chapter 155 anyway, in order to gain some sort of perspective on the whole before attempting the second 'authorized' reading. And since we have the author's word for it that 'this book consists of many books,' the possibility of reading the individual fragments of text experimentally in a completely random, aleatory order is clearly a tempting one. The hero of the realist story is one Horacio de Oliveira, an expatriate Argentinian intellectual down and out in Paris who searches in a somewhat desultory fashion for some pattern in life in an existentialist landscape characterized precisely by the random and aleatory. Oliveira eventually returns to Argentina, the pattern still undiscovered, and as the text peters out he is working in a lunatic asylum – shades of Watt and Céline's *Voyage* – and flirting with suicide. The reader, clearly, has the choice of emulating Oliveira's example or not, as he or she wishes. As its title suggests, *Rayuela* (or *Hopscotch*) is a game, one either played *with* the reader who believes that the ostensible rules of such games should be adhered to, or played *by* the reader who sees that the point of such rules is that they are there to be broken. The reading of the text, in other words, is foregrounded as part of the text itself, and the reader is offered – at his own risk, needless to say – a starring role as protagonist.

Italo Calvino takes the matter one step further in his *If on a Winter's Night a Traveler* (*Se una notte d'inverno un viaggiatore*, 1979), by incorporating the Reader as protagonist on the level of story as well as that of discourse. 'You are about to begin reading Italo Calvino's new novel, *If on a winter's night a traveler*. Relax. Concentrate. Dispel every other thought. Let the world around you fade. Best to close the door; the TV is always on in the next room '(3). 'You' is (or are) the hero of 'Italo Calvino's new novel,' which you have just sought out in a bookstore and are now preparing with keen anticipation to read. 'The novel [the embedded novel, that is to say; the novel we are reading is already well underway] begins in a railway station, a locomotive huffs, steam from a piston covers the opening of the chapter, a cloud of smoke hides part of the first paragraph' (10), we are informed in a typical confusion of story level and discourse level. It is a spy story, with passwords, identical suitcases to be secretly exchanged, and a mysterious and beautiful woman – 'Your attention, as reader, is now completely concentrated on the woman, already for several pages you have been circling around her,' we are advised by the first-person narrator. Unfortunately, apparently because of a binder's error, the developing story breaks off abruptly after only one signature, and 'you' have no recourse but to set off for the bookstore again to exchange your defective copy for a perfect one. You will never find it, for the copy you eventually take home with you, because of yet another error, will actually be *Outside the Town of Malbork* by the Polish writer Tazio Bazakbal rather than 'Italo Calvino's new novel.' You will find something else, however, for in the bookstore you encounter 'the Other Reader,' who is also attempting to trade in her defective copy, and thereby, of course, hangs yet another tale. Second-person you and third-person she join forces as a pair of literary sleuths, but are completely unsuccessful in tracking down either the Calvino or the Bazakbal, which also breaks off after its opening pages, as will all ten texts eventually tracked down in sequence by our intrepid pair of detectives – and whose titles together constitute an embryonic narrative themselves:

> If on a winter's night a traveler
> Outside the town of Malbork
> Leaning from the steep slope
> Without fear of wind or vertigo
> Looks down in the gathering shadow
> In a network of lines that enlace
> In a network of lines that intersect
> On the carpet of leaves illuminated by the moon
> Around an empty grave
> What story down there awaits its end?

Calvino's text is very much a book of openings, for all the stories in it are left awaiting their end – with one exception, of course. *Traveler* itself – or at any rate the *Traveler* that the empirical reader reads rather than the *Traveler* that the diegetic Reader reads – ends as a good love story should with the Reader and the Other Reader happily married, 'a great double bed' receiving their 'parallel readings' (260). As the novel draws to its close the Other Reader turns off her light and asks you to turn off yours too. 'And you say, "Just a moment, I've almost finished *If on a winter's night a traveler* by Italo Calvino"' (260). Since the ostensible point of the story is that the embedded

Traveler does not continue beyond its first chapter, the second-person Reader must obviously be just about to finish the same text that we as readers are just about to finish. The happy Reader thus not only attains both marital bliss and hermeneutic gratification but also achieves *en passant* the leap from the world of story to that of discourse whose impossibility constitutes the central dilemma of Kafka's Josef K., Beckett's Watt, and Pynchon's Oedipa.

There is, of course, no good reason (in its own terms) why *Traveler* should ever come to an end, for clearly the technique is infinitely extensible, a latter-day *Arabian Nights* in which the moment of climax is infinitely postponable. The moment of decision as to when to put out the light is a purely arbitrary one – as is Calvino's decision to parody only certain styles and not others, to embed the beginnings of only ten novels rather than fifteen or twenty or five, or to have their titles form a potential teasing narrative in their own right. Calvino brilliantly parodies a whole shelfful of modern literature, from gloomy Central European kitchen realism and metaphysical self-examination to Japanese erotica and James Bond thrillers, not to mention the completely trite love story in which the whole is framed. Calvino's reach is much wider than this, however, for the real text on which his parody is based is not just a collection of examples of individual literary styles but the institution of literary discourse itself. We meet not only the Reader and the Other Reader, but also a Non-Reader who uses books purely as objects to be incorporated in his sculptures, literary analysts who reduce books to lists of word frequencies, literary discussion groups who refuse to discuss anything but their own reactions to books, a senescent professor and a harried editor of a publishing house, a burnt-out author who dreads the computers that can simulate his books at the touch of a button, and a jetsetting villain straight out of a James Bond story who sets all the confusion in motion and turns out to be a lovesick multilingual translator – and whose status as winged messenger of the gods is clear, rejoicing as he does in the name of Ermes. *Traveler* is a book about books, a fiction about fiction, a narrative about narrative and its conventions. Those conventions are shown to be in some ways highly flexible, in other ways highly resistant to any attempt to circumvent them.

Traveler is very self-consciously about reading, but in a wider sense it is about the whole textual communication situation in general and its central element of postmodernist paradox in particular: the author is free to say anything he chooses in the text he constructs, as long as the reader agrees that that is that he is saying; the reader is free to find whatever meaning he can in that text as long as the text allows him to do so; the text itself is simultaneously the unchanging words on the page and the whole interactive and continually changing relationship between the world of the author and the world of the reader. Author and reader alike shape and are shaped by the text, shape and are shaped by each other. While the unchallenged authority of the author in the realist paradigm and that of the text in the modernist paradigm were perceived in terms of those models of reading as essentially unproblematic, the further shift of that authority towards the reader in the postmodernist paradigm has, paradoxically, been only a step on the way to the further relocation of authority in paradox itself. To this extent we can properly refer to even so obviously good-humoured a text as *Traveler* as essentially *entropic* parody, a structuration of uncertainty.

Author, Text, and Critic: Nabokov's *Pale Fire*

There are few texts in which this irreducible relationship of author, text, and reader is so clearly the focus as in Vladimir Nabokov's *Pale Fire* (1962). Nabokov's text, ostensibly a critical edition of a poem, is made up of two parts, a 27-page poem called 'Pale Fire' by the author John Shade, and a scholarly apparatus of close to 200 pages by the reader and critic Charles Kinbote, consisting of a Foreword, a Commentary, and an Index. The lover of poetry who turns first to the text of the 999-line poem will not be disappointed, for Shade's poem has many charms. The reader who conscientiously turns to the editor's Foreword, however, soon becomes aware of the disquietingly unscholarly nature of what is initially assumed – provisionally, at least – to be a scholarly text. After only a few pages the Foreword develops into a rambling account of Kinbote's difficulties as editor, not so much with the text, however, as with various people who have tried very hard to prevent him from editing it. In short, it very soon emerges that while Kinbote considers himself to have been the late poet's best friend, literary adviser, and even inspiration, Shade's wife and many of Kinbote's colleagues clearly consider Kinbote to be a lunatic. The Foreword ends with Kinbote's advice that the reader should now turn to his running commentary on the poem: 'Although these notes, in conformity with custom, come after the poem, the reader is advised to consult them first and then study the poem with their help, rereading them of course as he goes through its text, and perhaps, after having done with the poem, consulting them a third time so as to complete the picture' (18). Having duly studied the commentary, replete with increasingly less veiled references on Kinbote's part to his own colourful past, we find that Kinbote is really King Charles Xavier the Beloved of the 'distant northern land' (224) of Zembla, living incognito in American exile since the recent revolution that drove him out of his kingdom.

Shade, it further emerges, is now dead – shot down in cold blood, in fact, immediately after finishing the last lines of the poem, by an escaped inmate from an asylum for the criminally insane, one Jack Grey, who mistakes him for the judge who had him incarcerated. This is what we glean, at any rate, from reading between the lines of Kinbote's account, for according to Kinbote the attacker was really one Jakob Gradus, an assassin sent by Zemblan extremists to shoot the escaped king. Gradus, however, bungles the job, missing Kinbote at point-blank range and accidentally killing Shade instead. Kinbote, in the confusion, escapes with the now complete poem and eventually tricks Shade's widow into giving him permission to prepare it for publication. His interest in the poem is not merely scholarly: Kinbote, it emerges, has been assiduously cultivating Shade over the last nine months, though without directly revealing his identity, filling long walks with vibrant accounts of the glory that was Zembla, under the assumption that Shade's poem – for which Kinbote has suggested the title 'Solus Rex' (209) – would transpose his stories into enduring poetry. He is furious when he discovers that the poem at first seems to have nothing to do with Zembla at all, but on closer inspection of the poem – and especially of some variant readings that he has fortunately also saved from destruction – he discovers enough echoes and resonances of his talks with the poet to fill his two hundred pages of commentary. All of this, and much more besides, we discover from the commentary itself, which re-creates what Shade's poem failed to re-create, namely the richly convoluted tale of Kinbote's royal youth, lengthy reign, brutal overthrow, daring escape, tragic marriage, and multifarious pleasurable dallyings with kitchen boys, pages, young gentlemen of the court, and the officers and men of the palace guard. His commentary, in short, is flamboyantly a commentary not on what Shade wrote, much of which Kinbote finds only mediocre at best, but on what he did *not* write (but should have).

At any rate, this is a comfortably commonsense reading of Nabokov's text: Shade, the poet, indulgently tolerates Kinbote's wild imaginings and delusions of grandeur, and neither his poem nor his eventual death has anything at all to do with the unfortunate Kinbote, whose behaviour verges on the certifiably insane. This, indeed, is likely to be our second reading of *Pale Fire*, following on a quickly aborted first attempt to read it as a bona fide piece of textual edition. In the process, we notice, the relationship between the two texts has shifted significantly: where Shade's poem in our first abortive reading was the primary text and Kinbote's commentary clearly the secondary according to the traditional division of textual criticism, in our second reading Kinbote's 'commentary' is clearly a primary text itself as well, its dependence on Shade's poem a purely superficial affair – Kinbote frequently takes a completely unremarkable expression such as 'often' or 'my bedroom' as his cue for a long account of Zemblan matters with no relevance of any sort to the passage allegedly the object of the commentary. In this reading, in other words, we are dealing with two quite independent texts that only masquerade as text and commentary. It is when we take the next step and read both texts together as a single text, however, that the matter becomes really interesting.

The title *Pale Fire* is borrowed from Shakespeare's *Timon of Athens*: 'The sun's a thief, and with his great attraction / Robs the vast sea; the moon's an arrant thief, / And her pale fire she snatches from the sun' (4.3.442–4). This central motif of reflection is itself reflected throughout both Shade's poem and Kinbote's commentary, both of which contain multiple references to mirrors, window panes, glasses, and the like. Shade's poem opens with one of the most complex of these images of reflection: 'I was the shadow of the waxwing slain / By the false azure of the windowpane; / I was the smudge of ashen fluff – and I / Lived on, flew on, in the reflected sky. / And from the inside, too, I'd duplicate / Myself,' watching the reflected room superimposed at night on the snowy scene 'out in that crystal land' (23). Physical reflections, however, are themselves only a reflection of the complex interaction of the characters in Nabokov's text. Many of these could certainly be explained as merely the product of Kinbote's overheated imagination. He reveals the existence, for example, of an extremist revolutionary faction in Zembla called The Shadows – shades of Pynchon's Tristero – many of whose members have names that are mirror images of heroes of the royalist cause: the hero Odon has a Shadow counterpart (and half-brother) Nodo; the patriot Baron Radomir Mandevil has a Shadow cousin Baron Mirador Mandevil; Jakob Gradus the assassin is the Shadow counterpart of a 'mirror maker of genius' (223), Sudarg of Bokay, and so on. Jakob

Gradus himself could, of course, merely be Kinbote's transformation of the more prosaic Jack Grey, just as Izumrúd, the head of the Zemblan secret police, could be a more romantic version of Gerald Emerald, a young fellow instructor whom Kinbote detests. The King's tutors Beauchamp and Campbell, last seen playing a chess game to a draw (92), might merely be his invention too, and the name of the head of the department in which Kinbote teaches, Nattochdag (which seems to mean 'night and day' in Zemblan), might just be a coincidence. Gradus's name, Kinbote tells us, is related to the Zemblan *grados*, meaning 'tree,' which gives both shade and shadow, thus linking the dead poet to his Shadow assailant. But who is responsible for the multiple coincidence that John Shade, who is dead when the action of the narrative opens, writes a poem that is largely concerned with death, has a name that is an anagram of Hades, the land of grey shades – and is killed by a man whose name doubly echoes his own, Jack Grey? One answer, obviously, is that nobody is responsible – other than Nabokov, of course. Accidents happen, coincidences occur. Another possibility inviting consideration, however, is that *Pale Fire* is not the (fictive) work of two authors after all, as we have been assuming so far, but of one only: either Shade, who invents Kinbote, or Kinbote, who invents Shade, or a third party, who invents both of them.

The title – which applies to both Shade's poem and the whole text – is one initial reason for attributing the entire text to Shade, for example. Since the title suggests a relationship from the start we might speculate that Shade indeed creates his own 'explicator,' a comic Boswell to his own Johnson, a moon to his own sun, a lunatic pale fire that outshines its apparent origin. (Kinbote, by contrast – ostensibly, at any rate – neither understands the reason for the title nor knows its source. He suspects it may be *The Tempest* even though he has a Zemblan translation of *Timon* in his possession, and he several times uses variations of the phrase 'pale fire' in his commentary without any apparent awareness of its overtones.) The ostentatious reflection motif of the opening stanza – 'I duplicate myself' (23) – supports this assumption and is itself supported some pages later by the picture of 'the old man / Dying in a motel' who 'conjures in two tongues' (39). Shade's poem talks of finding 'Some kind of link-and-bobolink, some kind / Of correlated pattern in the game' (44) – ostensibly the game of life, with the forces that determine our fate 'Playing a game of worlds, promoting pawns / To ivory unicorns and ebon fauns; / ... Making ornaments / Of accidents and possibilities'

(45). Shade is an eighteenth-century scholar, author of a book on Pope, in whose *Dunciad* Zembla is the home of Dullness – the Zembla of *Pale Fire* is anything but dull. Nova Zembla in Swift's *Battle of the Books*, moreover, is the home of Criticism. Shade's description of his morning shave as ploughing 'Old Zembla's fields where my gray stubble grows' (48) may well be read as a reference to his intended invasion of both of these grey lands – Russian *zemlya* 'land' – parodically subverting the sobriety and self-importance of academic criticism. The Zemblan language is a 'tongue of the mirror' (172), as we are told in Kinbote's commentary, and the name of the country is 'a corruption ... of Semblerland, a land of reflections, of "re-semblers"' (187) – or of dissemblers, as we might add. In this reading the Gradus who makes his way 'through the entire length of the poem ... swinging down to the foot of the page from line to line as from branch to branch' (56) and 'kills' the poet just as the last line is written is no more than the work itself, which once completed 'gradually' displaces its uninteresting maker. (Shade, Gradus, and Kinbote, we notice, all have the same birthday, 5 July, with Gradus and Kinbote being born on the same day in 1915.) Shade's poem has as one of its central themes the possibility of life after death, and Shade's own invented death parodically bears out his dry forecast, 'I'm reasonably sure that we survive' (49). The butterfly that flits through the dying lines of the poem handily provides the reader with a classic symbol of metamorphosis and a reminder of the unreality of rigid dividing lines. But is the line in question here limited to that between life and death in metaphysical terms (as Shade's poem without the commentary might well lead us to think), or is the division between the poet and his commentator just as unreal?

This last question could, of course, be answered in the affirmative without necessarily implying Shade as the sole author. The situation could be exactly the other way around, for it could conceivably have been Kinbote, after all, who invented Shade for his own purposes, whether sane or mad. The text generously supplies us with supporting evidence for this possibility too. Casual references like that in the Foreword to 'the pale fire of the incinerator' (9) *could* be read as a hint to the reader on Kinbote's part (as sole author) rather than as evidence of his critical tin ear. Various references to Shade also take on a very different meaning if we see Kinbote as the sole author. Shade's unprepossessing physical self is contrasted to his poetic self at one point, culminating in the assertion that 'He was his own cancellation' (17), for example. Without Kinbote's commentary Shade's text 'simply has no human reality at all' (18) – a statement with which Shade might not have agreed, Kinbote notes, 'but, for better or worse, it is the commentator who has the last word' (19). The Index overtly blurs the identity of Kinbote and Shade in the entry for Shade, where the pronoun *his*, which should logically refer to Shade, in fact refers to Kinbote (223). Kinbote cites an alleged variant 'I like my name: Shade, *Ombre, almost "man"* / In Spanish ...' (124). The beginning of Shade's poem is synchronized with the beginning of Gradus's journey by Kinbote as being just 'a few minutes after midnight July 1, while I played chess' (53). Are Shade and *all* the other characters merely pawns and pieces in a chess game devised by Kinbote's paranoia and megalomania then, a game in which a psychotic Kinbote is indeed 'solus rex' (209), a lone king, surrounded by attackers? Shade is killed, Gradus commits suicide, as does also, apparently, Shade's daughter Hazel, who, Kinbote observes at one point without giving any supporting evidence, 'resembled me in certain respects' (138). Perhaps we can find the resemblance in the passage 'She had strange fears, strange fantasies, strange force / Of character' (32) and its continuation 'She twisted words ... '(32). Towards the end of his commentary Kinbote mentions his blinding headaches and black depressions, and the word suicide drops. Are the deaths of Shade, Hazel, Gradus, merely fantasized trial runs for a more real suicide yet to come?

Kinbote's name allegedly means 'regicide' in Zemblan: he reflects at one point that a king who voluntarily abandons his identity for the anonymity of exile is in a sense indeed a regicide – but so too, we might add, is a king who commits suicide. The alleged etymology of Kinbote's name leads us to a final alternative possibility, namely that both Shade and Kinbote are the figments of yet a third character's imagination. (In real-life terms, of course, this is indeed the situation, and the character in question is called Nabokov.) The reader is made aware only some half-way through the book of the existence of a Professor Botkin, who is referred to en passant, in an apparently gratuitous piece of information, as being fortunate enough not to work in the Russian Department (112), whose head Kinbote detests. Why, the reader may well ask, should Kinbote bother to describe Botkin, who up to this point has never even been mentioned before, as fortunate not to work in a particular department? The reader gifted with photographic recall may remember an earlier reference to certain names deriving from professions 'such as Rymer, Scrivener, Linner (one who illuminates parchments), Botkin (one who makes bottekins, fancy footwear) and thousands of others' (73) and possibly a later one to one of the gentlemanly ways to commit suicide, involving 'a bare botkin (note the correct spelling)' (157). Later it will emerge, oddly enough, that one of Kinbote's colleagues (a Professor Pardon, no less) has been under the impression that Kinbote was born in Russia rather than Zembla and that his name 'was a kind of anagram of Botkin or Botkine' (189) – a suggestion sarcastically rejected by Kinbote. In the Index we note that Botkin *is* 'an American scholar of Russian descent' and may or may not be surprised by the other subentries under the name Botkin, V., to wit: 'king-bot, maggot of extinct fly that once bred in mammoths and is thought to have hastened their phylogenetic end, 247; bottekin-maker, 71; *bot*, plop, and *boteliy*, big-bellied (Russ.); botkin or bodkin, a Danish stiletto' (216). Kinbote discovers that Shade's wife has referred to him in public as 'a king-sized botfly ... the monstrous parasite of a genius' (123) and even has to beg his own exiled Queen, who cannot recall his pseudonym, not to address any more letters from her villa in the south of France to 'Charles X. Kingbot' (182). And so on.

We might well be tempted at this point to cut further narratological tap-dancing short and accept gratefully that 'V. Botkin' is very likely indeed to be the intratextual representative of V. Nabokov and the 'real' author of both Shade's and Kinbote's texts. But the evidence, again, is far from conclusive: Botkin *might* perhaps be just Kinbote's real name (disavowed for whatever reason), and in that case – as Kinbote – he *might* be the author of the whole or, then again, he might not, as we have already seen. The point should be amply clear by now: while we can presumably be sure (we hope) that the real extratextual author of *Pale Fire* is Vladimir Nabokov, we cannot say conclusively, based on the available intratextual evidence, who the real intratextual author is at any given point and whether he remains constant throughout. Nabokov's game of mirrors ensures that we never gain any conclusive footing, any Archimedean point of leverage in the shifting sands of the narrative. Our common sense as readers will tell us that Kinbote's whole Zemblan scenario is obviously unreal – but this unreality is balanced against the 'reality' of an America that contains such places as New Wye (near Exe), Utana, Idoming, and Arcady as well as New York and Washington. The reader is constantly challenged to establish the relative validity of the conflicting authorial voices in the text, to *create* an authorial and authoritative voice, and in the end can only admit the impossibility of the task. Reality is no longer accessible, for in the end all is appearance only, the play of artifice, and the butterfly possibility of difference.

Language Speaks: Joyce's *Finnegans Wake*

If our first mode of entropic parody was character-based (represented by *La maison de rendez-vous*), and the second reader-based (represented to different degrees by both *Die Hornissen* and *Pale Fire*), the third and final of our three modes is language-based, and its most obvious and most brilliant exemplar to date is certainly James Joyce's *Finnegans Wake* (1939). Once again it should be made clear that these categories are in no way intended to be seen as exclusive. All literary narratives are to a greater or lesser extent both 'character-based' and 'reader-based,' and all are certainly and simultaneously 'language-based.' The reader-based entropic parodies that we have been looking at – *textes scriptibles*, as Barthes calls them – are certainly concerned with language, indeed they are essentially concerned with the language of the literary communication situation: the language of writing, of reading, of narrative. In *Finnegans Wake* Joyce deals with all of these, and also with the language of language itself. *Pale Fire* poses in an exemplary manner a question that is central to the reading of all entropic parody: Who speaks? *La maison de rendez-vous* and *Die Hornissen*, as we have seen, are also centrally concerned with this constitutive uncertainty. Our third mode of entropic parody, as represented by the *Wake*, not only subscribes forcefully to the same question, but introduces as well, and in an ostentatious form, a closely related question: *What* speaks?

If Flaubert cherished the ambition to write a book about nothing, Joyce went to the other extreme: *Finnegans Wake* is a book about everything. Most specifically, however, it is about itself, and its Irish stew of 'once current puns, quashed quotatoes, messes of mottage' (183) – which is another way of saying that it is about language, as even this brief example of its 'alphybettyformed verbage' (183) makes clear. Though usually claimed for the sake of taxonomic convenience as a member of the class 'English literature,' and though many of the words used in the text are indeed demonstrably English and may be found in dictionaries – good dictionaries, at any rate – of that language, the *Wake* is written less *in* the English language than *around* the English language. Its basic compositional unit is the lowly pun, and Joyce magisterially develops this once-despised trope – 'the lowest form of wit' – to an unsurpassable degree of multilingual, polyvalent virtuosity. Scholars have compiled wordlists of *Wake* vocabulary that include most of the known languages of the ancient and modern world, including (but certainly not limited to) English, Irish, French, Spanish, Italian, German, the Scandinavian languages, Russian, Arabic, Chinese, and Japanese (not to mention Latin, Greek, and Sanskrit, of course), to name but an insignificant few. It might be more accurate to say simply that the *Wake* is written not in English but in language and leave it at that.

The realistic motivation – if we need one – for this primeval linguistic soup is provided by the device of the dream, for all of the *Wake* can be read on one level as the dream of a bibulous innkeeper, appropriately named Porter, whose establishment is located in the village of Chapelizod, just outside Dublin. The only adequate summary of the *Wake* would be a word-for-word repetition of the whole, but one basic armature of the plot, insofar as one can isolate one, involves the fact that Mr Porter has a wife named Anna, a daughter named Isabel, and twin sons called Kevin and Jerry, and that he employs an old cleaning woman called Kate and an old man who helps behind the bar called Joe. Following on an evening of overindulgence as his own best customer, Mr Porter spends a long night uneasily dreaming of one thing and another, and the result is for one thing the story of human civilization and for another the text of *Finnegans Wake.* Mr Porter metamorphoses in his dream (which is simultaneously an element of the plot and the *Wake* itself) into Humphrey Chimpden Earwicker (otherwise HCE), his wife into Anna Livia Plurabelle (otherwise ALP), his daughter into Isolde, and his sons Kevin and Jerry into Shaun and Shem, or Mick and Nick, or Mutt and Jute, or whatever, for in Earwicker's dream nothing remains the same for very long. The *Wake* is characterized by the merging of identities, narratives, times, and places into other identities, narratives, times, and places, as one might expect in a dream – or in a narrative whose first word is 'riverrun' (3). By the same token, Earwicker's dream is not his alone either, for on another level of the narrative it reflects the endless rise and fall and rise again of civilizations in a perennial cycle of comings and goings, beginnings and endings – organized not around some notion of ineluctable historical progress, however, but around the eighteenth-century philosopher Giambattista Vico's cyclical theory of history in *The New Science* (1725). Vico's model of historical development posits four historical ages, an age of gods followed by an age of heroes, followed in turn by one of mere men, which degenerates in turn into chaos, but chaos is simultaneously a *ricorso*, in which the age of gods may again be reborn. The once strong are supplanted by the once weak, the rulers by the ruled, the fathers by the sons, who become fathers in their turn and ripe themselves for overthrow. Everyman Earwicker, as the Finnegan of the popular ballad (or the reborn Finn of Irish myth, Finn again), parodic god, hero, and fallen man simultaneously (not to mention Humpty Dumpty, alias the Cosmic Egg), may have fallen (metaphorically or otherwise) from the ladder and split his skull, but it will only take a splash of whiskey (Irish *uisce beatha* 'water of life') to wake him in the course of his own wake. If tipsy Finnegan's fall (like Earwicker's dream) was the result of drink, Earwicker's fall is shrouded in uncertainty, though (like Adam's) it seems to have much to do with women. Isabel-Isolde-Iseut-Issy, his daughter, is an object of guilty desire for Earwicker (alias Persse O'Reilly, via French *perce-oreille*), as Isolde (from whom Chapel-izod takes its name) once was for King Mark, who was supplanted by Tristan, as Earwicker will be by the battling brothers Shaun (the brashly successful man of affairs) and Shem (the introverted writer and failure), who also battle over possession of Issy. But Isolde is also young Anna, as Anna is young Old Kate, and Shaun-Shem is young Earwicker, as Earwicker is young Old Joe. And Earwicker is Dublin, as Anna is the River Liffey, on which Dublin stands. Earwicker is alpha, earth, sun, historical change, all men and father of all, as Anna is omega, water, moon, transhistorical constancy, all women and mother of all, guarantor of rebirth, 'Bringer of Pluralities' (104). And the more things change, the more they remain themselves – 'the old order changeth and lasts like the first' (486) – for the other philosopher of whom Joyce is able to make major use for his own purposes is Giordano Bruno, whose theory of the complementarity of opposites is wedded to Vico's cyclical theory of history to underpin the 'millwheeling vicociclometer' (614) that is the *Wake*, where all always 'moves in vicous cicles yet remews the same' (134).

Finnegans Wake is a repository of unending change in changelessness, a library of endless transformations – or as one strand of one of the stories has it, a rubbish dump of possibilities, a midden to be excavated. It is the story of a night, or of all nights – a 'scherzarade of one's thousand one nightinesses' (51) – and in order to escape from the logical denotative language of day Joyce invented his own connotative language of illogic and night and endless associative potential. The result is an astounding linguistic tour de force that will continue to keep a happily burgeoning *Wake* industry busy for generations to come. The result is also, clearly, a gigantic joke, an enormous literary and especially linguistic hoax of almost unimaginable proportions, this 'hoax that joke bilked' (511). (One would have to have a heart of stone to read it without laughing, as Oscar Wilde reportedly observed of *Little Dorrit*.) And the humour, beyond any argument, is certainly entropic, for in the world of the *Wake nothing* is fixed, stable, enduring, reliable, certain – least of all the language in which the text is composed. If the reader-based entropic parodies at which we have just been looking can be considered parodic of reading and writing, the *Wake*, that 'acomedy of letters' (425), goes one giant step further in that it is parodic of language itself, for 'every dimmed letter in it is a copy and not a few of the silbils and wholly words' (424), a comedy of 'blurry wards' (425) that 'by the coincidance of their contraries reamalgamerge in that indentity of undiscernibles' (49-50), in short 'the last word in stolentelling' (424). This is not to raise a claim for some unheard-of originality on the part of the *Wake*, for many texts are parodic of language in this sense for the length of a line or a paragraph or a page; what is truly unheard-of is the absolutely unreasonable consistency – and surely no *reasonable* person could ever have written a *Finnegans Wake* – with which essentially a single elementary comic device, the pun, usually applied (by reasonable people) for humorous effect to a single word or phrase, is vastly extended to a complex literary text of more than 600 pages, or some 300,000 words. Each pun reinforces and supports each of the others in a potentially infinite and self-supporting 'coincidance' (49) of signifiers, engendering an entropic proliferation of possible interpretations that is certainly inscribed as an integral part of the endlessly convoluted joke that Joyce built. Though Joyce, playing the role of 'Bygmester Finnegan' (4) himself, performed superhuman feats as master builder, however, he is of necessity well and truly effaced in this 'overgrown babeling' (6) in which the game of language plays itself endlessly out through his writing and through countless readers' readings.

Much parodic play is made in the *Wake* with the notion of totalization, of eventually reaching some millennial Archimedean point from which everything would fall into a single proper perspective and thus yield itself up to authoritative and definitive explanation. The text is full of lists and series of one sort or another that appear to be raising a claim to some power of summation. In general terms, of course, we could include in this complex the massive, pervasive presence of the various forms of intertextuality at work and at play in the text: references to and quotations and pseudoquotations from whole libraries of books (duly catalogued by *Wake* scholars), songs, proverbs, nursery rhymes, advertising slogans, street cries, and the like in 'lashons of languages' (29), 'anythongue athall' (117). The pervasive presence of the multiple languages themselves, of course, is

also suggestive of this apparent will to totalization. On a more specific scale we have a variety of devices that serve as parodic metaphors of totality, such as, for example, various versions of the musical
scale, whether ascending, as in 'Dont retch meat fat salt lard sinks
down' (260), or descending, as in 'Does she lag soft fall means rest
down?' (407). Similarly 'metandmorefussed' (513) numerical systems
put in guest appearances in 'minney combinaisies and permutandies'
(284), reduced to their 'comedy nominator' (283): 'Ya, da, tra, gathery,
pimp, shesses, shossafat, okodeboko, nine' (51), or 'Aun Do Tri Car
Cush Shay Shockt Ockt Ni Geg' (308). Alphabets dance to exotic
strains in this 'letteracettera' (339–40): 'Olives, beets, kimmels, dol-
lies, alfrids, beatties, cormacks and daltons' (19), or 'Prettimaid tints
may try their taunts: apple, bacchante, custard, dove, eskimo,
feldgrau' and so on down to 'vanilla, wisteria, xray, yesplease, zaza,
philomel, theerose' (247–8). Rainbows come out to play in multicol-
oured metaphors of completion, 'like a rudd yellan gruebleen
orangeman in his violet indigonation' (23). All the resources of world
history and geography are threatened with mobilization in a vast
mapping strategy that succeeds eventually only in a parodic mapping
of its own relativity, in which all times, all places, blur and merge. In
the endlessly shifting world of the Wake 'every person, place and
thing in the chaosmos of Alle anyway connected' is 'moving and
changing every part of the time' (118) in a continual 'passing of order
and order's coming' (277), 'order othered' (613), apparent chaos and ostensible cosmos inextricably interleaved in a self-reflecting, self-de-
constructing 'chaosmos.'

We find a perfect metaphor for Finnegans Wake and its play with
totalizing systems, parodically balancing totalization and incompletion, in the beneficent ordering system of Borges's Chinese encyclopaedia, in which totality and entropy are identical. In no text that
we have so far encountered is the relationship of chaos and cosmos,
order and entropy, so clearly defined as essentially one of play as it is
in the Wake. In thermodynamics the concept of entropy is predicated
on the erosion of certainty: order develops irreversibly into chaos. In
information theory entropy is of major theoretical interest precisely
because this irreversibility is not perceived to be absolute, because of
the potential exploitation of uncertainty: chaos can, in certain appropriate contexts, be teased into a provisional, hypothetical order, noise
can be transformed into information, and one of the most appropriate
contexts is the literary text. Entropic parody is the most overt expression of this literary exploitation of uncertainty, and Finnegans Wake

in turn is a key expression – *the* key expression – of one form of entropic parody, namely that form which is dominantly language-based. The linguistic intertextuality of the *Wake* constitutes a form of parodic glossolalia characterized by pandemic uncertainty – wall-to-wall language characterized by wall-to-wall uncertainty, flux, change, difference. Language, in the guise of the discrete languages of all times and places, is ostentatiously exploded, abraded, eroded, and this entropic dissolution is simultaneously and parodically reversed in a polysystem of recombinations exploiting sense and sound, similarity and difference, a concerted and paradoxical 'abnihilisation of the etym' (353) producing what the text itself calls 'uttermost confussion' (353), fission and fusion at once. Earwicker's fall – and Earwicker is everyman – is both mirrored in and mirror of this process of linguistic 'confussion.' The thunder of his fall – as Finnegan, Adam, Humpty Dumpty, peeping tom in the Phoenix Park – is repeatedly represented throughout the text by a thunderword of a hundred letters, different each time it occurs, and always composed of discrete, scrambled elements of dozens of different languages, ancient and modern. 'The hundredlettered name' is the 'last word of perfect language' (424), but it is also the first, for it is simultaneously the sound of the thunder with which a new cycle of human development is inaugurated in the Viconian system, fall and rise alike memorialized and celebrated in a fission-fusion of language.

Joyce's 'meanderthalltale' (19), 'a sequentiality of improbable possibles' (110) and 'piously forged palimpsests' (182), 'totalled in toldteld and teldtold in tittletell tattle' (597), both reflects and produces for the reader an endlessly proliferating and endlessly promising 'dividual chaos' (186). In every reading of every line 'we are once more as babes awondering in a wold made fresh where with the hen in the storyaboot we start from scratch' (336) in our decoding of these 'strangewrote anaglyptics' (419): 'In the buginning is the woid' (378), and in the end all ostensible answers are 'for teasers only' (284). Completing the last page of the book is only an illusory completion, suggesting in the end an only spuriously reassuring sense of *arche* and *telos*, beginning and end, origin and order. The writing of *Finnegans Wake* is overtly incomplete – the text breaks off, refusing closure, in the middle of a final sentence whose continuation is found only by turning to the first sentence of the text again, parodically prompting an endless circular reading of an infinite 'continuarration' (205). Our reading, even if we were 'that ideal reader suffering from an ideal insomnia' (120), can indeed never be complete. *Finnegans Wake* is uncontestably the best example we have, or are likely to have, of that master script of late-twentieth-century reading, the radically open text, the *texte scriptible*. If *Finnegans Wake* did not exist, indeed, it would surely be necessary to invent it if much of modern thinking about texts were not to be undermined: for, without any doubt, the *Wake* is *the* literary authority paradoxically but powerfully underwriting one of the most fundamental critical insights of our time, the threefold ramifications of which have massively contributed to a redrawing of the late-twentieth-century map of the literary communication situation: that all language refers first and foremost to other language, that all writing is rewriting, and that all reading can never be more than a pretext for further reading.

Conclusion

The experience of reading *Finnegans Wake* should serve as a salutary warning against ambitions of completion, totalization, closure. We have seen in part 1 of this book the pervasive effects of entropic modes of thinking on our twentieth-century perception of humour, and in part 2 the systemic effects of the consequent mutation of humour on our twentieth-century perception of the literary text. It may, however, still be worth repeating that the resulting notion of entropic comedy, the examination of whose various modes and submodes of articulation has occupied us throughout part 3, has *not* been advanced here as some radiant new paradigm of reading triumphantly supplanting earlier (and by definition less interesting) modes of coming to terms with literary texts. The concept of entropic comedy, it should be quite clear, is only one voice in the orchestra of contemporary literary criticism, one reader's way of making a particular kind of sense of a particular body of texts: the foregoing investigation raises no claim to provide answers to questions other than those it poses in its own terms – and even those answers are advanced as provisional rather than absolute, hypothetical rather than axiomatic, without any claim to any exclusive authority. What the concept of entropic comedy and its associated taxonomy of texts *can* usefully provide, it is suggested, is precisely a loose and flexible grid for purposes of provisional orientation, suggestive rather than prescriptive, inclusive rather than exclusive. It is not claimed that the texts we have examined in the final part of this book 'are' textbook examples of entropic satire or irony or parody in the exclusive sense that they can consequently 'be' nothing else; rather the endeavour has been to show that the texts examined here can be interestingly *read* as *functioning* in terms of these postulated modes of modern writing and reading. Read in another context they will take on a very different colouring, and it is entirely appropriate – and no matter for regret of any sort – that this should be so. For the reader is most in tune with his or her ideal role not when attempting to provide categorical, conclusive, once-and-for-all answers as to what a particular literary text really *means* or *is*, but when he or she is attempting to devise as many interesting questions as possible as to the nature of the literary text in particular and in general and in the context of the reader's own life and times.

I should also make it quite clear that the stance described in the previous paragraph is not at all an example merely of a becoming authorial modesty. Rather it is an essential component of the overall position advanced throughout this book. The ideal role of the ideal reader – at this particular point in history, that is, for other periods have had and no doubt will have their own ideal readers – is to be an incessant questioner, and that is why reading is so centrally important an activity, both for the individual and for the society in which he or she lives. Those of us who have the professional presumption to advise other readers how they might or might not read may or may not succeed in persuading some of them of the relative validity of our own particular reading. Any such success does not necessarily make us purveyors of truth. Literary theory – and every reading is always an application, conscious or otherwise, of some particular form of literary theory – can never be a serenely objective master discourse whose function is to state once and for all the real and unassailable truth about the texts we read, but must always remain instead the expression of a series of particular questions arising from a particular context. That context, in turn, is always and inescapably a function of the particular historical situation in which the questioner lives and reads. The single most important criterion for gauging the effectiveness of any particular branch of literary theory or mode of textual interpretation is that – rather than remaining blissfully limited to its immediate and fond progenitor – it should enable a certain sizeable group of readers to read a certain sizeable group of texts more interestingly. The crucial factor making a reading more interesting, in turn, is the degree of relevance of our reading for the particular context in which we perceive ourselves to be situated.

Every age, and our own Age of Entropy is certainly no exception, chooses its own canonical texts and its own reading of them. All reading, to this extent, is inescapably part of a great and never-ending exercise in mapping and remapping, a continued and continuing attempt on the part of individuals and communities to rewrite the answers of the past and thus redefine the questions of the present. This is the strongest and most central intellectual impulse of the human psyche, the same timeless drive that sent Faust on his emblematic quest to establish once and for all 'was die Welt im Innersten zusammenhält' / 'what holds the world together at its core.' We postmoderns, fortunate to live in interesting times, may well lack Faust's renaissance confidence in the existence of such final answers, but that is no reason at all to stop reformulating the questions.

Bibliography

Aristotle. *The Poetics.* Trans. Hamilton Fyfe. London: Heinemann 1927

Attridge, Derek, and Daniel Ferrer, eds. *Post-Structuralist Joyce: Essays from the French.* Cambridge: Cambridge University Press 1984

Bakhtin, Mikhail. *Problems of Dostoevsky's Poetics.* Ed. and trans. Caryl Emerson. Intro. Wayne C. Booth. Theory and History of Literature, vol. 8. Minneapolis: University of Minnesota Press 1984

– *Rabelais and His World.* Trans. Helene Iswolsky. Bloomington: Indiana University Press 1984

Bal, Mieke. *Narratology: Introduction to the Theory of Narrative.* Trans. Christine van Boheemen. Toronto: University of Toronto Press 1985

Barrett, William. *Irrational Man: A Study in Existential Philosophy.* Garden City, NY: Anchor-Doubleday 1962

Barth, John. *The Floating Opera.* New York: Bantam 1980

– 'The Literature of Replenishment: Postmodernist Fiction.' *Atlantic,* January 1980, 65–71

– *Lost in the Funhouse: Fiction for Print, Tape, Live Voice.* New York: Bantam 1981

Barthes, Roland. *Elements of Semiology.* Trans. Annette Lavers and Colin Smith. New York: Hill and Wang 1978

– *Image – Music – Text.* Essays selected and trans. Stephen Heath. New York: Hill and Wang 1977

– *The Pleasure of the Text.* Trans. Richard Miller. New York: Hill and Wang 1975

– *S/Z.* Trans. Richard Miller. New York: Hill and Wang 1974

Baudelaire, Charles. *Curiosités esthétiques.* Ed. Henri Lemaître. Paris: Garnier 1962

Beattie, James. 'An Essay on Laughter, and Ludicrous Composition.' In *Essays,* 583–705. Edinburgh: William Creech 1776

Beckett, Samuel. *Watt.* New York: Grove 1959

Belsey, Catherine. *Critical Practice*. New Accents. London, New York: Methuen 1980

Bergson, Henri. 'Laughter.' In Sypher, *Comedy*, 61–190

Booth, Wayne C. *The Rhetoric of Fiction*. Chicago: University of Chicago Press 1961

Borges, Jorge Luis. 'The Analytical Language of John Wilkins.' In *Borges: A Reader*, ed. Emir Rodriguez Monegal and Alastair Reid, 141–3. New York: Dutton 1981

Boston, Richard. *An Anatomy of Laughter*. London: Collins 1974

Bradbury, Malcolm, ed. *The Novel Today: Contemporary Writers on Modern Fiction*. Glasgow: Fontana-Collins 1977

Brée, Germaine. *Twentieth-Century French Literature*. Trans. Louise Guiney. Chicago, London: University of Chicago Press 1983

Breton, André. *Anthologie de l'humour noir*. Paris: Pauvert 1966

Brooke-Rose, Christine. *A Rhetoric of the Unreal: Studies in Narrative and Structure, Especially of the Fantastic*. Cambridge: Cambridge University Press 1983

Brooks, Cleanth. *The Well-Wrought Urn: Studies in the Structure of Poetry*. London: Dennis Dobson 1968

Brush, Stephen G. 'Thermodynamics and History.' *The Graduate Journal* 7 (1967): 477–565

Caillois, Roger. *Man, Play and Games*. Trans. Meyer Barash. New York: Free Press of Glencoe 1961

Calder, Nigel. *Einstein's Universe*. New York: Viking 1979

Calvino, Italo. *If on a Winter's Night a Traveler*. Trans. William Weaver. San Diego: Harcourt 1981

Campbell, Jeremy. *Grammatical Man: Information, Entropy, Language, and Life*. New York: Simon and Schuster 1982

Camus, Albert. *L'étranger*. Collection Folio. Paris: Gallimard 1980

– *The Outsider*. Trans. Stuart Gilbert. Harmondsworth, Eng.: Penguin 1971

Carlson, Richard S. *The Benign Humorists*. Hamden, CT: Archon Books 1975

Cazamian, Louis. *The Development of English Humor*. Durham, NC: Duke University Press 1952

Céline, Louis-Ferdinand. *Journey to the End of Night*. Trans. Ralph Manheim. New York: New Directions 1983

– *Voyage au bout de la nuit*. Collection Folio. Paris: Gallimard 1978

Chapman, A.J., and H.C. Foot. *It's a Funny Thing, Humour*. Oxford: Pergamon 1977

Chatman, Seymour. *Story and Discourse: Narrative Structure in Fiction and Film*. Ithaca, NY: Cornell University Press 1980

Cicero. *De oratore*. Trans. E.W. Sutton. London: Heinemann 1942

Clark, Hilary Anne. 'The Idea of a Fictional Encyclopaedia: *Finnegans Wake, Paradis, The Cantos.*' Doctoral dissertation, University of British Columbia, 1985

Collins, R.G. 'Nineteenth Century Literary Humour: The Wit and Warmth of Wiser Men?' *Mosaic 9*, no. 4 (1976): 1–42

Cortázar, Julio. *Hopscotch.* Trans. Gregory Rabassa. New York: Bard-Avon 1975

Culler, Jonathan. *On Deconstruction: Theory and Criticism after Structuralism.* Ithaca, NY: Cornell University Press 1982

– *The Pursuit of Signs: Semiotics, Literature, Deconstruction.* Ithaca, NY: Cornell University Press 1981

Darby, David. 'The Narrative Text as Palimpsest: Levels of Discourse in Peter Handke's *Die Hornissen.*' *Seminar* 23 (1987): 251–64

Darwin, Charles. *The Expression of the Emotions in Man and Animals.* Chicago: University of Chicago Press 1965

Davis, Douglas M. *The World of Black Humor.* New York: Dutton 1967

de Man, Paul. *Blindness and Insight: Essays in the Rhetoric of Contemporary Criticism.* Theory and History of Literature, vol. 7. Minneapolis: University of Minnesota Press 1983

Derrida, Jacques. *Of Grammatology.* Trans. Gayatri Chakravorty Spivak. Baltimore: Johns Hopkins University Press 1976

– *Writing and Difference.* Trans. Alan Bass. Chicago: University of Chicago Press 1978

Doležel, Lubomír. 'Kafka's Fictional World.' *Canadian Review of Comparative Literature* 11 (1984): 61–83

Donato, Eugenio. 'The Museum's Furnace: Notes toward a Conceptual Reading of *Bouvard and Pécuchet.*' In *Textual Strategies: Perspectives in Post-Structuralist Criticism,* 213–38. Ed. Josué V. Harari. Ithaca, NY: Cornell University Press 1979

Dostoyevsky, Fyodor. *Notes from Underground.* Trans. Andrew R. MacAndrew. New York: Signet 1961

Eagleton, Terry. *Literary Theory: An Introduction.* Minneapolis: University of Minnesota Press 1983

Eastman, Max. *Enjoyment of Laughter.* London: Hamilton 1937

Eco, Umberto. *The Name of the Rose.* Trans. William Weaver. New York: Harcourt 1983

– *The Role of the Reader: Explorations in the Semiotics of Texts.* Bloomington: Indiana University Press 1979

– *A Theory of Semiotics.* Bloomington: Indiana University Press 1979

Einstein, Albert. *Relativity: The Special and the General Theory: A Popular Exposition.* Trans. Robert W. Lawson. London: Methuen 1968

Eliot, T.S. *The Complete Poems and Plays 1909–1950.* New York: Harcourt 1971

Esslin, Martin. *The Theatre of the Absurd.* Garden City, NY: Anchor-Doubleday 1969

Fish, Stanley. *Is There a Text in This Class? The Authority of Interpretive Communities.* Cambridge, MA: Harvard University Press 1980

Flaubert, Gustave. *Bouvard et Pécuchet.* Ed. Claudine Gothot-Mersch. Collection Folio. Paris: Gallimard 1981

Foucault, Michel. *The Order of Things: An Archaeology of the Human Sciences.* [Trans. anon.] New York: Vintage 1973

Fowles, John. *The French Lieutenant's Woman.* New York: Signet-NAL 1970

Freud, Sigmund. *Beyond the Pleasure Principle.* In *Standard Edition* 18: 1–64

– 'Humour.' In *Standard Edition* 21: 159–66

– *Jokes and Their Relation to the Unconscious.* Trans. James Strachey. New York: Norton 1960

– *The Standard Edition of the Complete Psychological Works of Sigmund Freud.* Trans. under the general editorship of James Strachey. 24 vols. London: Hogarth Press 1966–75

Friedman, Bruce Jay, ed. *Black Humor.* New York: Bantam 1965

Fry, William F., Jr. *Sweet Madness: A Study of Humor.* Palo Alto, CA: Pacific Books 1963

Frye, Northrop. *Anatomy of Criticism: Four Essays.* New York: Atheneum 1966

García Márquez, Gabriel. *Cien años de soledad.* Buenos Aires: Editorial Sudamericana 1979

– *One Hundred Years of Solitude.* Trans. Gregory Rabassa. New York: Bard-Avon 1971

Gardner, Martin. *The Relativity Explosion.* New York: Vintage 1976

Genette, Gérard. *Narrative Discourse: An Essay in Method.* Trans. Jane E. Lewin. Foreword by Jonathan Culler. Ithaca, NY: Cornell University Press 1983

Gödel, Kurt. *On Formally Undecidable Propositions.* New York: Basic Books 1962

Goethe, Johann Wolfgang von. *Goethes Faust.* Ed. Erich Trunz. Hamburg: Wegner 1963

Goffmann, Erving. *Frame Analysis.* Harmondsworth, Eng.: Penguin 1974

Goldstein, J.H., and P.E. McGhee. *The Psychology of Humor.* New York: Academic Press 1972

Goncharov, Ivan. *Oblomov.* Trans. David Magarshack. Harmondsworth, Eng.: Penguin 1978

Graff, Gerald. 'The Myth of the Postmodernist Breakthrough.' In Bradbury
(ed.), *The Novel Today*, 217–49

Grass, Günter. *Die Blechtrommel.* Frankfurt am Main: Fischer Bücherei 1962
- *Dog Years.* Trans. Ralph Manheim. New York: Fawcett 1966
- *Hundejahre.* Neuwied: Luchterhand 1963
- *The Tin Drum.* Trans. Ralph Manheim. New York: Vintage 1964

Handke, Peter. *Die Hornissen.* Frankfurt: Suhrkamp 1978

Hawkes, Terence. *Structuralism and Semiotics.* Berkeley: University of
California Press 1977

Hazard, Paul. *The European Mind, 1680–1715.* Trans. J. Lewis May. London:
Hollis & Carter 1953

Hazlitt, William. 'On Wit and Humour.' In *Lectures on the English Comic
Writers*, 1–56. London: Templeman 1841

Heller, Joseph. *Catch-22.* New York: Dell 1962

Henniger, Gerd. *Brevier des schwarzen Humors.* Munich: dtv 1966
- 'Zur Genealogie des schwarzen Humors.' *Neue Deutsche Hefte* 13, no. 2
(1966): 18–34

Hobbes, Thomas. *The Leviathan.* Intro. A.D. Lindsay. London: Dent 1914

Hofstadter, Douglas R. *Gödel, Escher, Bach: An Eternal Golden Braid.*
New York: Vintage 1980

Hogben, Lancelot. *Mathematics for the Million.* New York: Norton 1983

Holland, Norman. *Laughing: A Psychology of Humor.* Ithaca, NY: Cornell
University Press 1982

Homer. *The Iliad of Homer.* Trans. Richmond Lattimore. Chicago: University of Chicago Press 1961

Huizinga, Johan. *Homo Ludens: A Study of the Play Element in Culture.*
Trans. R.F.C. Hull. London: Routledge 1949

Hutcheon, Linda. *Narcissistic Narrative: The Metafictional Paradox.*
Waterloo, ON: Wilfrid Laurier University Press 1980
- *A Theory of Parody: The Teachings of Twentieth-Century Art Forms.*
New York, London: Methuen 1985

Idt, Geneviève. *Sartre, La nausée: Analyse critique.* Profil d'une Oeuvre 18.
Paris: Hatier 1971

Iser, Wolfgang. *The Implied Reader: Patterns of Communication in Prose
Fiction from Bunyan to Beckett.* Baltimore: Johns Hopkins University
Press 1974

Jakobson, Roman. 'Closing Statement: Linguistics and Poetics.' In *Style in
Language*, ed. Thomas A. Sebeok, 350–77. Cambridge, MA: MIT Press 1960
- 'Two Aspects of Language and Two Types of Aphasic Disturbances.'
In Roman Jakobson and Morris Halle, *Fundamentals of Language*, 69–96.
The Hague: Mouton 1956

Jammer, Max. 'Entropy.' In *Dictionary of the History of Ideas*, ed. Philip P. Wiener, 5 vols, 2: 112–20. New York: Scribners 1973

Jefferson, Ann, and David Robey, eds. *Modern Literary Theory: A Comparative Introduction*. London: Batsford Academic 1982

Joyce, James. *Finnegans Wake*. New York: Viking 1971

Kafka, Franz. *The Penal Colony: Stories and Short Pieces*. Trans. Willa and Edwin Muir. New York: Schocken 1970

– *Der Prozess*. Frankfurt am Main: Fischer Bücherei 1964

– *The Trial*. Trans. Willa and Edwin Muir. New York: Schocken 1970

Kant, Immanuel. *Critique of Judgment*. Trans. J.H. Bernard. New York: Hafner 1966

Kayser, Wolfgang. *The Grotesque in Art and Literature*. Trans. Ulrich Weisstein. New York: McGraw-Hill 1966

Kenner, Hugh. *A Reader's Guide to Samuel Beckett*. London: Thames and Hudson 1973

Kline, Morris. *Mathematics: The Loss of Certainty*. Oxford, New York: Oxford University Press 1980

Knickerbocker, Conrad. 'Humor with a Mortal Sting.' In Davis, *World of Black Humor*, 299–305

Knox, Ronald A. 'On Humour and Satire.' In *Satire: Modern Essays in Criticism*, 52–65. Englewood Cliffs, NJ: Prentice-Hall 1971

Koestler, Arthur. *The Act of Creation*. London: Hutchinson 1964

– *The Call-Girls*. London: Pan 1976

– *Insight and Outlook: An Inquiry into the Common Foundations of Science, Art and Social Ethics*. New York: Macmillan 1949

Lacan, Jacques. *Ecrits: A Selection*. Trans. Alan Sheridan. New York: Norton 1977

Leibniz, Gottfried Wilhelm. *Theodicy*. Ed. Austin Farrar. Trans. E.M. Huggard. London: Routledge 1952

Lemon, Lee T., and Marion J. Reis, trans. *Russian Formalist Criticism: Four Essays*. Lincoln: University of Nebraska Press 1965

Lentricchia, Frank. *After the New Criticism*. Chicago: University of Chicago Press 1980

Lévi-Strauss, Claude. *The Savage Mind*. London: Weidenfeld & Nicolson 1966

– *Structural Anthropology*. Trans. Claire Jacobson and Brooke Grundfest Schoepf. Harmondsworth, Eng.: Penguin 1972

Lodge, David. *The Modes of Modern Writing: Metaphor, Metonymy and the Typology of Modern Literature*. London, New York: Edward Arnold 1977

– *Small World: An Academic Romance*. London: Secker and Warburg 1984

Lotman, Jurij. *The Structure of the Artistic Text*. Trans. Ronald Vroon.

Michigan Slavic Contributions 7. Ann Arbor: University of Michigan Press 1977

Lyons, John. *Semantics*. 2 vols. Cambridge: Cambridge University Press 1977

Lyotard, Jean-François. *The Postmodern Condition: A Report on Knowledge*. Trans. Geoff Bennington and Brian Massumi. Theory and History of Literature 10. Minneapolis: University of Minnesota Press 1984

MacCabe, Colin, ed. *James Joyce: New Perspectives*. Sussex: Harvester; Bloomington: Indiana University Press 1982

Mangel, Anne. 'Maxwell's Demon, Entropy, Information: *The Crying of Lot 49*.' In *Mindful Pleasures: Essays on Thomas Pynchon*, ed. George Levine and David Leverenz, 87–100. Boston, Toronto: Little, Brown and Company 1976

Marx, Karl, and Friedrich Engels. *Über Kunst und Literatur*. 2 vols. Berlin: Dietz 1967–8

Merchant, Moelwyn. *Comedy*. The Critical Idiom 21. London, New York: Methuen 1972

Mercier, Vivian. *The Irish Comic Tradition*. London: Oxford University Press 1969

– *A Reader's Guide to the New Novel from Queneau to Pinget*. New York: Farrar, Straus and Giroux 1971

Meredith, George. 'An Essay on Comedy.' In Sypher, *Comedy*, 3–57

Merivale, Patricia. 'The Flaunting of Artifice in Vladimir Nabokov and Jorge Luis Borges.' In *Nabokov: The Man and His Work*, ed. L.S. Dembo, 209–24. Madison: University of Wisconsin Press 1967

– '*Catch-22* and *The Secret Agent*: Mechanical Man, The Hole in the Centre, and the "Principle of Inbuilt Chaos."' *English Studies in Canada* 7 (1981): 426–37

Miller, J. Hillis. 'The Critic as Host.' *Critical Inquiry* 3 (1977): 439–48

Milner, G.B. 'Homo Ridens: Towards a Semiotic Theory of Humour and Laughter.' *Semiotica* 5 (1972): 1–30

Mistacco, Vicki. 'The Theory and Practice of Reading Nouveaux Romans: Robbe-Grillet's *Topologie d'une cité fantôme*.' In Suleiman and Crosman (eds), *Reader in the Text*, 371–400

Monro, D.H. *Argument of Laughter*. Melbourne: Melbourne University Press 1951

– 'Humor.' *The Encyclopedia of Philosophy*, ed. Paul Edwards, 8 vols, 4: 90–3. New York: Macmillan 1972

Morreall, John. *Taking Laughter Seriously*. Albany, NY: SUNY Press 1983

Nabokov, Vladimir. *Pale Fire*. New York: Berkeley 1972

The New Columbia Encyclopedia. Ed. William J. Harris and Judith S. Levey. New York, London: Columbia University Press 1975

Nietzsche, Friedrich. 'On Truth and Falsity in Their Ultramoral Sense.' In
   The Complete Works of Friedrich Nietzsche, ed. Oscar Levy, 18 vols, 2:
   171–92. New York: Russell 1964
– *Thus Spoke Zarathustra*. Trans. R.J. Hollingsworth. Harmondsworth,
   Eng.: Penguin 1976
Norris, Christopher. *Deconstruction: Theory and Practice*. London, New
   York: Methuen 1982
O'Brien, Flann. *At Swim-Two-Birds*. London: MacGibbon & Kee 1966
O'Neill, Patrick. 'The Comedy of Entropy: The Contexts of Black Humour.'
   Canadian Review of Comparative Literature 10 (1983): 145–66
– 'The Comedy of Stasis: Narration and Knowledge in Kafka's *Prozess*.' In
   Franz Kafka (1883–1983): His Craft and Thought, ed. Roman Struc and
   J.C. Yardley, 49–73. Waterloo, Ont.: Wilfrid Laurier University Press 1986
– 'On Playing with Worlds: The Sense of Humour and the Sense of
   Literature.' *Acta Litteraria Academiae Scientiarum Hungaricae* 29
   (1987): 31–8
Paterson, Janet M. 'Le roman "postmoderne": Mise au point et
   perspectives.' *Canadian Review of Comparative Literature* 13 (1986):
   238–55
Plato. *Philebus*. Ed. Harold N. Fowler. London: Heinemann 1925
– *Plato's Symposium or Supper*. London: Nonesuch Press 1924
Pollard, Arthur. *Satire*. The Critical Idiom 7. London: Methuen 1970
Popp, Walter. *History of Mathematics*. Trans. Maxim Bruckheimer. Milton
   Keynes, Eng.: Open University Press 1978
Porush, David. *The Soft Machine: Cybernetic Fiction*. New York: Methuen
   1985
Potts, L.J. *Comedy*. London: Hutchinson 1949
Pratt, Mary Louise. *Toward a Speech Act Theory of Literary Discourse*.
   Bloomington: Indiana University Press 1977
Prigogine, Ilya, and Isabelle Stengers. *Order out of Chaos: Man's New
   Dialogue with Nature*. New York: Bantam 1984
Pynchon, Thomas. *The Crying of Lot 49*. New York: Bantam 1967
– 'Entropy.' *Kenyon Review* 22 (1960): 277–92
Queneau, Raymond. *Exercices de style*. Paris: Gallimard 1947
The Ramayana. Trans. A. Menen. New York: Scribner 1954
Reddick, John. *The 'Danzig Trilogy' of Günter Grass*. New York, London:
   Harcourt 1975
Richter, Jean Paul. 'Vorschule der Ästhetik.' In *Werke*, ed. Norbert Miller,
   6 vols, 5: 7–456. Munich: Hanser 1963
Rilke, Rainer Maria. *Duino Elegies*. German text with English trans. by
   J.B. Leishman and Stephen Spender. New York: Norton 1963

Rimmon-Kenan, Shlomith. *Narrative Fiction: Contemporary Poetics.*
London: Methuen 1983
Robbe-Grillet, Alain. *La maison de rendez-vous.* Paris: Les Editions de
Minuit 1965
– *La Maison de Rendez-vous.* Trans. Richard Howard. New York: Grove
1966
– *Pour un nouveau roman.* Collection Idées. Paris: Gallimard 1964
Rose, Margaret A. *Parody//Meta-Fiction: An Analysis of Parody as a
Critical Mirror to the Writing and Reception of Fiction.* London: Croom
Helm 1979
Rousseau, Jean-Jacques. *Essai sur l'origine des langues.* Ed. Charles Porset.
Bordeaux: Ducros 1970
Sartre, Jean-Paul. *Nausea.* Trans. Lloyd Alexander. New York: New Direc-
tions 1969
– *La nausée.* Collection Folio. Paris: Gallimard 1980
Saussure, Ferdinand de. *Course in General Linguistics.* Trans. Wade Baskin.
New York: McGraw-Hill 1966
Schiller, Friedrich. *Naive and Sentimental Poetry.* Trans. Julius A. Elias.
New York: Ungar 1967
– *On the Aesthetic Education of Man in a Series of Letters.* Trans. E.M.
Wilkinson and L.A. Willoughby. Oxford: Clarendon Press 1967
Scholes, Robert. *Fabulation and Metafiction.* New Haven: Yale University
Press 1979
– *Semiotics and Interpretation.* New Haven: Yale University Press 1982
Schopenhauer, Arthur. *The World as Will and Idea.* Trans. R.B. Haldane
and J. Kemp. London: Trübner 1883
Schulz, Max F. 'Black Humor.' In *Encyclopedia of World Literature in the
20th Century,* ed. Frederick Ungar and Lina Mainiero, 4 vols, 4: 45–9.
New York: Ungar 1975
– *Black Humor Fiction of the Sixties.* Athens: Ohio University Press 1973
Serra, Cristóbal. *Antología del humor negro español.* Barcelona: Tusquets
1976
Serres, Michel. *Hermes: Literature, Science, Philosophy.* Baltimore: Johns
Hopkins University Press 1982
Sewell, Elizabeth. *The Field of Nonsense.* London: Chatto & Windus 1952
Shaftesbury, Anthony Ashley Cooper, Earl of. *Sensus Communis: An Essay
on the Freedom of Wit and Humor.* New York: Garland 1971
Shakespeare, William. *The Complete Works of William Shakespeare.* Ed.
W.J. Craig. Oxford: Clarendon, n.d.
Shipley, Joseph T., ed. *Dictionary of World Literature.* Totowa, NJ: Little-
field 1972

Shklovsky, Victor. 'Art as Technique.' In Lemon and Reis, *Russian Formalist Criticism*, 3–24 ·
– 'Sterne's *Tristram Shandy*: Stylistic Commentary.' In Lemon and Reis, *Russian Formalist Criticism*, 25–57
Slade, Joseph W. *Thomas Pynchon*. New York: Warner 1974
Spencer, Herbert. 'On the Physiology of Laughter.' In *Essays on Education and Kindred Subjects*, 301–12. London: Dent 1911
Sterne, Laurence. *Tristram Shandy*. New York: Signet 1960
Stevick, Philip. 'Scheherezade Runs out of Plots, Goes on Talking; The King, Puzzled, Listens: An Essay on New Fiction.' In Bradbury (ed.), *The Novel Today*, 186–216
Styan, J.L. *The Dark Comedy*. Cambridge: Cambridge University Press 1968
Suits, Bernard. *The Grasshopper: Games, Life and Utopia*. Toronto: University of Toronto Press 1978
Suleiman, Susan R., and Inge Crosman, eds. *The Reader in the Text: Essays on Audience and Interpretation*. Princeton, NJ: Princeton University Press 1980
Sypher, Wylie. 'Existentialism and Entropy.' In Davis, *World of Black Humor*, 338–47
– *Comedy*. Baltimore, London: Johns Hopkins University Press 1980
Tave, Stuart. *The Amiable Humorist: A Study in the Comic Theory and Criticism of the Eighteenth and Early Nineteenth Centuries*. Chicago: University of Chicago Press 1960
Todorov, Tzvetan. *Introduction to Poetics*. Trans. Richard Howard. Theory and History of Literature 1. Minneapolis: University of Minnesota Press 1981
Tompkins, Jane P., ed. *Reader-Response Criticism: From Formalism to Post-Structuralism*. Baltimore: Johns Hopkins University Press 1980
Vico, Giambattista. *The New Science*. Trans. Thomas Goddard Bergin and Max Harold Fisch. Ithaca: Cornell University Press 1968
Voltaire. *Romans et contes*. Ed. H. Bénac. Paris: Garnier 1967
Waugh, Patricia. *Metafiction: The Theory and Practice of Self-Conscious Fiction*. London, New York: Methuen 1984
Wellek, René. 'Literary Criticism.' In *What Is Criticism?* ed. Paul Hernadi, 297–321. Bloomington: Indiana University Press 1981
West, Nathanael. 'Miss Lonelyhearts.' In *The Complete Works of Nathanael West*, 63–140. London: Secker 1968
Whitrow, G.J. 'Entropy.' In *The Encyclopedia of Philosophy*, ed. Paul Edwards, 8 vols, 2: 526–9. New York: Macmillan 1967
Wiener, Norbert. *The Human Use of Human Beings: Cybernetics and Society*. Garden City, NY: Anchor-Doubleday 1954

Wilde, Oscar. *Plays*. Harmondsworth, Eng.: Penguin 1960
Wilson, Robert Rawdon. 'Godgames and Labyrinths: The Logic of
    Entrapment.' *Mosaic* 15, no. 4 (1982): 1–22
– 'In Palamedes' Shadow: Game and Play Concepts Today.' *Canadian
    Review of Comparative Literature* 12 (1985): 177–99
Wimsatt, William K., and Cleanth Brooks. *Literary Criticism: A Short
    History*. 2 vols. Chicago: University of Chicago Press 1978
Wittgenstein, Ludwig. *Philosophical Investigations / Philosophische
    Untersuchungen*. German text with English trans. by G.E.M. Anscombe.
    Oxford: Blackwell 1953
– *Tractatus Logico-Philosophicus*. German text with English trans. by C.K.
    Ogden. London: Routledge and Kegan Paul 1981
Yeats, William Butler. *The Collected Poems of W.B. Yeats*. London:
    Macmillan 1973
– *A Vision*. London: Macmillan 1937
Zukav, Gary. *The Dancing Wu Li Masters: An Overview of the New
    Physics*. New York: Morrow 1979

Index